Contents

✔ KT-382-208

Plan Your Trip — 4

Explore Sydney — 48

Understand Sydney — 193

Survival Guide — 217

Sydney Maps — 238

Sydney

"All you've got to do is decide to go
and the hardest part is over.

So go!"

TONY WHEELER, COFOUNDER – LONELY PLANET

4 1 0193358 0

(left) **Bondi to Coogee walk p160** Enjoy spectacular coastal views.

(above) **University of Sydney p110** Take a break in the quadrangle.

(right) **Taronga Zoo p81** Encounter native wildlife.

Manly
p168

Circular
Quay &
the Rocks
p52

Kings
Cross
& Potts
Point
p136

Sydney
Harbour
p69

Darling
Harbour
& Pyrmont
p102

City
Centre &
Haymarket
p85

Inner
West
p108

Surry Hills &
Darlinghurst
p122

Paddington &
Centennial
Park
p144

Bondi to
Coogee
p156

Welcome to Sydney

Book a window seat for your flight to Sydney: day or night, this city sure is good-lookin'. Scratch the surface and it only gets better.

Show Pony

Brash is the word that gets bandied around when it comes to describing the Harbour City, and let's face it, Sydney is one hot mess! Compared to its Australian sister cities, Sydney is loud, uncompromising and in your face. Fireworks displays are more dazzling here, heels are higher, bodies more buffed, contact sports more brutal, starlets shinier, drag queens glitzier and chefs more adventurous. Australia's best musos, foodies, actors, stockbrokers, models, writers and architects flock to the city to make their mark, and the effect is dazzling: a hyperenergetic, ambitious marketplace of the soul, where anything goes and everything usually does.

Making a Splash

Defined just as much by its rugged Pacific coastline as its exquisite harbour, Sydney relies on its coastal setting to replenish its reserves of charm; venture too far away from the water and the charm evaporates. Jump on a ferry and Sydney's your oyster – the harbour prises the city's two halves far enough apart to reveal an abundance of pearls. On the coast, Australia ends abruptly in sheer walls of sandstone punctuated by arcs of golden sand, which in summer are covered with bronzed bodies making the most of a climate that encourages outdoor fun.

After Dark

After a lazy Saturday at the beach, urbane Sydneysiders have a disco nap, hit the showers and head out again. There's always a new restaurant to try, undercover bar to hunt down, sports team to shout at, show to see or crazy party to attend. The city's pretensions to glamour are well balanced by a casualness that means a cool T-shirt and a tidy pair of jeans will get you in most places. But if you want to dress up and show off, there's plenty of opportunity for that among the sparkling lights of the harbour.

On the Wild Side

National parks ring the city and penetrate right into its heart. Large chunks of the harbour are still edged with bush, while parks cut their way through the skyscrapers and suburbs. Consequently, native critters turn up in the most surprising places. Great clouds of flying foxes pass overhead at twilight and spend the night rustling around in suburban fig trees, oversized spiders stake out the corners of lounge-room walls, possums rattle over the roofs of terrace houses, and sulphur-crested cockatoos bleat from the railings of urban balconies. At times Sydney's concrete jungle seems more like an actual one – and doesn't that just make it all the more exciting?

Why I Love Sydney

By Peter Dragicevich, Author

My visits to Sydney were becoming increasingly frequent before I decided to up sticks and move to the city in 1998. Sure, it was the glitzy side that first attracted me – the sense that there was always something thrilling going on somewhere, and if you turned the right corner, you could be part of it. That sense remains, but I've discovered much more to love: the lively food scene, endless days at the beach and the way Sydney's Indigenous and convict history is so often hidden in plain sight.

For more about our authors, see p264.

Above: Sydney Harbour Bridge (p55)

Sydney's
Top 10

Sydney Opera House (p54)

1 Striking, unique, curvalicious – is there a sexier building on the planet? Seeing such a recognisable object for the first time is always an odd experience. Depending on where you stand, the Opera House can seem smaller or bigger than you think it's going to be. It confounds expectations but it's never disappointing. Most of all, it's a supremely practical building, and what goes on inside (theatre, dance, concerts) can be almost as interesting as the famous exterior.

◉ Circular Quay & the Rocks

Sydney Harbour National Park (p74)

2 Spread out around the harbour, this unusual national park offers a widely varied set of experiences, all with a blissful harbour view. In this park it's equally possible to separate yourself from civilisation or to be surrounded by traffic. It incorporates harbour islands, secluded beaches, ancient rock art, lighthouses, untouched headlands and, right in the middle of the city, a historic cottage. You can kayak into otherwise inaccessible beaches or cycle along well-tended paths. Pack a picnic and disappear along the bushy trails. BELOW: HORNBY LIGHTHOUSE, SOUTH HEAD (P71)

◉ Sydney Harbour

3

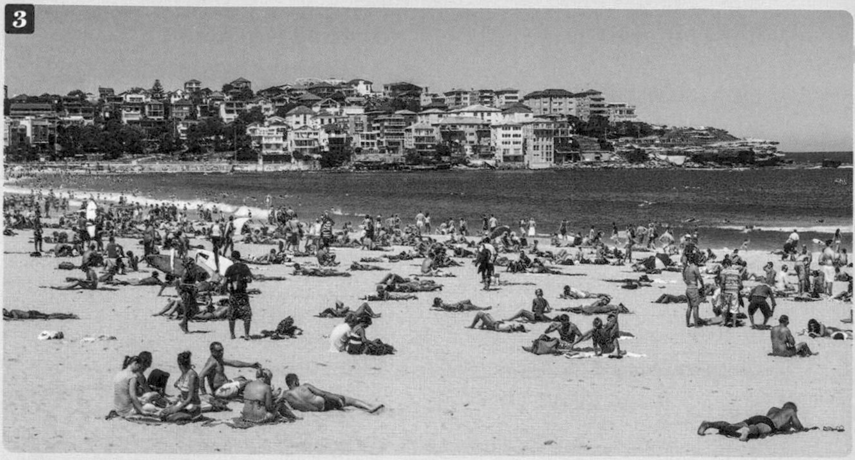

4

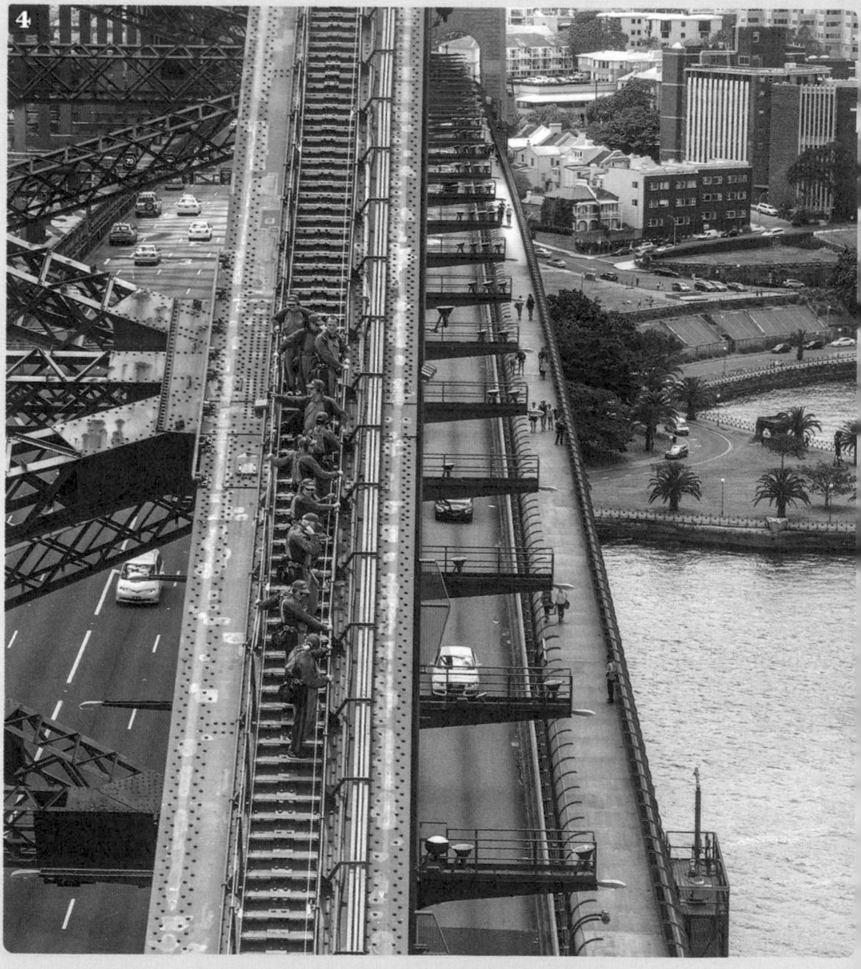

Bondi Beach *(p158)*

3 An essential Sydney experience, Bondi Beach offers munificent opportunities for lazing on the sand, lingering in bars and cafes, carving up the surf, splashing about in the shallows and swimming in sheltered pools. Every summer the world comes to Bondi, and what a wonderful world it is. The tightly arranged beach towels form a colourful mosaic, and a walk to the water can reveal a multitude of accents and languages. After dark, the action shifts to accomplished Italian restaurants, quirky bars and bustling pubs.

⊙ *Bondi to Coogee*

Sydney Harbour Bridge *(p55)*

4 Like the Opera House, Sydney's second-most-loved construction inhabits the intersection of practicality and great beauty. The centrepiece of the city's biggest celebrations, the bridge is at its best on New Year's Eve when it erupts in pyrotechnics and the image is beamed into lounge rooms the world over. The views it provides are magnificent, whether you're walking over it or joining a BridgeClimb expedition up and over its central rainbow of steel.

LEFT: A GROUP UNDERTAKING THE BRIDGECLIMB (P55)

⊙ *Circular Quay & the Rocks*

Royal Botanic Garden *(p56)*

5 Although the bustle of the city couldn't be closer, these spacious gardens are superbly tranquil – the only visible traffic being the little road-train that whisks people around and the purposeful procession of ferries on the harbour. Whether you're content to spread out a picnic on the lawn or you'd prefer to study the signs on the botanical specimens, it's an idyllic place in which to hang around for an hour or two.

⊙ *Circular Quay & the Rocks*

Sydney's Eateries *(p33)*

6 Eat to the beat of a city that's shaken off its colonial yoke, broken free of the tyranny of meat-and-two-veg and fallen in love with the flavours of the multitude of cultures that inhabit it. Sydney's dining scene has never been more diverse, inventive and downright exciting. Sure, it can be pretentious, fadish and a little too obsessed with celebrity chefs, but it wouldn't be Sydney if it weren't. It's assuredly not a case of style over substance – Sydney's quite capable of juggling both. BELOW: DINING AT CIRCULAR QUAY (P64)

✗ *Eating*

The Rocks *(p60)*

7 Australia's convict history began here with a squalid canvas shanty town on a rocky shore. Its raucous reputation lives on in atmospheric lanes lined with historic buildings, more than a few of them still operating as pubs. Sure, the place is overrun with tacky, overpriced stores and package tourists, but there are some great museums here as well. When it all gets too much, head through the convict-hewn Argyle Cut to the less frantically commercial Millers and Dawes Points.

◉ *Circular Quay & the Rocks*

6

Art Gallery of NSW *(p87)*

8 The Art Gallery of NSW's stately neoclassical building doesn't divulge the exuberance of the collection it contains. Step inside and a colourful world of creativity opens up, offering portals into Sydney's history, the outback and distant lands. There's certainly nothing stuffy about the place. All are welcome (including children, who are particularly well catered for), admission is free, and free guided tours help to break down any lingering belief that art is the province of a knowledgeable elite.

⊙ *City Centre & Haymarket*

Aboriginal Rock Art *(p159)*

9 It inevitably comes as a surprise to stumble across an art form that's so ancient in such a modern city, yet Sydney is built on top of a giant gallery. Until recently not much attention was paid to such things and much was covered over or destroyed. But with the dot paintings from distant deserts being celebrated, Sydneysiders have started to wake up to the treasure trove in their own backyard. Look for it on headlands around the harbour and on the coast and in nearby national parks. RIGHT: ABORIGINAL ROCK ART AT JIBBON HEAD (P181), ROYAL NATIONAL PARK

◉ *Bondi to Coogee*

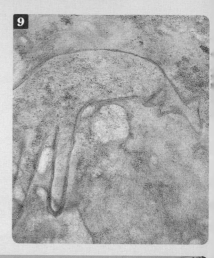

Taronga Zoo *(p81)*

10 A day trip to Taronga Zoo offers so much more than the zoo itself: running the gauntlet of didgeridoo players and living statues at Circular Quay; the ferry ride past the Opera House and out into the harbour; the cable car from the wharf to the top gate; the ever-present views of the city skyline as you make your way between the enclosures. And to cap it all off, the zoo is excellent, too.

◉ *Sydney Harbour*

What's New

Beyond the Lockout Zone

Tough new licensing laws affecting the inner city (1.30am lockouts and no alcohol to be served after 3am) have put a dampener on the raucous late-night drinking scene in traditional hotspots such as Kings Cross, Darlinghurst and Darling Harbour. The beneficiaries have been venues in the next ring of suburbs, including Newtown, Marrickville, Pyrmont, Double Bay and Bondi Beach.

Chippendale

The behipification of Chippendale continues apace, with the opening of One Central Park and hot new eatery Ester. (p110)

Darling Harbour

Old behemoths are being torn down to make way for new ones, while the Barangaroo casino and hotel development extends the precinct further north. (p102)

Opal Card

The city's integrated public transport smartcard is finally in place and starting to transform the way both locals and tourists traverse the city. (p218)

Grazing in Surry Hills

Just when you thought there couldn't possibly be any more excellent eateries in Surry Hills, along comes Reuben Hills, Sample Coffee, Devon, MoVida, the Devonshire and 4Fourteen. (p125)

Turning Japanese

The city's Japanese dining options are getting better and better, with the arrival of Cho Cho San, Ippudo Sydney, Saké and Sokyo. (p35)

Newtown Nightlife

Newtown is thriving, with an injection of kookiness courtesy of Mary's, Earl's Juke Joint, Midnight Special, Toyko Sing Song and Newtown Social Club. (p116)

Theatre Openings

Dramatic entrances to the Sydney stage include the Monkey Baa children's theatre in Darling Harbour and the wonderful Eternity Playhouse in Darlinghurst. (p42)

Matt Moran Expands

Between TV appearances, popular Aria chef Matt Moran has found time to open Chiswick Restaurant (p151) in Woolahra and Chiswick at the Gallery (p87) at the Art Gallery of NSW, and to revitalise Opera Bar (p65) at Circular Quay.

For more recommendations and reviews, see **lonelyplanet.com/sydney**

Need to Know

For more information, see Survival Guide (p217)

Currency
Australian dollar ($)

Language
English

Visas
The only visitors who do not require a visa in advance of arriving in Australia are New Zealanders. There are a variety of options.

Money
There are ATMs everywhere and major credit cards are widely accepted.

Mobile Phones
Most phones will accept local SIM cards. Quad-band US and Japanese handsets will work but need to be unlocked to accept a SIM.

Time
Eastern Standard Time (GMT/UTC plus 10 hours).

Tourist Information
Sydney Visitor Centre – The Rocks (Map p240; ☎02-8273 0000; www.bestof.com.au; cnr Argyle & Playfair Sts; ☐Circular Quay)

Daily Costs

Budget:
Less than $190
➡ Dorm beds: $22–52
➡ Return train trip: $8
➡ Hanging out at the beach: free
➡ Pizza, pasta, noodles or burgers: $8-15

Midrange:
$190–320
➡ Private room with own bathroom: $100–200
➡ Cafe breakfast: $15
➡ All-day public transport: maximum $15 using Opal card
➡ Two-course dinner with glass of wine: $45

Top End:
More than $320
➡ Four-star hotel: from $200
➡ Three-course dinner in top restaurant with wine: $120–200
➡ Opera ticket: $150
➡ Taxis: $50

Advance Planning
Three months before Book accommodation; make sure your passport, visa and travel insurance are in order.

One month before Book top restaurants; check to see if your visit coincides with any major events and book tickets.

A week before Top up your credit cards; check the Sydney news sites and events listings.

Useful Websites
Destination NSW (www.sydney. com) Official visitors' guide.

City of Sydney (www.cityof sydney.nsw.gov.au) Visitor information.

Sydney Morning Herald (www. smh.com.au) Daily newspaper.

Time Out (www.au.timeout. com/sydney) What's on information and reviews.

Urbanspoon (www.urbanspoon. com) Restaurant ratings.

Lonely Planet (www.lonely planet.com/sydney) Destination information.

WHEN TO GO

Peak season is Christmas until the end of January, coinciding with school holidays and hot weather. Spring (September to November) is dry and warm.

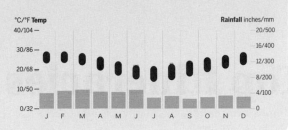

Arriving in Sydney

Sydney Airport Taxis to the city cost up to $55 and depart from the front of the terminals. Airport shuttles head to city hotels for around $15. Trains depart from beneath the terminal but charge a whopping $18 for the short journey into the city.

Central station Country and interstate trains arrive in Haymarket, in the heart of the city. Follow the signs downstairs to connect to local services or head to Railway Sq for buses.

Sydney Coach Terminal Long-distance coaches stop in front of Central station.

Overseas Passenger Terminal Many cruise ships pull in here, right in the centre of Circular Quay. There's a train station nearby.

For much more on **arrival** see p218

Getting Around

Grab yourself an Opal smartcard to get the best rates on all public transport modes.

➡ **Train** Generally the best way to get around, with reliable and reasonably frequent central services.

➡ **Bus** Buses will get you to all the places that trains don't go, such as Bondi and the Eastern Beaches, Vaucluse and Balmoral Beach.

➡ **Light Rail** Connects Central station, Pyrmont and Glebe, but nowhere else you're likely to go.

➡ **Ferries** An excellent way to see the harbour and the best option for getting from the city to Manly, Watsons Bay, Taronga Zoo and Balmain.

For much more on **getting around** see p219

Sleeping

Sydney is not a cheap city to stay in, and the Australian dollar provides little relief for international visitors. This is particularly true for midrange travellers; even many of the hostels charge over $100 for a private room with its own bathroom.

You're best to book well in advance, both to secure your top choice of accommodation and to take advantage of cheaper rates. Weekends are usually busier than weekdays, although the reverse can be true for some of the more business-focused places.

Useful Websites

➡ **Wotif** (www.wotif.com) Bookings, including 'mystery deals'.

➡ **Sydney.com** (www.sydney.com) Official tourism website, including accommodation listings.

➡ **Lonely Planet** (www.lonelyplanet.com/australia/sydney/hotels) Accommodation listings.

➡ **HomeCamp** (www.home-camp.com.au) Budget option; camp in suburban house gardens.

For much more on **sleeping** see p183

Top Itineraries

Day One

Circular Quay & the Rocks (p52)

☀ Why postpone joy? Start at Circular Quay and head directly to **Sydney Opera House**. Circle around it and follow the shoreline into the **Royal Botanic Garden**. Have a good look around and then continue around **Mrs Macquaries Point** and down to Woolloomooloo.

> ✕ **Lunch** Grab a pie at Harry's Cafe de Wheels (p141), a Sydney institution.

City Centre & Haymarket (p85)

☀ Head up to the **Art Gallery of NSW**. Take some time to explore the gallery then cross the **Domain** and cut through **Sydney Hospital** to Macquarie St. **Parliament House** is immediately to the right, while to the left is the **Mint** and **Hyde Park Barracks**. Cross into **Hyde Park** and head straight through its centre, crossing Park St and continuing on to the **Anzac Memorial**.

> ✕ **Dinner** Catch a cab to the Devonshire (p130), for relaxed, inventive fine dining.

Surry Hills & Darlinghurst (p122)

☾ After dinner, if you haven't booked tickets for a play at **Belvoir**, take a stroll along Crown St. There are plenty of good bars and pubs to stop at along the way.

Day Two

Bondi to Coogee (p156)

☀ Grab your swimming gear and head to the beach. Catch the bus to **Bondi** and spend some time strolling about and soaking it all in. If the weather's right, stop for a swim. Once you're done, take the clifftop path to **Tamarama** and on to **Bronte**.

> **Lunch** Detour slightly up to Bronte's excellent Three Blue Ducks (p164).

Bondi to Coogee (p156)

☀ Continue on the coastal path through **Waverley Cemetery** and down to **Clovelly**. This is a great spot to stop for a swim or a snorkel. Continuing on you'll pass **Gordons Bay** and **Dolphin Point** before you arrive at **Coogee Beach**. Stop for a drink on the rooftop of **Coogee Pavilion** then jump aboard a bus back to Bondi Junction. Shopaholics can have a brief whirl around **Westfield**.

> ✕ **Dinner** Fortify yourself for a Cross blinder at buzzy Ms G's (p140).

Kings Cross & Potts Point (p136)

☾ Everyone needs at least one trashy night up the Cross. Start with cocktails at **Jimmy Lik's** after dinner. Back it up with a tipple at **Bootleg**. Then **Sugarmill**, **Kings Cross Hotel**, **World Bar**...

Day Three

Sydney Harbour (p69)

 Take the scenic ferry ride from Circular Quay to **Watsons Bay**. Walk up to the **Gap**, to watch the waves pounding against the cliffs, then continue on to **Camp Cove** for a dip. Take the **South Head Heritage Trail** for sublime views of the city and the whole of the upper harbour.

> **Lunch** Pull up a pew with a view at Dunbar House (p81).

Circular Quay & the Rocks (p52)

Head back to Circular Quay and spend the afternoon exploring the Rocks. Start at the **Museum of Contemporary Art** and then head up into the network of narrow lanes to the **Rocks Discovery Museum**. Continue through the Argyle Cut to **Millers Point** and wander up **Observatory Hill**. Pop into one of Sydney's oldest pubs (maybe the **Lord Nelson** or **Hero of Waterloo**) and then cut down to **Walsh Bay** and double back under **Sydney Harbour Bridge**.

> **Dinner** Book well in advance for Sydney's top restaurant, Quay (p64).

Circular Quay & the Rocks (p52)

If last night was your trashy night, make this your glamorous one. Book a show at **Sydney Opera House** or Walsh Bay, or head straight to **Opera Bar** to be mesmerised by the lights sparkling on the water.

Day Four

Darling Harbour & Pyrmont (p102)

 Have a stroll around the waterfront and settle on whichever of the big attractions takes your fancy – perhaps the **Australian National Maritime Museum**, **Sydney Sea Life Aquarium** or **Wild Life Sydney Zoo**. Each of these will easily fill up an entire morning.

> **Lunch** For a cheap bite, pop up to Central Baking Depot (p95).

Sydney Harbour (p69)

Jump on the river service at King St Wharf and take an hour-long cruise upstream as far as **Sydney Olympic Park**. Take a stroll around **Newington Nature Reserve** until the next ferry arrives to whisk you back. Stop at **Cocktaoo Island** for a look at its art installations and the remnants of its convict and shipbuilding past. From here you can either catch a ferry to **Balmain**, or head straight back to Darling Harbour or Circular Quay.

> **Dinner** Have a final night of Modern Australian cuisine at Ester (p114).

Inner West (p108)

After dinner stroll up to King St, **Newtown**, and cruise the late-night bookshops and bars. A short pub-crawl could include **Corridor**, **Zanzibar**, **Courthouse Hotel**, **Midnight Special** and **Earl's Juke Joint**. Or continue on to **Newtown Social Club** to catch a band, or to the **Imperial** for the Priscilla drag show.

If You Like...

Parks & Gardens

Royal Botanic Garden Well-tended lawns, interesting botanical collections and ever-present harbour views add up to Sydney's most beautiful park. (p56)

Hyde Park A shady avenue of trees, lit with fairy lights at night, makes this an inviting place for a stroll. (p89)

Chinese Garden of Friendship A traditional arrangement of streams, ponds and paths to soothe the city's stresses. (p104)

The Domain The extensive lawns are used for large-scale public gatherings, while Mrs Macquaries Point offers unforgettable city views. (p88)

Centennial Park Formal bits, wild bits and a whir of joggers, cyclists and horse riders circling the central avenues. (p146)

Nielsen Park A tucked-away, leafy, harbourside park with a blissful shark-netted beach. (p74)

Museums

Australian National Maritime Museum Half the museum is moored outside; clamber through a submarine and into the hold of a tall ship. (p104)

Nicholson Museum The university's museum of antiquities is such a hidden gem that most Sydneysiders have never heard of it. (p110)

Sydney Jewish Museum An affecting little museum tracing the history of Judaism in Australia

MANFRED GOTTSCHALK / GETTY IMAGES ©

Archibald Memorial Fountain (p89) with St Mary's Cathedral in the background

but mainly devoted to the Holocaust. (p124)

Rocks Discovery Museum A warts-and-all primer for Australia's first proper neighbourhood. (p60)

Susannah Place Museum A reminder that history is as much about the people who lived in slum houses as those who lived in palaces. (p61)

Australian Museum The grand dame of Sydney museums, with historic collections of minerals and bones and an interesting Aboriginal section. (p125)

Art

Art Gallery of NSW Where the state stashes its greatest treasures; locals are well represented. (p87)

Museum of Contemporary Art Bringing edgy art to the heart of the city. (p60)

White Rabbit A fascinating private collection of contemporary Chinese art, free to all. (p110)

Australian Centre for Photography Not limited to traditional photography, the ACP displays digital, video and multimedia works as well. (p146)

Artspace On the bleeding edge (sometimes literally – ew) of Sydney's art scene. (p138)

Historic Buildings

Vaucluse House William Wentworth's Vaucluse mansion is a rare surviving colonial estate on the harbour's edge. (p74)

Elizabeth Bay House Another harbourside home, built in a gracious Georgian style in the heart of Lizzie Bay. (p138)

Hyde Park Barracks Museum Convict architect Francis Greenway's beautiful prison,

which houses a fascinating museum. (p88)

Old Government House Part of a cluster of important remnants of the early colony lingering in Parramatta. (p80)

Queen Victoria Building The most unrestrained and ornate survivor of the Victorian era. (p94)

Martin Place A stretch of grand bank buildings and the High Victorian former General Post Office, the most iconic building of its time. (p90)

Religious Buildings

St Mary's Cathedral Beamed in from Gothic Europe, the grand Catholic cathedral is awash with colour when the sun hits its stained glass. (p89)

Great Synagogue A mismatch of architectural styles, maybe, but a beautiful one. (p89)

St James' Church Francis Greenway's elegant, understated church is perhaps his crowning achievement. (p89)

Mary MacKillop Place A humble final resting place for Australia's only Catholic saint, with a small museum about her life. (p76)

Garrison Church Regimental flags brighten the cool interior of this sturdy sandstone church. (p62)

20th-Century Architecture

Sydney Opera House One of the world's most recognisable architectural treasures enhances the beauty of the harbour. (p54)

Sydney Harbour Bridge The city's favourite coathanger, the

For more top Sydney spots, see the following:

➡ Beaches (p30)

➡ Eating (p33)

➡ Drinking & Nightlife (p36)

➡ Gay & Lesbian Sydney (p39)

➡ Entertainment (p42)

➡ Shopping (p44)

➡ Sports & Activities (p46)

PLAN YOUR TRIP IF YOU LIKE...

bridge manages to be simultaneously practical, sturdy and surprisingly elegant. (p55)

Australia Square In 1968 this distinctive tower block raised the city's skyline to new heights. (p90)

Anzac Memorial Art-deco sensibilities lend grace and beauty to this solemn monument. (p89)

Zoos & Aquariums

Taronga Zoo A thoroughly modern establishment, housing its animals in spacious enclosures with million-dollar views. (p81)

Sydney Sea Life Aquarium Well laid out and fascinating, with giant sharks, rays and, most unusually, dugongs. (p104)

Wild Life Sydney Zoo Bringing the outback to the heart of Darling Harbour. (p104)

Manly Sea Life Sanctuary A slimmed down, cheaper version of the Aquarium, great for entertaining the kids on rainy days in Manly. (p170)

Views

Sydney Tower Eye Towering over absolutely everything, there's no better place to get an overview of the entire city. (p94)

O Bar Order a cocktail and enjoy the vista from the rotating bar at the top of the Australia Square tower. (p97)

Mrs Macquaries Point Jutting out into the harbour, offering the best ground-level views of the Opera House and the city skyline. (p56)

Observatory Hill Trudge up from the Rocks to this grassy knoll and gaze over Walsh Bay to the inner harbour. (p62)

Waverley Cemetery A great spot for gazing out to sea and shouting 'thar she blows' whenever you spot a whale. (p159)

Industrial Remnants

Powerhouse Museum The building once generated power for the tram network and is now a shrine to technology. (p110)

Cockatoo Island The detritus of defunct shipyards lends a sculptural quality to the island landscape. (p71)

Walsh Bay Elegant Edwardian warehouses, once part of a bustling port, now housing theatres, restaurants and apartments. (p62)

Woolloomooloo Finger Wharf The wool bales may have gone, but the winches and girders remain. (p138)

Carriageworks Cavernous brick train sheds converted into an edgy arts precinct. (p114)

National Parks

Sydney Harbour National Park Preserving the wild side of the city on numerous headlands and islands. (p74)

Blue Mountains National Park A vast blanket of forested wilderness guarding the city's western flank. (p178)

Royal National Park Secluded rivers and beaches amid bush and heath, to the city's south. (p180)

Ku-ring-gai Chase National Park This large untamed area to the north completes the circle of wilderness enclosing the city. (p181)

Lane Cove National Park Encircled by suburbia but rich in wildlife nonetheless. (p175)

Month by Month

January

The peak of the peak season with school holidays in full swing, taking advantage of the long, hot days. On average this is the hottest month.

☆ Field Day

Groove New Year's Day away in the Domain with well-known international and local acts from the indie end of the spectrum (www.fielddaynyd.com.au).

☆ Sydney Festival

Sydney's premier arts and culture festival (www.syd neyfestival.org.au) offers three weeks of music, theatre, visual art and 'happenings' around town.

☆ Flickerfest

Bondi's international short-film festival (www.flicker fest.com.au) offers shorts, docos, animation and work-shops over 10 days in mid-January at Bondi Pavilion.

☆ Australia Day

On 26 January Sydneysiders celebrate with picnics, barbe-cues and harbour fireworks and, increasingly, much flag waving and drunkenness.

☆ Ferrython

Part of the Sydney Festival, this delightfully insane Australia Day contest sees a fleet of bespangled ferries race around the harbour.

February

Almost as hot as January, but the kids are back at school, so the beaches are less crowded. From mid-February the Mardi Gras influx arrives.

☆ Chinese New Year

A 17-day Chinatown-based celebration (www.sydneychi nesenewyear.com) with food, fireworks, dragon dancers and dragon-boat races to see in the lunar new year.

☆ St Jerome's Laneway Festival

A one-day music festival (www.lanewayfestival.com. au) held in Rozelle, with the hippest international indie acts just as they're breaking.

☆ Future Music Festival

Dance-kids head to Royal Randwick Racecourse for this one-dayer in late Feb-ruary, featuring big-name EDM and hip-hop acts (www. futuremusicfestival.com.au).

March

March kicks off with the Mardi Gras parade. The temperature is still balmy, but it's traditionally Sydney's wettest month. Smells like wet drag queen.

☆ Sydney Gay & Lesbian Mardi Gras

A two-week festival culmi-nating in a massive parade and party (see p39) on the first Saturday in March.

☆ Taste of Sydney

A four-day ticketed event (www.tasteofsydney.com. au) full of famous chefs serving top food in Centen-nial Park in mid-March.

☆ St Patrick's Day

On March 17 (www.stpat ricksday.org.au) Sydney-siders add an 'O' to their surname and get blotto on Guinness in the Rocks.

April

As autumn progresses, showers are frequent, but it's not particularly cold. People make the most of the Easter weekend and the school holidays.

🎇 Sydney Royal Easter Show

This two-week fiesta (www.eastershow.com.au) features carnival rides, showbags and sugary horrors; held at Sydney Olympic Park.

🏃 Sydney Autumn Racing Carnival

Sydney's biggest horse-racing carnival (www.australianturfclub.com.au), held in March and April.

🔒 Fashion Week

The gaunt, pert and pubescent tread the catwalk in Carriageworks wearing local designer labels (www.mbffsydney.com.au).

☆ Sydney Comedy Festival

Wise guys and gals take to the stage at numerous venues for four weeks from late April (www.sydneycomedyfest.com.au).

May

Average high temperatures finally dip below 20°C and rainfall remains high, but Sydneysiders see it as an chance to pull out novels.

☆ Sydney Writers' Festival

The country's preeminent literary shindig (www.swf.org.au) runs for a week in various prime locations around the central city.

🎇 Vivid Sydney

Light installations and projections, performances and public talks; held over 18 days from late May (www.vividsydney.com).

June

Sunshine hours shrink to their lowest levels (an average of 5½ per day) as winter kicks in. The rugby league season keeps passions running hot.

☉ Biennale of Sydney

High-profile festival of art and ideas (www.biennaleofsydney.com.au) held between March and June in even-numbered years.

☆ Sydney Film Festival

Held (mostly) at the State Theatre, this excellent film festival (www.sff.org.au) screens art-house gems from Australia and the world.

July

Kids escape from school for the first two weeks of Sydney's coldest month, where the daily highs rarely strike above the mid-teens.

🏃 State of Origin Series

Rugby league fanatics consider this series of three matches between Queensland and New South Wales the pinnacle of the game.

August

August is chilly but dry – perfect for a run to the beach, but once you get there, you won't be tempted to get in.

🏃 City2Surf

On the second Sunday in August, over 80,000 people run the 14km from Hyde Park to Bondi Beach (www.city2surf.com.au).

September

Spring brings warming weather and sunny days. September is traditionally Sydney's driest month and daily highs scrape back above 20°C.

🏃 Sydney Running Festival

Includes a marathon, half-marathon, bridge run and family fun run (www.sydneyrunningfestival.com.au).

October

The pleasant spring weather continues. Workers get the Labour Day long weekend to enjoy it, while school students get the whole first week.

🍴 Crave Sydney International Food Festival

Month-long celebration of food and wine (www.goodfoodmonth.com), with dining events, cooking classes and night noodle markets.

☆ Manly Jazz

Held over the Labour Day long weekend, this long-standing festival (www.manly.nsw.gov.au/whatson/manlyjazz) features performances ranging from trad jazz to contemporary.

🏃 National Rugby League Grand Final

The NRL season (www.nrl.com.au) culminates with this clash on the Sunday of

Top: Mitzi Macintosh at the Sydney Gay & Lesbian Mardi Gras
Bottom: New Year's Eve fireworks

the long weekend. Sometimes falls in late September.

November

November is a great time to visit Sydney. It's usually the sunniest month, with temperatures warm but rarely scorching.

✷ Newtown Festival

All of the tribes of Newtown flock to Camperdown Memorial Rest Park in early November (www.newtowncentre.org).

◉ Sculpture by the Sea

For 17 days from late October, the clifftop trail from Bondi Beach to Tamarama transforms into a sculpture garden (www.sculptureby thesea.com).

December

Decembers in Sydney are hot and dry, and for the first three weeks the beaches are free of school holidayers. From Christmas onward things go crazy.

☆ Tropfest

The world's largest short-film festival (www.tropfest.com) is enjoyed from picnic blankets in Centennial Park on a day in early December.

🏃 Sydney Hobart Yacht Race

On Boxing Day, Sydney Harbour churns with competitors and onlookers for the start of the race (www.rolexsydneyhobart.com).

✷ New Year's Eve

Watch the harbour bridge erupt with pyrotechnic bedazzlement (www.sydney newyearseve.com).

Sydney with Kids

With boundless natural attractions and relaxed, outdoor living, kids love Sydney. Families can easily show their little ones a good time without suffering for it themselves with many great options that don't cost a cent: swim, wander and play all across the city.

Street performer at Darling Harbour (p102)

Attitudes

Australians are generally tolerant of children. Most restaurants welcome well-supervised children and many have high chairs and kids' menus, though avoid little hole-in-the-wall cafes in the inner city (no space). The only place you may come across a blanket ban on children is in some of the quieter B&Bs and boutique hotels.

Beaches & Pools

The calm waters of Sydney's harbour beaches are great for kids. If you're particularly paranoid about sharks, head to the netted areas at Murray Rose Pool (p75), Nielsen Park (p74), Balmoral (p81) and Manly Cove (p170). Most of Sydney's surf beaches have saltwater ocean pools like the spectacular Wiley's and McIvers Baths (p167).

There are also some excellent indoor public pools complete with slides and other watery attractions. Cook and Phillip Park Aquatic Centre (p101) in the centre of town is a lot of fun and the Australian Museum is right across the road or try the **Ian Thorpe Aquatic Centre** (Map p250; ✑02-9518 7220; www.itac.org.au; 458 Harris St; swim adult/child $7/5.20, fitness $19.20; ⊙6am-9pm; ⊠Exhibition Centre) next door to the Powerhouse.

Parks & Wildlife

Sydney's not short on places to let the kids off the leash. Most beaches have superb playgrounds and right in the middle of the city at Darling Harbour there's an incredible adventure park with water games, swings, slides and flying foxes. Once you're done you can hitch a ride on the mini train (p107) to Wild Life Sydney (p104) and the Sydney Aquarium (p104) or pop into the fascinating Maritime Museum (p104).

Better still is the ferry ride to the excellent Taronga Zoo (p81) or combine a trip to Manly with a visit to the penguins at the Sea Life Sanctuary (p170). For a less hectic wildlife experience, Featherdale Wildlife Park (p176) is *the* place for koala cuddles.

Theme Parks

If the kids are hounding you for some gut-churning highs visit Luna Park (p76), which has enough old-fashioned kitsch to impress the oldies. If it's a hot day consider a Spin and Swim ticket which includes entry to the harbourside North Sydney pool (p83). During summer the sprawling Wet'n'Wild (p176) water park in Sydney's west will impress the kids and clean out your wallet.

Active Pursuits

Bondi's Let's Go Surfing (p158) offers lessons for kids aged seven to 16 – but watch out, you may find that your offspring are suddenly much cooler than you are.

Bike tours are another good way to expend excess energy; try Bike Buffs (p68), Bonza Bike Tours (p68) or Manly Bike Tours (p176). Otherwise you can hire bikes (kids' bikes are widely available) and lead your own pack around Centennial Park (p155) or Sydney Olympic Park (p111), which also has an impressive high ropes adventure park for kids eight and up.

Sydney Harbour Kayaks (p83) welcomes 12-year-olds to its tours, as long as they're accompanied by an adult. They also rent kayaks to families with kids as young as three.

Wet-Weather Lifelines

Kids adore Ultimo's science and technology-focused Powerhouse Museum (p110), which has plenty of hands-on experiments, big chunks of machinery for budding engineers plus an interactive Wiggles exhibition. Close by at Darling Harbour, the tween set are likely to be quite distracted by Rihanna, Taylor Swift and Lady Gaga at Madame Tussauds (p104).

If the thought of dragging the kids around a gallery fills you with dread, you'll be surprised by the child-friendly Art Gallery of NSW (p87). The dynamic program includes free shows most Sundays, tailored discovery trails and self-guided, child-focused audio tours. There are also regular art safaris and creative workshops at the Museum of Contemporary Art (p60).

NEED TO KNOW

➡ For an extra cost, car-hire companies will supply and fit child safety seats (compulsory for children under seven).

➡ Most accommodation providers can provide cots, but try to arrange in advance.

➡ Mothers have a legal right to breastfeed in public.

The delights of the Opera House (p54) aren't restricted to adults. Catch the best in international children's theatre, school holiday shows and free Creative Play sessions. There's also a junior version of the popular Opera House Essential Tour.

Little astronomers might want to do some stargazing or see the Time Ball drop at the Sydney Observatory (p62).

Family & Children's Tickets

Most sights, entertainment venues and transport providers offer a discount of up to 50% off the full adult rate for children, although the upper age limit can vary widely (anything from 12 to 18 years of age). Many places also let under fives or under threes in for free. Family tickets are common at big attractions, generally covering two adults and two children.

Babysitting

Most big hotels offer babysitting services. Otherwise agencies can send babysitters to you, usually for a four-hour minimum (per hour from $25) and a booking fee (from $23); try **Nannies & Helpers** (☑02-9363 4221; www.nanniesandhelpers.com.au) or the **Wright Nanny** (☑02-9519 2928; www. thewrightnanny.com.au).

Resources

For an exhaustive list of events and activities for babies up to school-age kids, visit www.ellaslist.com.au or look out for the free *Sydney's Child* newspaper.

Like a Local

In most parts of Sydney, locals are firmly in the majority, even at that perennial tourist favourite Bondi Beach. Ditch the tour group, unstrap the bum bag (don't ever call it a fanny pack!) and step away from the Rocks – before you know it, you'll have blended right in.

Leona Edmiston store (p153), Paddington

Dining Out Like a Local

Unless it's a very special occasion locals don't dine at Circular Quay or the Rocks. And unless they have out-of-towners to entertain (or a child), they shun Darling Harbour as well. Those in-the-know head to reliable Surry Hills or to that just-opened place that everybody's been talking about in one of the inner suburbs or near the beaches. For those seeking cheap eats, Chinatown is a standby, or they'll rock up to their tried-and-true neighbourhood favourite or local pub.

But above all, locals head to cafes. Oh, the comfort of settling into the reliable local where staff make a decent flat white without bubbling the milk, serve consistently good food without charging the earth and always have a newspaper to read. For many urban Sydneysiders, brunch has replaced religious services as the main weekend ritual. And if not brunch, then yum cha.

Drinking Like a Local

Australians have a bad reputation for binge drinking, particularly when they're overseas, but generally you'll find Sydney pubs and bars pleasant places to be. Sure, Kings Cross can be unpleasant on weekends, but that is precisely the neighbourhood that soon-to-be-vomiting types gravitate towards. Licensing laws punish venues that serve drunks, so you're more likely to see this kind of behaviour on the streets than in the bars themselves.

The British-style local pub survives throughout the city, although you're less likely to see cross-generational family groupings in them than you would in the 'mother country'. The local passion for sport and the monopoly of coverage by pay-TV operators makes the pub a popular place whenever the local side is playing.

Hipsters gravitate to the new crop of small bars in Surry Hills, Darlinghurst, Newtown and the city, while those wanting to go all out might make for a cocktail bar with a harbour view.

Shopping Like a Local

The advent of the mega-mall has killed many a neighbourhood shopping strip. Once exclusively the province of supermarkets and chain stores, malls like giant Westfield Sydney and Westfield Bondi Junction have added designer boutiques and fancy dining to the mix. Paddington, the former go-to neighbourhood for fashion, is still holding on...just...and only around the Glenmore Road end. For a day of shopping escapism, the central city (mainly Pitt St) is the destination of choice, or lunch and a spot of browsing in the boutiques of Bondi Beach and Surry Hills.

Beachgoing Like a Local

By and large, Sydney's beaches are full of locals – even Bondi. Australia has one of the highest skin-cancer rates in the world – nearly four times greater than the USA's. Consequently, sunbaking is less popular than it used to be, and many locals will head to the beach early in the morning or late in the afternoon to avoid the worst of the sun. Once they get there, they'll lather up in extremely high SPF sunscreen and cover the kids in protective clothing. Sydneysiders aren't overly bothered by the possibility of shark attacks. The last fatal attack in the harbour was in 1963; surfers face more of a risk.

Local Obsessions
Sport

Enough already! Sports coverage takes up half the news broadcasts, a fair chunk of the daily paper and most of the weekend TV programming. Tribal affiliations run the deepest in rugby league, so knowing who to barrack for will stand you in good stead. If you're in the Eastern Suburbs (particularly the beaches), it's the mighty Roosters; in Surry Hills, Redfern or Erskineville, the Rabbitohs; in Balmain, the Tigers; in Cronulla, the Sharks; in Parramatta, the Eels; and in Manly, the Sea Eagles.

NEED TO KNOW

The city's premier eating guide is the annual *Good Food Guide* put out by the *Sydney Morning Herald*. The book awards 'chef's hats' in much the same way as Michelin awards stars: a 'three-hatted' restaurant is the pinnacle of good dining. The *SMH* also publishes *Good Cafe Guide* and *Good Pub Food Guide*. The *Good Food* section is published in the paper each Tuesday. The best and brightest of Sydney's food and drinking scene are also lauded annually by *Time Out Sydney*, an increasingly popular and regularly updated go-to for hot new restaurants and bars.

Food

Sydney foodies constantly read reviews, gossip about what's hot and what's gone off the boil, and hang out for the annual update of the *Good Food Guide* so they can religiously work their way through the places they haven't been to. Switch on the TV and chances are it'll either be a food or a sports show.

Property Prices

Did you hear how much an unrenovated one-bedroom terrace house went for last week in Erskineville? Don't worry, you soon will. With housing affordability extremely low, property obsession is at an all-time high.

Celebrities

Sure there are some fair-dinkum stars that live in Sydney, but Sydneysiders are just as fascinated by the personal lives of chefs, football players, radio jocks, former reality-TV contestants, all of the above's ex-partners and stylists, their local crime boss...

Keeping Fit

How much do you bench? I hear that jogging on the sand does wonders for the butt. Have you tried barre body yet? How's the diet going? You lost 5kg by going gluten-free!? Can't talk, gotta run. Yes, I am training for that half-marathon, you know.

For Free

Money, who needs it? In Sydney, many of the very best things in life really are free.

JAZZDOG / SHUTTERSTOCK ©

White Rabbit (p110) gallery

Beaches

Lazing on a surf-lifesaver-patrolled beach or diving into an ocean pool is part of the Australian birthright and one that's freely available to anyone who cares to roll out their towel. And if you forget to bring sunblock, ask the lifesavers for a complimentary squeeze.

Art

As well as free daily admission, the fabulous Art Gallery of NSW (p87) and the associated Brett Whiteley Studio (p124) offer free lecturers and films on Wednesday nights. While special exhibitions at the Museum of Contemporary Art (p60) are charged, most rooms are free. Another generous freebie is White Rabbit (p110), a stunning private collection of contemporary Chinese art.

Other excellent gallerwhite ries include Artspace (p138), the Australian Centre for Photography (p146), Sherman Contemporary Art Foundation (p146), Object Gallery (p124) and the student galleries at the University of Sydney (p110) and National Art School (p124).

The dozens of commercial galleries in Paddington, Woollahra and Danks St, Waterloo also welcome eager browsers.

Museums

Although the big museums charge, many of the smaller ones don't, such as Sydney University's secret trove of antiquities at the Nicholson Museum (p110).

The Rocks Discovery Museum (p60) provides an excellent introduction to Sydney's oldest neighbourhood, and you can follow this up with archaeological displays at The Big Dig (p61). Up the hill, Sydney Observatory (p62) has interesting exhibits and the Reserve Bank's **Museum of Australian Currency Notes** (Map p246; www.rba.gov.au/Museum; 65 Martin Pl; ⊙10am-4pm Mon-Fri; ⍰Martin Place) is also worth a look.

In Manly, visit the Manly Art Gallery & Museum (p170) and the museum at the old Quarantine Station (p171) on North Head.

Tours

Aside from the series of walking tours in our neighbourhood chapters you can enjoy free guided tours at the Art Gallery of NSW, Government House (p56) and the Royal Botanic Gardens. Additionally, Walsh Bay (p62) offers a downloadable self-guided wander around its historic wharves.

While they're only completely free to the most hard-hearted, both I'm Free (p101) and Peek Tours (p68) offer three-hour walking tours of the inner city, which the enthusiastic guides work for tips.

Classical Music

Enjoy the talent of classical musicians for nix at lunchtime on Wednesdays when the Sydney Conservatorium of Music (p57), St James' Church (p89) near Hyde Park and St Andrew's Cathedral (p94) offer regular concerts. The Town Hall has monthly lunchtime organ recitals.

Bus

Jump on bus 555 for a free loop around the inner city.

Wireless Internet

Unlike many countries, where free connections aren't hard to come by, you'll have to try a little harder for a cheap hook-up here. McDonald's, Starbucks, Gloria Jeans and public libraries are a good bet, along with some shopping centres, cafes and bars.

Significant Structures

Many of Sydney's most beautiful old buildings are open to the public, including Customs House (p57), The Mint (p88), St Mary's Cathedral (p89), the State Library (p88) and Town Hall (p94). For added entertainment, visit Parliament House (p88) on sitting days. Window-shoppers should peruse the exquisite Queen Victoria Building (p94) and the Strand Arcade (p99).

While you can't just go traipsing through the Opera House (p54) you can scramble all over it. Then you can walk over that other great icon, the Sydney Harbour Bridge (p55), and wander through Luna Park (p76; entry is free, rides are charged).

Cheap Alternatives

For views, zip up to Blu Bar (p66), on the 36th floor of the Shangri-La hotel, or the rotating O Bar (p97) on the 47th floor of the Australia Square tower. They're not cheap but a cocktail will cost less than the price of visiting Sydney Tower.

Rather than booking an expensive cruise, explore the harbour on a Manly ferry or take the Parramatta River service upstream.

For a taste of Sydney fine-dining **Marque** (Map p254; ☎02-9332 2225; www. marquerestaurant.com.au; 355 Crown St; 5/8 courses $120/165; ☉noon-3pm Fri, 6.30-10pm Mon-Sat; ☒Central) offers set three-course Friday lunches that are more than half off the price you'll pay for the regular menu while at Circular Quay, super star chef Matt Moran's Aria (p64) has a cheaper pre- and post-theatre menu.

ANDREW WATSON / GETTY IMAGES ©

Surf life-savers, Cronulla beach (p159)

⊙ Beaches

Whether you join the procession of the bronzed and the beautiful at Bondi, or surreptitiously slink into a deserted nook hidden within Sydney Harbour National Park, the beach is an essential part of the Sydney experience. Even in winter, watching the rollers break while you're strolling along the sand is exhilarating.

Beach Culture

In the mid-1990s an enthusiastic businesswoman obtained a concession to rent loungers on Tamarama Beach and offer waiter service. Needless to say, it didn't last long. Even at what was considered at the time to be Sydney's most glamorous beach, nobody was interested in that kind of malarkey.

For Australians, going to the beach is all about rolling out a towel on the sand with a minimum of fuss. And they're certainly not prepared to pay for the privilege. Sandy-toed ice-cream vendors are acceptable; martini luggers are not. In summer one of the more unusual sights is the little ice-cream boat pulling up to Lady Bay (and other harbour beaches) and a polite queue of nude gentlemen forming to purchase their icy poles.

Surf life-savers have a hallowed place in the culture and you'd do well to heed their instructions, not least of all because they're likely to be in your best interest. It's not coincidental that the spark for racist riots in Cronulla a few years back was an attack on this oh-so-Australian institution.

Ocean Pools

If you've got kids, or shark paranoia or surf just isn't your thing, you'll be pleased to hear that Sydney's blessed with a string of 40 man-made ocean pools up and down the coast, most of them free. Some, like Mahon Pool (p164), are what are known as bogey holes – natural-looking rock pools where you can safely splash about and snorkel, even while the surf surges in. Others are more like swimming pools; Bondi's Icebergs (p158) is a good example of this kind.

Surfing

Sydney has been synonymous with surfing ever since the Beach Boys effused about 'Australia's Narrabeen' in 'Surfin' USA' (Narrabeen is one of Sydney's northern beaches). For updates on what's breaking where, see www.coastalwatch.com or www.realsurf.com.

Beaches by Neighbourhood

➡ **Sydney Harbour** Lots of hidden coves and secret sandy spots; the best are out near the Heads.

➡ **Eastern Beaches** High cliffs frame a string of surf beaches, with excellent coffee and cold beer just a short stumble away.

➡ **Northern Beaches** A steady succession of magical surf beaches stretching 30km north from Manly to Palm Beach.

NEED TO KNOW

If you're not used to swimming at surf beaches, you may be unprepared for the dangers.

➡ Always swim between the red-and-yellow flags on life-saver-patrolled beaches. Not only are these areas patrolled, they're positioned away from dangerous rips and underwater holes. Plus you're much less likely to get clobbered by a surfboard.

➡ If you get into trouble, hold up your hand to signal the life-savers.

➡ Never swim under the influence of alcohol or other drugs.

➡ Due to pollution from stormwater drains, avoid swimming in the ocean for a day and in the harbour for three days after heavy rains. And on a related topic, don't drop rubbish – including cigarette butts – on the streets unless you don't mind swimming with it come the next rainfall.

PLAN YOUR TRIP BEACHES

Lonely Planet's Top Choices

Bondi Beach (p158) Australia's most iconic ocean beach.

Neilsen Park (p74) The pick of the harbour beaches surrounded by beautiful national park.

Gordon's Bay (p159) Despite the lack of beach, this is a magical swimming and snorkelling spot, reminiscent of a Mediterranean holiday.

Whale Beach (p182) Peachy-coloured sand and crashing waves; you've really left the city behind at this stunning Northern Beaches haven.

Murray Rose Pool (p75) The closest beach to the city is also one of Sydney's finest.

Best Harbour Beaches

Camp Cove (p71)

Chinamans Beach (p81)

Store Beach (p171)

Milk Beach (p74)

Best Ocean Beaches

Bronte Beach (p159)

Palm Beach (p182)

Manly Beach (p170)

Tamarama Beach (p159)

Whale Beach (p182)

Best Ocean Pools

Mahon Pool (p164)

Fairy Bower Beach (p170)

Giles Baths (p161)

Wylie's Baths (p167)

Bondi Icebergs (p158)

McIvers Baths (p167)

Best for Surfing

Curl Curl (p171)

Narrabeen (p182)

Tamarama Beach (p159)

Cronulla (p159)

Garie Beach (p181)

Best for Snorkelling

Gordons Bay (p167)

North Bondi (p158)

Camp Cove (p71)

Shelly Beach (p170)

Best Hidden Beaches

Store Beach (p171)

Parsley Bay (p74)

Washaway Beach (p171)

Best for Cafes

Bronte Beach (p159)

Manly Cove (p170)

Balmoral Beach (p81)

Palm Beach (p182)

Freshwater (p171)

Best for Bars

Watsons Bay (p71)

Manly Cove (p170)

Coogee Beach (p161)

Manly Beach (p170)

Best for Picnics

Parsley Bay (p74)

Balmoral Beach (p81)

Nielsen Park (p74)

Coogee Beach (p161)

Best for Public Tranport

Manly Cove (p170)

Manly Beach (p170)

Cronulla (p159)

Watsons Bay (p71)

Murray Rose (Redleaf) Pool (p75)

Ampersand Cafe & Bookstore (p150)

Eating

Sydney's cuisine rivals that of any great world city. Melbourne makes a big deal of its Mediterranean melting pot, but Sydney truly celebrates Australia's place on the Pacific Rim, marrying the freshest local ingredients with the flavours of Asia, the Americas and, of course, its colonial past.

Where to Eat

Sydney's top restaurants are properly pricey, but eating out needn't be expensive. There are plenty of ethnic eateries where you can grab a cheap, zingy pizza or a bowl of noodles. Cafes are a good bet for a solid, often adventurous and usually reasonably priced meal.

Cooking Courses

If your relationship with food goes beyond mere hunger, several seminars enable you to expand your culinary repertoire while

slipping some fine food and wine under your belt.

One of the city's best providores, **Simon Johnson** (☎02-8244 8220; www.simonjohnson. com; 24a Ralph St, Alexandria; courses $95; 🚍309-310), runs the excellent 'Talk Eat Drink' series of two-hour classes from its base 5km south of the city centre.

The Sydney Fish Market (p105) attracts 13,000 people per year to its fish-focused 'Sydney Seafood School' sessions ($90 to $165).

For a less highfalutin experience, **Bar-Be School** (☎1300 227 745; www.bbqschool.com.au;

NEED TO KNOW

Opening Hours

Many cafes and restaurants open seven days a week. If they do close, it's usually on a Sunday night or Monday. The standard opening hours are roughly as follows:

➜ Cafes: 8am–4pm

➜ Restaurants: lunch noon–3pm, dinner 6–10pm

Price Ranges

We've classified our eating reviews using the dollar symbols below, based on the prices of main courses.

$ under $15

$$ from $15 to $32

$$$ over $32

Reservations

Book at least a week ahead for the best restaurants, although you might sneak in with less notice, particularly for a midweek lunch. For 'iconic' restaurants, such as Quay and Tetsuya's, book a month ahead.

Conversely, many popular Sydney restaurants don't take bookings at all; if you're prepared to wait a couple of hours, you'll snaffle a table.

Tipping

Tipping isn't compulsory in Australia, but if the service is passable most folks tip 10% (particularly at better restaurants). If anything gets your goat, you don't have to tip at all. Tipping isn't expected at cafes where you order and pay at the counter, but there's often a jar where customers can sling loose change.

3hr classes $120) runs a series of sessions where you mull over the finer points of barbecuing meat and seafood, and then eat the results. The three-hour classes are held in various locations.

Self-Catering

Coles and Woolworths have supermarkets everywhere, many with attached liquor shops. Some are open 24 hours or until midnight. Excellent providores, with a handful of branches, include **Simon Johnson** (www.simonjohnson.com) and **Fratelli Fresh** (www.fratellifresh.com.au). Paddy's Markets (p101)

has a large produce section, while the Eveleigh Farmers' Market (p116) and EQ Village Markets (p154) are better for fancy fare.

Drinking & BYO

Most of Sydney's licensed restaurants have a respectable wine list, with an understandable emphasis on Australian product. There's almost always at least a handful of wines sold by the glass as well, and better establishments have sommeliers who can help you make the best possible food and wine match. Restaurant prices are usually about double as much as you'd pay in a bottle shop (liquor store).

Sydney is blessed with enlightened licensing laws that allow you to BYO (bring your own) wine and sometimes beer to those restaurants with a BYO licence. You'll usually be charged a corkage fee (even if your bottle's got a screw cap) at either a per-person or per-bottle rate, but it's generally cheaper than choosing off the wine list.

Eating by Neighbourhood

➜ **Circular Quay & the Rocks** (p64) Sydney's best and priciest fine-dining restaurants, many with a harbour view and a famous chef.

➜ **Sydney Harbour** (p81) A handful of gems make the most of harbourside locations.

➜ **City Centre & Haymarket** (p95) Ranges from expense-account fine dining to all-hours dim sum.

➜ **Darling Harbour & Pyrmont** (p105) Touristy and overpriced, with some notable exceptions.

➜ **Inner West** (p114) Affordable multicultural eateries and serious coffee temples, with the odd fine-diner thrown in.

➜ **Surry Hills & Darlinghurst** (p125) Sydney's gastronomic heartland, with chefs pushing boundaries in all directions for a mainly local clientele.

➜ **Kings Cross & Potts Point** (p138) Chilled-out neighbourhood cafes in leafy streets and a frantic strip of all-night takeaways.

➜ **Paddington & Centennial Park** (p150) Gastropubs, chic cafes and white-linen restaurants lurking along tree-lined back streets.

➜ **Bondi to Coogee** (p161) Cool cafes catering to surfers and beachside brunchsters, and a handful of prominent ocean-gazing establishments.

➜ **Manly** (p171) Plenty of average family-focused eateries and a clutch of good cafes and switched-on restaurants.

Lonely Planet's Top Choices

Quay (p64) Inventive fine dining with the best views in Sydney.

Tetsuya's (p96) A degustatory journey through multiple inventive courses.

Mr Wong (p95) Hip Cantonese joint with perpetual queues out the door.

Ester (p114) Informal but innovative Modern Australian dining.

Bourke Street Bakery (p125) Irresistible pastries, cakes and bread.

Best by Budget

$

Bourke Street Bakery (p125) A Surry Hills institution, now spreading through Sydney.

Mamak (p97) Golden flaky *roti* and tasty Malaysian curries.

Eveleigh Farmers' Market (p116) Graze your way through foodie nirvana.

Black Star Pastry (p116) Gourmet pies and delicious sweets.

Reuben Hills (p125) Great coffee and a Latin American–inflected menu.

$$

Mr Wong (p95) Mouthwatering dumplings, delectable duck and plenty of other Cantonese treats.

Ester (p114) An exemplar of contemporary Australian cooking.

Porteño (p127) Delicious slow-cooked meat and bucketloads of atmosphere.

Spice Temple (p96) Spicy delights from China's western provinces.

Longrain (p127) A modern Thai institution.

$$$

Quay (p64) Quite simply, one of the world's top restaurants.

Tetsuya's (p96) A culinary adventure awaits.

Rockpool (p96) Asian-influenced Aussie cooking at its best.

Devonshire (p130) Sophisticated European fare in the backstreets of Surry Hills.

Four in Hand (p151) Acclaimed nose-to-tail cooking in a wonderful old pub.

Best by Cuisine

Modern Australian

Quay (p64) Cutting-edge cuisine and unforgettable views.

Ester (p114) A moderately priced but extremely accomplished newcomer.

Rockpool (p96) This old-timer still pushes boundaries with highly inventive fusion-style fare.

Four in Hand (p151) A joyous celebration of all things meaty.

Est. (p96) White-linen fine-dining at its very finest.

Chinese

Mr Wong (p95) The tastes of Canton in a dimly lit, uber-hip, Sydney warehouse basement.

Ms G's (p140) Not entirely Chinese, but loud, brash and delicious regardless.

Spice Temple (p96) An upmarket tribute to the cuisines of Sichuan, Yunnan, Hunan, Jiangxi, Guangxi and Xingjiang.

Bar H (p127) Sophisticated but relaxed eatery, serving a winning mixture of Chinese and Japanese fare.

Din Tai Fung (p96) Popular branch of the acclaimed Taiwanese dumpling chain.

Japanese

Cho Cho San (p140) Chic Japanese-influenced decor and delicious *izakaya*-style bites.

Sokyo (p107) Toyko glam within the casino complex.

Saké (p65) Contemporary Japanese cuisine in a darkly glamorous setting.

Ippudo Sydney (p96) A raucous ramen house in the heart of Westfield Sydney.

Toko (p127) Superb modern Japanese tapas, sushi and char-grilled meat.

Thai

Longrain (p127) Perennially popular modern-Thai trailblazer.

Chat Thai (p97) Reasonably priced, loaded with flavour and constantly buzzing.

Spice I Am (p125) Super-fragrant and super-spicy traditional Thai fare.

French

Vincent (p151) Smart but affordable bistro serving all the Gallic classics.

Bathers' Pavilion (p82) Modern French with harbour views.

Bistro Moncur (p151) Uppercrust restaurant serving top-notch French favourites.

Italian

Icebergs Dining Room (p164) Top-end Mediterranean glamour with Bondi views.

A Tavola (p164) Delicious homemade pasta, loaded with flavour.

Pilu at Freshwater (p175) Sardinian restaurant known for its seafood and slow-roasted suckling pig.

Drinking & Nightlife

In a city where rum was once the main currency, it's little wonder that drinking plays a big part in the Sydney social scene – whether it's knocking back some tinnies at the beach, schmoozing after work or warming up for a night on the town. Sydney offers plenty of choice in drinking establishments, from the flashy to the trashy.

The Sydney Scene

Sydneysiders are generally gregarious and welcoming of visitors, and the easiest place to meet them is at the pub. Most inner-city suburbs have retained their historic corner pubs – an appealing facet of British life the colonists were loathe to leave behind. The addition of beer gardens has been an obvious improvement, as has the banning of smoking from all substantially enclosed licensed premises.

Until recently, NSW licensing laws made it hard to set up small wine bars and hole-in-the-wall cocktail lounges, but a recent relaxation has seen a blooming of such establishments, particularly in the city centre.

Poker machines ('pokies' in the local lingo) are the scourge of Sydney pubs, changing many a lovely local into a circus of flashing lights, beeps, whistles and hypnotised gamblers. It's a brave licensee who forgoes this cash cow in favour of a more pleasant drinking environment, but bigger complexes at least have the luxury of hiding them in the corner.

The cheapest places to drink are at the Returned & Services League (RSL) clubs. In a tourist-friendly irony, locals are barred unless they're members, but visitors who live more than 5km away are welcome (you'll need to bring proof).

Central Sydney Lockouts

In an effort to cut down on alcohol-fuelled violence, tough new licensing laws have been introduced to a large area of the central city bounded by the Rocks, Circular Quay, Woolloomooloo, Kings Cross, Darlinghurst, Haymarket and the eastern shores of Darling Harbour.

Within this zone, licensed venues are not permitted to admit people after 1.30am. However, if you arrive before then, the venue is permitted to continue serving you alcohol until 3am.

What to Wear

Sydney can be flashy, but it's also very casual. Men will nearly always get away with tidy jeans, T-shirts and trainers. Thongs (flip-flops, jandals), singlets (vests) and shorts are usually fine in pubs in the daytime, but incur the ire of security staff after dark. Women can generally wear whatever the hell they like, and many take this as an excuse to wear as little as possible.

A NIGHT ON THE TILES

Most of Sydney's older pubs are clad in glazed tiles, often with beautifully coloured art-nouveau designs. Why? Prior to drinking-law reform in the mid-1950s, pubs shut their doors at 6pm, before which after-work drinkers would storm in and chug down as many beers as quickly as possible – the six o'clock swill. Publicans discovered pretty quickly that it's easier to hose slopped beer, vomit and urine from glazed tiles.

Live Music & DJs

Since the 1950s Sydney has been hip to jazz, and in the 1970s and '80s, Aussie pub rock became a force to be reckoned with. Although Sydney fell into a house-induced haze in the '90s, live music is making a comeback. You can catch bands any night of the week in dozens of inner-city pubs. Check the free street mags (*The Music, Brag*) and the *Shortlist* section of Friday's *Sydney Morning Herald* for listings.

Sydney's obsession with dance music was born out of the gay scene's legendary shindigs: Mardi Gras, Sleaze Ball and numerous other megaparties. The crossover into mainstream culture in the 1990s coincided with the worldwide house and hip-hop explosion and a flood of ecstasy tablets.

If you feel like tying one on, you'll have no problems finding a place to do the tying. As well as a few world-class clubs, plenty of upmarket bars have DJs and dance floors. This isn't New York or London where you can party any night of the week, but if you just can't control your feet, there are plenty of options from Wednesday through Sunday.

Drinking & Nightlife by Neighbourhood

➡ **Circular Quay & the Rocks** (p65) Historic pubs and glam harbour-facing bars galore.

➡ **Sydney Harbour** (p82) Great old pubs in Balmain and a handful of prominent venues scattered about elsewhere.

➡ **City Centre & Haymarket** (p97) Fancy watering holes for after-work execs, and hip speakeasies in back alleys.

➡ **Darling Harbour & Pyrmont** (p107) Big brash booze dens full of suburban kids and suited city slickers.

➡ **Inner West** (p118) Diverse venues catering to students, bohemians, politicos, punks, lesbians, gay dudes and live-music lovers.

➡ **Surry Hills & Darlinghurst** (p131) Gay bars, hipster havens, schmickly renovated pubs and interesting little backstreet bars.

➡ **Kings Cross & Potts Point** (p141) Legendary locale for all things seedy, shady, trashy and boozy.

➡ **Paddington & Centennial Park** (p151) Upmarket old pubs and classy wine bars for would-be fashionistas.

NEED TO KNOW

Opening Hours

➡ Pubs and bars: roughly 11am–midnight; later on weekends and in livelier areas; some open 24 hours.

➡ Clubs: 10pm–5am Wednesday to Saturday; most aren't busy until after midnight.

➡ Venues within a designated central zone are unable to admit people after 1.30am or to serve them alcohol after 3am.

Beer Sizes

Traditional Sydney pubs serve middies (285mL) and schooners (425mL), while pints (570mL) are the domain of Anglo-Celtic theme pubs. Australian pubs abandoned pints long ago because beer would go warm in the summer heat before you'd finished your glass. Arm yourself with this invaluable local insight and order a schooner instead.

Tipping

Tipping in bars is very unusual, so you should feel under no obligation to do so. The only possible exceptions are where there has been a considerable amount of table service (more than just delivering drinks and clearing empties) or where fancy cocktails are concocted.

Door Policies

➡ It is against the law to serve people who are intoxicated and you won't be admitted to a venue if you appear drunk.

➡ If security staff suspect that you're under the legal drinking age (18), you'll be asked to present photo ID with proof of your age.

➡ Some gay bars have a 'no open-toed shoes' policy, ostensibly for safety (to avoid broken glass), but sometimes invoked to keep straight women out.

➡ **Bondi to Coogee** (p165) Big, boozy beach bars full of Brit backpackers, Irish larrikins and Latin lovers.

➡ **Manly** (p175) Large pubs with water views for a post-beach refresher or a weekend rave-up.

Lonely Planet's Top Choices

Baxter Inn (p97) Whiskies by the dozen in a back-alley hideaway.

Frankie's Pizza (p97) A hidden wonderland for indie-rock fans.

Watsons Bay Beach Club (p82) Our favourite spot for a sundowner on a balmy summer's day.

Wild Rover (p131) A modern-day speakeasy behind a nondescript Surry Hills shopfront.

Earl's Juke Joint (p118) Newtown's most happening spot for cocktails and craft beers.

Best Cocktails

Eau-de-Vie (p132) Serious cocktail wizardry in glam surrounds.

Hinky Dinks (p132) *Happy Days* are here again in this 1950s-themed cocktail bar.

Victoria Room (p132) Sip on something sophisticated in this forgotten outpost of the Raj.

Grandma's (p97) Kooky in the extreme, with tiki cocktails to boot.

Rook (p97) Sip a homemade infusion from this perch atop a city tower.

Best for Beer

Local Taphouse (p132) Sydney's beer specialists, offering craft beer tastings and regular special events.

Lord Nelson Brewery Hotel (p65) Boutique brewers occupying one of Sydney's oldest and most atmospheric pubs.

Redoak Boutique Beer Cafe (p98) The Sydney base of a much-awarded boutique brewery.

Harts Pub (p66) A low-key pub serving a great range of craft beers hidden in plain sight within the Rocks.

Welcome Hotel (p82) A popular stop on a Balmain/Rozelle pub crawl for craft beer lovers.

Best Wine Bars

121BC (p131) Gather around the communal table for fine wine and free-flowing bonhomie.

Wine Library (p152) Woollahra's smart set clink glasses at this stylish oasis on the Oxford St strip.

10 William Street (p151) A tiny slice of Italy on the fashion strip.

The Winery (p131) The greenest spot for a cheeky tipple, right in the heart of Surry Hills.

Bambini Wine Room (p98) A quiet retreat for sophisticated city types.

Best Views

O Bar (p97) Oh boy! The views from this revolving, 47th-floor cocktail bar are unforgettable.

Blu Bar on 36 (p66) Stylish surrounds at the top of the Shangri-La.

Opera Bar (p65) Like drinking in a postcard, at the base of the Opera House.

Glenmore at the Rocks (p65) Head up to the rooftop for those perfect Opera House views.

North Bondi RSL (p165) Cheap drinks, priceless views.

Best Heritage Pubs

Hero of Waterloo (p65) Our favourite creaky boozer has been serving drinks since 1843.

Lord Nelson Brewery Hotel (p65) Sydney's oldest pub? They've been pouring beer here since 1841.

Fortune of War (p65) Sydney's oldest pub? The Fortune's had a license since 1828, but was rebuilt in 1921.

Courthouse Hotel (p118) This cosy backstreet pub has been keeping Newtown lubricated since 1859.

Shakespeare Hotel (p132) As comfortable and familiar as your favourite T-shirt; circa 1879.

Best Outdoor Drinking

Watsons Bay Beach Club (p82) Sydney's best beachside beer garden, offering harbour views from multiple terraces.

Bucket List (p165) This Bondi Pavilion hotspot is a great place to case the passing parade.

Opera Bar (p65) Sydney's most glamorous beer garden, soaking in the sights of Circular Quay.

Zanzibar (p118) Catch the last rays of the day on the Inner West's coolest rooftop bar.

Beresford Hotel (p131) The architects have worked wonders, grafting a spacious beer garden onto this historic pub.

Gay & Lesbian Sydney

Gays and lesbians have migrated to Oz's Emerald City from all over Australia, New Zealand and the world, adding to a community that is visible, vibrant and an integral part of the city's social fabric. Locals will assure you that things aren't as exciting as they once were, but Sydney is still indisputably one of the world's great queer cities.

Social Acceptance

These days few Sydney dwellers even bat an eyelid at same-sex couples holding hands on the street, but the battle for acceptance has been long and protracted. As recently as the early 1990s, several murders were linked to hate crimes, and a stroll up Oxford St could result in a chorus of abuse from car windows. Sydney is now relatively safe, but it still pays to keep your wits about you, particularly at night.

PARTY TIME

Ain't no denying it, Sydney puts on a good party. By good, we mean big, lavish and flashy. Some party animals treat it like a professional sport, spending months preparing for the big fixtures, which can resemble endurance events.

While Mardi Gras is the city's main Gay Pride festival, Darlinghurst's Stonewall Hotel organises a minifestival around the traditional Stonewall commemorations in late June. Catering to more niche tastes, **Harbour City Bears** (www.harbourcitybears.com.au) runs **Bear Pride** (www.bearpride.com.au) in August, while **Leather Pride Week** (www.sydney leatherpride.org) is a moveable feast, but is usually held in winter.

The Birth of Mardi Gras

On 24 June 1978 a Sydney icon was violently born. There had been other gay-rights marches – in 1973 activists were arrested in Martin Place – but this one was different. Two thousand people followed a truck down Oxford St in a carnival-type atmosphere, encouraging punters to come out of the bars to join them.

After harassing the participants for much of the route, the police corralled the remaining marchers in Darlinghurst Rd, Kings Cross, beating and arresting 53 of them. Worse still, the names of all of the arrestees were published in the *Sydney Morning Herald* and many of them lost their jobs.

The following year 3000 people joined the march, dubbed the 'Gay Mardi Gras', and in 1981 the decision was made to move the event to summer. The parade still has a serious political edge; more than just a protest, the parade is considered by many to have helped transform Australian society into a more accepting place for lesbians and gay men.

Mardi Gras Today

The famous **Sydney Gay & Lesbian Mardi Gras** (www.mardigras.org.au) is now the biggest annual tourist-attracting date on the Australian calendar. While the straights focus on the parade, the gay and lesbian community throws itself wholeheartedly into the entire festival, including the blitzkrieg of partying that surrounds it. There's no better

NEED TO KNOW

Gay & Lesbian Press

Aside from *DNA*, all of the following are available for free from gay and lesbian venues, and from many gay-friendly cafes and shops. You won't have any trouble stumbling over them in Darlinghurst or Newtown.

DNA (www.dnamagazine.com.au) Monthly glossy gay men's magazine, available from newsagents.

LOTL (www.lotl.com) Monthly lesbian magazine, aka *Lesbians on the Loose*.

Star Observer (www.starobserver.com.au) Monthly magazine.

SX (www.gaynewsnetwork.com.au) Weekly newspaper.

Further Resources

ACON (www.acon.org.au) AIDS Council of New South Wales website.

Gay Sydney Hotels (www.gaysydneyhotels.com) Listings of gay and gay-friendly hotels.

Grindr (www.grindr.com) Probably Sydney's most popular gay dating app.

Pinkboard (www.pinkboard.com.au) Gay bulletin boards.

Same Same (www.samesame.com.au) News, events and lifestyle features.

Scruff (www.scruff.com) Hook-up app catering to rougher tastes; also very popular in Sydney.

Legal Matters

NSW's gays and lesbians enjoy legal protection from discrimination and vilification, and an equal age of consent (16 years). They can't legally marry, but they do have de-facto relationship rights.

time for the gay traveller to visit Sydney than the two-week lead-up to the parade and party, held on the first Saturday in March.

On the big night itself, the parade kicks off around sunset, preceded by the throbbing engines of hundreds of Dykes on Bikes. Heading up Oxford St from Hyde Park, it veers right into Flinders St, hooking into Moore Park Rd and culminating outside the party site in Driver Ave. The whole thing takes about 90 minutes to trundle through, and attracts up to half a million spectators ogling from the sidelines.

For the best views, make friends with someone who has an apartment above the street. If you're forced to stand on the street, bring a milk crate (oh so suddenly scarce) to get a better view. The gayest section of the crowd is between Crown St and the first part of Flinders St. If you're running late, the crowd thins out considerably near the end – although by this stage the participants' enthusiasm is on the wane. Another fun option is to volunteer as a marshal: you'll need to attend a few meetings and arrive hideously early on the day, but you'll get the best view and a discounted party ticket for your efforts.

You can also buy a ticket for the **Parade Sideshow**, positioned near the end of the route. Not only is this a handy option if you're heading to the party, but you'll also have seats, toilets and bars at your disposal and entertainment while you wait.

The legendary **Mardi Gras Party** (tickets $150 through www.ticketek.com.au) is an extravaganza in every sense of the word. With around 16,000 revellers, it stretches over several large halls, and showcases the best DJs and lighting design the world has to offer.

Gay & Lesbian Sydney by Neighbourhood

➡ **Sydney Harbour** Some of Sydney's most popular gay beaches including Lady Bay (p74) and Obelisk (p81).

➡ **Inner West** (p108) The fabled lesbian homeland, also popular with gay men.

➡ **Surry Hills & Darlinghurst** (p122) Sydney's main gay 'ghetto', with most of the bars, clubs and gay-targeted businesses.

➡ **Kings Cross & Potts Point** (p136) No gay venues but loads of gay guys live here.

➡ **Paddington & Centennial Park** (p144) The home of the Mardi Gras Party and lots of well-dressed dudes.

➡ **Bondi to Coogee** (p156) The beautiful boys gravitate to North Bondi.

Lonely Planet's Top Choices

Sydney Gay & Lesbian Mardi Gras (p39) Is there another city that embraces its pride festival with more fervour?

Beresford Hotel (p131) Sunday afternoons see an infestation of the bold and the beautiful.

Birdcage (p118) Lesbian night at Newtown's Zanzibar.

North Bondi (p158) Staking a claim to a stretch of Sydney's most iconic beach.

Arq (p133) One of the city's best nightclubs, gay or straight.

Best Regular Parties

Fag Tag (www.facebook.com/welovefagtag) Organised take-overs of straight bars, usually on Sundays in summer – lots of free fun.

Daywash (www.daywash.com.au) Regular day parties (usually noon to 10pm on a Sunday) held at Chinese Laundry (p98).

In the Dark (www.inthedark.com.au) Runs various parties, including DILF (who's your daddy?) and Swagger (RnB and hip hop).

Extra Dirty (www.extradirty.com.au) A chance for the leather, fetish and rubber crowd to delve into the darker reaches of their wardrobes.

Best Lesbian Hang-Outs

Birdcage (p118) Wednesday night takeover of Zanzibar's 2nd floor.

Sly Fox (p119) Hosts Sydney's longest-running lesbian night, every Wednesday.

McIvers Baths (p167) Coogee's legendary women-only sea baths.

Exchange Hotel (p133) Plenty of queer-friendly entertainment on multiple levels.

Best Gay Venues

Arq (p133) The city's hottest gay dance floor.

Imperial Hotel (p119) The legendary home of Priscilla.

Palms on Oxford (p133) Good-time, trashy, campy dance venue.

Midnight Shift (p133) Oxford St's longstanding bar and club.

Stonewall Hotel (p133) Several levels of shiny, happy people.

Best Gay-Friendly Straight Bars

Beresford Hotel (p131) Gay-friendly all the time, but on Sundays play spot-the-straight.

Sly Fox (p119) Working-class pub welcoming lesbians for many years.

Zanzibar (p118) Popular Newtown bar which plays host to one of Sydney's main lesbian nights.

Marlborough Hotel (p118) Home to Tokyo Sing Song, an underground hideout for the kooky and queer.

Green Park Hotel (p133) A proper local pub for Darling-hursters of all persuasions.

Best Beaches & Pools

North Bondi (p158) Where the buff lads work on their tans.

Lady Bay (p74) Pretty nudist beach tucked under South Head.

Obelisk (p81) Small, secluded nude beach with a busy, bushy hinterland.

McIvers Baths (p167) Women-only sea baths, extremely popular with the Sapphic set.

Murray Rose Pool (p75) The nearest harbour beach to the gay ghettos.

Best for Shopping

Bookshop Darlinghurst (p135) Longstanding gay bookshop and a great source of local information.

House of Priscilla (p135) One-stop-shop for gender illusionists.

Sax Fetish (p135) Racks of shiny black leather and rubber gear.

Gertrude & Alice (p166) Named after literary lesbians and packed with interesting reads.

Sappho Books, Cafe & Wine Bar (p114) Part bohemian cafe-bar, part rag-tag bookshop.

Best Gay-Friendly Hotels

Arts (p191) Midrange hotel, extremely handy for the Oxford St venues and Mardi Gras.

Medusa (p190) Darlinghurst boutique hotel, well positioned for eating, drinking and being Mary.

Adina Apartment Hotel Sydney (p187) Large chain which actively courts gay business.

Meriton Serviced Apartments Kent Street (p187) Bag yourself your own city pad.

☆ Entertainment

Take Sydney at face value and it's tempting to unfairly stereotype its good citizens as shallow and a little narcissistic. But take a closer look: the arts scene is thriving, sophisticated and progressive – it's not a complete accident that Sydney's definitive icon is an opera house!

Theatre

Sydney doesn't have a dedicated theatre district, but that doesn't mean theatre lovers miss out. The city offers a vigorous calendar of productions from Broadway shows to experimental theatre at venues across the inner city.

Classical Music

There's a passionate audience for classical music in Sydney. Without having the extensive repertoires of European cities, Sydney offers plenty of inspired classical performances – offering the perfect excuse to check out the interior of those famous harbourside sails.

Dance

Dance and Sydney's body-focused audiences go hand in hand (and cheek to cheek). Australian dancers have a reputation for awesome, fearless physical displays – and sometimes a lack of costume. Performances range from traditional ballet with tutus and bulging tights to edgy, liberating 'physical theatre'.

Opera

Despite its population of only 23 million, Australia has produced some of the world's most ear-catching opera singers, including Dames Nellie Melba and Joan Sutherland. The Opera House may be the adored symbol of Sydney, but supporting such a cost-heavy art form is difficult. New and more obscure works are staged, but it's the big opera hits that put bums on seats.

Cinema

Most suburbs have mainstream cinemas, while art-house cinemas hover around the inner city. Movie listings can be found in Sydney's daily newspapers. Come summer various outdoor screens pop up in scenic spots.

Entertainment by Neighbourhood

➡ **Circular Quay & the Rocks** (p66) Sydney's principal arts neighbourhood, containing the Opera House and Walsh Bay precinct.

➡ **Sydney Harbour** (p82) Ensemble Theatre and Sunset Cinema, both in North Sydney.

➡ **City Centre & Haymarket** (p98) Major concert venues and theatres.

➡ **Darling Harbour & Pyrmont** (p107) Sydney Lyric and Monkey Baa theatres, and a giant IMAX cinema.

➡ **Inner West** (p119) Edgy theatre stages and live-music venues.

➡ **Surry Hills & Darlinghurst** (p134) Some of Sydney's most interesting theatre companies.

➡ **Kings Cross & Potts Point** (p143) Pub theatre, musical theatre, jazz and comedy.

➡ **Paddington & Centennial Park** (p152) Art-house cinemas and a comedy club.

➡ **Bondi to Coogee** (p158) Theatre and cinema at Bondi Pavilion.

Lonely Planet's Top Choices

Sydney Opera House (p66) Don't miss the chance to see the House in action.

State Theatre (p99) We don't care what's on, visiting this beautiful place is a joy.

City Recital Hall (p98) The city's premier classical-music venue.

Metro Theatre (p99) The best place to watch touring bands.

Belvoir (p134) Consistently excellent productions in an intimate setting.

Best for Theatre

Sydney Theatre Company (p66) The top dog of the Sydney theatre scene.

Belvoir (p134) Consistently excellent company operating out of their own intimate venue.

SBW Stables Theatre (p134) A hothouse for new Australian plays.

New Theatre (p119) Small venue presenting both new and established works.

Bell Shakespeare (p66) This acclaimed company regularly brings the bard to the Opera House.

Best for Dance

Sydney Dance Company (p67) Australia's top contemporary company.

Bangarra Dance Theatre (p67) The country's finest Aboriginal performance company.

Australian Ballet (p67) Melbourne based but regularly at the Opera House.

Performance Space (p120) An edgy hub for new dance works.

Best Classical-Music Companies

Opera Australia (p67) Without which that white thing on the harbour would just be the Sydney House.

Sydney Symphony Orchestra (p67) The city's premier orchestra.

Australian Chamber Orchestra (p67) Smaller in scale but undiminished in quality.

Musica Viva Australia (p99) Exemplars of ensemble music.

Australian Brandenburg Orchestra (p99) Exponents of the baroque on period instruments.

Best Live Rock, Blues & Jazz

Oxford Art Factory (p134) Live indie bands, DJs and assorted bohemian happenings.

Newtown Social Club (p119) Local bands and regular international blow-ins.

Vanguard (p119) Cabaret-style setting for live performances from many genres.

Frankie's Pizza (p97) Lots of live music, including karaoke backed by a band.

Basement (p67) Originally just jazz, but now covering all manner of music styles.

Best Cinema Experiences

Sydney Film Festival (p22) Winter's the time for bunkering down in the gorgeous State Theatre.

NEED TO KNOW

Opening Hours
→ Box office: usually 9am–5pm Monday–Friday, plus two hours pre-performance.
→ Cinema sessions: 10.30am–9.30pm.

What's On Listings
Sydney Morning Herald Friday's 'Shortlist' section, also online at www.smh.com.au.

What's On Sydney (www.whatsonsydney.com)

What's On City of Sydney (http://whatson.cityofsydney.nsw.gov.au)

Time Out Sydney (www.au.timeout.com/sydney)

Ticketing Agencies
Moshtix (www.moshtix.com.au)

Ticketek (☎132 849; www.ticketek.com.au)

Ticketmaster (☎136 100; www.ticketmaster.com.au)

Tropfest (p205) The world's largest short-film festival.

OpenAir Cinema (p67) Watch movies by the water, with the Opera House stealing attention from the screen.

Moonlight Cinema (p152) Spread out a picnic blanket in Centennial Park.

Bondi Openair Cinema (p158) Another idyllic setting for an outdoor flick.

PLAN YOUR TRIP ENTERTAINMENT

🛍 Shopping

*Brash, hedonistic Sydney has elevated shopping to a universal panacea.
Feeling good? Let's go shopping. Feeling bad? Let's go shopping. Credit-card
bills getting you down? Let's go shopping... Many locals treat shopping as a
recreational activity rather than a necessity, evidenced by the teeming cash-
flapping masses at the city's weekend markets.*

Service

Retail service in Sydney is generally reasonable, although travellers from the USA might
find it a bit laid-back at times. Sycophancy
isn't the Australian way, but nor is snobbish-
ness. You shouldn't face condescension if
you rock into a boutique in your thongs and
a singlet, but nor will you be treated like a
princess just because you've splashed $5000
on daddy's credit card.

What to Buy

Want something quintessentially Australian
to take home? Head to the Rocks and dig up
some opals, an Akubra hat, a Driza-Bone coat
or some Blundstone boots. Aboriginal art is
globally popular.

Sydney has a thriving fashion scene, and
a summer dress or Speedos won't eat up luggage space. Ask at CD stores or bookshops
about local bands and authors, or grab a
Sydney-made DVD. Hunter Valley wine
makes a great gift – check your country's
duty-free allowance before buying.

Shipping Goods

Check with your airline about excess baggage rates – it may be cheaper than shipping
a parcel. For standard parcel-post rates,
enquire at any **post office** (www.auspost.com.
au). For big items, such as art or cases of
wine, some vendors arrange shipping for a
fee. Shipping companies operating out of
Sydney are listed in the **telephone directory**
(www.yellowpages.com.au).

Sales Taxes

Sales taxes are included in the advertised
price. Apart from the 10% goods and services
tax (GST), the only other sales duties are on
things such as alcohol and tobacco, which are
best bought at duty-free shops, such as those
at the airport. The GST tourist refund scheme
(p225) has mostly replaced traditional duty-
free shopping.

Shopping by Neighbourhood

➡ **Circular Quay & the Rocks** (p68) Overpriced
souvenirs, tourist-tat, opals and the like.

➡ **Sydney Harbour** (p83) The markets in Kirribilli
and Balmain are worth checking out.

➡ **City Centre & Haymarket** (p99) Sydney's
shopping heartland, catering to every taste and
budget.

➡ **Inner West** (p120) Excellent bookshops,
alternative boutiques and factory outlets.

➡ **Surry Hills & Darlinghurst** (p134) Secondhand
boutiques, design stores and gay partywear.

➡ **Paddington & Centennial Park** (p153) Art,
fashion and books.

➡ **Bondi to Coogee** (p166) Surfwear and gear, and
Sydney's best mall.

Lonely Planet's Top Choices

Strand Arcade (p99) Fashion retail at its finest.

Queen Victoria Building (p99) Regal surroundings add a sense of gravitas to any splurge.

Westfield Bondi Junction (p166) Huge range of stores, plenty of daddy daycare and a great food hall.

Westfield Sydney (p99) Bafflingly large complex incorporating top restaurants and two prestigious department stores.

Paddy's Markets (p101) Forget high fashion, head here for bargains and bustle.

Best Weekend Markets

Paddington Markets (p153) Sydney's most famous market, selling everything from clothing to palm-reading.

Bondi Markets (p166) Fruit and veg on Saturdays, assorted bric-a-brac on Sundays.

Glebe Markets (p120) One big counter-cultural get-together.

Eveleigh Farmers' Market (p116) Foodies flock here on Saturday mornings.

Kirribilli Markets (p83) Clothing, jewellery, art and fashion.

Best Bookshops

Gleebooks (p120) Sydney's best bookshop, with regular author talks.

Better Read Than Dead (p120) Well-presented and -stocked Newtown store.

Kinokuniya (p100) Sydney's biggest bookshop.

Ariel (p153) Great for art and design books, amongst other things.

Berkelouw Books (p153) New, secondhand and rare titles.

Best for Women's Clothes

Corner Shop (p153) Well-curated boutique with branches in Paddington and the Strand Arcade.

Poepke (p153) Small store with a good range of Australian and international designers.

Capital L (p153) A friendly boutique focusing on up-and-coming Australian designers.

Leona Edmiston (p153) Local designer with branches in Paddington, the Strand Arcade and the Westfield malls.

Sass & Bide (p153) Internationally known Aussie label, with branches in Paddington, the Strand Arcade and the Westfields.

Best for Men's Clothes

Blue Spinach (p135) Big labels at reduced prices.

Herringbone (p154) Finely tailored men's shirts.

Surfection (p166) Bloke's beachwear, including interesting tees and boardies.

Calibre (p154) Aussie designers producing schmick suits and shirts.

Deus Ex Machina (p121) Revhead gear, along with cool tees and jeans.

Best for Australiana

RM Williams (p100) Everything you need for the fair dinkum jackaroo look.

Strand Hatters (p100) Complete the Crocodile Dundee look with an Akubra hat.

NEED TO KNOW

Opening Hours

As a very general rule, shop opening hours are as follows:

➡ 9.30am–6pm Monday–Wednesday, Friday and Saturday

➡ 9.30am–9pm Thursday

➡ 11am–5pm Sunday

Bargaining & Sales

Haggling isn't part of Australia's commercial culture, though you could try at some of the grungier markets around the city, or if you're buying in bulk. Big-store sales usually happen in early January and July.

Warranties

Under local law, all purchases (including secondhand items) have an implied warranty that the goods are of merchantable quality (unless the customer is informed otherwise), are fit for the purpose supplied, and match the sample or description provided. If this is not the case, you are legally entitled to a refund.

Many suppliers (particularly of electrical goods) offer written warranties (guarantees) for fixed terms. Check that they apply worldwide and include service in your home country.

Australian Wine Centre (p68) Stock up on the top Aussie drops.

Opal Minded (p68) Opal aficionados love this place.

Opal Fields (p100) Longstanding opal jewellery designers.

Sports & Activities

Who wants to be stuck inside on a beautiful sunny day? Certainly not most Sydneysiders. Give them any excuse and they'll be stripping off nonessential clothing and hitting the city's beaches, parks and pools. With looking good such an obvious concern, the city has devised myriad ways to stay built, bronzed and beautiful. Oh, and healthy, too.

Spectator Sports

Sydneysiders like to stay in shape, but not everyone here is a Bondi lifesaver – plenty of people settle for watching rather than participating in the competitive collision of sporting life. On any given Sydney weekend there'll be all manner of balls being hurled, kicked and batted around. By far the most popular spectator sport is rugby league, but rugby union, Aussie Rules (the Australian Football League), soccer (the other football), cricket, netball, basketball and tennis all have their devotees.

Sailing

An introductory sailing lesson is a brilliant way to get out onto the harbour, though it's not for the budget-conscious. More experienced salts can skipper their own boat.

Diving

Sydney's best shore dives are at Gordons Bay, Clovelly; Shark Point, Clovelly; Shelly Beach, Manly; and Ship Rock, Cronulla. Other destinations include North Bondi, Camp Cove and Bare Island. Popular boat-dive sites include the grey nurse shark colony at Magic Point, off Maroubra; Wedding Cake Island, off Coogee; Sydney Heads; and off Royal National Park.

Cycling

An ever-increasing number of Sydney roads have designated cycle lanes, but some of these run between parked cars and moving traffic (watch for opening doors). If you're just cycling for fun and not commuting, opt for the long cycle paths at North Head (near Manly), Sydney Olympic Park and Centennial Park.

In-Line Skating & Skateboarding

The beachside promenades at Bondi and Manly are in-line skating hot spots, but Centennial Park is better for serious workouts. You can even skate across Sydney Harbour Bridge. There's a decent skate ramp at the south end of Bondi Beach, and a skate centre at Sydney Olympic Park.

Sports & Activities by Neighbourhood

➡ **Circular Quay & the Rocks** (p68) The starting point for several cycling and walking tours.

➡ **Sydney Harbour** (p83) Sail, jet-boat, kayak, swim or take a cruise.

➡ **City Centre & Haymarket** (p101) Walking tours and some great swimming pools.

➡ **Inner West** (p121) Take a dip in Victoria Park.

➡ **Paddington & Centennial Park** (p155) Watch the footy, the cricket or the gee-gees, or circle Centennial Park on a bike, horse or in-line skates.

➡ **Bondi to Coogee** (p167) Dive, snorkel, surf, swim, skateboard or kite-board.

➡ **Manly** (p176) Surf, kayak, cycle, snorkel or skate.

Lonely Planet's Top Choices

Let's Go Surfing (p158) Learn to surf at one of the world's most famous beaches.

Sydney Football Stadium (p155) Yell your head off at a rugby league match.

Store Beach (p171) Kayak from Manly to this isolated harbour beach, only accessible from the water.

Centennial Parklands Equestrian Centre (p155) Saddle up for a canter around Centennial Park.

Gordons Bay Underwater Nature Trail (p167) Explore the scenery beneath the waves.

Best Cycling Tours

Sydney Architecture Walks (p101) Architecture-themed cycles by guides who know their stuff.

BlueBananas (p101) The cheat's city tour, on an electric bike.

Bonza Bike Tours (p68) Various options for exploring the city and Manly.

Bike Buffs (p68) Harbourside rides departing from the Rocks.

Manly Bike Tours (p176) Two-hour bike tours around Manly.

Best Walking Tours

The Rocks Walking Tours (p68) Delve into the stories of Australia's oldest streets.

Sydney Architecture Walks (p101) Specialist tours on various themes.

I'm Free (p101) Three-hour city tours, run for tips.

Peek Tours (p68) Tour historic pubs around the Rocks.

The Rocks Ghost Tours (p68) Take a walk on the creepy side.

Best Swimming Pools

Bondi Icebergs Swimming Club (p158) Swim laps to the sound of crashing surf.

Andrew (Boy) Charlton Pool (p101) Saltwater swimming, right on the harbour.

North Sydney Olympic Pool (p83) The pool with the views.

Wylie's Baths (p167) Historic sea baths set into the rocky shoreline.

Sydney Olympic Park Aquatic Centre (p111) Indulge your Olympic fantasies.

Best Boat Trips

Champagne Sailing (p83) Charter a yacht and a skipper for a taste of the high life.

Manly Ocean Adventures (p176) Blast along the coast in search of whales.

Sailing Sydney (p83) Try your hand as an America's Cup yachtee.

Sydney Showboats (p84) Dinner cruises with high-kicking entertainment.

James Craig (p83) Sail into the past on a mighty tall ship.

NEED TO KNOW

Sports Seasons

Conveniently, the most popular spectator sports happen in winter, not interrupting the beach schedule too much. The netball season runs from about March to August, while the football season (rugby league, rugby union and Aussie Rules) continues until the beginning of October. Summer sports include cricket, tennis, sailing and surf lifesaving. Soccer is the exception, with a season lasting from August to February.

Transporting Bikes

Bicycles can travel on suburban trains for free if you have an Opal card or if it's a fold-up bike. If not, you'll need to buy a separate kid's ticket for your bike during peak hours; offpeak is free. Bikes also ride for free on Sydney's ferries but are banned from buses.

Best Kayak Tours

Sydney Harbour Kayaks (p83) Four-hour ecotours, departing from the Spit Bridge.

Natural Wanders (p83) Morning harbour paddles in the shadow of the bridge.

Manly Kayak Centre (p176) Take a three-hour tour or splash out on your own.

Explore Sydney

49

SYDNEY'S
TOP SIGHTS

Sydney
Opera House 54

Sydney
Harbour Bridge 55

Royal Botanic Garden 56

Art Gallery of NSW 87

Bondi Beach 158

Neighbourhoods at a Glance

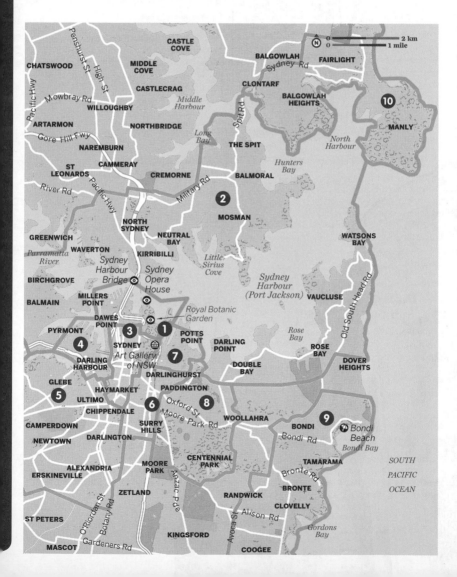

0 ———————— 2 km
0 ———————— 1 mile

CHATSWOOD

Penshurst St

High St

Pacific Hwy

Mowbray Rd

ARTARMON

Gore Hill Fwy

NAREMBURN

ST LEONARDS

Pacific Hwy

River Rd

GREENWICH

WAVERTON

Parramatta River

BIRCHGROVE

BALMAIN

MILLERS POINT

DAWES POINT

PYRMONT

4

DARLING HARBOUR

3

SYDNEY

Art Gallery of NSW

GLEBE

5

ULTIMO

HAYMARKET

CHIPPENDALE

CAMPERDOWN

NEWTOWN

DARLINGTON

ALEXANDRIA

ERSKINEVILLE

ST PETERS

O'Riordan St

Botany Rd

ZETLAND

MASCOT

Gardeners Rd

KINGSFORD

MIDDLE COVE

CASTLECRAG

WILLOUGHBY

NORTHBRIDGE

CAMMERAY

CREMORNE

NORTH SYDNEY

NEUTRAL BAY

KIRRIBILLI

Sydney Harbour Bridge

Sydney Opera House

Royal Botanic Garden

1

7

POTTS POINT

DARLINGHURST

PADDINGTON

8

Oxford St

Moore Park Rd

SURRY HILLS

6

MOORE PARK

Anzac Pde

CENTENNIAL PARK

CASTLE COVE

Middle Harbour

Long Bay

THE SPIT

Spit Rd

Military Rd

Little Sirius Cove

BALGOWLAH

Sydney Rd

CLONTARF

BALGOWLAH HEIGHTS

2

MOSMAN

Hunters Bay

BALMORAL

FAIRLIGHT

North Harbour

10

MANLY

WATSONS BAY

Sydney Harbour (Port Jackson)

VAUCLUSE

Rose Bay

DARLING POINT

DOUBLE BAY

ROSE BAY

DOVER HEIGHTS

Old South Head Rd

WOOLLAHRA

9

BONDI

Bondi Rd

Bondi Beach

Bondi Bay

TAMARAMA

Bronte Rd

BRONTE

CLOVELLY

Gordons Bay

RANDWICK

Alison Rd

Avoca St

COOGEE

SOUTH PACIFIC OCEAN

❶ Circular Quay & the Rocks p52

The birthplace of both the city and the modern nation, this compact area seamlessly combines the historic with the exuberantly modern. Join the tourist pilgrimage to the Opera House and Harbour Bridge then grab a schooner at a convict-era pub in the Rocks.

❷ Sydney Harbour p69

Stretching inland from the heads for 20km until it morphs into the Parramatta River, the harbour has shaped the local psyche for millennia, and today it's the city's sparkling playground. Its inlets, beaches, islands and shorefront parks provide endless swimming, sailing, picnicking and walking opportunities.

❸ City Centre & Haymarket p85

Sydney's central business district offers plenty of choices for upmarket shopping, eating and sightseeing, with gracious colonial buildings scattered among the skyscrapers and orderly parks providing breathing space. The breathless jumble of Haymarket and Chinatown provide the yin to the CBD's yang.

❹ Darling Harbour & Pyrmont p102

Unashamedly tourist focused, Darling Harbour will do its best to tempt you to its shoreline bars and restaurants with fireworks displays and a sprinkling of glitz. On its western flank, Pyrmont appears to be sinking under the weight of its casino and motorway flyovers.

❺ Inner West p108

Quietly bohemian Glebe and more loudly bohemian Newtown are the most well-known of the Inner West's tightly packed suburbs, grouped around the University of Sydney. All the essential hang-outs for students – bookshops, cafes and pubs – are present in abundance.

❻ Surry Hills & Darlinghurst p122

Sydney's hippest and gayest neighbourhoods are also home to its most interesting dining and bar scenes. For the most part, they're more gritty than pretty, and actual sights are thin on the ground, but there's still plenty to do and see here, especially after dark.

❼ Kings Cross & Potts Point p136

If Darling Harbour is Sydney dressing up nicely for tourists, the Cross is where it relaxes, scratches itself and belches. In equal parts thrilling and depressing but never boring, this is where you come for nighttime blinders or surprisingly pleasant daytime meanders.

❽ Paddington & Centennial Park p144

The next band of suburbs to the east is distinctly well-heeled – and in Paddington's case they're probably Manolo Blahniks. Despite taking a hit with the opening of the Westfield Bondi Junction mall just up the road, this is still Sydney's fashion and art heartland.

❾ Bondi to Coogee p156

Sydney sheds its suit and tie, ditches the strappy heels and chills out in the Eastern Beaches. Beach after golden-sand beach, alternating with sheer sandstone cliffs, are the classic vistas of this beautiful, laid-back and egalitarian stretch of the city.

❿ Manly p168

Sydney's only ferry destination boasting an ocean beach, Manly caps off the harbour with scrappy charm. The surf's good and as the gateway to the Northern Beaches, it makes a popular base for the board-riding brigade.

Circular Quay & the Rocks

CIRCULAR QUAY | THE ROCKS | DAWES POINT | MILLERS POINT

Neighbourhood Top Five

1 Coming face to face with the number-one visual symbol of the city, the **Sydney Opera House** (p54). On a sunny day it's postcard perfect, its curves and points a pinnacle of architectural expression.

2 Strolling the idyllic grounds of the **Royal Botanic Garden** (p56), with the harbour sparkling below.

3 Finding artistic inspiration at the **Museum of Contemporary Art** (p60).

4 Gazing on the harbour from amid the heavy metal of the **Sydney Harbour Bridge** (p55).

5 Letting the food and view seduce you at **Quay** (p64), or any of the other top harbourside restaurants.

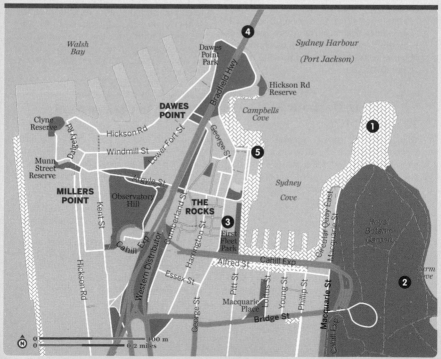

For more detail of this area, see Map p240 ➡

Explore Circular Quay & the Rocks

At some stage you'll almost certainly end up in this neck of the woods – you haven't really been to Sydney if you don't. Set aside the best part of a day to see the sights of this very touristy neighbourhood. Return at night to clink glasses at an upmarket restaurant, to down a beverage in a historic pub or to catch a show.

Nowadays Sydney Cove carries the weight of Sydney iconography, with the Harbour Bridge and the Opera House abutting each point of its horseshoe. Sensing photo opportunities, some of Sydney's swankiest hotels and restaurants are also here.

Circular Quay's promenade serves as a backdrop for buskers of mixed merit and locals disgorging from harbour ferries. The Rocks is unrecognisable from the squalid place it once was and it now serves as an 'olde worlde' tourist trap. Over the ridge is Millers Point, a low-key colonial district that makes a calming diversion from the harbourside tourist fray, and Dawes Point, a redeveloped maritime precinct.

Local Life

➡ **Performing arts** Sydneysiders put aside their aversion to this most touristy part of town to attend performances at the Sydney Opera House (p66) and the Walsh Bay theatres (p66).

➡ **Special occasion restaurants** For proposals, zero-ending birthdays or that one extravagant night out per year, restaurants such as Quay (p64) and Aria (p64) are never-fail options.

➡ **Parks** You're liable to see locals taking romantic strolls, letting the kids off the leash or shaking out a picnic blanket in the Royal Botanic Garden (p56) or Observatory Hill (p62).

Getting There & Away

➡ **Train** Circular Quay is one of the City Circle stations.
➡ **Ferry** Circular Quay is Sydney's ferry hub and has services to Double Bay, Watsons Bay, Manly, Taronga Zoo, Kirribilli, North Sydney, Milsons Point, Darling Harbour, Cockatoo Island, Balmain, Sydney Olympic Park and Parramatta, among others.
➡ **Bus** Circular Quay is the major terminus for routes including: 301–303 (Surry Hills); 324 and 325 (Kings Cross–Double Bay–Vaucluse–Watsons Bay); 333 and 389 (Darlinghurst–North Bondi); 373 and 374 (Coogee); 380 (Darlinghurst–Paddington–Bondi–Watsons Bay); 422, 423, 426 and 428 (Newtown); and 470 (Glebe).

Lonely Planet's Top Tip

The best way to avoid the city traffic is to travel here by train or ferry. If you really feel that you must bring the car, come on the weekend, as the Wilson parking building beneath the Opera House charges a set fee of $15 between 6am and 5pm (it's $55 during the week).

Best Places to Eat

➡ Quay (p64)
➡ Saké (p65)
➡ Aria (p64)
➡ Sailors Thai Canteen (p64)
➡ Cafe Sopra (p65)

For reviews, see p64 ➡

Best Places to Drink

➡ Lord Nelson Brewery Hotel (p65)
➡ Opera Bar (p65)
➡ Hero of Waterloo (p65)
➡ Glenmore at the Rocks (p65)
➡ Argyle (p65)

For reviews, see p65 ➡

Best Heritage Sights

➡ Rocks Discovery Museum (p60)
➡ Susannah Place Museum (p61)
➡ Government House (p56)
➡ Sydney Observatory (p62)
➡ The Big Dig (p61)

For reviews, see p56 ➡

TOP SIGHT
SYDNEY OPERA HOUSE

Gazing upon the Sydney Opera House with virgin eyes is a sure way to send a tingle down your spine. Gloriously curvaceous and pointy, the Opera House perches dramatically at the tip of Bennelong Point, waiting for its close-up. No matter from which angle you point a lens at it, it shamelessly mugs for the camera; it really doesn't have a bad side.

DON'T MISS...

→ Catching a performance – any performance

→ Taking a guided tour

PRACTICALITIES

→ Map p240

→ ☎ 02-9250 7250

→ www.sydneyopera house.com

→ Bennelong Point

→ tours adult/child $37/20

→ ⊙ tours 9am-5pm

→ ⓡ Circular Quay

Design & Construction

Danish architect Jørn Utzon's competition-winning 1956 design is Australia's most recognisable visual image (p212). It's said to have been inspired by billowing sails, orange segments, palm fronds and Mayan temples, and has been poetically likened to nuns in a rugby scrum, a typewriter stuffed with scallop shells and the sexual congress of turtles. It's not until you get close that you realise that the seemingly solid expanse of white is actually composed of tiles – 1,056,000 self-cleaning cream-coloured Swedish tiles, to be exact.

The Opera House's construction was itself truly operatic – so much so, it was dramatised as *The Eighth Wonder*, performed here by Opera Australia in 1995. The predicted four-year construction started in 1959. After a tumultuous clash of egos, delays, politicking, death and cost blow-outs, Utzon quit in disgust in 1966. The Opera House finally opened in 1973. Utzon and his son Jan were commissioned for renovations in 2004, but Utzon died in 2008 having never seen his finished masterpiece in the flesh.

Performances

Inside, dance, concerts, opera and theatre are staged in the **Concert Hall**, **Joan Sutherland Theatre**, **Drama Theatre** and **Playhouse**, while more intimate and left-of-centre shows inhabit the **Studio**. Companies regularly performing here include the Australian Ballet (p67), Australian Chamber Orchestra (p67), Bangarra Dance Theatre (p67), Opera Australia (p67), Sydney Symphony Orchestra (p67) and the Sydney Theatre Company (p66). The acoustics in the concert hall are superb; the internal aesthetics like the belly of a whale.

Most events (2400 of them annually!) sell out quickly, but partial-view tickets are often available on short notice. The free monthly *What's On* brochure lists upcoming events, including info on *Kids at the House* – a pint-sized entertainment roster of music, drama and dance.

Tours

The interiors don't live up to the promise of the dazzling exterior, but if you're curious to see inside, one-hour guided tours depart throughout the day. You can book ahead for tours in various languages, including Auslan sign language, and if you've got limited mobility, Access Tours can be arranged.

Not all tours can visit all theatres because of rehearsals, but you're more likely to see everything if you go early. A highlight is the **Utzon Room**, the only part of the Opera House to have an interior designed by the great man himself. For a more in-depth nosy around, the two-hour early-morning backstage tour ($165, departs 7am) includes the Green Room, stars' dressing rooms, stage and orchestra pit.

TOP SIGHT
SYDNEY HARBOUR BRIDGE

Whether they're driving over it, climbing up it, jogging across it, shooting fireworks off it or sailing under it, Sydneysiders adore their bridge and swarm around it like ants on ice cream. Dubbed the 'coathanger', it's a spookily big object – moving around town you'll catch sight of it out of the corner of your eye when you least expect it.

The Structure

At 134m high, 1149m long, 49m wide and 52,800 tonnes, the Sydney Harbour Bridge is the largest and heaviest (but not the longest) steel arch in the world. It links the Rocks with North Sydney, crossing the harbour at one of its narrowest points.

The two halves of chief engineer JJC Bradfield's mighty arch were built outwards from each shore. In 1930, after seven years of merciless toil by 1400 workers, the two arches were only centimetres apart when 100km/h winds set them swaying. The coathanger hung tough, the arch was bolted together and the bridge finally opened to the public two years later.

The bridge is the centrepiece of Sydney's major celebrations, particularly the New Year's Eve fireworks. In 2007, when it reached its 75th birthday, 250,000 people celebrated by walking across the great span.

Get Over It

The best way to experience the bridge is on foot – don't expect much of a view crossing by train or car (driving south there's a toll). Staircases access the bridge from both shores; a footpath runs along its eastern side.

BridgeClimb

Once only painters and daredevils scaled the Harbour Bridge – now anyone can do it (Bruce Springsteen, Bette Midler, 10-year-old kids...). Make your way through the **Bridge-Climb** (☑02-8274 7777; www.bridgeclimb.com; 3 Cumberland St; adult $218-348, child $148-228; ℝCircular Quay) departure lounge and the extensive training session, don your headset, an umbilical safety cord and a dandy grey jumpsuit (Elvis would be so proud) and up you go. If you're afraid of heights, the scariest part is crossing over the mesh catwalk while under the bridge; on the curved span itself the track is wide enough that you never see straight down.

Tours last 2¼ to 3½ hours – a preclimb toilet stop is a smart idea. If you're uncertain whether your nerve or bladder will hold that long, a 90-minute sampler is available but it only goes halfway and never reaches the summit. The priciest climbs are at dawn and sunset.

Pylon Lookout

The bridge's hefty pylons may look as though they're shouldering all the weight, but they're largely decorative – right down to their granite facing. There are awesome views from the top of the **Pylon Lookout** (☑02-9240 1100; www.pylonlookout.com.au; adult/child $13/6.50; ⊙10am-5pm; ℝCircular Quay), atop the southeast pylon, 200 steps above the bridge's footpath. Inside the pylon there are exhibits about the bridge's construction, including an eight-minute film which screens every 15 minutes.

DON'T MISS...

➡ Sunset from the top of the bridge
➡ The views from the Pylon Lookout

PRACTICALITIES

➡ Map p240
➡ ℝCircular Quay

CIRCULAR QUAY & THE ROCKS SYDNEY HARBOUR BRIDGE

TOP SIGHT
ROYAL BOTANIC GARDEN

This expansive park is the inner city's favourite picnic destination, jogging route and snuggling spot. Bordering Farm Cove, immediately east of the Opera House, the garden was established in 1816 and features plant life from Australia and around the world. It includes the site of the colony's first paltry vegetable patch.

DON'T MISS...

➡ Government House
➡ The rainforest walk
➡ The succulent garden

PRACTICALITIES

➡ Map p240
➡ 📞 02-9231 8111, 02-9231 8111
➡ www.rbgsyd.nsw. gov.au
➡ Mrs Macquaries Rd
➡ admission free
➡ ⏰ 7am-8pm Oct-Feb, to 5.30pm Mar-Sep
➡ 🚉 Circular Quay

Plants

Highlights include the **rose garden**, the **rainforest walk** and the **succulent garden**. There's also a begonia garden, herb garden, palm grove, pioneer garden, rare and threatened plants garden, bushland walk, Australian native rockery, fernery and an ever-popular camellia garden.

The garden's many magnificent mature trees are well labelled with genus and place of origin. Look for the rare **Wollemi pine**, an ancient tree only discovered in 1994 in a remote pocket of the Blue Mountains, the exact location of which has been kept a secret. In between all the greenery are ponds, fountains, lawns and numerous interesting sculptures, both modern and traditional.

Walks & Tours

Free 1½-hour **guided walks** depart at 10.30am daily from the information booth outside the Garden Shop. From March to November there's also an additional hour-long tour at 1pm on weekdays.

Long before the convicts arrived, this was an initiation ground for the Gadigal people. Book ahead for an **Aboriginal Heritage Tour** (📞02-9231 8134; adult/child $37/17; ⏰10am Fri), which covers local history, traditional plant uses and bush-food tastings. You can also download self-guided tours from the RBG website.

The park's paths are mostly wheelchair accessible. Estimated walking times on signs are pessimistic (if a sign says something is five minutes away, bank on two). If you're all walked out, take a ride on the **Choochoo Express** (www.choochoo.com.au; adult/child $10/5; ⏰11am-4pm), a trackless train that departs from Queen Elizabeth II Gate (nearest the Opera House) every half an hour.

Government House

Encased in English-style grounds within the gardens, **Government House** (📞02-9931 5222; www.sydneylivingmuseums.com.au; Macquarie St; ⏰grounds 10am-4pm, tours 10.30am-3pm Fri-Sun; 🚉Circular Quay) FREE is a Gothic sandstone mansion (built 1837–43) which serves as the official residence of the Governor of NSW. It's also used for hosting visiting heads of state and royalty. Unless there's a bigwig in town the interior can be accessed on a free guided tour; collect your ticket from the gatehouse. Disabled access is OK, but it's best to call in advance.

Mrs Macquaries Point

Adjoining the garden but officially part of The Domain, this peninsula forms the northeastern tip of Farm Cove and provides beautiful views over the bay to the Opera House and city skyline. It was named in 1810 after Elizabeth, Governor Macquarie's wife, who ordered a seat chiselled into the rock from which she could view the harbour. **Mrs Macquaries Chair**, as it's known, remains to this day.

Clouds of sulphur-crested cockatoos disturb the peace with their raucous caws during the day, while at night it's a romantic spot for an after-dinner stroll.

⊙ SIGHTS

⊙ Circular Quay

SYDNEY OPERA HOUSE BUILDING
See p54.

ROYAL BOTANIC GARDEN GARDENS
See p56.

SYDNEY CONSERVATORIUM OF MUSIC HISTORIC BUILDING
Map p240 (⊘02-93511222; www.music.usyd.edu.au; 1 Conservatorium Rd; ⛎Circular Quay) The castellated 'Con' was designed in 1817 by convict architect Francis Greenway as the stables and servants' quarters of Governor Macquarie's new government house. Partly because of the project's extravagance, Macquarie was ousted before the house could be completed. In 1915 the stables were converted into a music conservatorium, which amalgamated with the University of Sydney in 1990. Subsequent renovations (equally extravagant at $145 million) created five world-class performance venues.

JUSTICE & POLICE MUSEUM MUSEUM
Map p240 (⊘02-9252 1144; www.sydneyliving museums.com.au; cnr Albert & Phillip Sts; adult/child $10/5; ⛎10am-5pm Sat & Sun; ⛎Circular Quay) Occupying the old Water Police Station (1858), this mildly unnerving museum documents the city's dark and disreputable past through old police photographs and an often macabre collection of exhibits.

CUSTOMS HOUSE HISTORIC BUILDING
Map p240 (⊘02-9242 8555; www.sydney customshouse.com.au; 31 Alfred St; ⛎10am-7pm Mon-Fri, 11am-4pm Sat & Sun; ⛎Circular Quay) FREE This elegant harbourside edifice (1885) houses a bar, Cafe Sydney (p64), on the top floor, and the three-level **Customs House Library** (Map p240; ⊘02-9242 8555; 31 Alfred St; ⛎10am-7pm Mon-Fri, 11am-4pm Sat & Sun; ⛎Circular Quay), which has a great selection of international newspapers and magazines, internet access and interesting temporary exhibitions. In the lobby, look for the swastikas in the tiling (and the plaque explaining their symbolism), and a fascinating 1:500 model of the inner city under the glass floor.

MACQUARIE PLACE SQUARE
Map p240 (cnr Loftus & Bridge Sts; ⛎Circular Quay) Beneath some shady Moreton Bay fig trees a block or two back from the Quay is this little historic triangle. Look for the actual **cannon and anchor** from the First Fleet flagship (HMS *Sirius*), an ornate but defunct 1857 drinking fountain, a National Trust–classified gentlemen's *pissoir* (closed) and an 1818 **obelisk** erected 'to record that all the public roads leading to the interior of the colony are measured from it'.

The park is overlooked by the imposing 19th-century **Lands Department Building**; the north facade bears statues of Sturt, Hume, Leichhardt and other early Australian movers and shakers.

TANK STREAM FOUNTAIN FOUNTAIN
Map p240 (Herald Sq, Alfred St; ⛎Circular Quay) Designed by Stephen Walker, this four-part bronze fountain (1981) near Circular Quay

---

BENNELONG

Bennelong was born around 1764 into the Wangal tribe, the westerly neighbours of the Gadigal who lived around central Sydney. Captured in 1789, he was brought to Governor Arthur Phillip, who hoped to use Bennelong to understand the local Aboriginals' customs and language.

Bennelong took to life with the settlers, developing a taste for British food and alcohol, and learning to speak the language of his new 'masters'. Eventually he escaped, but he returned by 1791 when reassured that he would not be held against his will. He developed a strong friendship with Governor Phillip, who had a brick hut built for him on what is now Bennelong Point.

In 1792 Bennelong went on a 'civilising' trip to England, and returned in 1795 with a changed dress sense and altered behaviour. Described as good natured and 'stoutly made', Bennelong ultimately was no longer accepted by Aboriginal society and never really found happiness with his white friends either. He died a broken, dispossessed man in 1813, possibly as a result of his affection for the bottle.

MANFRED GOTTSCHALK / GETTY IMAGES ©

WARWICK KENT / GETTY IMAGES ©

QUAY
GRAND

DANITA DELIMONT / GETTY IMAGES ©

1. Circular Quay (p52)
Postcard-perfect vistas in the heart of iconic Sydney.

2. The Rocks (p60)
Stroll the alleys where Australia's convict history began.

3. Sydney Opera House (p54)
A technicolour transformation during the Vivid Sydney festival (p22).

4. Royal Botanic Garden (p56)
Walk among statues such as *Sweep Boy* in this expansive, tranquil green space.

WHERE IT ALL BEGAN

After dismissing Botany Bay as a site for the colony, Governor Phillip sailed the First Fleet into what James Cook had named Port Jackson (Warran in the local language) and dropped anchor at a horseshoe bay with an all-important freshwater stream running into it. Phillip astutely christened the bay Sydney Cove after the British Home Secretary, Baron Sydney of Chislehurst, who was responsible for the colonies.

The socioeconomic divide of the future city was foreshadowed when the convicts were allocated the rocky land to the west of the stream (known unimaginatively as the Rocks), while the governor and other officials pitched their tents to the east.

Built with convict labour between 1837 and 1844, Circular Quay was originally (and more accurately) called Semicircular Quay, and acted as the main port of Sydney. In the 1850s it was extended further, covering over the by then festering Tank Stream, which ran into the middle of the cove.

As time went on, whalers and sailors joined the ex-convicts at the Rocks – and inns and brothels sprang up to entertain them. With the settlement filthy and overcrowded, the nouveau riche started building houses on the upper slopes, their sewage flowing to the slums below. Residents sloshed through open sewers, and alleys festered with disease and drunken lawlessness. Thus began a long, steady decline.

Bubonic plague broke out in 1900, leading to the razing of entire streets, and Harbour Bridge construction in the 1920s wiped out even more. It wasn't until the 1970s that the Rocks' cultural and architectural heritage was finally recognised. Redevelopment saved many old buildings by converting them into tourist-focused businesses. Shops hocking Opera House key rings proliferate, but gritty history is never far below the surface if you know where to look.

incorporates dozens of sculptures of native Australian animals; play spot-the-echidna. The fountain is dedicated to 'all the children who have played around the Tank Stream', which now runs beneath the city.

⊙ The Rocks

MUSEUM OF
CONTEMPORARY ART   GALLERY

Map p240 (☑02-9245 2400; www.mca.com.au; 140 George St; ⊙10am-5pm Fri-Wed, to 9pm Thu; ⊠Circular Quay) FREE One of country's best and most challenging galleries, the MCA is a showcase for Australian and international contemporary art. Aboriginal art features prominently. The fab Gotham City–style art deco building bears the wounds of a redevelopment that has grafted on additional gallery space and a rooftop cafe/sculpture terrace – and ruined the George St facade in the process. Volunteer-led guided tours are offered at 11am and 1pm daily, and at 7pm Thursdays and 3pm on weekends.

KEN DONE GALLERY   GALLERY

Map p240 (www.kendone.com.au; 1 Hickson Rd; ⊙10am-5.30pm; ⊠Circular Quay) FREE The cheerful, quasi-childlike work of Sydney artist Ken Done is exhibited inside the lavishly restored Australian Steam Navigation Building. Expect luridly coloured Australian landscapes, Opera House renderings and comic minutiae from Done's days.

ROCKS DISCOVERY MUSEUM   MUSEUM

Map p240 (☑02-9240 8680; www.rocksdiscov erymuseum.com; Kendall Lane; ⊙10am-5pm; ⊠Circular Quay) FREE Divided into four chronological displays – Warrane (pre-1788), Colony (1788–1820), Port (1820–1900) and Transformations (1900 to the present) – this excellent museum digs deep into the Rocks' history and leads you on an artefact-rich tour. Sensitive attention is given to the Rocks' original inhabitants, the Gadigal people.

FOUNDATION PARK   PARK

Map p240 (Gloucester Walk; ⊠Circular Quay) Thought-provoking Foundation Park is set among the preserved ruins of 1870s houses, built against the cliff face. The oversized furniture by artist Peter Cole evokes the cramped conditions once experienced by working-class Rocks families. It's a great place to pause in the shade and enjoy the views over the roofs.

SUSANNAH PLACE MUSEUM MUSEUM

Map p240 (02-9241 1893; www.sydneyliving
museums.com.au; 58-64 Gloucester St; adult/
child $8/4; tours 2pm, 3pm & 4pm; Circular
Quay) Dating from 1844, this diminutive
terrace of four houses and a shop selling historical wares is a fascinating time
capsule of life in the Rocks since colonial
times. After you watch a short film about the
people who lived here, a guide will take you
through the claustrophobic homes, which
are decorated to reflect different periods in
their histories.

THE BIG DIG ARCHAEOLOGICAL SITE

Map p240 (www.thebigdig.com.au; 110 Cumberland
St; dusk-dawn; Circular Quay) FREE Before
the outbreak of bubonic plague in the early
20th century and the subsequent slum clear-
ances, this section of the Rocks was a war-
ren of houses connected by tiny lanes. It then
spent decades covered by a car park, until
1994 when archaeologists commenced what
turned into a 15-year dig, uncovering cobblestones, foundations and little treasures along
the way. Displays bring the ruins to life, including photos of children at play on the very
cobblestones on which you're standing.

ST PATRICK'S CHURCH CHURCH

Map p240 (02-9254 9855; www.stpatschurch
hill.org; 20 Grosvenor St; 9am-4.30pm; Wynyard) This attractive sandstone church
(1844) was built on land donated by William Davis, an Irishman transported for his
role in the 1798 uprisings. Inside it's incredibly quiet, which makes the brass altar, the
stained-glass windows and the colourful
statues of St Patrick, St Joan of Arc and St
Michael (complete with dragon) seem even

CIRCULAR QUAY & THE ROCKS SIGHTS

PEMULWUY'S WAR

Aboriginal resistance to European colonisation was a subject long glossed over in
Australian history books, although it began pretty much at first contact. Dutch sailors
in the early 17th century had violent run-ins on the Australian west coast, and after
Captain Cook came ashore in 1770 and had a rock chucked at him, he wrote of the
locals, 'all they seem'd to want was us to be gone'.

Pemulwuy, a member of the Bidjigal group of Dharug speakers from near Botany
Bay, very much wanted the British to be gone. He was around 20 years old when Cook
visited, and pushing 40 by the time Arthur Phillip and the new arrivals from the First
and Second Fleets had begun killing and kidnapping his countrymen and generally
acting like they owned the place.

Pemulwuy branded himself as a troublemaker in 1790 by spearing to death Governor Phillip's game shooter. Even though the shooter, John McIntyre, was a convict
who brutalised Aboriginal people, this didn't stop Phillip from threatening a bloody
revenge. He sent out the first-ever punitive force against the locals, at first with orders
to kill 10 Bidjigals and bring their heads back to Sydney in sacks. Phillip soon calmed
down and issued milder orders to capture six for possible hanging.

The mission was an utter flop in any case, and Pemulwuy's 12 years as leader
of the struggle against the British began in earnest. At first he limited his guerrilla
campaign to small, sporadic raids on farms, taking livestock and crops. He eventually worked up to leading attacks by groups of more than a hundred men – a huge
number by Aboriginal standards of the time.

During his lifetime Pemulwuy survived being shot, as well as having his skull frac-
tured in a rumble with the enormous 'Black Caesar', a bushranger of West Indian
descent. He thoroughly cemented his reputation in 1797 in a bloody battle against
soldiers and settlers at Parramatta. During the fracas, Pemulwuy took seven pellets
of buckshot to the head and body and went down. Bleeding severely and near death,
he was captured and placed in hospital. Within weeks he managed to escape, still
wearing the leg irons he'd been shackled with.

Pemulwuy's luck ran out in 1802, when he was ambushed and shot dead. It's not
entirely clear by whom, but this time there *was* a price on Pemulwuy's head – which
was cut off, pickled in alcohol and sent to England (a similar fate befell Yagan, an
Aboriginal resistance leader in southwestern Australia, some 30 years later). Pemulwuy's son Tedbury carried on the fight until 1805.

more striking. Guided tours are infrequent but worthwhile; visit the website for details.

Davis' home (on the site of the chapel-turned-cafe) was arguably the first Catholic chapel in Australia; it was used for clandestine devotions and secretly housed a consecrated host after the colony's only Catholic priest was deported in 1818.

◉ Dawes Point

SYDNEY HARBOUR BRIDGE   BRIDGE
See p55.

WALSH BAY   WATERFRONT
Map p240 (www.walshbaysydney.com.au; Hickson Rd; ℝWynyard) This section of Dawes Point waterfront was Sydney's busiest before the advent of container shipping and the construction of new port facilities at Botany Bay. The last decade has seen the Federation-era wharves here gentrified beyond belief, morphing into luxury hotels, apartments, theatre spaces, powerboat marinas and restaurants.

The self-guided 1.6km Walsh Bay Walk starts at Pier 2 and leads you through 11 stops, with interesting plaques and directions urging you onwards; download a guide from the Walsh Bay website. Pier 4 houses the Wharf Theatre, home to the renowned Sydney Theatre Company, Sydney Dance Company and Bangarra Dance Theatre.

GARRISON CHURCH   CHURCH
Map p240 (☎02-9247 1268; www.thegarrison church.org.au; 62 Lower Fort St; ⊗9am-5pm; ℝCircular Quay) Also known as Holy Trinity (1843), this chunky sandstone Anglican church on the western side of the Argyle Cut was the colony's first military church. Below a dark timber ceiling, the hushed interior is spangled with dusty, lank-hanging regimental flags. Australia's first prime minister, Edmund Barton, went to school here (the parish hall doubled as a schoolhouse).

◉ Millers Point

SYDNEY OBSERVATORY   OBSERVATORY
Map p240 (☎02-9921 3485; www.sydneyobser vatory.com.au; 1003 Upper Fort St; ⊗10am-5pm; ℝCircular Quay) FREE Built in the 1850s, Sydney's copper-domed, Italianate observatory squats atop pretty **Observatory Hill**, overlooking the harbour. Inside is a collection

🚶 Neighbourhood Walk
A Rock-Quay Road

START CADMAN'S COTTAGE
END ROYAL BOTANIC GARDEN
LENGTH 3.5KM; TWO HOURS

Start outside ❶**Cadman's Cottage**, inner-city Sydney's oldest house. It was built on a now-buried beach for Government Coxswain John Cadman (a boat and crew superintendent) in 1816. The Sydney Water Police detained criminals here in the 1840s and it was later converted into a home for retired sea captains.

Head north along Circular Quay West past the ❷**Overseas Passenger Terminal**, where multistorey luxury cruise ships regularly weigh anchor. For a killer harbour view, head up to the level-four observation deck in the turret on the northern end. Further along the quay are ❸**Campbell's Storehouses**, built in 1839 by Scottish merchant Robert Campbell to house his stash of tea, alcohol, sugar and fabric. Construction of the 11 warehouses didn't finish until 1861, and a brick storey was added in 1890. Such buildings were common around Circular Quay into the early 20th century, but most have been demolished since. These survivors now sustain a string of pricey restaurants.

Play spot-the-bridal-party as you loop past the ❹**Park Hyatt** (p186) and into the small park at the end of Dawes Point. Couples jet in from as far away as China and Korea to have their photos taken here in front of the perfect Opera House background.

As you pass under the harbour bridge, keep an eye out for Luna Park on the opposite shore. Walk past Walsh Bay's gentrified ❺**Edwardian wharves** and then cross the road and cut up the stairs (marked 'public stairs to Windmill St') just before the ❻**Roslyn Packer Theatre** (p66). Continue up the hill on teensy Ferry Lane. Near the top you'll find the foundations of ❼**Arthur Payne's house**; he was the first victim of the 1900 bubonic plague outbreak.

At the corner of Windmill St is the ❽**Hero of Waterloo** (p65), a contender for the title of Australia's oldest pub. Turn right on Lower Fort St and head to

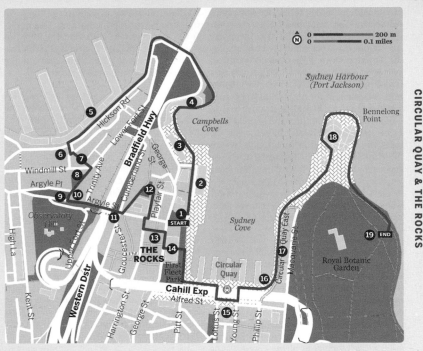

9 Argyle Place, a quiet, English-style village green lined with terraced houses.

Across the road is the handsome **10 Garrison Church** (p62). Hook left into Argyle St and stroll through the **11 Argyle Cut**. Convict labourers excavated this canyonlike section of road clear through the sandstone ridge that gave the Rocks its name. The work began in 1843 with hand tools, and was completed (with the aid of dynamite) in 1867. Just past the Cut take the stairs to the left and head along Gloucester Walk to **12 Foundation Park** (p60). Take the stairs down through the park, duck around the building at the bottom and exit onto Playfair St where there's a row of historic terraced houses.

Cross Argyle St into Harrington St then jag left into **13 Suez Canal**. One of few remaining such lanes, it tapers as it goes downhill until it's less than a metre wide (hence the name, which is also a pun on the word 'sewers'). Constructed in the 1840s, it was notorious as a lurking point for members of the Rocks Push, a street gang that relieved many a drunk of their wallet in the latter part of the 19th century. Where it intersects Nurses Walk look for the hoist jutting out of the building, once used for hauling goods to the upper floors.

Turn right into George St and cut through the **14 Museum of Contemporary Art** (p60). Exit onto Circular Quay and follow the waterline past the ferry wharves.

Cut underneath the train station to the fabulously renovated **15 Customs House** (p57). Stroll back to the water to check out the bad buskers and the plaques of the **16 Sydney Writers Walk**. This series of metal discs, set into the Circular Quay promenade, holds ruminations from prominent Australian writers and the odd literary visitor. The likes of Mark Twain, Germaine Greer, Peter Carey, Umberto Eco and Clive James wax lyrical on subjects ranging from Indigenous rights to the paradoxical nature of glass. Genres vary from eloquent poems addressing the human condition to a ditty about a meat pie by Barry Humphries.

Continue past the **17 Opera Quays** apartment and entertainment complex on Circular Quay East, which is disparagingly referred to by Sydneysiders as 'The Toaster'.

The heaven-sent sails of the **18 Sydney Opera House** (p54) are directly in front of you, adjacent to an unmissable perspective of the Sydney Harbour Bridge off to the left. Circumnavigate Bennelong Point, then follow the water's edge to the gates of the **19 Royal Botanic Garden** (p56).

of vintage apparatus, including Australia's oldest working telescope (1874). Also on offer are audiovisual displays, including Aboriginal sky stories and a virtual reality **3D Theatre** (www.sydneyobservatory.com.au; adult/child $10/8; ⊙2.30pm & 3.30pm daily, plus 11am & noon Sat & Sun; 🚊Circular Quay). Bookings are essential for night-time stargazing sessions (adult/child $18/12). If you're feeling more earthly, Observatory Hill is great for a picnic. Studded with huge Moreton Bay fig trees, the grassy hilltop buzzes with sweaty hill-climbing joggers, lunchtime CBD escapees and travellers taking time out from the Rocks below. The hill was the site of the colony's first windmill (1796), which ground wheat until someone stole its canvas sails and the structure collapsed.

SH ERVIN GALLERY   GALLERY
Map p240 (✆02-9258 0173; www.shervingallery.com.au; Watson Rd; adult/concession/under 12 $7/5/free; ⊙11am-5pm Tue-Sun; 🚊Wynyard) High on the hill inside the old Fort St School (1856), the SH Ervin Gallery exhibits invariably rewarding historical and contemporary Australian art. Annual mainstays include the Salon des Refusés (alternative Archibald Prize entries) and the Portia Geach Memorial Award. There's a cafe here, too.

✖ EATING

The charismatic back lanes of the Rocks are dotted with little eateries, from 24-hour pancake joints to white-linen palaces. Around the horseshoe from the Harbour Bridge to the Opera House you'll find dozens of upmarket restaurants, all with winning water views. It should come as no surprise that this most touristy of precincts is also the priciest. If at all possible, budget for at least one night where you can throw on your glad rags and let Sydney's showiness seduce you.

✖ Circular Quay

TRAMEZZINI ESPRESSO   CAFE $
Map p240 (✆02-9232 0422; 50 Bridge St; mains $4-8; ⊙6.30am-5pm Mon-Fri; 🚊Circular Quay) There aren't a lot of decent downtown places for a reasonably priced, healthy bite, so this Italian cafe in the foyer of the AMP building is worth remembering. Unsurprisingly, the clientele is extremely suity, but don't let that and all the ostentatious marble get in the way of a flat white and a zingy egg-and-parmesan breakfast roll.

ARIA   MODERN AUSTRALIAN $$$
Map p240 (✆02-9240 2255; www.ariarestaurant.com; 1 Macquarie St; lunch & pretheatre mains $46, 2-/3-/4-course dinner $105/130/155; ⊙noon-2.30pm Mon-Fri, 5.30-11pm daily; 🚊Circular Quay) Aria is a star in Sydney's fine-dining firmament, an award-winning combination of chef Matt Moran's stellar dishes, Opera House views and faultless service. A pretheatre à la carte menu is available before 7pm.

CAFE SYDNEY   MODERN AUSTRALIAN $$$
Map p240 (✆02-9251 8683; www.cafesydney.com; L5, Customs House, 31 Alfred St; mains $38-39; ⊙noon-11pm Mon-Fri, 5-11pm Sat, noon-3.30pm Sun; 🚊Circular Quay) This breezy, spacious restaurant on the Customs House roof has harbour views, an outdoor terrace, a glass ceiling, a cocktail bar and friendly staff. Seafood dishes dominate.

✖ The Rocks

SAILORS THAI CANTEEN   THAI $$
Map p240 (✆02-9251 2466; www.sailorsthai.com.au; 106 George St; mains $24-29; ⊙noon-3pm Mon-Fri, 5-10pm daily; 🚊Circular Quay) Wedge yourself into a gap between arts-community operators, politicians and media manoeuvrers at Sailors' long communal table and order from the fragrant menu of Thai street-food classics. The balcony tables fill up fast, but fortune might be smiling on you. Downstairs the vibe's more formal and the prices higher.

★QUAY   MODERN AUSTRALIAN $$$
Map p240 (✆02-9251 5600; www.quay.com.au; L3, Overseas Passenger Terminal; 3/4 courses $130/150; ⊙noon-2.30pm Tue-Fri, 6-10pm daily; 🚊Circular Quay) Quay is shamelessly guilty of breaking the rule that good views make for bad food. Chef Peter Gilmore never rests on his laurels, consistently delivering the exquisitely crafted, adventurous cuisine which has landed Quay on the prestigious World's Best Restaurants list. And the view? Like dining in a postcard.

★**SAKÉ** JAPANESE $$$
Map p240 (☎02-9259 5656; www.sakerestaurant. com.au; 12 Argyle St; mains $25-45; ⊘noon-3pm & 5.30-10.30pm; ☒Circular Quay) Colourful sake barrels and lots of dark wood contribute to the louche Oriental glamour of this large, buzzy restaurant. Solo travellers can prop themselves around the open kitchen and snack on delectable Wagyu dumplings and maki rolls, while couples tuck into multicourse banquets of contemporary Japanese cuisine (from $88).

✖ Dawes Point

CAFE SOPRA ITALIAN $$
Map p240 (www.fratellifresh.com.au; 16 Hickson Rd; mains $20-30; ⊘noon-3pm & 6-10pm; ☒Wynyard) Branches of this acclaimed Italian restaurant, paired with the associated Fratelli Fresh providore, have been popping up all over town. This one's easily the best place to eat in Walsh Bay.

🍷 DRINKING & 🍸 NIGHTLIFE

The Rocks has been intoxicated since convict times, with several local pubs dating back to settlement days. It's very touristy (George St in particular) but it's still an interesting place for a brew or two. Circular Quay's eastern shore is lined with modern bars serving pricey drinks, with tables spilling across the promenade. Note, most venues in these parts stick to traditional pub hours and close their doors around midnight. The entire area is covered by the inner city's lockout laws, meaning that nobody's permitted to enter a licensed venue after 1.30am. Only a handful of places stay open until 3am.

🍷 Circular Quay

★**OPERA BAR** BAR, LIVE MUSIC
Map p240 (www.operabar.com.au; lower concourse, Sydney Opera House; ⊘11.30am-midnight Mon-Fri, 9am-midnight Sat & Sun; ☒Circular Quay) Right on the harbour with the Opera House on one side and the Harbour Bridge on the other, this perfectly positioned terrace manages a very Sydney marriage of the laid-back and the sophisticated. A recent takeover by celebrity chef Matt Moran has shifted the food up a notch. There's live music or DJs most nights.

🍷 The Rocks

★**LORD NELSON BREWERY HOTEL** PUB, BREWERY
Map p240 (☎02-9251 4044; 19 Kent St; ⊘11am-11pm; ☒Circular Quay) Built in 1836 and converted into a pub in 1841, this atmospheric sandstone boozer is one of three claiming to be Sydney's oldest (all using slightly different criteria). The on-site brewery cooks up its own natural ales (try the Old Admiral).

★**HERO OF WATERLOO** PUB
Map p240 (www.heroofwaterloo.com.au; 81 Lower Fort St; ⊘10am-11pm; ☒Circular Quay) Enter this rough-hewn 1843 sandstone pub to meet some locals, chat up the Irish bar staff and grab an earful of the swing, folk and Celtic bands (Friday to Sunday). Downstairs is a dungeon where, in days gone by, drinkers would sleep off a heavy night before being shanghaied to the high seas via a tunnel leading straight to the harbour.

★**GLENMORE AT THE ROCKS** PUB
Map p240 (www.theglenmore.com.au; 96 Cumberland St; ⊘11am-midnight; ☎; ☒Circular Quay) Downstairs it's a predictably nice old Rocks pub, but head up to the rooftop and the views are beyond fabulous: Opera House, harbour and city skyline all present and accounted for. It gets rammed up here on the weekends, with DJs, good food and plenty of wine by the glass.

ARGYLE BAR
Map p240 (☎02-9247 5500; www.theargylerocks. com; 18 Argyle St; ⊘11am-midnight Sun-Wed, to 3am Thu-Sat; ☒Circular Quay) This mammoth conglomeration of five bars is spread through the historic sandstone Argyle Stores buildings, including a cobblestone courtyard and underground cellars resonating with DJ beats. The decor ranges from rococo couches to white extruded plastic tables, all offset with kooky chandeliers and moody lighting. Great bar food, too.

FORTUNE OF WAR PUB
Map p240 (www.fortuneofwar.com.au; 137 George St; ⊘9am-midnight Sun-Thu, to 3am Fri & Sat; ☒Circular Quay) This 1828 drinking den

CIRCULAR QUAY & THE ROCKS ENTERTAINMENT

retains much of its original charm and, by the looks of things, some of the original punters, too. There's live music on Thursday, Friday and Saturday nights and on weekend afternoons.

HARTS PUB   PUB
Map p240 (www.hartspub.com; cnr Essex & Gloucester Sts; ⊘noon-midnight; ⍰Circular Quay) Pouring a range of craft beers, Harts is frequented by locals drawn by the beer, the rugby tipping competition and some of Sydney's best pub food.

AUSTRALIAN HOTEL   PUB
Map p240 (www.australianheritagehotel.com; 100 Cumberland St; ⊘11am-midnight; ⍰Circular Quay) Not only is this pub architecturally notable (c 1913), it also boasts a bonza selection of fair dinkum Ocker (local) beer and wine. Keeping with the antipodean theme, the kitchen fires up pizzas topped with kangaroo and saltwater crocodile ($17 to $27).

BLU BAR ON 36   COCKTAIL BAR
Map p240 (www.shangri-la.com; Level 36, 176 Cumberland St; ⊘5pm-midnight; ⍰Circular Quay) The drinks may be pricey, but it's well worth heading up to the top of the Shangri-La hotel for the views, which seem to stretch all the way to New Zealand. The dress code is officially 'smart casual', but err on the side of smart if you can't handle rejection.

🍷 Dawes Point

HARBOUR VIEW HOTEL   PUB
Map p240 (☑02-9252 4111; www.harbourview. com.au; 18 Lower Fort St; ⊘11am-midnight Mon-Sat, to 10pm Sun; 🐾; ⍰Circular Quay) Built in the 1920s, the curvilicious Harbour View was the main boozer for the Harbour Bridge construction crew. These days it fulfils the same duties for the BridgeClimbers – wave to them from the 2nd-floor balcony as they traverse the lofty girders. The Tooth's KB Lager listed on the tiles out the front is long gone, but there's plenty of Heineken and James Squire on tap.

☆ ENTERTAINMENT

With the Opera House as its centrepiece, it follows that this neighbourhood is the locus of Sydney's performing-arts scene. Most of the big companies are based here, taking advantage of the area's seven world-class stages. The ratio of theatre luvvies and dance bunnies to the general population is higher in Walsh Bay (home to four major companies and two excellent theatre complexes) than anywhere else in the city. If you're keen to spot famous thespians, there are few better locales.

★ SYDNEY OPERA HOUSE   PERFORMING ARTS
Map p240 (☑02-9250 7777; www.sydney operahouse.com; Bennelong Point; ⍰Circular Quay) The glamorous jewel at the heart of Australian performance, Sydney's famous opera house has five main stages. Opera may have star billing, but theatre, comedy, music and dance are all performed here.

SYDNEY THEATRE COMPANY   THEATRE
Map p240 (STC; ☑02-9250 1777; www.syd neytheatre.com.au; Pier 4/5, 15 Hickson Rd; ⊘box office 9am-8.30pm Mon-Fri, 11am-8.30pm Sat, 2hr before show Sun; ⍰Wynyard) Established in 1978, the STC is Sydney theatre's top dog and has played an important part in the careers of many famous Australian actors (especially Cate Blanchett, who was co-artistic director from 2008 to 2013). Tours of the company's Wharf and Roslyn Packer theatres are held at 10.30am every Tuesday ($10). Performances are also staged at the Opera House.

ROSLYN PACKER
THEATRE WALSH BAY   THEATRE
Map p240 (☑02-9250 1999; www.sydneytheatre. org.au; 22 Hickson Rd; ⍰Wynyard) Opened in 2004, this is the most significant theatre built in the city since the Sydney Opera House. The state-of-the-art facility seats 850 and is managed by the Sydney Theatre Company. The Sydney Dance Company and a host of other troupes also perform here.

WHARF THEATRES   THEATRE
Map p240 (☑02-9250 1777; www.sydneytheatre. com.au; Pier 4/5, 15 Hickson Rd; ⍰Wynyard) 🐾 The Sydney Theatre Company stages intimate performances in two small theatres in the beautiful Edwardian pier building they share with Bangarra and the Sydney Dance Company.

BELL SHAKESPEARE   THEATRE
(☑02-8298 9000; www.bellshakespeare.com.au; tickets $75-79) Australia's Shakespeare specialists stage their Sydney performances

in the Opera House. Their repertoire occasionally deviates from the bard to the likes of Marlowe and Molière.

OPERA AUSTRALIA   OPERA

(☑9318 8200; www.opera-australia.org.au; Sydney Opera House; tickets $49-199; ⛴Circular Quay) Opera Australia is the big player in Oz opera, staging over 600 performances a year. The company's Sydney shows are performed in the Opera House, unless they're staging a big outdoor extraganza on the harbour or in the Domain.

BANGARRA DANCE THEATRE   DANCE

Map p240 (☑02-9251 5333; www.bangarra.com.au; Pier 4/5, 15 Hickson Rd; tickets $30-93; ⛴Wynyard) Bangarra is hailed as Australia's finest Aboriginal performance company. Artistic director Stephen Page conjures a fusion of contemporary themes, indigenous traditions and Western technique. When not touring internationally, the company performs at the Opera House or at their own small theatre in Walsh Bay.

SYDNEY DANCE COMPANY   DANCE

Map p240 (SDC; ☑02-9221 4811; www.sydneydancecompany.com; Pier 4/5, 15 Hickson Rd; ⛴Wynyard) Australia's number-one contemporary-dance company has been staging wildly modern, sexy, sometimes shocking works for nearly 40 years. Performances are usually held across the street at the Roslyn Packer Theatre, or at Carriageworks.

AUSTRALIAN BALLET   DANCE

(☑1300 369 741; www.australianballet.com.au; tickets $39-289) The Melbourne-based Australian Ballet performs a wide repertoire of classical as well as contemporary works. See them twinkle their toes at the Opera House or the Capitol Theatre.

SYDNEY SYMPHONY
ORCHESTRA   CLASSICAL MUSIC

(☑02-8215 4600; www.sydneysymphony.com) The SSO plays around 150 concerts annually with famous local and international musicians. Catch them at the Sydney Opera House or the City Recital Hall.

AUSTRALIAN
CHAMBER ORCHESTRA   CLASSICAL MUSIC

(☑02-8274 3888; www.aco.com.au; tickets $46-127) Since 1975 the ACO has been making chamber music sexy and adventurous, especially under the tutelage of artistic di-

rector and lead violinist Richard Tognetti. Concerts are staged throughout the year at the Opera House and City Recital Hall.

SYDNEY CONSERVATORIUM
OF MUSIC   CLASSICAL MUSIC

Map p240 (☑02-9351 1222; www.music.usyd.edu.au; Conservatorium Rd; ⛴Circular Quay) This historic venue showcases the talents of its students and their teachers. Choral, jazz, operatic and chamber concerts happen from March to November, along with free lunchtime recitals on Wednesday at 1.10pm.

SYDNEY
PHILHARMONIA CHOIRS   CLASSICAL MUSIC

(☑02-9251 2024; www.sydneyphilharmonia.com.au; tickets $40-100) If you want your world walloped by hundreds of enthusiastic voices, this is your choir. It also has the 100-voice Symphony Chorus, the 32-voice Chamber Singers and the youth-focused Vox. Internationally renowned, the choirs usually perform at the Opera House or St Mary's Cathedral.

BASEMENT   LIVE MUSIC

Map p240 (☑02-9251 2797; www.thebasement.com.au; 7 Macquarie Pl; admission $8-60; ⛴Circular Quay) Once solely a jazz venue, the Basement now hosts international and local musicians working in many disciplines and genres. Dinner-and-show tickets net you a table by the stage, guaranteeing a better view than the standing-only area by the bar.

OPENAIR CINEMA   CINEMA

(www.stgeorgeopenair.com.au; Mrs Macquaries Rd; tickets $37; ⊙Jan & Feb; ⛴Circular Quay) Right on the harbour, the outdoor three-storey screen here comes with surround sound, sunsets, skyline and swanky food and wine. Most tickets are purchased in advance, but a limited number of tickets go on sale at the door each night at 6.30pm; check the website for details.

DENDY OPERA QUAYS   CINEMA

Map p240 (☑02-9247 3800; www.dendy.com.au; 2 Circular Quay East; adult/child $20/14; ⊙sessions 9.30am-9.30pm; ⛴Circular Quay) When the harbour glare and squawking seagulls get too much, follow the scent of popcorn into the dark folds of this plush cinema. Screening first-run, independent world films, it's augmented by friendly attendants and a cafe/bar.

🛍 SHOPPING

Not a place the locals would ever choose for a shopping spree, this 'hood caters mainly to the tastes of wealthy tourists. If you're in the market for some opals, duty-free stuff or tacky souvenirs, this is the place for you.

AUSTRALIAN WINE CENTRE — WINE
Map p240 (www.australianwinecentre.com; Goldfields House, 1 Alfred St; ⊙10am-8pm Mon-Sat, to 6.30pm Sun; 🚇Circular Quay) This multilingual basement store is packed with quality Australian wine, beer and spirits. Smaller producers are well represented, along with a staggering range of prestigious Penfolds Grange wines. International shipping can be arranged.

OPAL MINDED — JEWELLERY
Map p240 (www.opalminded.com; 55 George St; ⊙9am-6.30pm; 🚇Circular Quay) As good a place as any to stock up on that quintessential piece of Aussie bling.

GANNON HOUSE — ART
Map p240 (📞02-9251 4474; www.gannonhousegallery.com; 45 Argyle St; 🚇Circular Quay) Specialising in contemporary Australian and Aboriginal art, Gannon House purchases works directly from artists and Aboriginal communities. You'll find the work of prominent artists such as Gloria Petyarre here, alongside lesser-known names.

THE ROCKS MARKETS — MARKET
Map p240 (www.therocksmarket.com; George St; ⊙9am-3pm Fri, 10am-5pm Sat & Sun; 🚇Circular Quay) Under a long white canopy, the 150 stalls at this weekend market are a little on the tacky side, but there are some gems to be uncovered. The Friday 'Foodies Market' is more fulfilling (and filling).

HERRINGBONE — CLOTHING
Map p240 (www.herringbone.com; 7 Macquarie Pl; ⊙9am-6pm Mon-Wed & Fri, to 8pm Thu, 10am-5pm Sat, 11am-4pm Sun; 🚇Circular Quay) Branch of the Sydney shirt company, whose products combine Australian design and Italian fabrics.

🤸 SPORTS & ACTIVITIES

Circular Quay is the departure point for many Sydney Harbour boating activities (p83), such as Tribal Warrior, Whale Watching Sydney, Captain Cook Cruises and Matilda Cruises.

BONZA BIKE TOURS — CYCLING
Map p240 (📞02-9247 8800; www.bonzabiketours.com; 30 Harrington St; 🚇Circular Quay) These bike boffins run a 2½-hour Sydney Highlights tour (adult/child $66/79) and a four-hour Sydney Classic tour ($119/99). Other tours tackle the Harbour Bridge and Manly. They also hire bikes (per hour/half-day/day $15/35/50).

BIKE BUFFS — CYCLING
(📞0414 960 332; www.bikebuffs.com.au; adult/child $95/70; 🚇Circular Quay) Offers daily four-hour, two-wheeled tours around the harbourside sights (including jaunts over the Harbour Bridge), departing from Argyle Place. They also hire bikes (per half-day/day/week $35/60/295).

THE ROCKS WALKING TOURS — WALKING TOUR
Map p240 (📞02-9247 6678; www.rockswalkingtours.com.au; cnr Argyle & Harrington Sts; adult/child/family $25/12/62; ⊙10.30am & 1.30pm; 🚇Circular Quay) Regular 90-minute tours through the historic Rocks, with plenty of not-so-tall tales and interesting minutiae.

PEEK TOURS — WALKING TOUR
(📞0420 244 756; www.peektours.com.au; 🚇Circular Quay) If you find that a cool beverage makes local history easier to digest, this crew will lead you on a two-hour tour of the Rocks, stopping in historic pubs ($60, including a drink at each). They also offer a 90-minute walking tour of Bondi Beach ($40) and other guided walks on request.

THE ROCKS GHOST TOURS — WALKING TOUR
(📞02-9241 1283; www.ghosttours.com.au; adult $42; ⊙6.45pm Apr-Sep, 7.45pm Oct-Mar; 🚇Circular Quay) If you like your spine chilled and your pulse slightly quickened (they're more creepy than properly scary), join one of these two-hour tours, departing from outside Cadman's Cottage nightly. Tours run rain or shine (ponchos provided); bookings essential.

Sydney Harbour

HARBOUR ISLANDS | WATSONS BAY | VAUCLUSE | DOUBLE BAY | DARLING POINT | BALMAIN | NORTH SYDNEY | MOSMAN

Neighbourhood Top Five

1 Catching a ferry to **Watsons Bay** (p71) and spending an afternoon exploring South Head and lying around Camp Cove before claiming a spot at the pub as the sun sinks over the city.

2 Gaining a glimpse into the busy world of the **Parramatta River** (p80) from a ferry's prow.

3 Sneaking down to secluded **Shark Beach** (p74) for a picnic and a swim.

4 Exploring the detritus of industry and incarceration on **Cockatoo Island** (p71).

5 Meeting the native critters at **Taronga Zoo** (p81) – the zoo with the view.

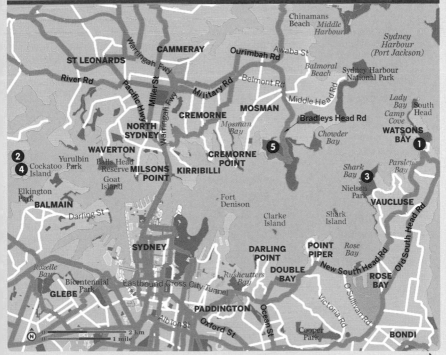

For more detail of this area, see Map p242 ➡

Lonely Planet's Top Tip

There's no need to shell out on a pricey cruise when you can see exactly the same sights from a ferry. Board a ferry to Watsons Bay and then back it up with the river service to Parramatta. You'll cover far more distance than the average cruise and all for a maximum of $15 on an Opal transport card. Unless of course you prefer your views accompanied by commentary, cocktails, dinner or showgirls...

✕ Best Places to Eat

➡ Riverview Hotel & Dining (p82)

➡ Bathers' Pavilion (p82)

➡ Adriano Zumbo (p81)

➡ Tea Room Gunners Barracks (p82)

➡ Kazbah (p82)

For reviews, see p81

♞ Best Places to Drink

➡ Watsons Bay Beach Club (p82)

➡ Golden Sheaf Hotel (p82)

➡ Welcome Hotel (p82)

➡ London Hotel (p82)

For reviews, see p82 ➡

◉ Best Beaches

➡ Shark Beach (p74)

➡ Camp Cove (p71)

➡ Balmoral Beach (p81)

➡ Parsley Bay (p74)

➡ Lady Bay (p74)

For reviews, see p71 ➡

Explore: Sydney Harbour

Sure, it's a stretch to call this large, disparate area a 'neighbourhood', but the harbour is such an integral part of the Sydney experience that we felt it was worth highlighting in this way.

Catch a ferry at Circular Quay for a short hop around the lower North Shore, or allocate half a day to exploring Watsons Bay or heading upriver to Parramatta. Sydney's wealthiest homes are huddled around the harbour in exclusive nooks such as Vaucluse, Point Piper and Darling Point in the Eastern Suburbs and Mosman on the North Shore. Even former working-class bastions such as Balmain, west of the city, are now among the city's most desirable addresses.

Due to its military use, large chunks of the scrub-covered coast have been left much as the First Fleet would have found it. The navy still controls some of the land, but most has been turned over to Sydney Harbour National Park. If you fancy a wilderness walk in the heart of the city, pick a slice to explore and jump on a ferry.

Local Life

➡ **Ferries** There are worse ways of getting to work than cruising on the harbour. For those living close to the water, this is the commute of choice.

➡ **Beaches** Many of the harbour beaches are local treasures, frequented only by those who live in the immediate surrounds.

➡ **Wharves** Dedicated fisherfolk congregate at their favourite spots to try their luck at hooking the big one.

Getting There & Away

➡ **Ferry** Most of the places around Sydney Harbour can be reached by ferries from Circular Quay, the major exceptions being Vaucluse and Balmoral.

➡ **Train** Useful stations include Circular Quay, Edgecliff (for Double Bay), Parramatta, Milsons Point, North Sydney and Waverton (for Balls Point).

➡ **Bus** Buses are the only public transport reaching Vaucluse and Balmoral. Useful routes from Circular Quay include 325 (Kings Cross–Double Bay–Rose Bay–Vaucluse–Watsons Bay), 380 (Darlinghurst–Paddington–Bondi–Watsons Bay). The following routes all head from Wynyard through North Sydney and Mosman: 176–180 (for Spit Bridge), 244 (for Obelisk and Cobblers Beach) and 245 (for Balmoral). Bus 229 (for Chinamans Beach) leaves from Milsons Point.

➡ **Parking** A car will come in particularly handy for getting to Vaucluse, Balmoral and Obelisk. Street parking shouldn't be difficult to find, but in busy areas it's often metered.

◉ SIGHTS

◉ Harbour Islands

COCKATOO ISLAND   ISLAND
Map p242 (⌂02-8969 2100; www.cockatoo island.gov.au; ⬛Cockatoo Island) Studded with photogenic industrial relics, convict architecture and art installations, fascinating Cockatoo Island (Wareamah) opened to the public in 2007 and now has regular ferry services, a campground, rental accommodation, a cafe and a bar. Information boards and audioguides ($5) explain the island's time as a prison, shipyard and naval base.

A spooky tunnel passes clear through the middle of the island and you can also explore the remains of the prison. During WWII most of the old sandstone buildings were stripped of their roofs and converted into bomb shelters. Solitary confinement cells were unearthed here recently after being filled in and forgotten in the 1890s.

GOAT ISLAND   ISLAND
Map p242 (⌂02-9253 0888; www.nationalparks. nsw.gov.au; tour adult/child $38/29) Goat Island, west of the Harbour Bridge, has been a shipyard, quarantine station and gunpowder depot in its previous lives. Heritage tours are offered for groups of 20 or more (see the national parks website for details).

FORT DENISON   FORTRESS
Map p242 (www.fortdenison.com.au; tour $16/14; ⊙tours 11am, 12.15pm, 1.45pm & 2.45pm) Called Mat-te-wan-ye (rocky island) by the Gadigal people, in colonial times the small fortified island off Mrs Macquaries Pt was a sorry site of suffering, used to isolate recalcitrant convicts. It was nicknamed 'Pinchgut' for its meagre rations. Fears of a Russian invasion during the mid-19th-century Crimean War led to its fortification. The NPWS offers tours of the Martello tower (cheaper if prebooked with your ferry ticket), although plenty of people just pop over to visit the cafe. Both Captain Cook Cruises (p84) and Manly Fast Ferry (p220) have several services per day heading to the island from Darling Harbour and Circular Quay.

SHARK ISLAND   ISLAND
Map p242 (www.nationalparks.nsw.gov.au; ferry adult/child $20/17) Little Shark Island, off Rose Bay, makes a great picnic getaway.

There's not a lot here except for toilets and drinking water – and at 250m by 100m, you'll soon have explored every inch of it. Captain Cook Cruises (p84) runs four ferries per day to the island from Circular Quay (Jetty 6) and Darling Harbour (Pier 26).

◉ Watsons Bay

The narrow peninsula ending in South Head is one of Sydney's most sublime spots. Approaching from Bondi, as Old South Head Rd leaves the sheer ocean cliffs to descend to Watsons Bay, the view of Sydney Harbour is breathtaking.

WATSONS BAY   AREA
Map p242 (⬛Watsons Bay) Watsons Bay, east of the city centre and north of Bondi, was once a small fishing village, as evidenced by the tiny heritage cottages that pepper the suburb's narrow streets (and now cost a fortune). While you're here, tradition demands that you sit in the beer garden at the Watsons Bay Hotel at sunset and watch the sun dissolve behind the disembodied Harbour Bridge, jutting up above Bradley's Head. On the ocean side, **The Gap** is a dramatic clifftop lookout where proposals and suicides happen with similar frequency.

CAMP COVE   BEACH
Map p242 (Cliff St; ⬛Watsons Bay) Immediately north of Watsons Bay, this small swimming beach is popular with both families and topless sunbathers. When Governor Phillip realised Botany Bay didn't cut it as a site for a convict colony, he sailed north into Sydney Harbour, dropped anchor and sunk his boots into Camp Cove's gorgeous golden sand on 21 January 1788.

SOUTH HEAD   NATIONAL PARK
Map p242 (www.nationalparks.nsw.gov.au; Cliff St; ⊙5am-10pm; ⬛Watsons Bay) At the northern end of Camp Cove, the **South Head Heritage Trail** kicks off, leading into a section of Sydney Harbour National Park distinguished by harbour views and crashing surf. It passes old battlements and a path heading down to Lady Bay (p74), before continuing on to the candy-striped **Hornby Lighthouse** and the sandstone **Lightkeepers' Cottages** (1858).

Sydney Harbour

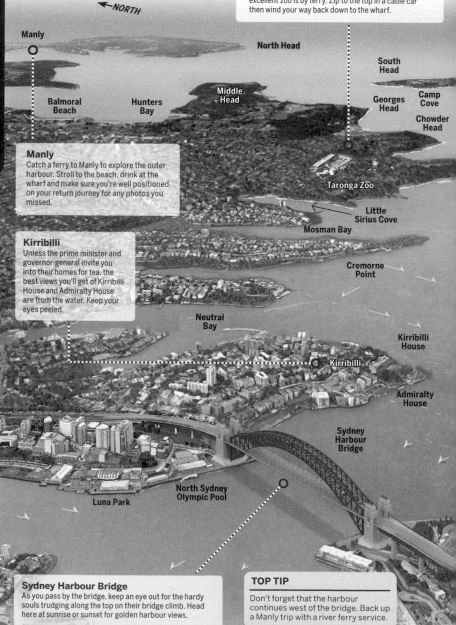

←NORTH

Taronga Zoo
Even if you've hired a car, the best way to reach this excellent zoo is by ferry. Zip to the top in a cable car then wind your way back down to the wharf.

Manly

North Head

South Head

Balmoral Beach

Hunters Bay

Middle Head

Georges Head

Camp Cove

Chowder Head

Manly
Catch a ferry to Manly to explore the outer harbour. Stroll to the beach, drink at the wharf and make sure you're well positioned on your return journey for any photos you missed.

Taronga Zoo

Little Sirius Cove

Mosman Bay

Kirribilli
Unless the prime minister and governor-general invite you into their homes for tea, the best views you'll get of Kirribilli House and Admiralty House are from the water. Keep your eyes peeled.

Cremorne Point

Neutral Bay

Kirribilli House

Kirribilli

Admiralty House

Sydney Harbour Bridge

North Sydney Olympic Pool

Luna Park

Sydney Harbour Bridge
As you pass by the bridge, keep an eye out for the hardy souls trudging along the top on their bridge climb. Head here at sunrise or sunset for golden harbour views.

TOP TIP
Don't forget that the harbour continues west of the bridge. Back up a Manly trip with a river ferry service.

Watsons Bay
Imagine Watsons Bay as the isolated fishing village it once was as you pull into its sheltered wharf. Stroll around South Head for views up the harbour and over ocean-battered cliffs.

Fort Denison
Known as Pinchgut, this fortified speck was once a place of fearsome punishment. The bodies of executed convicts were left to hang here as a grisly warning to all; the local Aborigines were horrified.

FERRIES
Circular Quay is the hub for state-run Sydney Ferries; nine separate routes leave from here, journeying to 38 different wharves.

Watsons Bay

Macquarie Lighthouse

Vaucluse Bay

Shark Bay

Rose Bay

Bradleys Head

Shark Island

Point Piper

Double Bay

Darling Point

Clark Island

Garden Island

Naval Base

Elizabeth Bay

Fort Denison

Mrs Macquaries Point

Potts Point

Woolloomooloo Finger Wharf

Sydney Opera House

Government House

Farm Cove

Royal Botanic Gardens

Circular Quay

The Rocks

Sydney Opera House
You can clamber all over it and walk around it, but nothing beats the perspective you get as your ferry glides past the Opera House's dazzling sails. Have your camera at the ready.

Circular Quay
Circular Quay has been at the centre of Sydney life since the First Fleet dropped anchor here in 1788. Book your ferry ticket, check the indicator boards for the correct pier and get onboard.

GUARDIANS OF THE SHORELINE

Sydney Harbour National Park (www.nationalparks.nsw.gov.au) protects large swathes of bushland around the harbour shoreline, plus several harbour islands. In among the greenery you'll find walking tracks, scenic lookouts, Aboriginal carvings, beaches and a handful of historic sites. The park incorporates South Head (p71) and Nielsen Park on the south side of the harbour, but most of the park is on the North Shore – including Bradleys Head, Middle Head, Dobroyd Head and North Head (p170).

LADY BAY   BEACH

Map p242 (Cliff St; 🚢 Watsons Bay) Also known as Lady Jane, this diminutive gay nudist beach sits at the bottom of a cliff, on top of which (somewhat ironically) is a Royal Australian Navy facility. To get here, follow the clifftop walking track from (somewhat aptly named) Camp Cove. All together now: 'In the navy...'

⊙ Vaucluse

Vaucluse is immediately south of Watsons Bay, taking up the middle section of the peninsula that forms South Head. There are no ferries, so it's best reached by New South Head Rd, which is the continuation of William St; bus services are frequent.

PARSLEY BAY   BEACH

Map p242 (enter near 80a Hopetoun Ave; 🚌 325) A hidden gem, this little bay has a calm swimming beach, a lawn dotted with sandstone sculptures for picnics and play, and a cute suspension bridge. Keep an eye out for water dragons (native reptiles) as you walk down through the bush.

VAUCLUSE HOUSE   HISTORIC BUILDING

Map p242 (📞 02-9388 7922; www.sydneyliving museums.com.au; Wentworth Rd; adult/child $8/4; ⏲ 11am-4pm Fri-Sun; 🚌 325) Construction of this imposing, turreted specimen of Gothic Australiana, set amid 10 hectares of lush gardens, commenced in 1805, but the house was tinkered with into the 1860s. Decorated with beautiful European period pieces including Bohemian glass, heavy oak Jacobean furniture and Meissen china, the house offers visitors a rare glimpse into early Sydney colonial life, as lived by the well-to-do.

Vaucluse was occupied from 1827 to 1862 by William Charles Wentworth, his wife Sarah and their children. The son of a convict mother, Wentworth became a barrister and cowrote the first New South Wales colonial constitution. However, his democratic leanings kept him estranged from high society: he held the 'outrageous' view that Australian-born colonials were the equals of the English, and that political and legal rights should be extended to emancipists (freed convicts). Wentworth was also an intrepid explorer. In 1831 he was part of the first European expedition to cross the Blue Mountains.

NIELSEN PARK   PARK, BEACH

Map p242 (Shark Beach; Vaucluse Rd; 🚌 325) Something of a hidden gem, this gorgeous harbourside park with a sandy beach was once part of the then 206-hectare Vaucluse House estate. Secluded beneath the trees is Greycliffe House, a gracious 1851 Gothic sandstone pile (not open to visitors), which serves as the headquarters of Sydney Harbour National Park.

Despite the beach's ominous name – there's really nothing to worry about – there's a shark net to put paranoid swimmers at ease. Visit on a weekday when it's not too busy: just mums with kids, retirees and slackers taking sickies from work.

MILK BEACH   BEACH

Map p242 (52 Vaucluse Rd; 🚌 325) The only thing to distract you from serious beach time at divine Milk Beach are seaplanes and the glistening Sydney skyline. With wow-worthy harbour views and limited access down a steep bush path, this isolated stretch of sand at the base of Hermit Bay is still one of the city's best kept secrets. Heritage-listed Strickland House is out back, and clear, warm waters in front, at this tiny parcel of harbourside paradise.

It's also known for its annual New Year's Day party.

MACQUARIE LIGHTHOUSE   LIGHTHOUSE

Map p242 (Old South Head Rd; 🚌 380) When the original Francis Greenway–designed lighthouse (1818) fell into disrepair and was dismantled, the current lighthouse (1883) was built in front of it as an exact replica. It's a pretty spot, with grassy lawns, heavenly ocean views and a clifftop trail extending to Bondi. Before the lighthouse was built, a series of fires were lit along this coast to keeps ships away from the cliffs.

◉ Double Bay

DOUBLE BAY AREA
Map p242 (🚇Double Bay) An odd thing has happened to Double Bay recently. Once the bastion of blue-rinse ladies and flashy, nouveau-riche types, it's now the clubbing locale of choice for young Sydneysiders escaping the lockouts and early closure of the city bars. It's a suburb in transition, with the reopening of the InterContinental hotel (where Michael Hutchence met his untimely demise) adding a bit of razzle-dazzle, new restaurants shaking up what was a tired eating scene, and a whole lot of new bars and clubs.

Immediately to the west, Edgecliff is a nondescript transport hub centred on New South Head Rd, sheltering the moneyed mansions of Darling Point – one of Sydney's richest nooks.

MURRAY ROSE POOL BEACH
Map p242 (Redleaf Pool; 536 New South Head Rd; 🚇Double Bay) FREE Not really a pool at all, family-friendly Murray Rose (named after a champion Olympic swimmer) is the closest swimming spot to the city – as such, it attracts an urbane cross-section of inner-eastern locals. A boardwalk runs around the top of the shark net, and there are two sought-after floating pontoons. The neighbouring Seven Shillings Beach is a semi-private stretch of sand that runs around the Point Piper waterfront. From here there are spectacular views towards the bridge.

◉ Darling Point

LINDESAY HISTORIC BUILDING
Map p242 (🕿02-9363 2401; www.nationaltrust.com.au; 1 Carthona Ave; tour $10; ⊗tours 10am, 11am & noon, 1st Thu of the month; 🚇Darling Point) Lindesay is rarely open, but, aside from Nicole Kidman inviting you in for tea, this is probably your best chance to look inside an actual Darling Point mansion. Built in 1834, it's still got its Georgian interiors, servants' quarters and long lawn overlook-ing the harbour. Lindesay is positioned directly above the Darling Point ferry stop.

◉ Balmain

The conjoined suburbs of Balmain, Rozelle and Birchgrove sit on their own peninsula, immediately west of the city centre. There are frequent ferry services to each of three wharves: Balmain East, Balmain (Thames St) and Birchgrove.

BALMAIN AREA
Map p242 (🚇Balmain East) Once a tough, working-class neighbourhood, Balmain now rivals Paddington in Victorian-era desirability – with the added advantage of being surrounded by water and city-bound ferries. Darling St traverses the spine of Balmain's peninsula, and makes for a decent pub crawl. Balmain's frangipani-scented streets contain dozens of historically significant buildings, most of which are privately owned.

The most notable is the graciously proportioned **Hampton Villa** (12b Grafton St; 🚇Balmain), a Georgian villa (1847). NSW Premier Sir Henry Parkes, the 'Father of Federation', lived here from 1888 to 1892. Nearby is the squat, shingle-roofed **Clontarf Cottage** (4 Wallace St; 🚇Balmain), an impressively restored house (1844) saved from demolition by protests in the late 1980s; and the semiderelict **St Mary's Hall** (7 Adolphus St; 🚇Balmain), built around 1851. Darling St has the **Watch House** (179 Darling St; 🚇Balmain), Sydney's oldest surviving lockup (1854); **Waterman's Cottage** (12 Darling St; 🚇Balmain East), built in 1841; and **Cathermore** (50 Darling St; 🚇Balmain East), Balmain's first bakery (1841), which later became the Waterford Arms pub.

YURULBIN POINT PARK
Map p242 (Louisa Rd; 🚇Birchgrove) On the northern tip of the Balmain peninsula (technically Birchgrove), this narrow point stretches to within 300m of the North Shore. Once called Long Nose Point, it was a shipyard until 1971, when it became a public park. It reverted to its Indigenous name (meaning 'swift running water') in 1994.

ELKINGTON PARK PARK
Map p242 (cnr Glassop & White Sts; 🚌433) If Balmain's historic cuteness doesn't float your boat, head to Elkington Park, named in 1883 after a local politician. At the

SYDNEY HARBOUR SIGHTS

bottom of the escarpment, the magnificently restored late-Victorian (1884) timber enclosure at the tidal **Dawn Fraser Baths** (⏱02-9555 1903; www.lpac.nsw.gov.au/Dawn-Fraser-Baths/; Elkington Park, Fitzroy Ave; adult/child $4.80/$3.30; ⏱7.15am-6.30pm Oct-Apr; ⏰433) picturesquely protects swimmers from underwater undesirables. Australia's all-conquering 1956–64 Olympian Dawn Fraser sacrificed her youth here swimming laps.

❂ North Sydney

BALLS HEAD RESERVE   PARK
Map p242 (Balls Head Rd; ⏰Waverton) Scruffy, bushy Balls Head Reserve not only has great views of the harbour, the city skyline and the industrial relics on Goat Island, it also has a wiggly waterline and inland paths, ancient Aboriginal rock paintings and carvings (although they're not easily discernible), and barbecue facilities.

From Waverton Station turn left and follow Bay Rd, which becomes Balls Head Rd. It's a 10-minute walk.

As on the Manly Scenic Walkway, it's easy to shut yourself off amid the sandstone and scrub here and imagine how Sydney must have been before European settlement.

MARY MACKILLOP PLACE   CHURCH, MUSEUM
Map p242 (⏱02-8912 4878; www.marymackillopplace.org.au; 7 Mount St; adult/child $9/6; ⏱10am-4pm; ⏰North Sydney) This museum tells the life story of St Mary of the Cross (aka Mary MacKillop), Australia's only Catholic saint. Born in Melbourne in 1842, she was a dedicated and outspoken educator, and a pioneer who prevailed over conservative hierarchical ideals, despite being excommunicated for six months. You'll find her tomb inside the chapel.

The museum has interesting interactive displays and a kookily whimsical Nuns on the Run automaton, proving that the Josephites (the order that MacKillop founded) have a sense of humour.

LUNA PARK   AMUSEMENT PARK
Map p242 (⏱02-9922 6644; www.lunaparksydney.com; 1 Olympic Dr; ⏱11am-10pm Fri & Sat, 2-6pm Sun, 11am-4pm Mon; ⏰Milsons Point) **FREE** A sinister chip-toothed clown face forms the entrance to this old-fashioned amusement park overlooking Sydney Har-

bour. It's one of several 1930s features, including the Coney Island funhouse, a pretty carousel and the nausea-inducing rotor. You can purchase a two-ride pass ($16), or buy a height-based unlimited-ride pass (from $30, cheaper if purchased online). Hours are extended during school and public holidays.

KIRRIBILLI POINT   AREA
Map p242 (⏰Kirribilli) The Sydney residences of Australia's governor general and prime minister are located on Kirribilli Point, east of the Sydney Harbour Bridge. When in town, the PM gets some shut-eye in the Gothic Revival–style **Kirribilli House**, built in 1854, while the GG bunkers down in **Admiralty House**, built in 1846. Admiralty House is nearer the bridge and is the one everyone dreams of living in (if it came without the job). Both houses are better spotted from the water than by peering through the lightly fortified gates (this ain't the White House).

Squeezed between the Harbour Bridge and the politicians, the diminutive **Dr Mary Booth Reserve Foreshore Walkway** (⏰Milsons Point) offers great views of the Opera House and the city skyline.

CREMORNE POINT   POINT
Map p242 (⏰Cremorne Point) Cremorne Point (technically Robertsons Point; Woolwarrajurng to the Eora people) is a beaut spot for a picnic on grassy **Cremorne Reserve** (⏰Cremorne Point), or for a swim in the free saltwater MacCallum Pool. The harbour views from here are downright delicious (especially when the New Year's Eve fireworks are erupting). Ferries chug past, newspaper readers flip pages – it's pretty darn chilled out.

MAY GIBBS' NUTCOTE   MUSEUM
Map p242 (⏱02-9953 4453; www.nutcote.org; 5 Wallaringa Ave; adult/child $10/4; ⏱11am-3pm Wed-Sun; ⏰Neutral Bay) Spanish Mission–style Nutcote (1925) is the former home of author and illustrator May Gibbs, who wrote the much-loved Australian children's book *Snugglepot & Cuddlepie*. It's now restored to its 1930s glory and houses a museum devoted to her life and work. Cheery volunteer guides will show you around, and there are beautiful gardens, a tearoom and a gift shop. It's a five-minute walk from the wharf.

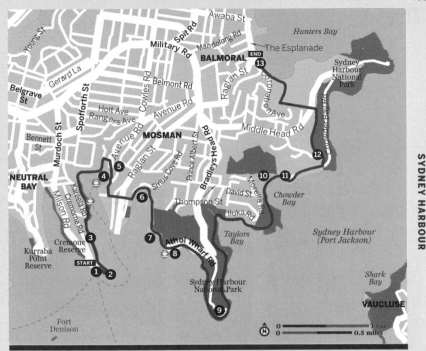

🏃 Neighbourhood Walk
North Shore Harbour Hustle

START CREMORNE POINT
END BALMORAL BEACH
LENGTH 13KM; FOUR HOURS

Ride the ferry from Circular Quay to chilled-out ❶ **Cremorne Point**, surrounded by the native shrub of Cremorne Reserve. Wander out to the ❷ **tip of the point** for brilliant city views. Heading north, you'll trundle past the well-tended plots of palms, ferns and philodendrons in ❸ **Lex & Ruby's Garden**, named after the local couple who planted it and lovingly tended it for decades.

Keep walking around the other side of exclusive ❹ **Mosman Bay**. Check out the historic stone building called the ❺ **Barn**, an early colonial structure that's now a scout hall. Just beyond is the Wharf Store; go up the stairs to Mosman St and follow Trumfield Lane to McLeod St. Turn left, scoot across Musgrave St and take the stairs down to the other side, then cross Raglan St, where more stairs descend to the shore.

Wind around ❻ **Little Sirius Cove** and take the stone steps onto a shoreline path, which runs around Taronga Zoo. Before you reach the zoo entrance, take the stairs down to ❼ **Whiting Beach**, a secluded sandy bay. Further along the lush, shady path is the ❽ **Taronga Zoo** (p81) entrance and ferry wharf.

Keep following the path into Sydney Harbour National Park where you'll link up with a bush track that leads to the tip of ❾ **Bradleys Head**, offering great views of South Head. Next up are Chowder Head, ❿ **Clifton Gardens Reserve** and ⓫ **Headland Park**, which occupies the site of an old naval base above Chowder Bay.

Head up to the lookout near the ⓬ **Tea Room Gunners Barracks** (p82), which has a glorious cityscape panorama and views over the battlements that once defended Sydney from threats both real and imagined. From here, pick up the track that darts through bushy scrubland before angling left, crossing Middle Head Rd and heading past some magnificently gnarled red gum trees. It will eventually head down some steps and pop you out near ⓭ **Balmoral Beach**.

3

1. Taronga Zoo (p81)
Encounter over 4000 animals and take in magnificent harbour views.

2. Cockatoo Island (p71)
The site of a 19th-century penal establishment now hosts cutting-edge arts and cultural events.

3. The Gap (p71)
Sweeping ocean panoramas from a dramatic clifftop.

4. Watsons Bay (p71)
This picturesque harbourside suburb was once a fishing village.

WORTH A DETOUR

PARRAMATTA RIVER

Sydney Harbour gets all the attention but a jaunt upriver to the geographical centre of the metropolis is just as interesting. As you pass old industrial sites and gaze into millionaires' backyards, a window opens onto a watery world in the heart of Sydney where school rowing crews get put through their paces, groups of mates glide past on yachts, solo kayakers work up a sweat and Mediterranean men fish off the wharves at night.

In geological terms the harbour is actually a drowned river valley, which makes it very hard to distinguish what's harbour and what's river, but as you glide past Cockatoo Island, where the Parramatta and Lane Cove Rivers meet, it's river all the way.

The ferry from Circular Quay to Parramatta takes about 1¼ hours (adult/child $7.60/3.80), although on some low tides the boats stop at Rydalmere, one wharf earlier, and a bus continues from there. If you feel like making a day of it, Sydney Olympic Park (p111) and Parramatta both have a smattering of interesting sights. And if you want to speed up your return trip, both are connected to the train network.

In Parramatta, make your first stop the **Parramatta Heritage & Visitor Information Centre** (p225) and grab a map of key sights. The centre is a museum in its own right, with temporary exhibits by local artists, as well as a permanent exhibition on Parramatta's history and culture.

The second European settlement in Australia, Parramatta was founded by First Fleet convict labour when Sydney Cove proved to be lousy for growing vegies. Originally called Rose Hill (despite the nearest roses being half a world away), the town became known by what is actually a mis-hearing of its Darug Aboriginal name, Burramatta. It roughly translates to 'place of the eels'; the slippery critters are now the mascot of Parramatta's rugby league team.

Although Sydney's reserves of glamour are running dry by the time you get this far west, there are some interesting historic sights to visit.

Old Government House (🖉02-9635 8149; www.nationaltrust.org.au; Parramatta Park; adult/child $10/8; ⊗10am-4pm Tue-Sun; 🚆Parramatta) The country residence of the early governors, this elegant Georgian Palladian building is now a preciously maintained museum furnished with original colonial furniture. It dates from 1799, making it the oldest remaining public building in Australia. Phone for details of monthly ghost nights.

Elizabeth Farm (🖉02-9635 9488; www.sydneylivingmuseums.com.au; 70 Alice St; adult/child $8/4; ⊗10.30am-3.30pm Sat & Sun; 🚆Rosehill) Elizabeth Farm contains part of Australia's oldest surviving European home (1793), built by renegade pastoralist and rum trader John Macarthur. Heralded as the founder of Australia's wool industry, Macarthur was a ruthless capitalist whose politicking made him immensely wealthy and a thorn in the side of successive governors. The pretty homestead is now a hands-on museum where you can recline on the reproduction furniture and thumb voyeuristically through Elizabeth Macarthur's letters.

Hambledon Cottage (🖉02-9635 6924; www.parramattahistorical.org.au; 63 Hassall St; adult/child $6/2; ⊗11am-4pm Thu-Sun; 🚊Parramatta) Surrounded by 200-year-old camphor laurels and English oaks, this historic cottage was built in 1824 for the Macarthurs' daughter's governess and was later used as weekend lodgings. It narrowly escaped being flattened to make way for a car park in the 1980s. Nowadays it houses a small museum dedicated to its owners and occupants.

Experiment Farm Cottage (🖉02-9635 5655; www.nationaltrust.org.au; 9 Ruse St; adult/child $8/4; ⊗10.30am-3.30pm Wed-Sun; 🚆Harris Park) Built in 1835, this colonial bungalow stands on the site of Australia's first official land grant. In 1789 Governor Phillip allocated 12 hectares to emancipated convict James Ruse as an experiment to see how long it would take Ruse to wean himself off government supplies. The experiment was a success, and Ruse became Australia's first private farmer. The house is furnished with pieces from the National Trust's collection of early colonial furniture.

◉ Mosman

TARONGA ZOO   ZOO
Map p242 (☎02-9969 2777; www.taronga.org.au;
Bradleys Head Rd; adult/child $46/23; ⊙9.30am-
5pm; 🚢Taronga Zoo) 🍴 A 12-minute ferry
ride from Circular Quay, Taronga Zoo has
75 hectares of bushy harbour hillside full
of kangaroos, koalas and similarly hirsute
Australians, and imported guests. The zoo's
4000 critters have million-dollar harbour
views, but seem blissfully unaware of the
privilege. Highlights include the nocturnal platypus habitat, the Great Southern
Oceans section and the Asian elephant
display. Feedings and encounters happen
throughout the day, while in summer, twilight concerts jazz things up.

Tours include **Nura Diya** (www.taron-
ga.org.au; 90min tour adult/child $99/69;
⊙9.45am Mon, Wed & Fri), where Indigenous
guides introduce you to native animals and
share Dreaming stories about them, giving
an insight into traditional Aboriginal life;
advance bookings essential. **Roar & Snore**
(☎02-9978 4791; www.taronga.org.au; adult/
child $320/205) is an overnight family ex-
perience that includes a night-time safari,
a buffet dinner, breakfast and tents under
the stars.

Catching the ferry is part of the fun,
and given that parking is expensive (per
day $17), it's well worth considering. From
the wharf, the Sky Safari cable car or a bus
will whisk you to the main entrance, from
which you can traverse the zoo downhill
back to the ferry. A Zoo Pass (adult/child/
family $53/27/148) from Circular Quay
includes return ferry rides, the bus or
cable-car ride to the top and zoo admission. Disabled access is good, even when
arriving by ferry.

OBELISK   BEACH
Map p242 (Chowder Bay Rd; 🚌244) An isolated
gay and nudist beach surrounded by bushland in the Middle Head section of Sydney
Harbour National Park. It loses the sun
quickly in the afternoon (making it chilly
for the nudists).

COBBLERS BEACH   BEACH
Map p242 (Cobblers Beach Rd; 🚌244) A nude
and secluded beach on the other side of
Middle Head from its partner in crime,
Obelisk.

BALMORAL BEACH   BEACH
Map p242 (The Esplanade; 🚌245) The beachy
enclave of Balmoral faces off with Manly
across Middle Harbour, and has some good
restaurants and a beaut swimming beach.
Split in two by an unfeasibly picturesque
rocky outcrop, Balmoral attracts picnicking
North Shore families. Swimmers migrate to
the shark-netted southern end.

CHINAMANS BEACH   BEACH
Map p242 (Cyprian St; 🚌229) Gorgeous, peaceful and serene, despite its proximity to busy
Balmoral; it's a photogenic location for a
swim.

🍴 EATING

**The best harbour restaurants dip their
feet in the water, with some offering
amazing views of the city.**

🍴 Watsons Bay

DUNBAR HOUSE   CAFE $$
Map p242 (☎02-9337 1226; www.dunbarhouse.
com.au; 9 Marine Pde, Watsons Bay; breakfast
$11-17, lunch $18-29; ⊙8am-3.30pm; 🚢Wat-
sons Bay) This meticulously restored 1830s
mansion is a gorgeous spot for brunch,
particularly if you can score one of the
harbour-view tables on the verandah.
Bookings are recommended on weekends.

DOYLES ON THE BEACH   SEAFOOD $$$
Map p242 (☎02-9337 2007; www.doyles.com.
au; 11 Marine Pde, Watsons Bay; mains $39-62;
⊙noon-3pm & 5.30-8.30pm; 🚢Watsons Bay)
There may well be better places for seafood,
but few can compete with Doyles' location
or its history – this restaurant first opened
in 1885. Catching the harbour ferry to Watsons Bay for a seafood lunch is a quintessential Sydney experience.

🍴 Balmain

ADRIANO ZUMBO   BAKERY $
Map p242 (www.adrianozumbo.com; 296 Darling
St, Balmain; sweets $2.50-10; ⊙8am-6pm; 🚢Bal-
main) Crafty Adriano gets up at 3am every
day to bake the amazing edibles on sale in
his superskinny patisserie. The slenderness
of the shop will be inversely proportionate

to the girth of your waistline if you visit too often: the macarons are as astonishing to look at as they are to eat.

RIVERVIEW HOTEL
& DINING
MODERN BRITISH $$

Map p242 (☑02-9810 1151; www.theriverview hotel.com.au; 29 Birchgrove Rd, Balmain; pizzas $20-22, mains $28-33; ☉noon-11pm; ☐Balmain) The Riv's head chef, Brad Sloane, worked under the legendary Marco Pierre White in London. British expats flock here to try his nose-to-tail dishes in the elegant upstairs dining room, while locals are equally keen on the pizzas served in the downstairs bar.

KAZBAH
NORTH AFRICAN $$

Map p242 (☑02-9555 7067; www.kazbah.com. au; 379 Darling St, Balmain; breakfast $12-23, lunch $19-29, dinner $28-34; ☉8am-3pm Sat & Sun, 11.30am-3pm Tue-Fri, 5.30-9.30pm Tue-Sat; ☐Balmain) Rock the Kazbah for weekend brunch or a peppy dinner. On hot summer days the windows fold out to the street. Generous serves feature plenty of eggplant, tahini, hummus and cumin; leave room for sweets.

✗ Mosman

TEA ROOM GUNNERS
BARRACKS
CAFE $$

Map p242 (☑02-8962 5900; www.gunnersbar racks.com.au; Suakin Dr, Georges Heights, Mosman; mains $14-29; ☉10am-5pm Mon-Fri, to 3pm Sat & Sun; ☐244) With a lengthy tea menu, this is a refined spot for a morning or afternoon cuppa and cake. On weekdays, the lunch menu is full of substantial Modern Australian meals.

BATHERS' PAVILION
MODERN FRENCH $$$

Map p242 (☑02-9969 5050; www.bathersspa vilion.com.au; 4 The Esplanade, Balmoral Beach; restaurant mains $50, cafe $23-34; ☉noon-3pm & 6.30-11pm; ☑; ☐245) Spanish Mission–style architecture, harbour views and outstanding food collide at one of Sydney's most enduringly popular restaurants. The seasonal menu focuses on produce from small local providers, with plenty of seafood; there's also a full vegetarian menu. Under the same roof, Bathers' Café opens for breakfast at 7am, serving equally scrumptious fare (including delicious pizza) at more democratic prices.

🍷 DRINKING & NIGHTLIFE

★WATSONS BAY BEACH CLUB
PUB

Map p242 (www.watsonsbayhotel.com.au; 1 Military Rd, Watsons Bay; ☉10am-midnight Mon-Sat, to 10pm Sun; ☐Watsons Bay) One of the great pleasures in life is languishing in the rowdy beer garden of the Watsons Bay Hotel, mere metres from the ferry wharf, after a day at the beach. Stay to watch the sun go down over the city.

GOLDEN SHEAF HOTEL
PUB

Map p242 (☑02-9327 5877; www.goldensheaf. com.au; 429 New South Head Rd, Double Bay; ☉10am-1am; ☐Double Bay) This noble, rambling old brick pub has a shady beer garden, a sports bar with pool tables, a bistro, a cocktail bar, a rooftop terrace and a dance floor. The musical mandate includes lots of live music and DJs. An impressive memorabilia wall includes autographed photos and albums from the likes of the Beatles and Bowie.

WELCOME HOTEL
PUB

Map p242 (☑02-9810 1323; www.thewelcome hotel.com.au; 91 Evans St, Rozelle; ☉11.30am-11.30pm Mon-Sat, noon-10pm Sun; ☐441-445) If you get lost in the backstreets of Rozelle, you might find yourself chowing down in the Welcome Hotel's acclaimed Italian restaurant, or working your way through the craft beer selection in the palm-shaded courtyard. You might even get to commune with Winston, the resident foxhound ghost.

LONDON HOTEL
PUB

Map p242 (☑02-9555 1377; www.londonhotel. com.au; 234 Darling St, Balmain; ☉11am-midnight Mon-Sat, noon-10pm Sun; ☐Balmain) The Harbour Bridge views from the London's long balcony are quintessentially Sydney – about as far from London as you can get. There's a great range of Oz beers on tap, plus a few quality overseas interlopers.

☆ ENTERTAINMENT

ENSEMBLE THEATRE
THEATRE

Map p242 (☑02-9929 0644; www.ensemble.com. au; 78 McDougall St, Kirribilli; ☐North Sydney) The long-running Ensemble presents mainstream theatre by overseas and Australian playwrights (think David Williamson and David Hare), generally with well-known Australian actors.

HAYDEN ORPHEUM
PICTURE PALACE
CINEMA

Map p242 (☎02-9908 4344; www.orpheum. com.au; 380 Military Rd, Cremorne; adult/child $20/15; ⊙sessions 10.30am-8.50pm; 🚌244) Return to cinema's golden age at this fab art deco gem (1935). It still has its original Wurlitzer organ, which gets a workout at special events.

IMB SUNSET CINEMA
CINEMA

Map p242 (www.sunsetcinema.com.au; North Sydney Oval, Miller St, North Sydney; adult/child $18/12; ⊙mid-Jan–Mar; 🚊North Sydney) The lure of big outdoor movie screens is too good for Sydneysiders to pass up on long, hot summer nights.

 **SHOPPING**

KIRRIBILLI MARKETS
MARKET

Map p242 (www.kirribillimarkets.com; Burton Street Tunnel, Kirribilli; 🚊Milsons Point) Kirribilli's general market (7am to 3pm, 4th Saturday of the month) offers exotic foods and lively harbourside hubbub, and sells everything from vintage clothes to kids' gear and all kinds of jewellery. Their other monthly market (9am to 3pm, 2nd Sunday of the month) has an area for art and design, and a separate zone for fashion.

BALMAIN MARKET
MARKET

Map p242 (www.balmainmarket.com.au; 223 Darling St, Balmain; ⊙8.30am-4pm Sat; 🚢Balmain) This small market is set in the shady grounds of St Andrews Congregational Church. Stalls sell arts, crafts, books, clothing, jewellery, plants, and fruit and veg. From the Balmain ferry wharf, head up Thames St to Darling St and turn left.

🏃 SPORTS & ACTIVITIES

CHAMPAGNE SAILING
SAILING

(☎02-9948 1578; www.champagnesailing.com.au; 4hr charters $1200) If you've got champagne tastes or ever fancied re-creating Duran Duran's *Rio* video, charter a 10m catamaran and muster your 20 best friends to split the bill.

SAILING SYDNEY
SAILING

Map p250 (☎1300 670 008; www.sailingsydney. net; King St Wharf 9; adult/child $129/99; 🚢Darling Harbour) Learn the ropes on a 2½-hour cruise on an actual America's Cup yacht.

JAMES CRAIG
SAILING

Map p250 (☎02-9298 3888; www.shf.org.au; Wharf 7, Pyrmont; adult/child $150/50; 🚢Pyrmont Bay) The *James Craig* is a hulking three-masted iron barque built in England in 1874 that's normally moored outside the Maritime Museum. It sails out beyond the heads roughly twice-monthly (bookings essential). Trips include morning tea, lunch, afternoon tea and a sea shanty or three.

EASTSAIL
SAILING

Map p242 (☎02-9327 1166; www.eastsail.com. au; d'Albora Marina, New Beach Rd, Rushcutters Bay; 🚊Edgecliff) Nobody ever said that yachting was a cheap sport. Take the two-day Start Yachting course for $615, or arrange a charter.

SYDNEY HARBOUR KAYAKS
KAYAKING

Map p242 (☎02-9960 4389; www.sydneyharbourkayaks.com.au; Smiths Boat Shed, 81 Parriwi Rd, Mosman; ⊙9am-5pm Mon-Fri, 7.30am-5pm Sat & Sun; 🚌173-180) Rents kayaks (from $20 per hour) and stand-up paddleboards (from $25), and leads four-hour ecotours ($99) from near the Spit Bridge.

NATURAL WANDERS
KAYAKING

Map p242 (☎0427 225 072; www.kayaksydney.com; Lavender Bay wharf; tours $65-150; 🚊Milsons Point) Offers exhilarating morning tours around the Harbour Bridge, Lavender Bay, Balmain and Birchgrove.

NORTH SYDNEY OLYMPIC POOL
SWIMMING

Map p242 (☎02-9955 2309; www.northsydney.nsw.gov.au; 4 Alfred St South; adult/child $7.10/3.50; ⊙5.30am-9pm Mon-Fri, 7am-7pm Sat & Sun; 🚊Milsons Point/Luna Park) Next to Luna Park is this art deco, Olympic-sized outdoor pool, plus a 25m indoor pool, kids' splash zones, a gym ($18.50 with pool access), a crèche and a cafe, all with unbelievable harbour views.

HARBOUR JET
BOAT TOUR

Map p250 (☎1300 887 373; www.harbourjet. com; King St Wharf 9; adult/child from $85/50; 🚢Darling Harbour) One of several jet-boat operators (Sydney Jet, Oz Jet Boating, Thunder Jet – take your pick), these guys run a 35-minute white-knuckle ride with 270-degree spins, fishtails and 75km/h power stops that'll test how long it's been since you had breakfast.

SYDNEY SHOWBOATS
CRUISE

Map p250 (🖉02-8296 7388; www.sydneyshow boats.com.au; King St Wharf 5; from $125; 🚢Darling Harbour) Settle in for a three-hour, three-course dinner cruise on this paddlesteamer, complete with cabaret singers, showgirls flashing their knickers, and a personal magician for your table. Very, very camp.

WHALE WATCHING SYDNEY
CRUISE

(🖉02-9583 1199; www.whalewatchingsydney. net) Humpback and southern right whales habitually shunt up and down the Sydney coastline, sometimes venturing into the harbour. Between mid-May and December, WWS runs three-hour tours (adult/child $94/59) beyond the heads. For a faster, more thrilling ride, they also offer two-hour jet-boat expeditions ($60/40). Boats depart from Jetty 6, Circular Quay or from Cockle Bay Wharf, Darling Harbour.

CAPTAIN COOK CRUISES
CRUISE

Map p240 (🖉02-9206 1111; www.captaincook. com.au; Wharf 6, Circular Quay; 🚢Circular Quay) As well as ritzy lunch and dinner cruises, this crew offers the aquatic version of a hop-on/hop-off bus tour, stopping at Watsons Bay, Taronga Zoo, Garden Island, Circular Quay, Luna Park and Darling Harbour.

MAGISTIC CRUISES
CRUISE

Map p250 (🖉02-8296 7222; www.magisticcruis es.com.au; King St Wharf 5; 🚢Darling Harbour) The fancy Magistic floaters take you on a range of cruises, ranging from the one-hour sightseeing cruise (from $25) offering all the harbour icons to two-hour lunch ($76) and dinner (from $100) cruises with a seafood buffet. Cruises also depart from Wharf 6 at Circular Quay.

MATILDA CRUISES
CRUISE

(🖉02-8270 5188; www.matilda.com.au) Not waltzing but sailing, Matilda offers various cruise options on plush catamarans, including breakfast (from $55), coffee ($55), lunch (from $77), cocktail ($42) and dinner (from $85) cruises, and a hop-on/hop-off harbour circuit (from $40). Boats depart from Jetty 6, Circular Quay and Pier 26, Darling Harbour.

TRIBAL WARRIOR
CULTURAL TOUR

Map p240 (🖉02-9699 3491; www.tribalwarrior. org; Eastern Pontoon, Circular Quay; adult/child $45/30; 🚢Circular Quay) 🍃 Learn about and experience Aboriginal culture and history on this three-hour cruise, stopping at Goat Island for a cultural performance and a guided walk. You'll also be contributing to a worthwhile community self-sufficiency project. Bookings essential.

SYDNEY BY SEAPLANE
SCENIC FLIGHTS

Map p242 (🖉1300 720 995; www.sydneybysea plane.com; Rose Bay Marina, 594 New South Head Rd, Rose Bay; 15min/30min/45min/1hr flights per person $190/260/445/525; 🚢Rose Bay) Scenic flights over Sydney Harbour and the Northern Beaches. Fly-and-dine packages are available for picnics in obscure places. Departs from Rose Bay and Palm Beach.

SYDNEY SEAPLANES
SCENIC FLIGHTS

Map p242 (🖉1300 732 752; www.seaplanes.com. au; Seaplane Base, Lyne Park, Rose Bay; 15/30min flights per person $200/265; 🚢Rose Bay) Aerial excitement meets epicurean delight when you take a seaplane flight from Rose Bay to remote **Berowra Waters Inn** (🖉02-9456 1027; www.berowrawatersinn.com; East or West public wharves; menu per person $175; 🕘noon-2pm Fri-Sun, 6-10pm Fri & Sat) on the Hawkesbury (per person $585) or **Jonah's** (🖉02-9974 5599; www.jonahs.com.au; 69 Bynya Rd, Whale Beach; breakfast $50, mains $49; 🕘7.30-9am, noon-2.30pm & 6.30-11pm; 🚌L90) at Whale Beach ($535). Also offers scenic flights around Sydney Harbour.

City Centre & Haymarket

MACQUARIE ST | THE DOMAIN | HYDE PARK | CITY CENTRE | HAYMARKET

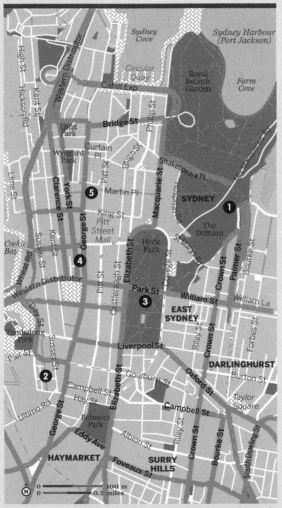

Neighbourhood Top Five

❶ Being transported into colonial vistas, Victorian parlours, Buddhist temples, postwar streets, the heart of the outback and the imaginations of generations of artists at the **Art Gallery of NSW** (p87).

❷ Shopping and eating your way through the vibrant streets of **Chinatown** (p94).

❸ Promenading through the green tunnel at the heart of elegant **Hyde Park** (p89).

❹ Enjoying a right royal shopping spree within the grand confines of the **Queen Victoria Building** (p94).

❺ Admiring the grand bastions of commerce lining **Martin Place** (p90).

For more detail of this area, see Map p245 and p246 ➡

Lonely Planet's Top Tip

If jetlag or other lifestyle choices leave you with the midnight munchies, Haymarket is the best place in the city to be. Restaurants, even some of the very best ones, stay open late here (Chat Thai's open until 2am, for example) and on Chinatown's Dixon St you can find noodles to slurp at any time of night. Just don't expect service with a smile at 5am.

✖ Best Places to Eat

➡ Tetsuya's (p96)

➡ Rockpool (p96)

➡ Mr Wong (p95)

➡ Mamak (p97)

➡ Ippudo Sydney (p96)

For reviews, see p95 ➡

♟ Best Places to Drink

➡ Baxter Inn (p97)

➡ Frankie's Pizza (p97)

➡ Grandma's (p97)

➡ Marble Bar (p97)

➡ O Bar (p97)

For reviews, see p97 ➡

🔒 Best Shopping

➡ Strand Arcade (p99)

➡ Queen Victoria Building (p99)

➡ Westfield Sydney (p99)

➡ Paddy's Markets (p101)

➡ David Jones (p100)

For reviews, see p99 ➡

Explore: City Centre & Haymarket

Before suburban sprawl started in earnest in the mid-19th century, this area (along with the Rocks) *was* Sydney. Today it's a towering Central Business District (CBD) with skyscrapers shadowing sandstone buildings and churches.

Clinging to the CBD fringes are museums, gracious colonial buildings and leafy retreats. The strip of greenery from Hyde Park through the Domain to the Royal Botanic Garden counterpoints the clash and throb of Sydney's commerce. Allocate at least a day to explore it properly, and a night to hit some of the ritzy restaurants and hidden bars. Shopaholics might need longer.

Wedged into the Haymarket district, Sydney's Chinatown is a tight nest of restaurants, shops and aroma-filled alleyways, centred on Dixon St. No longer just Chinese, the area is truly pan-Asian. Head here for cheap eats any time of the day or night.

Chinatown now extends towards Central station, an area that's become the epicentre of backpacker megahostels, with their attendant bars, internet cafes and international buzz. It's not the prettiest part of town, but it is indeed central.

Local Life

➡ **Weekday lunch** On sunny days, office workers swarm out of their climate-controlled, strip-lit cells and into the parks. Fitness freaks with showers in their tower jog straight to the Domain to work up a sweat.

➡ **Yum cha** Despite the larger restaurants seating hundreds of dumpling devotees, there always seems to be queues in Chinatown on weekend mornings.

➡ **Pitt Street Mall** Serious suburban shoppers descend on Sydney's retail ground zero on weekends.

Getting There & Away

➡ **Train** The best option for getting here by far, with City Circle stations at Central, Town Hall, Wynyard, St James and Museum. Additionally, the Eastern Suburbs and Illawarra line stops at Martin Place.

➡ **Bus** Numerous routes head to/from the Rocks and Circular Quay. Routes to the North Shore operate from Wynyard Park. Railway Sq is a major bus hub.

➡ **Light rail** City stops include Central, Capitol Square and Paddy's Market, a handy option if you're coming from Glebe or Pyrmont.

➡ **Parking** Street parking is almost nonexistent, but the city council operates a large underground car park on Goulburn St (corner Elizabeth St; per hour/day $9/49, $10 on Saturdays and Sundays and after 5pm).

TOP SIGHT
ART GALLERY OF NSW

With its classical Greek frontage and modern rear end, the Art Gallery of NSW plays a prominent and gregarious role in Sydney society. Blockbuster international touring exhibitions arrive regularly and there's an outstanding permanent collection of Australian art, including a substantial Indigenous collection. The gallery also plays host to a lively line-up of lectures, concerts, celebrity talks and children's activities.

Collection & Layout

As you enter, the galleries to the left are devoted to 20th- and 21st-century **Australian works** (featuring the likes of Brett Whiteley, Sidney Nolan, Grace Cossington Smith and James Gleeson), while to the right the central room contains local 19th-century art (Arthur Streeton, Tom Roberts). Either side of this is the **European art collection**, split into 15th to 19th century (Constable, Gainsborough, Rubens), and 19th and 20th century (Degas, Van Gogh, Monet, Rodin).

At the rear of this level is the most recent venture by celebrity chef Matt Moran, **Chiswick at the Gallery** (☏02-9225 1819; www.chiswickrestaurant.com.au; Art Gallery Rd; weekday mains $27-35, weekend $32-38; ⊘noon-3.30pm Thu-Tue, to 9pm Wed; ℞St James). Directly opposite is a room filled with ceramics and religious art from the well-regarded **Asian collection**. The remainder of the Asian collection (Chinese, Korean and Japanese art) is directly below on lower level 1, by the cafe. Lower level 2 has the constantly changing **Modern** (Picasso, Gormley, Bacon), **Contemporary** (Gilbert & George, Jeff Koons, Sol LeWitt) and **Photography** galleries. Head down again for the **Yiribana Gallery** containing the Aboriginal and Torres Strait Islander collection (Binyinyuwuy, Tom Djawa, Brenda L Croft).

A range of free guided tours is offered on different themes and in various languages; enquire at the desk or check the website.

Art Prizes

The gallery's most famous annual show coincides with the unfailingly controversial Archibald, Wynne and Sulman Prizes (usually held between July and September; admission $12).

The $75,000 **Archibald Prize** for portraiture is the one that garners the most attention, with its lure of celebrity subjects. It's so popular that it's generated three spin-offs: the **Salon des Refusés** at the SH Ervin Gallery; the highly irreverent **Bald Archies**; and the **Packing Room Prize** (judged by the guys who unload the crates, and generally echoing the public's preference for a famous face, realistically drawn).

The $35,000 **Wynne Prize** for landscape painting or figure sculpture and the $30,000 **Sir John Sulman Prize** for subject or mural painting don't usually cause as much consternation. Neither does the **Artexpress** exhibition of the year's best school student art, usually held between February and April (admission free).

Gallery Kids

Junior art-lovers can follow tailored trails and attend free performances (2.30pm Sundays). Tours for Tots are held monthly on Tuesdays and Thursdays ($20).

DON'T MISS...

➡ Yiribana Gallery
➡ *The Balcony 2* (1975), by Brett Whiteley
➡ *Fire's On* (1891), by Arthur Streeton
➡ *Nude in a Rocking Chair* (1956), by Pablo Picasso
➡ *Haft* (2007), by Antony Gormley

PRACTICALITIES

➡ Map p246
➡ ☏1800 679 278
➡ www.artgallery.nsw.gov.au
➡ admission free
➡ Art Gallery Rd
➡ ⊘10am-5pm Thu-Tue, to 10pm Wed
➡ ℞St James

CITY CENTRE & HAYMARKET ART GALLERY OF NSW

◉ SIGHTS

◉ Macquarie St & the Domain

ART GALLERY OF NSW · GALLERY
See p87.

DOMAIN · PARK
Map p246 (www.rbgsyd.nsw.gov.au; Art Gallery Rd; 🚇St James) Administered by the Royal Botanic Garden, the Domain is a large grassy tract east of Macquarie St, set aside by Governor Phillip in 1788 for public recreation. Phillip's intent rings true: today's city workers use the space to work up a sweat or eat their lunch. Large-scale public events are also held here. Sculptures dot the park, including a reclining Henry Moore figure, and Brett Whiteley's *Almost Once* (1991) – two giant matches, one burnt – rising from the ground near the Art Gallery of NSW.

On the lawn in front of the gallery you can listen to religious zealots, nutters, political extremists, homophobes, hippies and academics express their earnest opinions at the by turns entertaining and enraging **Speakers' Corner** (www.speakerscorner.org. au; ⏰2-5pm Sun). Some of them have something interesting to say; most are just plain mad. Either way, it makes for an interesting afternoon. BYO soapbox.

STATE LIBRARY OF NSW · LIBRARY
Map p246 (📞02-9273 1414; www.sl.nsw.gov.au; Macquarie St; ⏰9am-8pm Mon-Thu, 10am-5pm Fri-Sun; 🚇Martin Pl) FREE Among the State Library's over five million tomes are James Cook's and Joseph Banks' journals and William Bligh's log from the mutinous HMAV *Bounty*. It's worth dropping in to peruse the temporary exhibitions in the galleries, and the elaborately sculpted bronze doors and grand atrium of the neoclassical Mitchell Wing (1910); note the map of Tasman's journeys in the mosaic floor. The main reading room is an elegant temple of knowledge clad in milky marble.

Outside, on the Macquarie St side of the building, is a sculpture of explorer Matthew Flinders; look for his intrepid cat Trim on the windowsill behind.

PARLIAMENT HOUSE · HISTORIC BUILDING
Map p246 (📞02-9230 2111; www.parliament. nsw.gov.au; 6 Macquarie St; ⏰9am-5pm Mon-Fri; 🚇Martin Pl) FREE Twin of the nearby Mint, the venerable Parliament House (1816) has been home to the Parliament of New South Wales since 1829, making it the world's oldest continually operating parliament building. And like the Mint, its front section (which now blends into a modern addition on the eastern side) was part of the Rum Hospital (built in exchange for a monopoly on the rum trade).

You need to pass through a metal detector to access the inner sanctum, where you can check out art exhibitions in the lobby and the historical display in the wood-panelled Jubilee Room. On nonsitting days both assembly chambers are open, but when Parliament is sitting, you're restricted to the Public Gallery.

SYDNEY HOSPITAL · HISTORIC BUILDING
Map p246 (📞02-9382 7111; www.seslhd.health. nsw.gov.au/SHSEH; 8 Macquarie St; 🚇Martin Place) Originally the Rum Hospital, built by two Sydney merchants in return for a monopoly on the rum trade, Australia's oldest hospital has a grand Victorian sandstone facade and a chequered history. You can't wander around inside, but the central courtyard with its kitsch enamelled fountain studded with submissive swans is open to the public. The weathered-looking Gothic Nightingale Wing (1869) was the site of Australia's first Nightingale School of Nursing. In provocative recline out the front of the hospital is the pig-ugly bronze statue *Il Porcellino* (1968), a copy of a Florentine statue of a boar. Rubbing its snout is said to bring good luck.

THE MINT · HISTORIC BUILDING
Map p246 (www.sydneylivingmuseums.com.au; 10 Macquarie St; ⏰9am-5pm Mon-Fri; 🚇Martin Pl) FREE The stately Mint building (1816) was originally the southern wing of the infamous Rum Hospital, built by two Sydney merchants in return for a monopoly on the rum trade (Sydney's currency in those days). It became a branch of the Royal Mint in 1854, the first outside England. It's now head office for the Historic Houses Trust, with a small historical collection and an upstairs cafe. There's not a whole lot to see or do, but it's a worthwhile diversion nonetheless.

HYDE PARK BARRACKS MUSEUM · MUSEUM
Map p246 (📞02-8239 2311; www.sydneyliving museums.com.au; Queens Sq, Macquarie St; adult/child $10/5; ⏰10am-5pm; 🚇St James) Convict architect Francis Greenway designed this squarish, decorously Georgian

structure (1819) as convict quarters. Between 1819 and 1848, 50,000 men and boys did time here, most of whom had been sentenced by British courts to transportation to Australia for property crime. It later became an immigration depot, a women's asylum and a law court. These days it's a fascinating (if not entirely cheerful) museum, focusing on the barracks' history and the archaeological efforts that helped reveal it.

In 2010 it was one of the Australian convict sites to be inscribed on the Unesco World Heritage List. Inside you can learn about the offences for which convicts were transported to Australia, some of which seem astoundingly petty today.

ST JAMES' CHURCH — CHURCH
Map p246 (☑02-8227 1300; www.sjks.org.au; 173 King St; ☉10am-4pm Mon-Fri, 9am-1pm Sat, 7am-4pm Sun; ⓡSt James) Built from convict-made bricks, Sydney's oldest church (1819) is widely considered to be architect Francis Greenway's masterpiece. It was originally designed as a courthouse, but the brief changed and the cells became the crypt. Check out the dark-wood choir loft, the sparkling copper dome, the crypt and the 1950s stained-glass 'Creation Window'.

Free classical concerts happen at 1.15pm on Wednesdays between March and December. See the website or call for details on daily services.

⊙ Hyde Park

HYDE PARK — PARK
Map p246 (Elizabeth St; ⓡSt James & Museum) Formal but much-loved Hyde Park has manicured gardens and a tree-formed tunnel running down its spine which looks particularly pretty at night, illuminated by fairy lights. The park's northern end is crowned by the richly symbolic art deco **Archibald Memorial Fountain** (Map p246; ⓡSt James), featuring Greek mythological figures, while at the other end is the Anzac Memorial.

ST MARY'S CATHEDRAL — CHURCH
Map p246 (☑02-9220 0400; www.stmarys cathedral.org.au; St Marys Rd; crypt $5; ☉6.30am-6.30pm; ⓡSt James) Built to last, this 106m-long Gothic Revival–style cathedral was begun in 1868, consecrated in 1905 and substantially finished in 1928, but the massive, 75m-high spires weren't added until 2000. The crypt has an impressive terrazzo

WHAT'S IN A NAME?
Details of the original Sydney settlement are still hinted at through place names: Bridge St once spanned the Tank Stream, Sydney's first water supply, which trickled into Sydney Cove (now Circular Quay); crops were planted at Farm Cove to feed the early convicts and marines, the latter of which were housed at the top of Barrack St; Market St was the site of the first produce markets, which later moved south to Haymarket.

mosaic floor depicting the Creation, inspired by the Celtic-style illuminations of the *Book of Kells*.

The best time to visit is in the early morning and late afternoon, when the sun streams through the side stained-glass windows (made in Birmingham, England). That's because this cathedral has an unusual north–south orientation rather than the traditional east–west one (facing the rising sun), due to its size and the lie of the land.

GREAT SYNAGOGUE — SYNAGOGUE
Map p246 (☑02-9267 2477; www.greatsyna gogue.org.au; 187a Elizabeth St; tours adult/child $10/5; ☉tours noon Thu & 1st & 3rd Tue; ⓡSt James) The heritage-listed Great Synagogue (1878) is the spiritual home of Sydney's oldest Jewish congregation, established in 1831. It's considered the Mother Synagogue of Australia and is architecturally the most important in the southern hemisphere, combining Romanesque, Gothic, Moorish and Byzantine elements. Tours include the AM Rosenblum Museum's artefacts and a video presentation on Jewish beliefs, traditions and history in Australia.

Look out for the starry gold-leaf ceiling (supported by 12 arches representing the tribes of Israel) and the French Gothic wrought-iron gates.

ANZAC MEMORIAL — MEMORIAL
Map p246 (www.anzacmemorial.nsw.gov.au; Hyde Park; ☉9am-5pm; ⓡMuseum) FREE Fronted by the Pool of Remembrance, this dignified art deco memorial (1934) commemorates the soldiers of the Australia and New Zealand Army Corps (Anzacs) who served in WWI. The interior dome is studded with 120,000 stars – one for each New South Welsh man and woman who served. These

twinkle above Rayner Hoff's poignant sculpture *Sacrifice,* featuring a naked soldier draped over a shield and sword. There's also a small museum downstairs where a 13-minute film screens every 30 minutes. Pines at the southwestern entry grew from seeds gathered at Gallipoli in Turkey, the site of the Anzacs' most renowned WWI campaign.

⊙ City Centre

MUSEUM OF SYDNEY MUSEUM
Map p246 (MoS; ✏02-9251 5988; www.sydney livingmuseums.com.au; cnr Phillip & Bridge Sts; adult/child $10/5; ⊙9.30am-5pm; ℝCircular Quay) Built on the site of Sydney's first (and infamously pungent) Government House, the MoS is a fragmented, story-telling museum, which uses state-of-the-art installations to explore the city's people, places, cultures and evolution. The history of the indigenous Eora people is highlighted – touching on the millennia of continuous occupation of this place. Be sure to open some of the many stainless-steel and glass drawers (they close themselves).

In the forecourt, check out the disarming *Edge of Trees* sculpture by Janet Laurence and Fiona Foley. There's a cool cafe, too.

GOVERNORS PHILLIP & MACQUARIE TOWERS BUILDINGS
Map p246 (cnr Phillip, Young & Bent Sts; ℝCircular Quay) Clad in steel, granite and glass, Governor Phillip Tower (1993) is one of Sydney's tallest buildings (254m including antennae). Its distinctive metallic-bladed top has earned it the nickname 'the Milk Crate'. It's propped up on zinc-plated columns for a monumental 10 storeys before the tower proper begins. At 145m, neighbouring Governor Macquarie Tower (1994) is a comparative pipsqueak.

These towers were part of the redevelopment of the site of Governor Phillip's first Government House, which had been semi-derelict for 50 years. At the block's northern end the house's remnant foundations were converted into First Government House Plaza and the Museum of Sydney.

AUSTRALIA SQUARE BUILDING
Map p246 (www.australiasquare.com.au; 264 George St; ℝWynyard) Generally acknowledged as Australia's first major office tower, Australia Square (1968) was designed by archi-phenomenon Harry Seidler. His 50-storey design assumes a distinctive cylindrical form, with an open plaza at the base and shops below. A vibrant Sol LeWitt lobby mural (2004) replaced a rare Le Corbusier tapestry that hung here for decades before the building's owner auctioned it off. Head up to O Bar (p97) on the rotating 47th floor – jaw-dropping views for the price of a martini.

ST PHILIP'S CHURCH CHURCH
Map p246 (✏02-9247 1071; www.yorkstreet anglican.com; 3 York St; ℝWynyard) Completed in 1856 by architect Edmund Blacket in High Victorian Gothic style, St Philip's is the latest incarnation of a line descending from Sydney's original Anglican parish church (1793). It's an unobtrusive structure dwarfed by surrounding skyscrapers and is usually kept locked outside of Sunday services and special events.

MARTIN PLACE SQUARE
Map p246 (ℝMartin Pl) Studded with imposing edifices, long, lean Martin Place was closed to traffic in 1971, forming a terraced pedestrian mall complete with fountains and areas for public gatherings. It's the closest thing to a main civic square that Sydney has. In 2014 the Lindt cafe at 53 Martin Pl was the site of a 16-hour siege, ending in the death of two hostages and the gunman. At the time of writing, a permanent memorial to the victims was being planned.

As iconic in its time as the Opera House, **GPO Sydney** (www.gposydney.com; 1 Martin Pl), built in 1874, is a beautiful colonnaded Victorian palazzo that was once Sydney's General Post Office. It has since been gutted, stabbed with office towers and transformed into the Westin Sydney hotel, swanky shops, restaurants and bars. Inspired by Italian Renaissance palaces, architect James Barnet caused a minor fracas by basing the faces carved on the sandstone facade on local identities. Queen Victoria dominates the central white-marble statuary, surrounded by allegorical figures. Under a staircase in the basement there is a small historical display and a pipe housing the dribbling remnants of the Tank Stream.

Built in 1916, 12-storey **5 Martin Place** (www.5martinplace.com.au) was Australia's first steel-framed 'skyscraper'. At the time of writing, it was in the process of a major redevelopment, with a glass tower being grafted on to it. A **Commonwealth Bank branch** (48 Martin Pl) has taken over the old

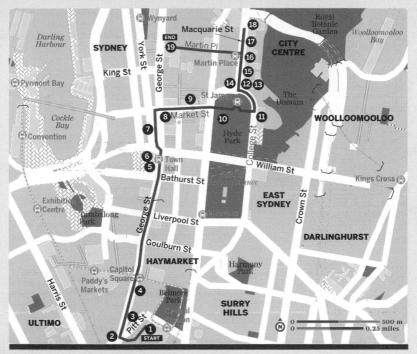

Neighbourhood Walk
Urban Canyons

START CENTRAL STATION
END MARTIN PLACE
LENGTH 3KM; ONE HOUR

Start in the main concourse of ❶**Central Station** (p95). Take the George St exit, turn left and walk through the small park down to ❷**Railway Square**, with its DNA-strand towers. Cross Pitt St and head onto George St. Step off Sydney's main drag into the calming 1845 sandstone ❸**Christ Church St Lawrence**. Check the thickness of your moral fibre before George St lures you into a saucy stew of sex clubs and porn shops.

Respite comes in the form of the elaborate Victoriana of the ❹**Haymarket library** and three blocks later ❺**St Andrew's Cathedral** (p94), ❻**Sydney Town Hall** (p94) and the ❼**Queen Victoria Building** (p94). Walk through the QVB and duck right into Market St. On your right is the extraordinarily extravagant ❽**State Theatre** (p94); stop to scan the foyer.

Trundle past the macrospindle of ❾**Sydney Tower** (p94), its base hidden within the Westfield Sydney complex, and

into verdant ❿**Hyde Park** (p89). As you cut across, check out the giant chessboard and the splendiferous fountain.

Across College St, skateboarders career around the sturdily buttressed ⓫**St Mary's Cathedral** (p89). Curve north from here around the top of Hyde Park under the watchful gaze of ⓬**Prince Albert**, then angle right into Macquarie St.

Governor Lachlan Macquarie commissioned convicted forger Francis Greenway to design this illustrious strip in the early 19th century. Greenway's ⓭**Hyde Park Barracks** (p88) and ⓮**St James' Church** (p89) guard the southern end. In quick succession on the right as you continue north are ⓯**The Mint** (p88), ⓰**Sydney Hospital** (p88), ⓱**Parliament House** (p88) and the ⓲**State Library of NSW** (p88). Cross the road and head into ⓳**Martin Place** – sadly, it's now famous as the site of a day-long seige in December 2014. Roam through the foyers and dodge the skateboarders along this pedestrian mall. Channel Seven news is filmed live behind the glass of the Colonial Centre, on the right past Elizabeth St.

RICHARD CUMMINS / GETTY IMAGES ©

1. Shopping in Chinatown (p99)
Browse the bargains on Dixon St.

2. Art Gallery of NSW (p87)
From Brett Whiteley to Pablo Picasso, the gallery's collection is vast.

3. Queen Victoria Building (p94 & p99)
Balconies, domes, stained glass and 200 speciality stores make for a glamorous shopping experience.

4. Hyde Park (p89)
The park's Archibald Memorial Fountain features Greek mythological figures.

State Savings Bank building: it's a beaut example of interwar beaux-arts architecture, featuring green-marble Ionian columns and an enclosed brass-and-marble teller area.

Near the George St end of Martin Place you'll find the **Cenotaph**, commemorating Australia's war dead. Abutting Martin Place on George St is the former **Commercial Banking Corporation of Sydney** – an impressive marbled edifice, worth a look if you're passing by.

SYDNEY TOWER EYE   TOWER

Map p246 (⏱1800 258 693; www.sydneytower eye.com.au; 100 Market St; adult/child $27/16, Skywalk adult/child $70/49; ⊗9am-9.30pm; ⊠St James) The 309m-tall Sydney Tower (built 1970–1981) offers unbeatable 360-degree views from the observation level 250m up – and even better ones for the daredevils braving the Skywalk on its roof. The visit starts with the 4D Experience – a short 3D film giving you a bird's-eye view (a parakeet's to be exact) of city, surf, harbour and what lies beneath the water, accompanied by mist sprays and bubbles; it's actually pretty darn cool.

Luke Skywalker aspirations? Don a spiffy 'skysuit' and take the **Skywalk**: shackle yourself to the safety rail and step onto two glass-floored viewing platforms outside Sydney Tower's observation deck, 268m above the street. It's no place for the weak bowelled...

Tickets are cheaper online, or as part of a Sydney Attractions Pass.

STATE THEATRE   BUILDING

Map p246 (⏱136 100; www.statetheatre.com.au; 49 Market St; tours adult/child $23/15; ⊗tours 10am & 1pm Mon-Wed; ⊠St James) The ostentatiously ornate State (1929) is Sydney's most beautiful theatre. Originally built as a movie palace during Hollywood's heyday, it's now a National Trust–classified building, dripping with gilt and velveteen. Live shows (musicals, comedy, middle-of-the-road bands) take the stage, except during the Sydney Film Festival in June.

QUEEN VICTORIA BUILDING   HISTORIC BUILDING

Map p246 (QVB; ⏱02-9264 9209; www.qvb. com.au; 455 George St; tours $15; ⊗11am-5pm Sun, 9am-6pm Mon-Wed, Fri & Sat, 9am-9pm Thu; ⊠Town Hall) Unbelievably, this High Victorian masterpiece (1898) was repeatedly slated for demolition before it was restored in the mid-1980s. Occupying an entire city block on the site of the city's first markets, the QVB is a Venetian Romanesque temple to the gods of retail.

Sure, the 200 speciality shops are great, but check out the wrought-iron balconies, the Byzantine copper domes, the stained-glass shopfronts, the mosaic floors, the replica crown jewels, the ballroom, the tinkling baby grand and the hyperkitsch animated Royal Clock (featuring the Battle of Hastings and an hourly beheading of Charles I). Informative 45-minute tours (11.30am Tuesday, Thursday and Saturday) depart from the concierge desk on the ground floor.

Outside there's an imposing statue of Queen Vic herself. Nearby is a wishing well featuring a bronze replica of her beloved pooch, Islay, which disconcertingly speaks in the baritone voice of former radio rabble-rouser John Laws.

SYDNEY TOWN HALL   HISTORIC BUILDING

Map p246 (www.sydneytownhall.com.au; 483 George St; ⊗8am-6pm Mon-Fri; ⊠Town Hall) Mansard roofs, sandstone turrets, wrought-iron trimmings and over-the-top balustrades: the French Second Empire wedding-cake exterior of the Town Hall (built 1868–89) is something to behold. Unless there's something on, you can explore the halls off the main entrance. The wood-lined concert hall has a humongous pipe organ with nearly 9000 pipes; it was once the largest in the world. It's used regularly for recitals, some of which are free.

ST ANDREW'S CATHEDRAL   CHURCH

Map p246 (⏱02-9265 1661; www.sydneycathe dral.com; cnr George & Bathurst Sts; ⊗10am-4pm Mon, Tue, Fri & Sat, 8am-7.30pm Wed & Sun, 10am-6.30pm Thu; ⊠Town Hall) Sporting beautiful stained glass and twin spires inspired by England's York Minster, squat St Andrew's Anglican is the oldest cathedral in Australia (1868). Music is a big deal here; refer to the website for details of free lunchtime organ recitals, concert band performances and 'Young Music' concerts during school terms. The accomplished St Andy's choir warbles at various services.

⊙ Haymarket

CHINATOWN   AREA

Map p245 (www.sydney-chinatown.info; ⊠Town Hall) With a discordant soundtrack of blaring Canto pop, Dixon St is the heart and soul of Chinatown: a narrow, shady pedestrian mall with a string of restaurants and their urgently attendant spruikers. The ornate dragon gates *(paifang)* at either end are topped with fake bamboo tiles, golden Chinese calligraphy (with English translations), ornamental lions to keep evil spirits at bay and a fair amount of pigeon poo.

This is actually Sydney's third Chinatown: the first was in The Rocks in the late 19th century before it moved to the Darling Harbour end of Market St. Dixon St's Chinatown dates from the 1920s. Look for the fake-bamboo awnings guarded by dragons, dogs and lions, and kooky upturned-wok lighting fixtures.

On Hay St, the surreal **Golden Water Mouth** (Map p245; Hay St; ⊠Town Hall) sculpture drips with gilt and water. Formed from a eucalyptus trunk from Condobolin, the destination of many gold-rush-era Chinese, its feng shui is supposed to promote positive energy and good luck. A little further down Hay St, Paddy's Markets (p101) fills the lower level of a hefty brick building. It started out in the mid-19th century with mainly European traders, but the tightly packed market stalls are more evocative of present-day Vietnam these days.

CENTRAL STATION   BUILDING

Map p245 (Eddy Ave; ⊠Central Station) Sydney's main railway station was built in 1906 on top of an old convent and cemetery (watch out for ghosts). The 75m Gothic clock tower was added 15 years later. The main sandstone concourse has an impressive vaulted roof and is the terminus for intercity and country trains. Suburban trains chug into the outdoor platforms downstairs on the Surry Hills side.

As you're pulling into Central from the south, look for the ornate disused **Mortuary Station** (1869) on your left.

✖ EATING

Without harbour views, Sydney's central-city restaurants tend to be discreet, upmarket spots – perfect for secret handshakes over million-dollar deals. Some have beaten geography by perching themselves atop towers. Expect a reverse gradation of prices, starting high at the water and dropping considerably as you head inland.

Chinatown is your best bet for a cheap, satisfying meal – especially after midnight. Chinese food dominates, but you'll also find superb Vietnamese, Malaysian, Korean and Thai. There's also a tiny Spanish Quarter on Liverpool St just west of George St; Little Korea along Pitt St near Liverpool St; and Thaitown on Campbell St.

✖ City Centre

CENTRAL BAKING DEPOT   BAKERY $

Map p246 (www.centralbakingdepot.com.au; 37-39 Erskine St; items $5-13; ⊙7am-4pm Mon-Sat; ⊠Wynyard) CBD produces quality baked goods right in the heart of the CBD (Central Business District). Drop by for a savoury snack (pies, sausage rolls, croissants, pizza slices, sandwiches), or a sweet treat with coffee. Seating is limited to a modest scattering of tables and a window bench.

SYDNEY MADANG   KOREAN $

Map p246 (371a Pitt St; mains $13-20; ⊙11.30am-midnight; ⊠Museum) Down a teensy Little Korea lane is this backdoor gem – an authentic barbecue joint that's low on interior charisma but high on quality and quantity. Noisy, cramped and chaotic, yes, but the chilli seafood soup will have you coming back tomorrow.

LE GRAND CAFÉ   FRENCH, CAFE $

Map p246 (www.afsydney.com.au/about/le-grand-cafe; 257 Clarence St; mains $10-15; ⊙8am-6.15pm Mon-Thu, to 4.30pm Fri, to 2pm Sat; ⊠Town Hall) All we can say about this cafe in the foyer of the Harry Seidler–designed Alliance Française building is *ooh la la*. The classic French snacks (think pastries, baguettes and croque-monsieur) are delicious, and the surrounds are extremely smart.

★MR WONG   CHINESE $$

Map p246 (☑02-9240 3000; www.merivale.com.au/mrwong; 3 Bridge Lane; mains $25-38; ⊙noon-3pm & 5.30-11pm; ⊠Wynyard) Dumpling junkies shuffle down a dirty lane and into the bowels of an old warehouse for a taste of Mr Wong's deliciously addictive Cantonese fare. There's a dark-edged glamour to the cavernous basement dining room. Despite seating 240, there are often queues out the door.

SPICE TEMPLE
CHINESE $$

Map p246 (📱02-8078 1888; www.rockpool.com;
10 Bligh St; dishes $14-45; 🕐noon-3pm Mon-Fri,
6-10.30pm Mon-Sat; 🍴; 🚇Martin Place) Tucked
away in the basement of his Rockpool Bar
& Grill is Neil Perry's darkly atmospheric
temple to the cuisine of China's western
provinces, especially Sichuan, Yunnan, Hu-
nan, Jiangxi, Guangxi and Xingjiang. Ex-
pect plenty of heat and lots of thrills.

IPPUDO SYDNEY
JAPANESE $$

Map p246 (📱02-8078 7020; www.ippudo.com.
au; L5 Westfield Sydney, 188 Pitt St; mains $15-
25; 🕐11am-10pm; 🚇St James) An exuber-
ant chorus of welcome greets guests on
arrival at this wonderful ramen house,
tucked away near the Westfield food court.
Founded in Fukuoka in 1985 and now in 11
countries, the Sydney branch serves all the
soupy, noodley favourites.

ALPHA
GREEK $$

Map p246 (📱02-9098 1111; www.alpharestau
rant.com.au; 238 Castlereagh St; mains $19-35;
🕐noon-3pm & 6-10pm; 🚇Museum) Located
directly across from the Greek consulate
in the grand dining room of the Hellenic
Club, this wonderful restaurant brings all
the zing and drama of the Mediterranean
to the heart of the city. Chef Peter Conis-
tis' menu covers the classics, with his own
unique tweaks.

DIN TAI FUNG
CHINESE $$

Map p245 (www.dintaifung.com.au; L1, World Sq,
644 George St; dishes $11-19; 🕐11.30am-2.30pm
& 5.30-9pm; 🚇Museum) The noodles and
buns are great, but it's the dumplings that
made this Taiwanese chain famous, delivering an explosion of fabulously flavoursome
broth as you bite into their delicate casings.
Come early, come hungry, come prepared
to share your table. They also have stalls in
The Star (p105) and Westfield Sydney (p99)
food courts.

ASH ST CELLAR
MODERN AUSTRALIAN $$

Map p246 (📱02-9240 3000; www.merivale.com
.au/ashstcellar; 1 Ash St; large plates $18-26;
🕐8.30am-11pm Mon-Fri; 🚇Wynyard) Part of
the so-hot-right-now Ivy complex, Ash
St Cellar is an urbane lane-side wine bar
that does excellent cheese, charcuterie and
shared plates. Sit outside if it's not too gusty
and agonise over the 200-plus wines on the
list. Despite the suits sweeping through, the
vibe is relaxed and unhurried.

★TETSUYA'S
FRENCH, JAPANESE $$$

Map p246 (📱02-9267 2900; www.tetsuyas.com;
529 Kent St; degustation $220; 🕐noon-3pm Sat,
6-10pm Tue-Sat; 🚇Town Hall) Down a clandestine security driveway, this extraordinary
restaurant is for those seeking a culinary
journey rather than a simple stuffed belly.
Settle in for 10-plus courses of French- and
Japanese-inflected food from the creative
genius of Japanese-born Tetsuya Wakuda.
Book way ahead.

ROCKPOOL
MODERN AUSTRALIAN $$$

Map p246 (📱02-9252 1888; www.rockpool.com;
11 Bridge St; lunch mains $35-55, 9-/10-course
dinner $145/165; 🕐noon-3pm Mon-Fri, 6-11pm
Mon-Sat; 🚇Circular Quay) The Neil Perry
empire now stretches to eight acclaimed
restaurants in three cities, and this grand
dining room is the mothership. After 25
years, Rockpool's creations still manage to
wow diners. Expect crafty, contemporary
cuisine with Asian influences, faultless
service and an alluring wine list.

EST.
MODERN AUSTRALIAN $$$

Map p246 (📱02-9240 3000; www.merivale.com.
au/est; L1, 252 George St; 4-course lunch/dinner
$118/155, degustation $180; 🕐noon-2.30pm Fri,
6-10pm Mon-Sat; 🚇Wynyard) Pressed-tin ceilings, huge columns, oversized windows and
modern furniture make the interior design
almost as interesting as the food. This is
Sydney fine dining at its best; thick wallet and fancy threads a must. Seafood fills
around half of the slots on the menu.

ROCKPOOL BAR & GRILL
STEAK $$$

Map p246 (📱02-8078 1900; www.rockpool.
com; 66 Hunter St; mains $26-115; 🕐noon-3pm
Mon-Fri, 6-11pm Mon-Sat; 🚇Martin Place) You'll
feel like a 1930s Manhattan stockbroker
when you dine at this sleek operation in
the art deco City Mutual Building. The
bar is famous for its dry-aged, full-blood
Wagyu burger (make sure you order a side
of the hand-cut fat chips), but carnivores
will be equally enamoured with the suc-
culent steaks, stews and fish dishes served
in the grill.

SEPIA
JAPANESE, FUSION $$$

Map p246 (📱02-9283 1990; www.sepiarestau
rant.com.au; 201 Sussex St; 4 courses/degustation
$160/190; 🕐noon-3pm Fri & Sat, 6-10pm Tue-Sat;
🚇Town Hall) There's nothing washed out or
brown-tinged about Sepia's food: Martin
Benn's picture-perfect creations are pre-

sented in glorious technicolour, with each taste worth a thousand words. A Japanese sensibility permeates the boundary-pushing menu, earning Sepia the city's top dining gong.

✕ Haymarket

MAMAK
MALAYSIAN $

Map p245 (www.mamak.com.au; 15 Goulburn St; mains $6-17; ⊙11.30am-2.30pm & 5.30-10pm Mon-Thu, to 2am Fri & Sat; ⊠Town Hall) Get here early (from 5.30pm) if you want to score a table without queuing, because this eat-and-run Malaysian joint is one of the most popular cheapies in the city. The satays are cooked over charcoal and are particularly delicious when accompanied by a flaky golden roti.

CHAT THAI
THAI $$

Map p245 (☑02-9211 1808; www.chatthai.com.au; 20 Campbell St; mains $10-20; ⊙10am-2am; ⊠Central) Cooler than your average Thai joint, this Thaitown linchpin is so popular that a list is posted outside for you to affix your name to should you want a table. Expat Thais flock here for the dishes that don't make it onto your average suburban Thai restaurant menu – particularly the more unusual sweets.

🍷⚓ DRINKING & NIGHTLIFE

The city centre has long been known for upmarket, after-work booze rooms, none of which you would describe as cosy locals. Some are worth checking out for their views, cocktails, sassy decor or historical interest; most are what you might call 'drycleaners' – good places to pick up suits. More interesting are the speakeasy-style places lurking in the most unlikely back alleys and basements. The entire city centre is subject to 1.30am lockouts and a complete ban on alcohol sales after 3am.

★BAXTER INN
BAR

Map p246 (www.thebaxterinn.com; 152-156 Clarence St; ⊙4pm-1am Mon-Sat; ⊠Town Hall) Yes, it really is down that dark lane and through that unmarked door (it's easier to find if there's a queue; otherwise look for the bouncer lurking nearby). Whisky's the main poison and the friendly bar staff really know their stuff.

★FRANKIE'S PIZZA
BAR

Map p246 (www.frankiespizzabytheslice.com; 50 Hunter St; ⊙4pm-3am Sun-Thu, noon-3am Fri & Sat; ⊠Martin Place) Descend the stairs and you'll think you're in a 1970s pizzeria, complete with plastic grapevines, snapshots covering the walls and tasty $6 pizza slices. But open the nondescript door in the corner and an indie wonderland reveals itself. Bands play here at least four nights a week (join them on Tuesdays for live karaoke) and there's another bar hidden below.

GRANDMA'S
COCKTAIL BAR

Map p246 (www.grandmasbarsydney.com; basement, 275 Clarence St; ⊙3pm-midnight Mon-Fri, 5pm-1am Sat; ⊠Town Hall) Billing itself as a 'retrosexual haven of cosmopolitan kitsch and faded granny glamour', Grandma's hits the mark. A stag's head greets you on the stairs and ushers you into a tiny subterranean world of parrot wallpaper and tiki cocktails. Someone's suprisingly cool granny must be very proud.

MARBLE BAR
BAR

Map p246 (www.marblebarsydney.com.au; basement, 488 George St; ⊙4pm-midnight Sun-Thu, to 2am Fri & Sat; ⊠Town Hall) Built for a staggering £32,000 in 1893 as part of the Adams Hotel on Pitt St, this ornate underground bar is one of the best places in town for putting on the ritz (even if this is the Hilton). Musos play anything from jazz to funk, Wednesday to Saturday.

When the Adams was demolished in 1968, every marble slab, wood carving and bronze capital was dismantled, restored, then reassembled here.

O BAR
COCKTAIL BAR

Map p246 (www.obardining.com.au; Level 47, Australia Sq, 264 George St; ⊙5pm-late; ⊠Wynyard) At around $20, the cocktails at this 47th-floor revolving bar aren't cheap, but they're still cheaper than admission to Sydney Tower – and it's considerably more glamorous. The views are truly wonderful.

ROOK
COCKTAIL BAR

Map p246 (www.therook.com.au; L7, 56-58 York St; ⊙noon-midnight Mon-Fri, 4pm to midnight Sat; ⊠St James) Seemingly designed for one-time grungsters turned stockbrokers, this covered rooftop bar has an artfully dishevelled look and serves a mean cocktail. It's not cheap though. Is spending $50 on lobster thermidor and then following it up with a deep-fried Mars Bar the ultimate ironic statement?

ESTABLISHMENT
BAR

Map p246 (www.merivale.com/establishmentbar; 252 George St; ⊙11am-late Mon-Sat, noon-10pm Sun; ☒Wynyard) Establishment's cashed-up crush proves that the art of swilling cocktails after a hard city day is not lost. Sit at the majestic marble bar or in the swish courtyard, or be absorbed by a leather lounge as stockbrokers scribble their phone numbers on the backs of coasters for flirty new aquaintances.

GOOD GOD SMALL CLUB
BAR, CLUB

Map p246 (www.goodgodgoodgod.com; 55 Liverpool St; front bar free, club varies; ⊙5-11pm Wed, to 1am Thu, to 3am Fri & Sat; ☒Town Hall) In a defunct underground taverna near Chinatown, Good God's rear dancetaria hosts everything from live indie bands to Jamaican reggae, '50s soul, rockabilly and tropical house music. Its success lies in the focus on great music rather than glamorous surrounds.

SLIP INN & CHINESE LAUNDRY
PUB, CLUB

Map p246 (www.merivale.com.au/chineselaundry; 111 Sussex St; club $20-30; ⊙11am-late Mon-Fri, 4pm-late Sat; ☒Wynyard) Slip in to this warren of moody rooms on the edge of Darling Harbour and bump hips with the kids. There are bars, pool tables, a beer garden and Mexican food, courtesy of El Loco. On Friday and Saturday nights the bass cranks up at the attached Chinese Laundry nightclub.

SPICE CELLAR
BAR, CLUB

Map p246 (www.thespicecellar.com.au; 58 Elizabeth St; ⊙bar 4pm-late Wed-Fri, 7pm-late Sat, club 9pm-late Thu-Sun; ☒Martin Place) Saunter down to this stylish underground bunker for cocktails in the lounge bar. The attached club has one of Sydney's hottest little dance floors, which despite its size attracts the occasional turntable legend to its decks.

IVY
BAR, CLUB

Map p246 (☎02-9254 8100; www.merivale. com/ivy; L1, 330 George St; ⊙noon-late Mon-Fri, 6.30pm-late Sat; ☒Wynyard) Hidden down a lane off George St, Ivy is a scarily fashionable complex of bars, restaurants, discreet lounges...even a swimming pool. It's also Sydney's most hyped venue; expect lengthy queues of suburban kids teetering on unfeasibly high heels, waiting to shed up to $40 on a Saturday for entry to Sydney's hottest club night, Pacha.

BAMBINI WINE ROOM
WINE BAR

Map p246 (www.bambinitrust.com.au; 185 Elizabeth St; ⊙3-10pm Mon-Fri, 5.30-11pm Sat; ☒St James) Don't worry, this bar doesn't sell wine to *bambini* – it's a very grown-up, European affair. The tiny dark-wood-panelled room is the sort of place where you'd expect to see Oscar Wilde holding court in the corner. It has an extensive wine list, slick table service, free almonds and breadsticks, and disembodied postmodern cornices dangling from above.

BAVARIAN BIER CAFÉ
BEER HALL

Map p246 (☎02-8297 4111; www.bavarianbier cafe.com; 24 York St; ⊙11am-midnight; ☒Wynyard) Stepping in the door here you'll feel as though you've put your head inside an enormous chandelier – sparkling racks of steins dangle above the central bar, waiting to be filled with litres of Löwenbrau. Soak it all up with some bratwurst, sauerkraut and a schnitzel at long *bierhalle* tables. Also at Manly Wharf (p175) and the Entertainment Quarter.

REDOAK BOUTIQUE BEER CAFE
BEER HALL

Map p246 (☎02-9262 3303; www.redoak.com. au; 201 Clarence St; ⊙noon-late Mon-Sat; ☒Wynyard) With over 20 craft beers available, this place should keep you off the streets for a while. Pull up a stool among the international crew and work your way through the much-awarded list. If things start to slip away from you, slow your descent with a meal.

☆ ENTERTAINMENT

★CITY RECITAL HALL
CLASSICAL MUSIC

Map p246 (☎02-8256 2222; www.cityrecitalhall. com; 2 Angel Pl; ⊙box office 9am-5pm Mon-Fri; ☒Martin Pl) Based on the classic configuration of the 19th-century European concert hall, this custom-built 1200-seat venue boasts near-perfect acoustics. Catch top-flight companies such as Musica Viva, the Australian Brandenburg Orchestra and the Australian Chamber Orchestra here.

★ **STATE THEATRE**   THEATRE

Map p246 (☑02-9373 6655; www.statetheatre. com.au; 49 Market St; ®St James) The beautiful 2000-seat State Theatre is a lavish, gilt-ridden, chandelier-dangling palace. It hosts the Sydney Film Festival, concerts, comedy, opera, musicals and the odd celebrity chef.

★ **METRO THEATRE**   LIVE MUSIC

Map p246 (☑02-9550 3666; www.metrothea tre.com.au; 624 George St; ®Town Hall) Easily Sydney's best venue for catching local and alternative international acts in intimate, well-ventilated, easy-seeing comfort. Other offerings include comedy, cabaret and dance parties.

MUSICA VIVA
AUSTRALIA   CLASSICAL MUSIC

(☑1800 688 482; www.mva.org.au) Musica Viva is the largest presenter of ensemble music in the world, providing over 2000 concerts around Australia annually in a number of musical styles (including chamber music, a cappella, experimental and jazz). Sydney concerts are normally held at the City Recital Hall.

AUSTRALIAN BRANDENBURG
ORCHESTRA   CLASSICAL MUSIC

(☑02-9328 7581; www.brandenburg.com.au; tickets $71-166) The ABO is a distinguished part of Australia's artistic landscape, playing baroque and classical music on period-perfect instruments. Leading international guest artists appear frequently. Performances are usually held at the City Recital Hall.

PINCHGUT OPERA   OPERA

(www.pinchgutopera.com.au) This small player stages two intimate, oft-overlooked chamber operas every July and December at the City Recital Hall.

CAPITOL THEATRE   THEATRE

Map p245 (☑1300 558 878; www.capitoltheatre. com.au; 13 Campbell St; ®Central) Lavishly restored, this large city theatre is home to long-running musicals (*Wicked, Les Miserables, Matilda*) and the occasional ballet or big-name concert.

🛍 SHOPPING

Sydneysiders head to the city when they've got something special to buy or when some serious retail therapy is required. The city centre's upmarket stores – centred on Pitt St Mall, Market St and George St – offer plenty of choice for gifts and treats. Shopping is one of Chinatown's big drawcards, with countless bargains of the 'Made in China/Taiwan/Korea' variety. The insane buzz of Paddy's Markets is half the fun.

🛍 City Centre

★ **STRAND ARCADE**   SHOPPING CENTRE

Map p246 (www.strandarcade.com.au; 412 George St; ⊗9am-5.30pm Mon-Wed & Fri, to 8pm Thu, 9am-4pm Sat, 11am-4pm Sun; ®St James) Constructed in 1891, the Strand rivals the QVB in the ornateness stakes. The three floors of designer fashions, Australiana and old-world coffee shops will make your short-cut through here considerably longer.

Top Australian designers commune and collude on the upper levels: Alannah Hill (www.alannahhill.com.au), Corner Shop (p153), Dinosaur Designs (p154), Leona Edmiston (p153), Love+Hatred (p100), Sass & Bide (p153), Scanlan Theodore (p153) and Strand Hatters (p100).

★ **QUEEN VICTORIA**
BUILDING   SHOPPING CENTRE

Map p246 (QVB; www.qvb.com.au; 455 George St; ⊗11am-5pm Sun, 9am-6pm Mon-Wed, Fri & Sat, 9am-9pm Thu; ®Town Hall) The magnificent QVB takes up a whole block and boasts nearly 200 shops on five levels. It's a High Victorian masterpiece – without doubt Sydney's most beautiful shopping centre.

★ **WESTFIELD SYDNEY**   MALL

Map p246 (www.westfield.com.au/sydney; 188 Pitt St Mall; ⊗9.30am-6.30pm Fri-Wed, to 9pm Thu; ®St James) The city's most glamorous shopping mall is a bafflingly large complex gobbling up Sydney Tower and a fair chunk of Pitt St Mall. The 5th-floor food court is excellent. Stores include Calibre (p154), Jurlique (p100), Leona Edmiston (p153), RM Williams (p100), Sass & Bide (p153) and Zimmermann (p154).

STRAND HATTERS
ACCESSORIES

Map p246 (📞02-9231 6884; www.strandhatters.com.au; Strand Arcade, 412 George St; ⊘11am-4pm Sun, 9am-5.30pm Mon-Wed, Fri & Sat, to 8pm Thu; 🚇St James) Got a cold or wet head, or a serious case of the *Crocodile Dundees*? Strand Hatters will cover your crown with a classically Australian Akubra bush hat (made from rabbit felt). Staff will block and steam hats to customer requirements (crocodile-teeth hatbands cost extra).

LOVE+HATRED
JEWELLERY

Map p246 (📞02-9233 3441; www.loveandhatred.com.au; L1, Strand Arcade, 412 George St; ⊘noon-4pm Sun, 10am-5.30pm Mon-Wed, Fri & Sat, to 8pm Thu; 🚇St James) This plush, sensual, wood-panelled shop is aglow with custom-made jewellery by Sydney designer Giovanni D'Ercole. Sapphire rings, natural pearls and rose-gold pieces manifest an unostentatious, mystic blend of Celtic, art nouveau and contemporary styles.

OPAL FIELDS
JEWELLERY

Map p246 (www.opalfields.com.au; L2 QVB, 455 George St; 🚇Town Hall) Billing itself as 'the world's largest opal retailer', this family firm has been turning out jewellery designs incorporating Australia's most famous gemstone for over 30 years. They also have a store at the airport.

DAVID JONES
DEPARTMENT STORE

Map p246 (www.davidjones.com.au; 86-108 Castlereagh St; ⊘9.30am-7pm Sat-Wed, to 9pm Thu & Fri; 🚇St James) DJs is Sydney's premier department store, occupying two enormous city buildings. The Castlereagh St store has women's and children's clothing; Market St has menswear, electrical goods and a highbrow food court. David Jones also takes up a sizeable chunk of Westfield Bondi Junction (p166).

MYER
DEPARTMENT STORE

Map p246 (📞02-9238 9111; www.myer.com.au; 436 George St; ⊘9am-7pm Fri-Wed, to 9pm Thu; 🚇St James) At seven storeys, Myer (formerly Grace Bros) is one of Sydney's largest stores and a prime venue for after-Christmas sales. It's marginally less swanky than David Jones, but you'll still find plenty of high-quality goods and some slick cafes. There's another branch at Westfield Bondi Junction (p166).

KINOKUNIYA
BOOKS

Map p246 (📞02-9262 7996; www.kinokuniya.com; L2, The Galeries, 500 George St; ⊘10am-7pm Fri-Wed, 10am-9pm Thu; 🚇Town Hall) This outpost of the Japanese chain is the largest bookshop in Sydney, with over 300,000 titles. The comics section is a magnet for geeky teens – the imported Chinese, Japanese and European magazine section isn't. There's a cool little cafe here, too.

DYMOCKS
BOOKS

Map p246 (📞02-9235 0155; www.dymocks.com.au; 424 George St; ⊘9am-7pm Fri-Wed, to 9pm Thu; 🚇St James) Heavy on the bestsellers, this mammoth, mainstream bookshop has more than 250,000 titles spread over three floors (including a helluva lot of Lonely Planet guides). Stationery and a cafe, too.

RM WILLIAMS
CLOTHING, ACCESSORIES

Map p246 (www.rmwilliams.com.au; 389 George St; ⊘9am-6pm Fri-Wed, to 9pm Thu; 🚇Wynyard) Urban cowboys and country folk can't get enough of this hard-wearing outback gear. It's the kind of stuff politicians don when they want to seem 'fair dinkum' about something. Prime-ministerial favourites include Driza-Bone oilskin jackets, Akubra hats, moleskin jeans and leather work boots. There are also branches in Westfield Sydney (p99) and Westfield Bondi Junction (p166).

KINGS COMICS
BOOKS

Map p246 (www.kingscomics.com; 310 Pitt St; ⊘9am-6.30pm Fri-Wed, to 8pm Thu; 🚇Town Hall) Like a tractor beam for geeks (and we use that term with all due respect), Kings drags them in with its collection of comics, manga, graphic novels, toys, collectibles and, we're sorry to say, apparel.

HEY PRESTO MAGIC STUDIO
MAGIC

Map p246 (www.heyprestomagic.com.au; 84 Pitt St; ⊘10am-5pm Mon-Wed, Fri & Sat, to 8pm Thu; 🚇Wynyard) If you've ever wanted to pull a rabbit out of a hat, here's where you'll find the hat. Beautiful assistants not provided.

JURLIQUE
BEAUTY

Map p246 (📞02-9235 0928; www.jurlique.com.au; Mid City Centre, 420 George St; ⊘11am-5pm Sun, 9am-6pm Mon-Wed, Fri & Sat, to 9pm Thu; 🚇St James) An international success story, this plant-based skincare range from South Australia is a decadent treat. There's another branch in Westfield Sydney (p99).

🛕 Haymarket

★ PADDY'S MARKETS   MARKET
Map p245 (www.paddysmarkets.com.au; 9-13 Hay St; ☺10am-6pm Wed-Sun; ⓡCentral) Cavernous, 1000-stall Paddy's is the Sydney equivalent of Istanbul's Grand Bazaar, but swap the hookahs and carpets for mobile-phone covers, Eminem T-shirts and cheap sneakers. Pick up a VB singlet for Uncle Bruce or wander the aisles in capitalist awe.

MARKET CITY   SHOPPING CENTRE
Map p245 (www.marketcity.com.au; 9-13 Hay St; ☺10am-7pm; ⓡCentral) This large shopping centre above Paddy's Markets includes a big food court, heaps of discount fashion outlet shops (cheap Converse anyone?), a supermarket and video-game parlours.

🏃 SPORTS & ACTIVITIES

ANDREW (BOY) CHARLTON POOL   SWIMMING
(☎02-9358 6686; www.abcpool.org; 1c Mrs Macquaries Rd; adult/child $6/4.50; ☺6am-7pm Sep-Mar; ⓡMartin Place) Sydney's best saltwater pool – smack bang next to the harbour – is a magnet for water-loving gays, straights, parents and fashionistas. Serious lap swimmers rule the pool, so maintain your lane. Wheelchair accessible.

COOK & PHILLIP PARK   SWIMMING
Map p246 (www.cookandphillip.org.au; 4 College St; adult/child $7/5.20; ☺6am-10pm Mon-Fri, 7am-8pm Sat & Sun; ⓡSt James) This Olympic-sized indoor pool has a hydrotherapy area and a gym ($20 including pool use), plus yoga, pilates, a basketball court, swimming lessons and a wave pool for cooling off the kids.

I'M FREE   WALKING TOUR
Map p246 (☎0405 515 654; www.imfree.com.au; 483 George St; ☺10.30am, 2.30pm & 6.00pm; ⓡTown Hall) FREE Departing thrice daily from the square off George St between the Town Hall and St Andrew's Cathedral (no bookings taken – just show up), these highly rated three-hour tours are nominally free but are run by enthusiastic young guides for tips. The route takes in The Rocks, Circular Quay, Martin Place, Pitt St and Hyde Park. They also have a Rocks tour, departing at 6pm outside Cadman's Cottage.

SYDNEY ARCHITECTURE WALKS   WALKING TOUR
(☎0403 888 390; www.sydneyarchitecture.org; adult/student walk $49/35, cycle incl bike $120/110) These bright young archi-buffs run two 3½-hour cycling tours and five themed two-hour walking tours (The City; Utzon and the Sydney Opera House; Harbourings; Art, Place and Landscape; and Modern Sydney).

BLUEBANANAS   CYCLING
Map p246 (☎02-9114 8488; www.bluebananas.com.au; 281 Clarence St; ⓡTown Hall) Take some of the puff out of a guided cycling tour on an electric bike. Options include the 1½-hour Bike the Bridge tour ($59) and the 2½-hour Sydney City Tour ($99).

CITY CENTRE & HAYMARKET SPORTS & ACTIVITIES

Darling Harbour & Pyrmont

Neighbourhood Top Five

1 Escaping the hustle and bustle of the city within the tranquil paths of the **Chinese Garden of Friendship** (p104).

2 Facing your fears in the underwater tunnels passing through the shark tanks at **Sydney Sea Life Aquarium** (p104).

3 Meeting the stars of the Australian bush in the heart of the city at **Wild Life Sydney Zoo** (p104).

4 Being eyed up by pelicans while gorging on fish and chips at **Sydney Fish Market** (p105).

5 Exploring the innards of the historic ships and submarine at the **Australian National Maritime Museum** (p104).

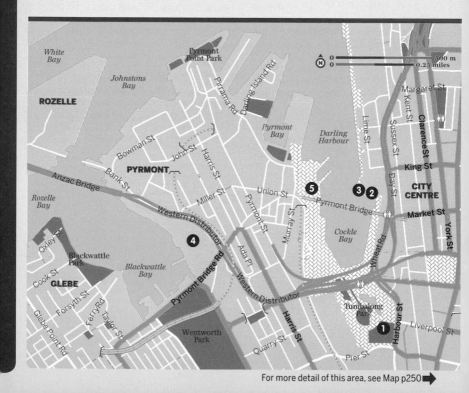

For more detail of this area, see Map p250 ➡

Explore: Darling Harbour & Pyrmont

Dotted between the flyovers and fountains of Sydney's purpose-built tourist hub (opened for the bicentennial in 1988) are some of the city's highest-profile paid attractions. Every other inch of this former dockland is given over to visitor amusements, bars and restaurants. Firework displays occur with alarming frequency; most Saturday nights go off with a bang.

Darling Harbour is currently in the grip of a major redevelopment involving the demolition of many of its 1980s edifices and the building of a giant convention centre. At the same time, the precinct is spreading north along its eastern shore with the rapid construction of the Barangaroo complex of office towers, waterside parks and entertainment venues. When it's finished Sydney's second mega-casino will glare across the water at its competitor, The Star, which has also recently been redeveloped.

In the meantime, it's business as usual for all of the other operators. If you're after a slice of real Sydney life you won't find it here, but it's still worth allocating an hour for a walkabout.

Local Life

➡ **Sydney Fish Market** Sydneysiders head to this market (p105) to stock up for dinner parties or to indulge in fish and chips by the water's edge.

➡ **Tumbalong Park playground** The inner city's best playground is always busy.

➡ **Harris St** The closest thing to a local shopping strip; pick up fancy deli goods from the branch of Simon Johnson at number 181.

Getting There & Away

➡ **Train** The eastern edge of Darling Harbour is within walking distance of Town Hall station. For King St Wharf, Wynyard station is closer.

➡ **Light Rail** If you're heading to Pyrmont from Central or Glebe, light rail is your best option. Convenient stops include Exhibition, Convention, Pyrmont Bay, The Star and Fish Market.

➡ **Ferry** Balmain services chug from Circular Quay to Darling Harbour and Pyrmont Bay. Parramatta River services also stop at Darling Harbour.

➡ **Bus** Bus 443 heads from Circular Quay to the Maritime Museum via George and Harris Sts.

➡ **Parking** Try Harbourside car park, under the Novotel (enter 100 Murray St; per hour/day $12/33).

Lonely Planet's Top Tip

Sydney Sea Life Aquarium, Wild Life Sydney Zoo, Madame Tussauds, Sydney Tower Eye and Manly Sea Life Sanctuary are all owned by the same people. You'll save a pretty penny on admission by purchasing a combo ticket, available in almost every permutation of attractions.

✕ Best Places to Eat

➡ Sokyo (p107)
➡ Adriano Zumbo (p105)
➡ Cafe Morso (p107)
➡ Flying Fish (p107)
➡ Sydney Fish Market (p105)

For reviews, see p105 ➡

🍷 Best Places to Drink

➡ Flying Fish (p107)
➡ Loft (p107)
➡ Cargo Bar (p107)

For reviews, see p107 ➡

◉ Best with Kids

➡ Sydney Sea Life Aquarium (p104)
➡ Tumbalong Park (p104)
➡ Monkey Baa Theatre Company (p107)
➡ Wild Life Sydney Zoo (p104)
➡ Darling Harbour Mini Train (p107)

For reviews, see p104 ➡

DARLING HARBOUR & PYRMONT

SIGHTS

Darling Harbour

WILD LIFE SYDNEY ZOO   ZOO
Map p250 (02-9333 9245; www.wildlifesyd ney.com.au; Aquarium Pier; adult/child $40/28; 9.30am-7pm; Town Hall) Complementing its sister and neighbour, Sea Life, this complex houses an impressive collection of Australian native reptiles, butterflies, spiders, snakes and mammals (including kangaroos and koalas). The nocturnal section is particularly good, bringing out the extrovert in the quolls, potoroos, echidnas and possums. As interesting as Wild Life is, it's not a patch on Taronga Zoo. Still, it's worth considering as part of a combo with Sea Life, or if you're short on time. Tickets are cheaper online.

MADAME TUSSAUDS   MUSEUM
Map p250 (www.madametussauds.com/sydney; Aquarium Pier; adult/child $40/28; 9.30am-8pm; Town Hall) In this celebrity-obsessed age, it's hardly surprising that Madame Tussauds' hyperrealistic waxwork dummies are just as popular now as when the eponymous madame lugged her macabre haul of French revolution death masks to London in 1803. Where else do mere mortals get to strike a pose with Hugh Jackman and cosy up to Kylie?

SYDNEY SEA LIFE AQUARIUM   AQUARIUM
Map p250 (02-8251 7800; www.sydneyaquar ium.com.au; Aquarium Pier; adult/child $40/28; 9.30am-8pm; Town Hall) As well as regular wall-mounted tanks and ground-level enclosures, this impressive complex has two large pools that you can walk through, safely enclosed in Perspex tunnels, as an intimidating array of sharks and rays pass overhead. Other highlights include clownfish (howdy, Nemo), platypuses, moon jellyfish (in a disco-lit tube), sea dragons and the swoon-worthy finale: the two-million-litre Great Barrier Reef tank.

★CHINESE GARDEN OF FRIENDSHIP   GARDENS
Map p250 (02-9240 8888; www.chinesegarden. com.au; Harbour St; adult/child $6/3; 9.30am-5pm; Town Hall) Built according to Taoist principles, the Chinese Garden of Friendship is usually an oasis of tranquillity – although construction noise from Darling Harbour's redevelopment can intrude from time to time. Designed by architects from Guangzhou (Sydney's sister city) for Australia's bicentenary in 1988, the garden interweaves pavilions, waterfalls, lakes, paths and lush plant life.

TUMBALONG PARK   PARK
Map p250 (Town Hall) Flanked by the new Darling Walk development, this grassy circle on Darling Harbour's southern rump is set up for family fun. Sunbakers and frisbee-throwers occupy the lawns; tourists dunk their feet in fountains on hot summer afternoons; and there's an excellent children's playground with a 21m flying fox.

AUSTRALIAN NATIONAL MARITIME MUSEUM   MUSEUM
Map p250 (02-9298 3777; www.anmm.gov.au; 2 Murray St; adult/child $7/3.50; 9.30am-5pm; Pyrmont Bay) Beneath an Utzon-like roof

---

CHINESE SYDNEY

Chinese immigrants started to come to Australia around 1840, when convict transportation ceased and labouring jobs became freely available. Initially they were considered a solution to labour shortages, but as gold-rush fever took hold, racial intolerance grew. The tireless Chinese were seen as threats, and state entry restrictions were enforced from the early 19th century into much of the 20th century.

In 1861 the New South Wales Government enacted the 'White Australia Policy', aimed at reducing the influx of Chinese. This included a ban on naturalisation, work-permit restrictions and acts such as the 1861 *Chinese Immigration Regulation & Restriction Act* (an immigrant tax). As a result of this policy (and the fact that many Chinese returned to China after the gold rush), the Chinese population remained low. The White Australia Policy wasn't completely dismantled until 1973.

Sydney's Chinese community eventually gravitated to Dixon St near Darling Harbour, an area once known for opium and gambling but now better known for tasty and great-value food. Today people of Chinese extraction make up 6.5% of Sydney's population, with well over half of these born in Australia.

(a low-rent Opera House?), the Maritime Museum sails through Australia's inextricable relationship with the sea. Exhibitions range from Indigenous canoes to surf culture, to the navy. Entry includes free tours and there are kids' activities on Sundays. The 'big ticket' (adult/child $27/16) includes entry to the vessels moored outside, including the submarine HMAS *Onslow,* the destroyer HMAS *Vampire* and an 1874 square rigger, the *James Craig,* which periodically offers sailing trips (p83).

☉ Pyrmont

THE STAR   CASINO
Map p250 (☎02-9777 9000; www.star.com. au; 80 Pyrmont St; ☉24hr; ☒The Star) After a name change and a $961-million renovation, the Star reopened in late 2011 amid much hype and hoopla. The complex includes high-profile restaurants, bars, a nightclub, an excellent food court, a light rail station and high-end shops.

SYDNEY FISH MARKET   MARKET
Map p250 (☎02-9004 1108; www.sydneyfishmar ket.com.au; Bank St; ☉7am-4pm; ☒Fish Market) This piscatorial precinct on Blackwattle Bay shifts over 15 million kilograms of seafood annually, and has retail outlets, restaurants, a sushi bar, an oyster bar and a highly regarded cooking school. Chefs, locals and overfed seagulls haggle over mud crabs, Balmain bugs, lobsters and slabs of salmon at the daily fish auction, which kicks off at 5.30am weekdays. Check it out on a behind-the-scenes tour (adult/child $30/10).

ANZAC BRIDGE   BRIDGE
Map p250 (Western Distributor) Completed in 1996, Sydney's other eye-catching bridge spans Johnstons Bay, connecting Pyrmont and Rozelle. It's the longest cable bridge in Australia (345m), and affords some magic views as you truck into the city from the west. The two main towers are shaped like needle eyes, with the road as the thread.

For a sea-level perspective, take the pathway between Blackwattle Bay and Bicentennial Park (p110).

EATING

Rows of restaurants line Darling Harbour, many of them pairing their sea views with seafood. Most are pricey tourist-driven
affairs that are good but not outstanding. Since reopening, The Star has sought to assert itself as Sydney's fine-dining mecca. There are some truly excellent restaurants here, but we're not sure the atmosphere justifies the prices.

✗ Darling Harbour

KAZBAH   NORTH AFRICAN $$
Map p250 (☎02-9555 7067; www.kazbah.com. au; The Promenade, Harbourside; lunch $10-29, dinner $28-35; ☉11.30am-3pm & 5.30-9.30pm; ☒Convention) Rock the Kazbah for beautifully presented, tasty dishes from the Maghreb and Middle East, including exceptional tagines. There's a good value 'express lunch' menu for those short on time or cash. The original restaurant in Balmain (p82) is that suburb's best eatery.

ZAAFFRAN   INDIAN $$
Map p250 (☎02-9211 8900; www.zaaffran.com. au; L2, Harbourside; mains $20-35; ☉noon-2.30pm & 6-10.15pm; ☒; ☒Convention) In a city with a gazillion cheap Indian joints, Zaaffran is a stand-out. Authentic and innovative curries by chef Vikrant Kapoor are served up with awesome views across Darling Harbour's sparkle and sheen. Book a terrace seat and launch yourself into the tiger prawn coconut curry. There's a good vegetarian selection, too.

✗ Pyrmont

ADRIANO ZUMBO   BAKERY $
Map p250 (www.adrianozumbo.com; Café Court, The Star, 80 Pyrmont St; sweets $2.50-10; ☉11am-9pm Sun, to 11pm Mon-Sat; ☒The Star) The man who introduced Sydney to the macaron has indulged his Willy Wonka fantasies in this concept shop, where baked treats are artfully displayed amid pink neon. The macarons (or zumbarons, as they're known here), tarts, pastries and cakes are as astonishing to look at as they are to eat.

CAFÉ COURT   FOOD COURT $
Map p250 (www.star.com.au; ground fl, The Star; mains $10-18; ☉11am-9pm Sun & Mon, to 11pm Tue-Sat; ☒The Star) The Star has done a great job of filling its ground-floor food court with some of the best operators of their kind, such as Din Tai Fung (p96) for dumplings, Messina (p130) for gelato and Adriano Zumbo for sweet delights.

DARLING HARBOUR & PYRMONT EATING

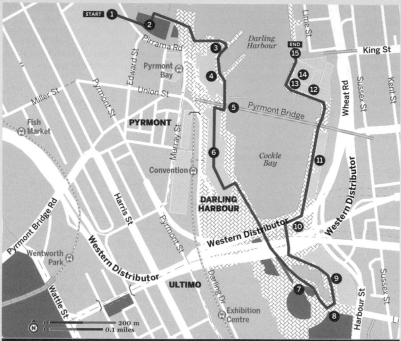

🏃 Neighbourhood Walk
A Darling Harbour Dawdle

START THE STAR
END KING STREET WHARF
LENGTH 3KM; 1½ HOURS

Catch the light rail to **❶ The Star** and try to negotiate your way out of the casino complex without haemorrhaging money or piling on pounds at Adriano Zumbo's luscious patisserie. Cross over and stroll through **❷ Pyrmont Bay Park** and then turn right. As you enter Darling Harbour you'll pass the **❸ Welcome Wall**, celebrating immigration to Australia, and the little lighthouse, moored ships and submarine that form part of the **❹ Australian National Maritime Museum** (p104). Cross under the 1902 **❺ Pyrmont Bridge** (the world's first electric swing bridge, doncha know) and zoom through the **❻ Harbourside** shopping centre.

Depending on when you visit, the next part of Darling Harbour is likely to be in the throes of a major redevelopment, replacing the giant convention centre which once stood here with an even more colossal one.

Duck under the freeway and continue strolling through **❼ Tumbalong Park**

(p104) to the **❽ Chinese Garden of Friendship** (p104), arguably the most tranquil spot in the city. Soak up the Zen over tea and cake in the teahouse.

Boomerang back past glassy **❾ Darling Walk** and the giant **❿ IMAX cinema** and trace the waterline past the restaurants and bars of **⓫ Cockle Bay Wharf**; keep an eye out for the frolicking storks. After scooting under Pyrmont Bridge again you'll pass Darling Harbour's big attractions in quick succession: **⓬ Sydney Sea Life Aquarium** (p104), **⓭ Madame Tussauds** (p104) and **⓮ Wild Life Sydney Zoo** (p104). Listen out for the squawks of the native birds in the giant netted aviary.

Continuing along the waterline, **⓯ King Street Wharf** is lined with still more restaurants and bars. North of here the Barangaroo entertainment, casino and residential complex is being built in earnest. Depending on it's progress you may be able to continue your waterfront stroll. Otherwise, reward your walking efforts with a beer and a bite at any of the establishments that took your fancy along the way.

CAFE MORSO
CAFE **$$**
Map p250 ([☎]02-9692 0111; www.cafemorso.com.au; Jones Bay Wharf; breakfast $16-19, lunch $17-27; [☉]7am-4pm; [🚋]The Star) The most popular eatery along Jones Bay Wharf, Morso lures black-clad, laptop-focused business bods and yacht skippers. Sassy breakfasts morph into proper cooked lunches, or you can just grab a sandwich (around $8).

SOKYO
JAPANESE **$$$**
Map p250 ([☎]02-9657 9161; www.star.com.au/sokyo; The Star, 80 Pyrmont St; breakfast $23-38, set lunch $45, mains $30-58; [☉]7-10.30am & 5.30-11pm daily, noon-3pm Thu-Sat; [🚋]The Star) Bringing an injection of Toyko glam to the edge of the casino complex, Sokyo serves well-crafted sushi and sashimi, delicate tempura and sophisticated mains. It also dishes up Sydney's best Japanese-style breakfast.

FLYING FISH
SEAFOOD **$$$**
Map p250 ([☎]02-9518 6677; www.flyingfish.com.au; Jones Bay Wharf; mains $47-49; [☉]noon-2.30pm daily, 6-10.30pm Mon-Sat; [🚋]The Star) Beyond the architects and investment groups along Jones Bay Wharf is this romantic seafood restaurant. The city lights work their magic all too easily here, aided by excellent food and an indulgent cocktail list.

🍷 DRINKING & NIGHTLIFE

Darling Harbour's bright lights herald a slew of glitzy bars that get more clublike as the night progresses. More brash than classy, they attract a buttoned-up, high-heeled, boozy crowd.

LOFT
BAR
Map p250 ([☎]02-9299 4770; www.theloftsydney.com; 3 Lime St, King St Wharf; [☉]4pm-1am Mon-Thu, noon-3am Fri & Sat, noon-1am Sun; [🚋]Wynyard) The Loft is far from lofty – it's more like an open-plan office space – but the walls fold back and disappear, sweeping your eye out across Darling Harbour and beyond. Interior design is Moroccan chic and service is snappy. Book for high tea at high noon on Saturday and Sunday. Live music on Fridays.

CARGO BAR
BAR
Map p250 ([☎]02-9262 1777; www.cargobar.com.au; 52 The Promenade, King St Wharf; [☉]11am-midnight Sun-Thu, to 3am Fri & Sat; [🚋]Wynyard) This pioneering King Street Wharf bar still lures beautiful boys, babes and backpackers. Before the drinkers descend, savour

the harbour views, tasty pizzas and salads. DJs fire things up on the weekend.

HOME
CLUB, BAR
Map p250 (www.homesydney.com; 1 Wheat Rd, Cockle Bay Wharf; [🚋]Town Hall) Welcome to the pleasuredome: a three-level, 2100-capacity timber and glass 'prow' that's home to a dance floor, countless bars, outdoor balconies, and sonics that make other clubs sound like transistor radios. You can catch live music most nights at the attached Tokio Hotel bar downstairs (tokiohotellive.com.au).

☆ ENTERTAINMENT

MONKEY BAA THEATRE COMPANY
THEATRE
Map p250 ([☎]02-8624 9340; www.monkeybaa.com.au; 1 Harbour St; tickets $25; [🚋]Town Hall) If you can drag them away from the neighbouring playground, bring your budding culture vultures here to watch Australian children's books come to life. This company devises and stages their own adaptations.

SYDNEY LYRIC
THEATRE
Map p250 ([☎]02-9509 3600; www.sydneylyric.com.au; The Star, Pirrama Rd; [🚋]The Star) This 2000-seat theatre within the casino stages big-name musicals and occasional concerts.

IMAX
CINEMA
Map p250 ([☎]02-9281 3300; www.imax.com.au; 31 Wheat Rd; adult/child short $23/17, feature $34/24; [☉]sessions 10am-10pm; [🚋]Town Hall) It's big bucks for a 45-minute movie, but everything about IMAX is big, and this is reputedly the biggest IMAX in the world. The eight-storey screen shimmers with kid-friendly documentaries and blockbuster features.

🏃 SPORTS & ACTIVITIES

Darling Harbour and Pyrmont are departure points for many harbour-based activities. James Craig (p83), Sailing Sydney (p83), Magistic Cruises (p84), Sydney Showboats (p84) and Harbour Jet (p83) are based here.

DARLING HARBOUR MINI TRAIN
TOUR
([☎]0408 290 515; adult/child $5/4; [☉]10am-5pm) This people mover 'train' tootles around Darling Harbour (signal the driver to jump on board). It's good for the kids and for resting your legs.

DARLING HARBOUR & PYRMONT DRINKING & NIGHTLIFE

Inner West

ULTIMO | CHIPPENDALE | GLEBE | CAMPERDOWN | DARLINGTON | NEWTOWN | ENMORE | ERSKINEVILLE

Neighbourhood Top Five

1 Grazing your way around the farmers market, scoffing at conceptual art or being mystified by an avant-garde performance within the capacious **Carriageworks** (p114) complex.

2 Gawking at ancient booty in Sydney University's fascinating **Nicholson Museum** (p110).

3 Challenging your cultural stereotypes and expanding your mind at **White Rabbit** (p110).

4 Catching a gig at the **Vanguard** (p119) or any of the Inner West's other live-music hot-spots.

5 Getting down with the brown at **Campos** (p117), king of the coffee-bean scene.

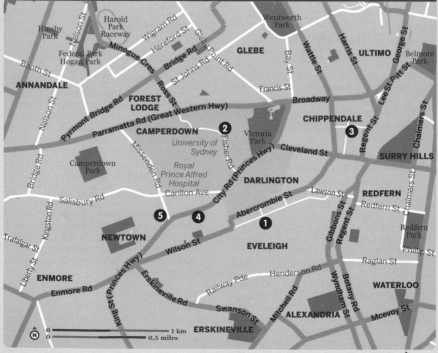

For more detail of this area, see Map p252

Explore: Inner West

The Inner West is a sociological stew of students, goths, urban hippies, artists, Mediterranean immigrants and sexual subculturists. At its heart is Sydney University, a bastion of old-world architecture that dominates the tiny suburbs of Camperdown, Darlington and Chippendale.

Between the university and Rozelle Bay, Glebe is home to a long-established Aboriginal community, students, lesbians, New Agers and cool bookstores. The First Fleet's chaplain was granted 160 hectares of church land here (technically a 'glebe'). Mansions began to sprout in 1826, but after 1855 the church leased its remaining land for downmarket housing, which degenerated into slums. In the mid-1970s Gough Whitlam's federal government bought the whole estate and rejuvenated the area for low-income families, many of whom have lived here for generations.

Where stoners and home renovators collide, Newtown shadows sinuous King St, lined with quirky boutiques, bookshops, yoga studios, cafes and Thai restaurants. It's definitely climbing the social rungs, but Newtown is still free-thinking and bolshy. Erskineville is similar but more upmarket, with an endearing village vibe and an outcrop of pubs and cafes.

Local Life

➡ **Camperdown Park** When the sun shines, the Newtown tribes descend with their picnic rugs. Even the goths brave the risk of absorbing vitamin D, unpacking their baskets in the adjacent cemetery.

➡ **Pubs** The centre of Inner Western social life, whether for watching the footy, grabbing a cheap meal, checking out a band, catching up with mates or hooking up.

➡ **Markets** Yummy mummies stock up on organic whatnots at Eveleigh (p116), while hippy chicks peruse preloved frocks at Glebe (p120).

Getting There & Away

➡ **Train** Newtown is well served by trains, with four stations (Macdonaldtown, Newtown, Erskineville and St Peters) on three train lines (Inner West, South and Bankstown). Redfern station is handy for Darlington, Chippendale and parts of Camperdown.

➡ **Light Rail** Glebe has two light rail stops (Glebe and Jubilee Park); walk uphill and you'll reach Glebe Point Rd. The best stop for Ultimo is Paddy's Market.

➡ **Bus** Dozens of buses from the city ply Glebe Point Rd (370, 431–433), Parramatta Rd (413, 436–440, 461, 480–483, M10) and City Rd/King St (352, 370, 422–428, M30).

➡ **Parking** Street parking is generally available. Watch out for the maze of one-way streets around Newtown.

Lonely Planet's Top Tip

Tucked between Central station, Surry Hills and Sydney University, the tiny suburb of Chippendale is one to watch. The 2009 opening of the White Rabbit gallery (p110) was an early herald of what is steadily turning into one of Sydney's coolest neighbourhoods. Now, as the Jean Nouvel/Sir Norman Foster–driven Central Park complex of sustainable plant-covered towers and terraces is taking shape, fantastic new eateries and bars are already springing up.

✖ Best Places to Eat

➡ Ester (p114)
➡ Eveleigh Farmers' Market (p116)
➡ Black Star Pastry (p116)
➡ Glebe Point Diner (p116)
➡ Boathouse on Blackwattle Bay (p116)

For reviews, see p114 ➡

🍷 Best Places to Drink

➡ Earl's Juke Joint (p118)
➡ Midnight Special (p118)
➡ Friend in Hand Hotel (p118)
➡ Corridor (p118)
➡ Zanzibar (p118)

For reviews, see p118 ➡

✖ Best for Coffee

➡ Campos (p117)
➡ Fleetwood Macchiato (p117)
➡ Mecca Espresso (p114)
➡ Black Star Pastry (p116)
➡ Luxe (p117)

For reviews, see p114 ➡

INNER WEST

◉ SIGHTS

◉ Ultimo

POWERHOUSE MUSEUM
MUSEUM

Map p252 (☎02-9217 0111; www.powerhouse museum.com; 500 Harris St; adult/child $15/8; ☺9.30am-5pm; 🚇Paddy's Markets) A short walk from Darling Harbour, this science and design museum whirs away inside the former power station for Sydney's defunct, original tram network. High-voltage interactive demonstrations wow school groups with the low-down on how lightning strikes, magnets grab and engines growl. It's a huge hit with kids but equally popular with adults, touching on subjects such as fashion and furniture design. Disabled access is good.

◉ Chippendale

CENTRAL PARK
AREA

Map p252 (www.centralparksydney.com; Broadway; 🚇Central Station) Occupying the site of an old brewery, this work-in-progress residential and shopping development will eventually cover 6,500 sq metres, and is already revitalising the central fringe suburb of Chippendale. Most impressive is Jean Nouvel's award-winning, vertical garden-covered tower, **One Central Park** (2013, 117m). The cantilevered roof has been designed to reflect sunlight onto the greenery below. A striking new Frank Gehry building is being built on the University of Technology campus across Broadway.

WHITE RABBIT
GALLERY

Map p252 (www.whiterabbitcollection.org; 30 Balfour St; ☺10am-5pm Wed-Sun, closed Feb & Aug; 🚇Redfern) **FREE** If you're an art lover or a bit of a Mad Hatter, this particular rabbit hole will leave you grinning like a Cheshire Cat. There are so many works in this private collection of cutting-edge, contemporary Chinese art, that only a fraction can be displayed at one time. Who knew that the People's Republic was turning out work that was so edgy, funny, sexy and idiosyncratic?

◉ Glebe

SZE YUP TEMPLE
TEMPLE

Map p252 (☎02-9660 6465; 2 Edward St; ☺10am-5pm; 🚇Jubilee Park) This humble backstreet temple was opened in 1898 by immigrants from the Sze Yup area of China. It's dedicated to 3rd-century folk hero Kwan Ti, whose embroidered, green-robed image, flanked by two guards, takes centre stage on the altar. Known for his loyalty, physical prowess and masculinity, he is looked to by supplicants as a wise judge, guide and protector.

At Chinese New Year it's a hectic place: kids' laughter in the forecourt is offset by solemn offerings of incense and fruit at the altar. Respectful visitors are welcome (take your shoes off before entering).

JUBILEE & BICENTENNIAL PARKS
PARK

Map p252 (Glebe Point Rd; 🚇Jubilee Park) These two rolling, grassy parks merge together to offer some tasty views across Rozelle Bay, and of both the Anzac and Harbour Bridges. Massive fig and palm trees dot the lawns. A path leads from here along the shoreline to Blackwattle Bay, passing the Victorian Italianate **Bellevue Cottage** (1896) and a park built around the templelike ruins of an industrial incinerator.

◉ Camperdown

UNIVERSITY OF SYDNEY
UNIVERSITY

Map p252 (☎02-9351 2222; www.sydney.edu.au; Parramatta Rd; 🚌422-440) Australia's oldest tertiary institution (1850) has over 49,000 students and even boasts its own postcode. You don't need to have a PhD to grab a free campus map and wander around. Flanked by two grand halls that wouldn't be out of place in Harry Potter's beloved Hogwarts, the **Quadrangle** has a Gothic Revival design that tips its mortarboard towards the stately colleges of Oxford. It's well worth seeking out the august collections of the Nicholson Museum, University Art Gallery and Macleay Museum.

NICHOLSON MUSEUM
MUSEUM

Map p252 (www.sydney.edu.au/museums; University Pl; ☺10am-4.30pm Mon-Fri, noon-4pm 1st Sat of month; 🚌422-440) **FREE** Within the University of Sydney's quadrangle, this museum is a must-see for ancient-history geeks. Inside is an amazing accumulation of Greek, Roman, Cypriot, Egyptian and Near Eastern antiquities, including Padiashaikhet the mummy. It was founded in 1860 by orphan-made-good Sir Charles Nicholson, a key figure in the establishment of both the university and the Australian Museum (p125).

MACLEAY MUSEUM
MUSEUM

Map p252 (www.sydney.edu.au/museums; Science Rd; ⏱10am-4.30pm Mon-Fri, noon-4pm 1st Sat of month; 📷422-440) FREE The University of Sydney's natural history museum is the oldest of its kind in Australia, having its roots in the collection of the Macleay family (of Elizabeth Bay House (p138) fame). There's also a historic photographic collection and an early assemblage of Aboriginal, Torres Strait and Pacific Island cultural material.

UNIVERSITY ART GALLERY
GALLERY

Map p252 (www.sydney.edu.au/museums; Science Rd; ⏱10am-4.30pm Mon-Fri, noon-4pm 1st Sat of month; 📷422-440) FREE Founded at the same time as the university, this gallery has accumulated over 7000 works of Australian, Asian and European art. Alongside the likes of Goya and Chagall are a swag of important Australian artists: Sidney Nolan, Arthur Boyd, Grace Cossington Smith, Arthur Streeton, James Gleeson, Margaret Preston, Russell Drysdale and Jeffrey Smart.

WORTH A DETOUR

SYDNEY OLYMPIC PARK

More than just Olympic nostalgia, the 640-hectare Sydney Olympic Park, 14km west of the city centre, is a sprawling sustainable world unto itself. Each year 850 million litres of water are captured in the park's water features, reducing its demand on city water by half, and banks of solar panels generate much of the site's electricity. In the post-Olympic years the surrounding land has been transformed into nature reserves, 35km of cycleways and residential enclaves.

In the shadow of the main Olympic stadium is **Games Memories**, an outdoor multimedia installation consisting of 480 decorated poles. Nearby, the silver flying saucer which burst into Olympic flame has been converted into a **fountain**.

The train deposits you at the heart of the complex, near the main venues. It's also possible to arrive by ferry, though the wharf is at the far northern tip of the complex, next to the **Newington Nature Reserve**. From here it's a 3.5km walk (about 45 minutes) to ANZ Stadium, or you can catch bus 526 (16 minutes, departs hourly). The best way to explore the entire complex is by bike.

ANZ Stadium (📞02-8765 2300; www.anzstadium.com.au; Olympic Blvd; tours adult/child $29/19; ⏱tours 11am, 1pm & 3pm daily, gantry 9am Fri-Wed; 🚆Olympic Park) The former Stadium Australia was custom-built for the 2000 Olympics at a cost of $690 million. It could originally accommodate 110,000 people, but following the games its capacity was reduced to a more manageable 83,500. A colourful sculpture of native feathers spirals over its main entrance and on big match days (such as the NRL Grand Final), the atmosphere is electric. Apart from the regular venue tours, daredevils can walk along the gantry, 45m above the pitch (adult/child $49/19).

Brickpit Ring Walk (Australia Ave; ⏱sunrise-sunset; 🚆Olympic Park) This brightly coloured circular walkway is supported by what look like metal chopsticks, lifting it 18m above the water filling an abandoned brickworks. Three billion bricks were made here between 1911 and 1988. Built into the loop are multimedia exhibits about the brick workers and their amphibious replacements, including the endangered green and golden bell frog.

Bike Hire @ Sydney Olympic Park (📞02-9746 1572; www.bikehiresydneyolympicpark. com.au; Bicentennial Park; mountain bike per 1/2/4/8/24hr $15/20/30/40/50; ⏱8.30am-5.30pm; 🚆Olympic Park) Rents bikes and tandems every day from Bicentennial Park (1.4km from Olympic Park train station). Also rents bikes from Blaxland Riverside Park (1.5km west along the river from the ferry wharf) on weekends and school holidays.

Aquatic Centre (📞02-9752 3666; www.aquaticcentre.com.au; Olympic Blvd; adult/child $7/6; ⏱5am-9pm Mon-Fri, 6am-7pm Sat & Sun; 🚆Olympic Park) Indulge your Ian Thorpe or Misty Hyman fantasies in the actual record-shattering pool which was used in the 2000 Olympics. There's also a leisure pool with a whirlpool in one corner, a state-of-the-art gym, a cafe and a swim shop. Wheelchair accessible.

INNER WEST SIGHTS

BJANKA KADIC / ALAMY ®

OLIVER STREWE / GETTY IMAGES ©

1. Carriageworks (p114)
Cavernous, Victorian-era train sheds have been transformed into an edgy arts precinct.

2. Nicholson Museum (p110)
Ancient history is the speciality of this museum, located in the University of Sydney's quadrangle.

3. King St (p120)
Shop this Newtown street for interesting boutiques and retro stores, including Faster Pussycat (p121).

4. Better Read Than Dead (p120)
Pick up some new reads at this electic Newtown bookshop.

LONELY PLANET ®

VICTORIA PARK   PARK

Map p252 (cnr Parramatta & City Rds; ℝRedfern) The green gateway to the Inner West and the University of Sydney, Victoria Park is a 9-hectare grassy wedge revolving around pondlike **Lake Northam** and Victoria Park Pool (p121). Each February, 75,000 people descend on the park for the Mardi Gras Fair Day: dog shows, live performances and the 'Miss Fair Day' drag competition.

⊙ Darlington

CARRIAGEWORKS   ARTS CENTRE

Map p252 (www.carriageworks.com.au; 245 Wilson St; ⊙10am-6pm; ℝRedfern) FREE Built between 1880 and 1889, this intriguing group of huge Victorian-era workshops was part of the Eveleigh Railyards. The rail workers chugged out in 1988 and in 2007 the artists pranced in. It's now home to various avant-garde arts and performance projects. Anna Schwartz Gallery (p121) is here, alongside Performance Space (p120) and the Eveleigh Farmers' Market (p116).

⊙ Newtown

CAMPERDOWN CEMETERY   CEMETERY

Map p252 (☑02-9557 2043; www.neac.com. au; 189 Church St; tours $10; ⊙sunrise-sunset, tours 11.30am 1st Sun of the month Feb-Dec; ℝNewtown) Take a self-guided tour beyond the monstrous 1848 fig tree into this dark, eerily unkempt cemetery next to St Stephens Church. Famous Australians buried here between 1849 and 1942 include Eliza Donnithorne, the inspiration for Miss Havisham in Dickens' *Great Expectations*.

✗ EATING

Newtown's King St is among the city's most diverse eat streets, with Thai restaurants sitting alongside Vietnamese, Macedonian, Lebanese and Mexican. And when it comes to coffee culture, all roads point to the Inner West.

✗ Ultimo

MECCA ESPRESSO   CAFE $

Map p252 (www.meccaultimo.com; 646 Harris St; mains $10-14; ⊙7am-4pm Mon-Sat; ℝCentral) ◤ Mecca has devotees cramming its indus-

trial interior – more for the transcendent coffee than the food, it's fair to say – but there are tasty cooked breakfasts, salads and some Middle Eastern–flavoured mains.

SYDNEY KOPITIAM   MALAYSIAN $

Map p252 (☑02-9282 9883; 594 Harris St; mains $10-15; ⊙noon-3pm daily, 6-9.30pm Tue-Sun; ℝPaddy's Market) Kopitiam (meaning 'coffee shop') isn't going to win design awards (low ceiling, daggy tiled floor, plastic furniture and Malaysian Airlines tourism posters), but the great-value, authentic Malaysian soups, stir-fries and curries are spectacular.

✗ Chippendale

★ESTER   MODERN AUSTRALIAN $$

Map p252 (☑02-8068 8279; www.ester-restaurant.com.au; 46 Meagher St; mains $26-36; ⊙noon-5pm Sun, noon-3pm Fri, 6pm-late Tue-Sat; ℝRedfern) Ester breaks the trend for hip new eateries by accepting bookings, but in other respects it exemplifies Sydney's contemporary dining scene: informal but not sloppy; innovative without being overly gimmicky; hip, but never try-hard. Influences straddle continents and dishes are made to be shared. If humanly possible, make room for dessert.

✗ Glebe

SAPPHO BOOKS, CAFE & WINE BAR   CAFE $

Map p252 (☑02-9552 4498; www.sapphobooks. com.au; 51 Glebe Point Rd; tapas $5-12, mains $8-19; ⊙9am-7pm Sun, 7.30am-7pm Mon & Tue, to 10pm Wed-Sat; ◤; ℝGlebe) Sequestered in the back of a raggedy bookshop, Sappho is a beaut bohemian garden cafe-bar, its walls scrawled with generations of graffiti. The coffee's excellent and there's a tasty array of cooked breakfasts, salads, and toasted ciabatta and wraps to choose between. Wine and tapas kick in after 6pm, often accompanied by live music. There's a full vegan menu, too.

SONOMA   BAKERY, CAFE $

Map p252 (www.sonoma.com.au; 215a Glebe Point Rd; mains $9-15; ⊙7am-4pm Mon-Sat, 7.30am-2pm Sun; ℝGlebe) Glebe branch of a popular chain of sourdough bakery cafes (p150).

YUGA   CAFE $$

Map p252 (☑02-9692 8604; www.yugaflora. com.au; 172 St Johns Rd; breakfast $12-16, lunch $12-20; ⊙7am-4pm; ℝGlebe) What a sweet-smelling combo: a florist *and* a cafe that's

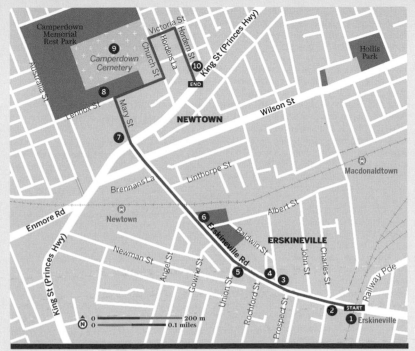

Neighbourhood Walk
Social-History Stroll

START ERSKINEVILLE STATION
END KING ST
LENGTH 1.5KM; ONE HOUR

Exiting **1 Erskineville train station**, turn left and cruise through Erskineville Village. On your left you'll pass the lavishly tiled **2 Rose of Australia** (p119) pub, and on your right the defunct **3 Erskineville Town Hall** and the art-deco **4 Erskineville Hotel**. Cinematic déjà vu? You may recognise the **5 Imperial Hotel** (p119) on the Union St corner as the spot from which the bus departed in *The Adventures of Priscilla, Queen of the Desert*. In June 1931 this unassuming side street was the setting for the 'Battle of Union St', one of several Great Depression eviction clashes. Hundreds of people gathered and jeered as police brutally evicted residents who had barricaded themselves inside a house.

Another socialist landmark, **6 Green Bans Park**, just before the railway bridge on Erskineville Rd, owes its existence to the construction workers' green bans of the 1980s and '90s. Ceramic tiles tell the story

of the 1992 union ban that led to this land being retained as a community park. Similar green bans saved Woolloomooloo's Finger Wharf and parts of the Rocks.

Cross the bridge and truck up to King St, Newtown. Across the road is a **7 Martin Luther King mural**. Although it was painted without permission in 1991 by a group of artists calling themselves Unmitigated Audacity Productions, it's become a much-loved symbol of Newtown – so much so that the local council awarded it heritage protection in 2014.

Cut down Mary St to the narrowest slice of **8 Camperdown Memorial Rest Park**, Newtown's green meeting place. Turn right on Lennox St then left into Church St; the evocatively ramshackle **9 Camperdown Cemetery** is on your left. Grab a self-guided tour pamphlet from the box near the gate and go exploring.

Leaving the cemetery go straight ahead on Victoria St then turn right into Hordern St, before hanging left onto **10 King Street**, Newtown's pulsing thoroughfare. Above shop level the largely extant facades tie the streetscape to its past.

stylish, reasonably priced and friendly. The menu at sophisticated and serene Yuga starts with Aussie breakfasts and morphs into Italian lunches.

GLEBE POINT DINER   MODERN AUSTRALIAN **$$$**
Map p252 (☑02-9660 2646; www.glebepoint diner.com.au; 407 Glebe Point Rd; mains $29-39; ⊙12-3pm Thu-Sun, 6-11pm Mon-Sat; 🚌Jubilee Park) A sensational neighbourhood diner where only the best local produce is used and everything – from the home-baked bread and hand-churned butter to the nougat finale – is made from scratch. The food is creative and comforting at the same time; a rare combination.

BOATHOUSE ON BLACKWATTLE BAY   SEAFOOD **$$$**
Map p252 (☑02-9518 9011; www.boathouse.net. au; 123 Ferry Rd; ⊙noon-3pm Fri-Sun, 6-11pm Tue-Sun; 🚌Glebe) The best restaurant in Glebe, and one of the best seafood restaurants in Sydney. Offerings range from oysters so fresh you'd think you shucked them yourself, to a snapper pie that'll go straight to the top of your favourite-dish list. Amazing Anzac Bridge views; reservations essential.

✖ Camperdown

DEUS CAFE   CAFE **$$**
Map p252 (☑02-9519 3669; www.deuscustoms. com; 98-104 Parramatta Rd; breakfast & lunch $8-18, dinner $26-32; ⊙8.30am-9.30pm Sun & Mon, 7.30am-4pm Tue-Sat; 🚌436-440) Strewn with vintage motorcycles and kooky two-

wheelin' art, Deus Cafe is an extension of an eccentric motorbike shop on frenzied Parramatta Rd. Start the day with a classic: a Triumph Bonneville T100 or eggs Benedict with a high-revving coffee. Hearty mains (burgers, steak sandwiches, fish and chips) kick in as the day progresses.

✖ Darlington

EVELEIGH FARMERS' MARKET   MARKET **$**
Map p252 (www.eveleighmarket.com.au; Carriageworks, 245 Wilson St; ⊙8am-1pm Sat; 🚌Redfern) Over 70 regular stallholders sell their goodies at Sydney's best farmers' market, held in a heritage-listed railway workshop. Food and coffee stands do a brisk business; celebrity chef Kylie Kwong can often be spotted cooking up a storm.

✖ Newtown

BLACK STAR PASTRY   BAKERY **$**
Map p252 (www.blackstarpastry.com.au; 277 Australia St; mains $7-10; ⊙7am-5pm; 🚌Newtown) Wise folks follow the black star to pay homage to excellent coffee, a large selection of sweet things and a few very good savoury things (gourmet pies and the like). There are only a couple of tables; it's more a snack-and-run or picnic-in-the-park kind of place.

MARY'S   BURGERS **$**
Map p252 (6 Mary St; mains $14; ⊙4pm-midnight Mon-Sat, noon-10pm Sun; 🚌Newtown) Not put off by the grungy aesthetics, the ear-splitting heavy metal or the fact that the

---

WORTH A DETOUR

LEICHHARDT

The main drag of Leichhardt (affectionately referred to as Dykeheart by the local lesbians) is famous for its Italian restaurants and improbable piazza. Italians form a substantial and visible part of the suburb's population.

Italian Forum (www.theitalianforum.com.au; 23 Norton St; ⊙10am-10pm; 🚌Petersham) This re-created mustard and maroon Italian piazza has copped its fair share of criticism, and yes, it's totally Disney-goes-to-Rome, but the Italian Forum is a reliable place for a strong coffee, some pasta or a pair of expensive sunglasses. Immaculate waiters without a hair out of place deliver your gelato or macchiato as the kids play Caligula. Remember to say 'ciao' whenever possible.

Grappa (☑02-9560 6090; www.grappa.com.au; 267-277 Norton St; mains $25-40; ⊙noon-3pm Tue-Fri & Sun, 6-10pm Tue-Sun; 🚌Leichhardt North) Grappa – with its open kitchen, snazzy bar and cream leather seats – is the setting for rich, succulent dishes (such as baked snapper in a rock-salt crust) and bounteous wood-fired pizzas. If it's warm, sit outside on the terrace, sip chianti and think of Tuscany. Ahhh, Tuscany...

building was previously a sexual health clinic and a Masonic Temple? Then head up to the mezzanine of this dimly lit hipster bar for some of the best burgers and fried chicken in town.

CAMPOS
CAFE $

Map p252 (🖉02-9516 3361; www.camposcoffee. com; 193 Missenden Rd; pastries $4; ⊗7am-4pm; 🚇Macdonaldtown) Trying to squeeze into crowded Campos can be a challenge. Bean fiends come from miles around – hat-wearing students, window-seat daydreamers and doctors on a break from the hospital – all gagging for a shot of Campos Superior Blend. Food is limited to tasty pastries.

VARGABAR ESPRESSO
CAFE $

Map p252 (🖉02-9517 1932; www.vargabarnew town.com.au; 10 Wilson St; mains $10-16; ⊗7am-6pm; 🛜; 🚇Newtown) 🥖 A diminutive dark-pink cafe with an electric-blue coffee machine, Varga trades on big breakfasts and generates too many hard decisions for 7am. The pesto scrambled eggs or the polenta porridge? Both?

GUZMAN Y GOMEZ
MEXICAN $

Map p252 (🖉02-9517 1533; www.guzman ygomez.com; 175 King St; mains $8-15; ⊗11am-11pm; 🚇Macdonaldtown) A spicy alternative for fast-food aficionados, this zippy blue-and-yellow diner uses fresh local produce to whip up tacos, burritos and quesadillas. Everything's marinated and grilled daily. Look out for other branches around Sydney.

LUXE
CAFE $$

Map p252 (www.luxesydney.com.au; 191 Missenden Rd; breakfast $8-20, lunch $11-22; ⊗8am-4pm; 🚇Macdonaldtown) Campos, next door, might be the pinnacle of Sydney's caffeine culture, but if you want to sit down, read the paper and eat something more substantial, Luxe is the dux. The menu stretches to cooked brekkies, pasta and burgers, and the counter of this industrial-chic bakery-cafe is chocka with chunky sandwiches, moist cakes and delicate tarts.

BLOODWOOD
MODERN AUSTRALIAN $$

Map p252 (🖉02-9557 7699; www.bloodwood newtown.com; 416 King St; dishes $9-30; ⊗5-11pm Mon-Fri, noon-11pm Sat & Sun; 🚇Newtown) Relax over a few drinks and a progression of small plates (we love those polenta chips!) in the front bar, or make your way to the rear to enjoy soundly conceived and expertly cooked dishes from across the globe.

The decor is industrial-chic and the vibe is alternative – very Newtown.

THAI POTHONG
THAI $$

Map p252 (🖉02-9550 6277; www.thaipothong. com.au; 294 King St; mains $15-31; ⊗noon-3pm & 6-10.30pm; 🖉; 🚇Newtown) The menu at this crowd-pleasing restaurant is predictable and the usual crowd of golden Buddhas festoons the walls, but the mood is oddly romantic. Pull up a window seat and watch the Newtowners pass by.

GREEN GOURMET
VEGAN $$

Map p252 (🖉02-9519 5330; www.greengourmet. com.au; 115 King St; mains $13-25; ⊗noon-3pm & 6-10pm; 🖉; 🚇Macdonaldtown) Green Gourmet delivers buffet and à la carte vegan Chinese food, including yum cha, noodles, rice, salads and a whole virtual farmyard of mock-meat dishes. It's alcohol-free, too.

THANH BINH
VIETNAMESE $$

Map p252 (🖉02-9557 1175; www.thanhbinh.com. au; 111 King St; mains $15-28; ⊗5.30-11pm Mon-Fri, noon-11pm Sat & Sun; 🚇Macdonaldtown) If you're used to Vietnamese restaurants where everything is prerolled and ready to be shovelled into your mouth, you haven't really had Vietnamese food. Here, playing with your food is part of the fun. Load up your prawn cracker, soak your rice paper, pluck your herbs and launch into a wrapping, rolling, dipping and feasting frenzy.

🍴 Enmore

COW & THE MOON
ICE CREAM $

Map p252 (181 Enmore Rd; small gelati $5; ⊗9am-11pm; 🚇Newtown) Forget the diet and slink into this cool corner cafe, where an array of sinful truffles and tasty tarts beckons seductively. Ignore them and head straight for the world's best gelato – the title this humble little place won in 2014 at the Gelato World Tour title in Rimini, Italy.

🍴 Erskineville

FLEETWOOD MACCHIATO
CAFE $

Map p252 (43 Erskineville Rd; mains $9-18; ⊗7am-3pm; 🖉; 🚇Erskineville) The best name for a cafe ever? We think so. Luckily Fleetwood Macchiato backs it up with excellent coffee, delicious cooked breakfasts, tasty sandwiches and homemade cakes, preserves, pickles, yogurt and mayonnaise.

🍺 DRINKING & NIGHTLIFE

Devotees of the comfortable, atmospheric local pub rejoice! The Inner West has plenty of pubs in varying degrees of gentrification, ranging from 'not at all' to 'within an inch of its life'. A thirsty student population sustains a barrage of bars and live-music venues, while a sizeable lesbian and gay community also makes its presence felt. Night owls can take heart that the Inner West is outside the central city's restricted alcohol zone – meaning no lockouts.

🍷 Glebe

FRIEND IN HAND HOTEL   PUB
Map p252 (☑02-9660 2326; www.friendinhand.com.au; 58 Cowper St; ☺10am-10pm Sun, 8am-midnight Mon-Sat; 🐾; 🚍Glebe) At heart Friend in Hand is still a working-class pub with a resident loud-mouth cockatoo and a cast of grizzly old-timers and local larrikins propping up the bar. But then there's all the other stuff: live music, life drawing, poetry readings, crab racing, comedy nights. Strewth Beryl, bet you weren't expecting that.

AB HOTEL   PUB
Map p252 (☑02-9660 1417; www.abhotel.com.au; 225 Glebe Point Rd; ☺10am-midnight Mon-Sat, to 10pm Sun; 🐾; 🚍Glebe) An old fave with a $5-million facelift, the former Ancient Briton still screens the horses in the front bar, but now there's also a cute courtyard and live fish swimming around inside the upstairs bar.

🍷 Newtown

★EARL'S JUKE JOINT   BAR
Map p252 (407 King St; ☺4pm-midnight Mon-Sat, to 10pm Sun; 🚍Newtown) The current it-bar of the minute, swinging Earl's serves craft beers and killer cocktails to the Newtown hiperati.

MIDNIGHT SPECIAL   BAR
Map p252 (www.themidnightspecial.com.au; 44 Enmore Rd; ☺5pm-midnight Tue-Sat, to 10pm Sun; 🚍Newtown) Band posters and paper lanterns decorate the black walls of this groovy little bar. Musicians take to the tiny stage a couple of nights a week.

CORRIDOR   COCKTAIL BAR
Map p252 (www.corridorbar.com.au; 153a King St; ☺5pm-midnight Mon, 3pm-midnight Tue-Sun; 🚍Newtown) The name exaggerates this bar's skinniness, but not by much. Downstairs the bartenders serve old-fashioned cocktails and a good range of wine, while upstairs there's interesting art (for sale) and a tiny deck. There's live music most nights.

ZANZIBAR   BAR
Map p252 (☑02-9519 1511; www.zanzibarnewtown.com.au; 323 King St; ☺10am-4am Mon-Sat, 11am-midnight Sun; 🚍Newtown) Eastern opulence continues all the way to the roof at this late-night Newtown bar with a winged art deco facade. Catch the sunset from the rooftop, settle into a cushioned couch or shoot pool in the funky downstairs bar. On Wednesday nights the Birdcage lesbian night takes over the 2nd floor.

MARLBOROUGH HOTEL   PUB, CLUB
Map p252 (☑02-9519 1222; www.marlboroughhotel.com.au; 145 King St; ☺10am-4am Mon-Sat, noon-midnight Sun; 🚍Macdonaldtown) One of many great old art deco pubs in Newtown, the Marly has a front sports bar with live bands on weekends and a shady beer garden. Head upstairs for soul food and rockabilly bands at Miss Peaches, or downstairs for all sorts of kooky happenings at the Tokyo Sing Song nightclub.

COURTHOUSE HOTEL   PUB
Map p252 (202 Australia St; ☺10am-midnight Mon-Sat, to 10pm Sun; 🚍Newtown) What a brilliant pub! A block back from the King St fray, the 150-year-old Courthouse is the kind of place where everyone from pool-playing goth lesbians to magistrates can have a beer and feel right at home. How ironic – a complete absence of social judgement in a pub called the Courthouse. Good pub grub, too.

BANK HOTEL   PUB
Map p252 (www.bankhotel.com.au; 324 King St; ☺11am-1am Sun-Thu, to 4am Fri & Sat; 🚍Newtown) There's been bags of cash splashed about the Bank, but it still attracts a kooky crowd – they just don't wear their Ugg boots to the pub anymore. The portfolio includes a rooftop terrace and cocktail bar. DJs and live musicians entertain on the weekends.

MARRICKVILLE

Once the slightly frumpy western neighbour of Newtown and Enmore, the suburb of Marrickville has gradually attracted bohemians, artists, students and kooks forced out of Newtown by rising rents. Alongside a great set of pubs and bars (some of which host live music), cafes are Marrickville's new claim to fame. The latest *Sydney Morning Herald Good Cafe Guide* gave its highest possible rating to three Marrickville cafes and named **Cornersmith** (314 Illawarra St) as the best in Sydney.

We suggest you explore the neighbourhood under your own steam. Jump off the train at Marrickville station, turn right and head up Illawarra Rd.

The eclectic **Camelot Lounge** (www.camelotlounge.wordpress.com; 19 Marrickville Rd; ⓡSydenham) hosts jazz, world music, blues, folk, comedy, cabaret and all manner of other weird stuff.

🍸 Enmore

SLY FOX
PUB

Map p252 (www.theslyfoxhotel.com; 199 Enmore Rd; ⓢ10am-3am Mon-Thu, to 6am Fri & Sat; ⓡNewtown) By day this crafty canine is a typical blue-collar pub, but on Wednesday nights it transforms into Sydney's premier lesbian bar. As the week slides to an end it reinvents itself yet again, this time as a live-music venue. DJs take up the baton until everyone's booted out into the dawn.

🍸 Erskineville

IMPERIAL HOTEL
GAY, CLUB

Map p252 (www.theimperialhotel.com.au; 35 Erskineville Rd; admission free-$15; ⓢ3pm-midnight Sun-Thu, to 5am Fri & Sat; ⓡErskineville) The art deco Imperial is legendary as the setting for *The Adventures of Priscilla, Queen of the Desert*. The front bar is a lively place for pool-shooting and cruising, with the action shifting to the cellar club late on a Saturday night. But it's in the cabaret bar that the legacy of Priscilla is kept alive.

HIVE
BAR

Map p252 (②02-9519 9911; www.thehivebar.com.au; 93 Erskineville Rd; ⓢnoon-midnight Mon-Sat, 11am-10pm Sun; ⓡErskineville) 🌿 In increasingly groovy Erskineville village, this breezy little corner bar lures the neighbourhood's hipsters with food, cocktails, DJs spinning funk and soul, crazy murals and a quiet bolthole upstairs. Order a few plates to share over a glass of vino and pull up a footpath table.

ROSE OF AUSTRALIA
PUB

Map p252 (②02-9565 1441; www.roseofaustralia.com; 1 Swanson St; ⓢ10am-10pm Sun & Mon, to midnight Tue-Sat; ⓡErskineville) The extensive renovations to this old corner pub haven't dented the tiled front bar's charm. Locals of all persuasions hang out here, catching some afternoon rays at the street-side tables, a footy game on the big screens or a meal upstairs.

 ENTERTAINMENT

VANGUARD
LIVE MUSIC

Map p252 (②02-9557 7992; www.thevanguard.com.au; 42 King St; ⓡMacdonaldtown) Intimate 1920s-themed Vanguard stages live music most nights (including some well-known names), as well as burlesque, comedy and classic-movie screenings. Most seats are reserved for dinner-and-show diners.

NEWTOWN SOCIAL CLUB
LIVE MUSIC

Map p252 (②1300 724 867; www.newtownsocialclub.com; 387 King St; ⓢ7pm-midnight Tue-Thu, noon-2am Fri & Sat, noon-10pm Sun; ⓢ; ⓡNewtown) The legendary Sandringham Hotel (aka the 'Sando', where God used to drink, according to local band The Whitlams) may have changed names but if anything it has heightened its commitment to live music. Gigs range from local bands on the make to indie luminaries such as Gruff Rhys and Stephen Malkmus.

NEW THEATRE
THEATRE

Map p252 (②02-9519 3403; www.newtheatre.org.au; 542 King St; tickets $17-32; ⓡSt Peters) Australia's oldest continuously performing theatre (since 1932), Newtown's eclectic New Theatre produces new dramas as well as more established pieces.

SEYMOUR CENTRE
PERFORMING ARTS

Map p252 (⌂02-9351 7940; www.seymourcen
tre.com; cnr City Rd & Cleveland St; ⍰Redfern)
Behind a glass curtain wall on an insanely
busy intersection, this Sydney Uni–affiliated
theatre (actually, four theatres) shows an
eclectic selection of plays, cabaret, comedy
and musicals.

ENMORE THEATRE
LIVE MUSIC

Map p252 (⌂02-9550 3666; www.enmore
theatre.com.au; 130 Enmore Rd; ⊙box office
9am-6pm Mon-Fri, 10am-4pm Sat; ⍰Newtown)
Originally a vaudeville playhouse, the ele-
gantly wasted, 2500-capacity Enmore now
hosts such acts as Paolo Nutini, Wilco and
PJ Harvey, plus theatre, ballet and comedy.

PERFORMANCE SPACE
PERFORMING ARTS

Map p252 (⌂02-8571 9111; www.performance
space.com.au; Carriageworks, 245 Wilson St;
⍰Redfern) This edgy artists' hub stages
performances of new dance, acrobatic and
multimedia works – basically anything that
can be lumped under the broad umbrella of
'the Arts'.

DENDY NEWTOWN
CINEMA

Map p252 (⌂02-9550 5699; www.dendy.com.
au; 261 King St; adult/child $20/14; ⊙sessions
9.30am-9.30pm; ⍰Newtown) Follow the but-
tery scent of popcorn into the dark folds of
this plush cinema, screening first-run, independent world films.

🛍 SHOPPING

**Newtown and Glebe are hot spots for
anything punky, alternative, socialist,
greenie, intellectual or noir. King St,
Newtown, has interesting boutiques,
secondhand stores and (along with Glebe
Point Rd) the city's best bookstores.
New homewares stores strike the fear
of gentrification into the hearts of long-
term locals.**

GLEBE MARKETS
MARKET

Map p252 (www.glebemarkets.com.au; Glebe
Public School, cnr Glebe Point Rd & Derby Pl;
⊙10am-4pm Sat; ⍰Glebe) The best of the
west; Sydney's dreadlocked, shoeless,
inner-city contingent beats a course to this
crowded hippy-ish market.

GLEEBOOKS
BOOKS

Map p252 (⌂02-9660 2333; www.gleebooks.
com.au; 49 Glebe Point Rd; ⊙9am-7pm Sun-Wed,
to 9pm Thu-Sat; ⍰Glebe) Generally regarded
as Sydney's best bookshop, Gleebooks'
aisles are full of politics, arts and general
fiction, and staff really know their stuff.
Check their calendar for author talks and
book launches. There's a separate secondhand store at 191 Glebe Point Rd.

BETTER READ THAN DEAD
BOOKS

Map p252 (⌂02-9557 8700; www.betterread.
com.au; 265 King St; ⊙9.30am-9pm; ⍰Newtown)
This just might be our favourite Sydney
bookshop, and not just because of the pithy
name and the great selection of Lonely

LOCAL KNOWLEDGE

ALEXANDRIA OUTLETS

The semi-industrial area of Alexandria, east of Erskineville, is known for its factory-
outlet shops. Most are spread along the busy McEvoy St strip. You can easily walk there
from Erskineville station in about 15 minutes or from Green Square station in about 10.

Victoria's Basement (Map p252; ⌂02-9557 1954; www.victoriasbasement.com.au; cnr
Euston Rd & Harley St; ⊙9am-6pm Fri-Wed, to 8pm Thu; ⍰Erskineville) This huge warehouse (on the 1st floor, not in the basement) is packed to overflowing with high-quality
kitchen and tableware at bargain-basement prices (wedding and house-warming gifts
aplenty). Despite a ban on shopping-tour buses it's always frantic on weekends. The
full-price branch is in the QVB (p99).

Oxford (Map p252; ⌂02-9318 1718; www.oxfordshop.com.au; 111 McEvoy St; ⊙9am-5pm;
⍰Green Square) A bargain outlet for a big local brand, Oxford stocks reasonably priced
but stylish mens- and womenswear, including well-tailored shirts, suits and ties. For
its latest range head to the stores scattered all over Sydney.

Seafolly (Map p252; ⌂02-9690 1955; www.seafolly.com.au; 111-117 McEvoy St; ⊙9am-5pm;
⍰Green Square) Here's where the famous Aussie women's swimwear label sells its
sexy seconds, samples and discontinued lines. As well as bikinis to battle over, there
are bargain sarongs, board shorts and tracksuits to be had.

Planet titles. Nobody seems to mind if you waste hours perusing the beautifully presented aisles, stacked with high-, middle- and deliciously low-brow reading materials.

GOULD'S BOOK ARCADE
BOOKS

Map p252 (☑02-9519 8947; www.gouldsbooks. com; 32 King St; ☺10am-10.30pm; ☒Macdonaldtown) Possibly the world's scariest secondhand bookstore: the floor-to-ceiling racks and stacks threaten to bury you under a ton of Stalinist analysis. All manner of musty out-of-print books are stocked, along with cassettes, records and even video tapes (VHS and Beta!).

FASTER PUSSYCAT
CLOTHING, ACCESSORIES

Map p252 (☑02-9519 1744; www.fasterpussycat online.com; 431a King St; ☺11am-6pm; ☒Newtown) Inspired by 'trash pop culture, hot rods and rock and roll', this cool cat coughs up clothing and accessories for all genders and ages (including baby punkwear) in several shades of Newtown black.

QUICK BROWN FOX
CLOTHING, ACCESSORIES

Map p252 (☑02-9519 6622; www.quickbrown fox.com.au; 231 King St; ☺10.30am-6.30pm; ☒Newtown) No lazy dogs here – just plenty of fast-looking, tanned vixens snapping up funky vintage fashions that veer from 'hello, boys!' cuteness to indecent-exposure sexiness. Catchy patterns and fabrics, chic boots and bags.

DEUS EX MACHINA
CLOTHING, ACCESSORIES

Map p252 (☑02-8594 2800; www.deuscustoms. com; 102-104 Parramatta Rd; ☺9am-5pm; ☒436-440) With a name translating to 'God is in the machine', this kooky showroom is crammed with classic and custom-made motorcycles and surfboards. A hybrid workshop, cafe and offbeat boutique, it stocks men's and women's threads, including Deus-branded jeans, tees and shorts.

C'S FLASHBACK
CLOTHING

Map p252 (☑02-9565 4343; www.csflashback. com.au; 180 King St; ☺10am-6pm; ☒Macdonaldtown) Specialises in trippy secondhand clothes, just like it's Surry Hills (p135) sister.

RECLAIM
HOMEWARES, GIFTS

Map p252 (www.reclaim.net.au; 356 King St; ☺10am-6pm; ☒Newtown) Absolutely the place to shop for Iggy Pop throw cushions, antique tea sets, quirky homewares and funky gifts. It's all put together by local singer Monica Trapaga (of Monica and the Moochers).

BEEHIVE GALLERY
CRAFTS

Map p252 (☑02-9550 2515; www.beehivegallery. com.au; 441 King St; ☺11am-5pm Tue, Wed & Fri-Sun, to 7pm Thu; ☒Newtown) If it's handmade or Japanese, it has a home in this store.

EGG RECORDS
MUSIC

Map p252 (☑02-9550 6056; www.eggrecords online.com; 3 Wilson St; ☺10am-6pm; ☒Newtown) There's something a bit too cool about this secondhand and new music store, but it's the perfect place to, say, complete your collection of 1980s David Bowie 12-inch singles, or pick up a Cramps T-shirt or a Gene Simmons figurine.

HOLY KITSCH!
GIFTS

Map p252 (4 Enmore Rd; ☺noon-6pm; ☒Newtown) Colourful Mexican paraphernalia; there's another branch in Surry Hills (p134).

BROADWAY SHOPPING CENTRE
SHOPPING CENTRE

Map p252 (www.broadway.com.au; 1 Bay St; ☺10am-7pm Fri-Wed, to 9pm Thu; ☒; ☒Central) Inside the rejuvenated Grace Bros building (check out the cool old globes above the facade), this centre has dozens of shops, a food court, a cinema complex and two supermarkets.

ANNA SCHWARTZ GALLERY
ARTS

Map p252 (www.annaschwartzgallery.com; Carriageworks, 245 Wilson Street; ☺10am-6pm Wed-Fri, 1-5pm Sat) One of Sydney's leading commercial galleries, focused on contemporary works.

🏃 SPORTS & ACTIVITIES

VICTORIA PARK POOL
SWIMMING

Map p252 (☑02-9518 4800; www.vppool.com.au; cnr Parramatta & City Rds; adult/child $6/4.50; ☺6am-7pm; ☒431-440) This 50m heated outdoor pool in Victoria Park serves as Newtown and Glebe's beach. There's also a gym ($18 with pool access), crèche, cafe and swim shop.

INNER CITY CYCLES
CYCLING

Map p252 (☑02-9660 6605; www.innercity cycles.com.au; 151 Glebe Point Rd; hire per day/weekend/week $33/55/88; ☺9.30am-6pm Mon-Wed & Fri, 9.30am-8pm Thu, 9am-4pm Sat, 11am-3pm Sun; ☒Glebe) Hires bikes and performs repairs.

Surry Hills & Darlinghurst

Neighbourhood Top Five

1 Eating your way around Sydney's gastronomic heartland, starting with the slow-cooked meat at **Porteño** (p127) and then returning again and again to sample the variety of tastes the neighbourhood has to offer.

2 Grabbing a cocktail at **Pocket** (p132) and then exploring Darlinghurst's thriving small-bar scene.

3 Examining the sobering displays and video testimonies at the **Sydney Jewish Museum** (p124).

4 Soaking up the atmosphere of **Oxford Street**, Sydney's gay strip – at its best around Mardi Gras.

5 Perking up at **Sample Coffee** (p125) or any of Surry Hills' numerous temples to the coffee bean.

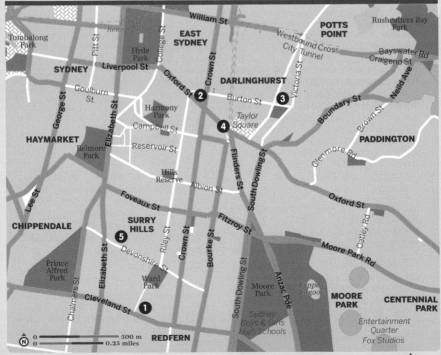

For more detail of this area, see Map p254 ➡

Explore: Surry Hills & Darlinghurst

Surry Hills bears absolutely no resemblance to the beautiful hills of Surrey, England, from which it takes its name. And these days it also bears little resemblance to the tightly knit, working-class community so evocatively documented in Ruth Park's classic Depression-era novels set here. The rows of Victorian terrace houses remain, but they're now home to a mishmash of inner-city hipsters, foodies and gay guys who keep the many excellent neighbourhood restaurants and bars in business.

The warehouses lining Surry Hills' moody lower canyons, near Central station, are the remnants of the local rag trade and print industry. They now contain coffee shops, art galleries, interior-design outlets and apartments.

Immediately east of the city, Darlinghurst is synonymous with Sydney's vibrant and visible gay community. The shabby lower end of Oxford St has traditionally been Sydney's sequinned mile, and while it's seen better days, it's still home to most of the city's gay venues and the Mardi Gras parade. Downhill from here, Darlinghurst morphs into East Sydney, with what remains of a tiny Italian enclave centred on Stanley St.

Local Life

→ **Brunch** The neighbourhood's cafes are popular at the best of times, but come the weekend, they heave.
→ **Sunday sessions** Squeezing the last drop of drinking time out of a weekend is a cherished tradition in these parts. Pubs with beer gardens fill up on sunny Sunday afternoons and stay busy into the evening.
→ **Eat streets** Restaurants cluster on Surry Hills' Crown and Holt Sts, Darlinghurst's Victoria St and East Sydney's Stanley St.

Getting There & Away

→ **Train** A train station is seldom more than a kilometre away. Exit at Museum for East Sydney and the blocks around Oxford St; Central for the rest of Surry Hills; and Kings Cross for the northern and eastern reaches of Darlinghurst.
→ **Bus** Numerous buses traverse Cleveland, Crown, Albion, Oxford, Liverpool and Flinders Sts. Useful routes include 339 (the Rocks to Clovelly via Albion and Flinders), 355 (Newtown to Bondi Junction via Cleveland), 372 (Central to Coogee via Elizabeth and Cleveland) and 373/377 (Circular Quay to Coogee/Maroubra via Oxford and Flinders).
→ **Car** Street parking is usually possible, but it's often metered and limited in duration. Don't leave valuables visible.

Lonely Planet's Top Tip

Many of the neighbourhood's hippest eateries – including Bodega (p127), Buffalo Dining Club (p130), House (p127), Lucio Pizzeria (p131), Porteño (p127) and Spice I Am (p125) – don't take bookings. To avoid a lengthy wait, turn up early (around 6pm). You'll need to have your whole party present to secure a table. Otherwise put your name on the list and wait at a nearby bar until called.

Best Places to Eat

→ Devonshire (p130)
→ Porteño (p127)
→ 4Fourteen (p130)
→ Devon (p127)
→ Bourke Street Bakery (p125)

For reviews, see p125 →

Best Places to Drink

→ Wild Rover (p131)
→ Local Taphouse (p132)
→ Pocket (p132)
→ Hinky Dinks (p132)
→ Shady Pines Saloon (p132)

For reviews, see p131 →

Best Gay Venues

→ Palms On Oxford (p133)
→ Arq (p133)
→ Midnight Shift (p133)
→ Stonewall Hotel (p133)
→ Oxford Hotel (p133)

For reviews, see p133 →

◉ SIGHTS

◉ Surry Hills

BRETT WHITELEY STUDIO   GALLERY
Map p254 (✆1800 679 278; www.brettwhiteley.org; 2 Raper St; ◷10am-4pm Fri-Sun; ⊠Central) FREE Acclaimed local artist Brett Whiteley (1939–1992) lived fast and without restraint. His hard-to-find studio (look for the signs on Devonshire St) has been preserved as a gallery for some of his best work. At the door is a miniature of his famous sculpture *Almost Once,* which you can see in all its glory in the Domain.

OBJECT GALLERY   GALLERY
Map p254 (✆02-9361 4511; www.object.com.au; 415 Bourke St; ◷11am-5pm Wed-Sat; ⊠Central) FREE Inside the cylindrical former St Margaret's Hospital chapel (a 1958 modernist classic by architect Ken Woolley), nonprofit Object presents innovative exhibitions of new craft and design from Australia and overseas. Furniture, fashion, textiles and glass festoon three levels.

◉ Darlinghurst

TAYLOR SQUARE   SQUARE
Map p254 (cnr Oxford & Bourke Sts; ⊠Museum) You know it's been a rough night if you wake up in Taylor Sq – a vaguely defined paved area straddling the gay hub of Oxford St. The stern Greek Revival Darlinghurst Courthouse (1842) watches the goings-on, no doubt disapprovingly. Near the courthouse is a heritage-listed Edwardian underground toilet (closed), while on the Surry Hills side a sporadic fountain shoots enemas at unsuspecting passers-by. Continuing the theme are metre-high suppository-like sculptures, housing an outdoor gallery of sorts.

NATIONAL
ART SCHOOL   HISTORIC SITE, GALLERY
Map p254 (www.nas.edu.au; Forbes St; ◷gallery 11am-5pm Mon-Sat; ⊠Kings Cross) FREE From 1841 to 1912 these sandstone buildings were Darlinghurst Gaol: writer Henry Lawson was incarcerated here several times for debt (he called the place 'Starvinghurst'). If today's art students think they've got it tough, they should spare a thought for the 732 prisoners who were crammed in here, or the 76 who were hanged.

The central circular building was the chapel. A tiny former morgue near the Burton St exit has creepy skull-and-crossbone carvings. There's also an excellent on-site gallery showcasing students' work.

GREEN PARK   PARK
Map p254 (cnr Victoria & Burton Sts; ⊠Kings Cross) Once the residence of Alexander Green, hangman of Darlinghurst Gaol, Green Park is a cheery space during the day, but as the many syringe-disposal bins attest, it's best avoided nocturnally. At the top of the slope, the inverted pink triangular prism backed by black pillars is the Gay & Lesbian Holocaust Memorial.

The memorial was founded by the late Dr Kitty Fischer, who as a young Jewish girl in Auschwitz was kept alive by food smuggled to her by a gay inmate forced to wear the pink triangle. In a lower corner of the park is the Victor Chang Memorial – before he was murdered in 1991, he was a famed heart surgeon who worked at neighbouring St Vincent's Hospital.

SYDNEY JEWISH MUSEUM   MUSEUM
Map p254 (✆02-9360 7999; www.sydneyjewishmuseum.com.au; 148 Darlinghurst Rd; adult/child $10/7; ◷10am-4pm Sun-Thu, to 2pm Fri; ⊠Kings Cross) Created largely as a Holocaust memorial, this museum examines Australian Jewish history, culture and tradition, from the time of the First Fleet (which included 16 known Jews), to the immediate aftermath of WWII (when Australia became home to the greatest number of Holocaust survivors per capita, after Israel), to the present day. Allow at least two hours to take it all in. Free 45-minute tours leave at noon on Monday, Wednesday, Friday and Sunday.

Video testimony and touch-screen computers are used to good effect. The sobering Holocaust section includes a moving Children's Memorial.

ST JOHN'S CHURCH   CHURCH
Map p254 (✆02-9360 6844; www.stjohnsanglican.org.au; 120 Darlinghurst Rd; ◷10am-2pm Mon-Fri; ⊠Kings Cross) Grab a pamphlet inside this lovely sandstone church (1858) for an interesting 10-minute, self-guided tour. It makes for a hushed escape from the urban jangle of Darlinghurst Rd and the car wash next door. The Anglican congregation runs the Rough Edges Community Centre, working with the area's many homeless.

AUSTRALIAN MUSEUM   MUSEUM

Map p254 (☑02-9320 6000; www.australian museum.net.au; 6 College St; adult/child $15/8; ☺9.30am-5pm; ☒Museum) This natural-history museum, established just 40 years after the First Fleet dropped anchor, has endeavoured to shrug off its museum-that-should-be-in-a-museum feel by jazzing things up a little. Hence dusty taxidermy has been interspersed with video projections and a terrarium with live snakes, while dinosaur skeletons cosy up to life-size re-creations. Yet it's the most old-fashioned sections that are arguably the most interesting – the large collection of crystals and precious stones, and the hall of skeletons.

The latter has an intriguingly bizarre tableau of a skeletal man riding a horse, and another sitting in a comfy chair next to his underfed pets.

Also worthwhile is the Indigenous Australians section, covering Aboriginal history and spirituality, from Dreaming stories to videos of the Freedom Rides of the 1960s. There are also displays on extinct megafauna (giant wombats – simultaneously cuddly and terrifying), and a sad 'where are they now' exhibit featuring stuffed remains and video footage of recently extinct species.

EATING

Scruffy Surry Hills' transformation into Sydney's foodie nirvana was sudden, roughly commencing with the 1999 opening of the Eastern Distributor, which made peaceful tree-lined backstreets out of Crown and Bourke Sts (once the main routes to the airport). Some of the city's top-rated restaurants now inhabit surprising nooks amid terrace houses and former warehouses, with new places opening all the time.

✘ Surry Hills

★BOURKE STREET BAKERY   BAKERY $

Map p254 (www.bourkestreetbakery.com.au; 633 Bourke St; items $5-14; ☺8am-5pm; ☒Central) Queuing outside this teensy bakery is an essential Surry Hills experience. It sells a tempting selection of pastries, cakes, bread and sandwiches, along with sausage rolls which are near legendary in these parts. There are a few tables inside but on a fine day you're better off on the street.

REUBEN HILLS   CAFE $

Map p254 (www.reubenhills.com.au; 61 Albion St; mains $12-18; ☺7am-4pm; ☎; ☒Central) An industrial fit-out and Latin American menu await here at Reuben Hills (aka hipster central). Fantastic single-origin coffee and fried chicken, but the eggs, tacos and *baleadas* (Honduran tortillas) are no slouches, either.

SAMPLE COFFEE   CAFE $

Map p254 (www.samplecoffee.com.au; 118 Devonshire St; items $3-5; ☺6.30am-4pm Mon-Fri; ☒Central) If the alpine scene on the wall induces the urge to yodel, quickly shove one of Sample's deliciously moist muffins in your mouth. The food is limited to some lovely sweet things to go with coffee, which is the real star of the show here. Enter from Holt St.

LE MONDE   CAFE $

Map p254 (www.lemondecafe.com.au; 83 Foveaux St; mains $9-18; ☺6.30am-4pm Mon-Fri, 7.30am-2pm Sat; ☒Central) Some of Sydney's best breakfasts are served between the demure dark wooden walls of this small streetside cafe. Top-notch coffee and a terrific selection of tea will gear you up to face the world.

SPICE I AM   THAI $

Map p254 (www.spiceiam.com; 90 Wentworth Ave; mains $12-19; ☺11.30am-3.30pm & 5.45-10pm Tue-Sun; ☑; ☒Central) Once the preserve of expat Thais, this little red-hot chilli pepper now has queues out the door. No wonder, as everything we've tried from the 70-plus dishes on the menu is superfragrant and superspicy. It's been so successful that they've opened the upmarket version in Darlinghurst (p130).

FORMAGGI OCELLO   CAFE $

Map p254 (☑02-9357 7878; www.ocello.com. au; 425 Bourke St; mains $9-16; ☺10am-6.30pm; ☒Central) Like lactose? Then Formaggi Ocello is for you. Display even the slightest hint of dairy devotion and you'll have the staff at your elbow. Cheeses are mostly Italian, Spanish and French, with some top Aussie selections, too. Check out the humongous cheese wheels in the ageing room. Also serves soups, salads, panini, wine and coffee.

BANGBANG   CAFE $

Map p254 (113 Reservoir St; mains $10-20; ☺8am-4pm; ☒Central) If anyone knows the value of a restorative breakfast it's a DJ; this

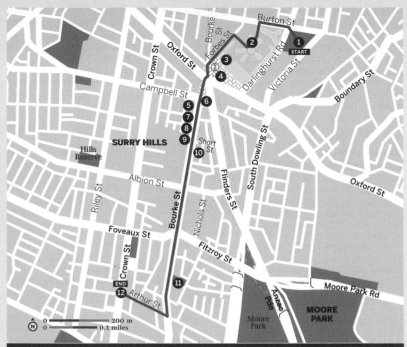

Neighbourhood Walk
'Hurst to Hills Hike

START GREEN PARK
END CROWN ST
LENGTH 1.5KM; 40 MINUTES

This largely residential neighbourhood isn't big on sights, but it's liberally peppered with awesome pubs, bars, cafes and restaurants (see our reviews for recommendations). ❶ **Green Park** (p124) sits at the start of the Victoria St restaurant strip, flanked by the Sydney Jewish Museum, St Vincent's Hospital and Sacred Heart Hospice. Both the hospital and the hospice found themselves at the front line of the AIDS epidemic in the 1980s.

Head west on Burton St, following the sandstone walls of the ❷ **National Art School** (p124) – formerly Darlinghurst Gaol. As you enter, look for the creepy morgue on your right. Turn right at the circular chapel, exit onto Forbes St and head left past the ❸ **Darlinghurst Courthouse** and enter ❹ **Taylor Square** (p124), the heart of Sydney's main gay strip, Oxford St. Cross over to the Surry Hills side. Before you continue up Bourke St, note the art deco ❺ **Belgenny apartment building** and the ❻ antique

red post box. The first block of Bourke St harbours reminders of the neighbourhood's once-prominent Greek community. ❼ **Christopher's Cake Shop** has been selling Greek sweets since 1955. A few doors down is ❽ **St Sophia's Greek Orthodox Church**.

Shuffle along Bourke St to the old St Margaret's Hospital site, now housing the ❾ **Object Gallery** (p124). Pricey apartments and restaurants stand in contrast to the sandstone ❿ **Wesleyan Chapel** (1847) across the road, where the Edward Eager Lodge assists the Hills' homeless.

Continuing along Bourke St you'll pass some interesting houses, including a sandstone-and-brick Georgian block and some hefty Victorian terraces. Just after number 454, blink-and-you'll-miss-it ⓫ **Fred Miller Park** is unremarkable except that it commemorates a very Surry Hills character. Miller (1926–1992) was a plumber turned Labor politician who was a staunch supporter of gay rights, despite being straight himself. Hook right into Arthur St, which spits you out onto ⓬ **Crown Street**, Surry Hills' main cafe, bar and hipster strip.

stylish little cafe is run by one (the head-phones mural is the giveaway). Settle into a shiny silver saddle seat and enjoy.

PORTEÑO
ARGENTINE **$$**

Map p254 (⌨02-8399 1440; www.porteno.com.au; 358 Cleveland St; sharing plates $15-48; ⊙6pm-midnight Tue-Sat; ⓡCentral) Lamb and suckling pig are spit-roasted for eight hours before the doors even open at this acclaimed and extremely hip restaurant, devoted to the robust meatiness of Argentine cuisine. Arrive early to avoid a lengthy wait, although there's no hardship in hanging out upstairs at the very cool Gardel's Bar until a table comes free.

DEVON
CAFE **$$**

Map p254 (www.devoncafe.com.au; 76 Devonshire St; mains $14-21; ⊙7am-4.30pm daily, 6-10pm Thu-Sat) If it's boring old bacon and eggs you're after, look elsewhere. Devon shamelessly plunders the cuisines of 'multicultural Australia' to deliver an extremely creative menu, with plenty of twists on old favourites. There's even an 'Ogre's Happy Meal' (ox-tongue, apparently – we weren't tempted).

LONGRAIN
THAI **$$**

Map p254 (⌨02-9280 2888; www.longrain.com; 85 Commonwealth St; mains $18-38; ⊙noon-2.30pm Fri, 6-11pm daily; ⓡCentral) Devotees flock to this century-old, wedge-shaped printing-press building to feast on fragrant modern Thai dishes, and to sip delicately flavoured and utterly delicious cocktails. Sit at shared tables or at the bar.

BODEGA
TAPAS **$$**

Map p254 (⌨02-9212 7766; www.bodegatapas.com; 216 Commonwealth St; tapas $12-28; ⊙noon-2pm Fri, 6-10pm Tue-Sat; ⓡCentral) The coolest progeny of Sydney's tapas explosion, Bodega has a casual vibe, good-lookin' staff and a funky matador mural. Dishes vary widely in size and price. Wash 'em down with Spanish and South American wine, sherry, port or beer, and plenty of Latin gusto.

MOVIDA
SPANISH **$$**

Map p254 (⌨02-8964 7642; www.movida.com.au; 50 Holt St; tapas $5-13, raciones $17-26, mains $29; ⊙noon-late Mon-Sat; ⓡCentral) A Sydney incarnation of a Melbourne legend, MoVida serves top-notch tapas and raciones (larger shared plates), and a great selection of Spanish wines. Book well ahead for a table or get in early for a seat by the bar.

BAR H
ASIAN **$$**

Map p254 (⌨02-9280 1980; www.barhsurryhills.com; 80 Campbell St; dishes $10-34; ⊙6-10.30pm Mon-Sat, 10am-3pm Sun; ⓡMuseum) Marrying Chinese and Japanese dishes with native Australian bush ingredients, this sexy, shiny, black-walled corner eatery is completely unique and extremely impressive. Dishes range considerably in size and are designed to be shared; confer with your waiter about quantities.

SINGLE ORIGIN ROASTERS
CAFE **$$**

Map p254 (⌨02-9211 0665; www.singleorigin.com.au; 60-64 Reservoir St; mains $13-17; ⊙6.30am-4pm Mon-Fri; ⓡCentral) ✐ Unshaven graphic artists roll cigarettes at little outdoor tables in the bricky hollows of deepest Surry Hills, while inside impassioned, bouncing-off-the-walls caffeine fiends prepare their beloved brews, along with a tasty selection of cafe fare.

FOURATEFIVE
CAFE **$$**

Map p254 (www.fouratefive.com; 485 Crown St; mains $10-19; ⊙7am-3.30pm Mon-Sat, 9.30am-2.30pm Sun; ✐; ⓡCentral) Band posters and kooky art fill the walls of this excellent post-grunge cafe. The vibe is chilled and the food is a crowd-pleasing mix of cooked breakfasts, fancy sandwiches, salads and burgers. The tables on the street fill up quickly.

TOKO
JAPANESE **$$**

Map p254 (⌨02-9357 6100; www.toko.com.au; 490 Crown St; dishes $12-31; ⊙noon-3pm Tue-Fri, 6-11pm Mon-Sat; ⓡCentral) Toko dishes up superb modern Japanese *otsumami* (tapas) such as soft-shell crab, sweet eggplant miso and meaty options from the *robata* (charcoal grill). Settle into a communal table and expect to spend around $30 on food – more if you're a sashimi junkie.

EL LOCO
MEXICAN **$$**

Map p254 (www.merivale.com.au/elloco; 64 Foveaux St; mains $10-18; ⊙noon-midnight Mon-Thu, to 3am Fri & Sat, to 10pm Sun; ⓡCentral) As much as we lament the passing of live rock at the Excelsior Hotel, we have to admit that the hip Mexican cantina that's taken over the band room is pretty darn cool. The food's tasty, inventive and, at $5 per taco, fantastic value.

HOUSE
THAI **$$**

Map p254 (⌨02-9280 0364; www.spiceiam.com; 202 Elizabeth St; mains $11-19; ⊙11.30am-10.30pm; ⓡCentral) On a sticky Sydney

1. Liverpool St, Darlinghurst (p135)
For high-end recycled fashion, step inside the vivid storefront of Blue Spinach.

2. Green Park (p124)
Take a break from the city bustle in this Darlinghurst park.

3. Taylor Square (p124)
Admire the bold hues of Reko Rennie's *Always Was, Always Will Be* mural.

4. Object Gallery (p124)
Explore innovative craft and design in a former hospital chapel.

night, House's lantern-strung courtyard really feels like Southeast Asia, not least because of the constant traffic passing. Specialising in the street food of the Issan region of northeast Thailand, the food is deliciously authentic – when they say spicy, believe them.

BOOK KITCHEN
CAFE $$

Map p254 (☑0420 239 469; www.thebook kitchen.com.au; 255 Devonshire St; brunch $11-20, dinner $18-24; ⊗8am-4pm Sun-Tue, to 11pm Wed-Sat; ☎; ◙Central) Nobody's cooking the books here. They're all too busy preparing inventive meals or delivering them to your table with a smile. Grab a table on the sunny footpath or inside the brick warehouse, where food books line the walls, waiting to be sold raw.

DEVONSHIRE
MODERN EUROPEAN $$$

Map p254 (☑02-9698 9427; www.thedevonshire. com.au; 204 Devonshire St; mains $37; ⊗noon-2.30pm Fri, 6-10pm Tue-Sat; ◙Central) It's a long way from a two-Michelin-starred Mayfair restaurant to grungy old Devonshire St for chef Jeremy Bentley, although cuisinewise, perhaps not as far as you'd think. His food is simply extraordinary – complex, precisely presented and full of flavour. And while there's white linen on the tables, the atmosphere isn't the least bit starchy.

4FOURTEEN
MODERN AUSTRALIAN $$$

Map p254 (☑02-9331 5399; www.4fourteen. com.au; 414 Bourke St; mains $30-42; ⊗noon-3pm Tue-Sun, 6-11pm Tue-Sat; ◙Central) When he's not busy terrorising contestants on TV cooking shows, Irish-born chef Colin Fassnidge can be found cranking out hearty, meaty dishes at one of his Sydney eateries, the newest of which is this big, fun, buzzy place. Solo diners should grab a seat by the kitchen for dinner with a show.

✗ Darlinghurst

MESSINA
ICE CREAM $

Map p254 (www.gelatomessina.com; 241 Victoria St; 2 scoops $6; ⊗noon-11pm; ◙Kings Cross) Join the queues of people who look like they never eat ice cream at the counter of Sydney's most popular gelato shop. Clearly even the beautiful people can't resist quirky flavours such as figs in Marsala and salted caramel. The attached dessert bar serves sundaes.

PABLO'S VICE
CAFE $

Map p254 (www.facebook.com/pablosvice; 3/257 Crown St; mains $7-15; ⊗7am-4.30pm Mon-Sat; ◙Museum) A tiny triangular kitchen half-buried below street level with three tables bolted to the wall outside. Big enough for the best coffee in Darlinghurst? You betcha! Grab a seat and unkempt staff will serve you a croissant, salad, wrap, sandwich or cooked breakfast.

BAR COLUZZI
CAFE $

Map p254 (www.facebook.com/barcoluzzidar linghurst; 322 Victoria St; mains $6-12; ⊗5am-7pm Mon-Thu, to 10pm Fri & Sat; ◙Kings Cross) Legendary Coluzzi has been here since 1957 and still attracts an oddball mix of old Italian gents, lycra-clad cyclists, judges, Kings Cross dealers, Darlinghurst gays, students and suits. The food's simple and the coffee's strong.

DON DON
JAPANESE $

Map p254 (☑02-9331 3544; 80 Oxford St; mains $11-15; ⊗11.30am-10pm; ◙Museum) For years we've thumbed our way through diminutive Don Don's photo menu, discovering consistently delicious dishes. Expect everything from *katsudon* (rice with deep-fried chicken, beef or pork, egg and condiments) to sashimi, mostly served with rice, miso and Japanese pickles on the side. Be prepared to queue.

BUFFALO DINING CLUB
ITALIAN $$

Map p254 (www.buffalodiningclub.com.au; 116 Surrey St; mains $20; ⊗noon-11pm Wed-Sun; ◙Kings Cross) Describing itself as a mozzarella bar, this tiny but massively popular eatery limits its output to high-quality antipasto plates and three types of pasta. The kitchen takes up a good half of the downstairs space, but there are extra tables above; expect to queue.

BILLS
CAFE $$

Map p254 (www.bills.com.au; 433 Liverpool St; mains $14-25; ⊗7.30am-2.30pm; ◙Kings Cross) Bill Granger almost single-handedly started the Sydney craze for stylish brunching. This sunny corner cafe with its newspaper-strewn communal table was the original; there are other branches in Surry Hills and Bondi Beach.

SPICE I AM
THAI $$

Map p254 (☑02-9332 2445; 296-300 Victoria St; mains $18-30; ⊗11.30am-3.30pm Thu-Sun, 5.45-10.30pm daily; ☑; ◙Kings Cross) The proper

sit-down restaurant version of the legendary Surry Hills cheapie (p125).

LUCIO PIZZERIA PIZZA $$
Map p254 (www.luciopizzeria.com.au; 248
Palmer St; pizzas $17-24; ◷6-10pm Wed-Mon;
▣Museum) One of a cluster of eateries in an
attractive courtyard off Palmer St, Lucio's
has impeccable Italian credentials: the
pizzas are cooked in a wood-fired oven and
are authentically Neopolitan; Peroni is the
tipple of choice; and statement sunglasses
are much in evidence on the outdoor tables.
No bookings, so get here early or be prepared to queue.

A TAVOLA ITALIAN $$
Map p254 (✆02-9331 7871; www.atavola.com.
au; 348 Victoria St; mains $24-37; ◷noon-3pm &
6-11pm Mon-Sat; ▣Kings Cross) At this classy
pasta joint, the menu only has a handful of dishes to choose from, augmented
by wonderfully fresh specials chalked up
daily. Before each service starts, the long
communal table doubles as the main pasta-
making workbench.

RED LANTERN ON RILEY VIETNAMESE $$$
Map p254 (✆02-9698 4355; www.redlantern.
com.au; 60 Riley St; mains $36-39; ◷noon-3pm
Thu & Fri, 6-10pm daily; ▣Museum) 🍴 This
atmospheric eatery is run by television
presenters Luke Nguyen (*Luke Nguyen's
Vietnam*), Mark Jensen (*Ready Steady
Cook*) and sister/wife Pauline Nguyen
(author of the excellent *Secrets of the Red
Lantern* cookbook-cum-autobiography). It
serves modern takes on classic Vietnamese dishes.

🍷 DRINKING &
🍸 NIGHTLIFE

**Once upon a time this neighbourhood
was known for its grungy live-music pubs
and high-octane gay scene. Many of the
music venues have subsequently been
converted into chic bar-restaurants
and the gay bars have eased up on the
gas, but this area still contains some of
Sydney's best nightspots. You just have
to look harder to find them. The 'small
bar' phenomenon has taken off here,
with many of Sydney's best lurking
down the most unlikely lanes.**

🍷 Surry Hills

★WILD ROVER BAR
Map p254 (www.thewildrover.com.au; 75 Campbell
St; ◷4pm-midnight Mon-Sat, to 10pm Sun; ▣Cen-
tral) Look for the old sign on the window
reading 'Gestetner's Surry Hills Shirt Warehouse' and enter this supremely cool brick-
lined speakeasy, where a big range of craft
beer is served in chrome steins. Live bands
play upstairs a couple of nights a week.

THE WINERY WINE BAR
Map p254 (www.thewinerysurryhills.com.au; 285a
Crown St; ◷noon-midnight; ▣Museum) Set
back from the road in the leafy grounds
of a historic water reservoir, this wine bar
serves dozens of wines by the glass to the
swankier Surry Hills set. Sit for a while
and you'll notice all kinds of kitsch touches
lurking in the greenery: headless statues,
upside-down parrots, iron koalas.

TIO'S CERVECERIA BAR
Map p254 (4-14 Foster St; ◷5pm-midnight;
▣Museum) Tio likes tequila. Heaps of different types. And wrestling, Catholic kitsch
and *Day of the Dead* paraphernalia. Surry
Hills skaters, beard-wearers and baby-doll
babes love him right back.

VASCO COCKTAIL BAR
Map p254 (www.vascobar.com; 421 Cleveland
St; ◷5pm-midnight Tue-Sat; ▣372) Like the
much, much hipper and better-looking Italian cousin of a Hard Rock Cafe, Vasco serves
beer, wine and rock-themed cocktails in a
room lined with band photos and guitars.
Order a plate of *salumi* or pasta to snack on
as you sip your 'Monkey Gone to Heaven',
while Jagger sneers on the screen.

BERESFORD HOTEL PUB
Map p254 (www.merivale.com.au/theberesford
hotel; 354 Bourke St; ◷noon-midnight; ▣Cen-
tral) The once-grungy Beresford (circa
1870) has turned into a superslick architectural tractor beam designed to reel in
the beautiful people. The crowd will make
you feel either inadequate or right at home,
depending on how the mirror is treating
you. There's a vast new beer garden, and
upstairs is a schmick live-music/club space.

121BC WINE BAR
Map p254 (www.121bc.com.au; 4/50 Holt St;
◷5pm-midnight Tue-Sat; ▣Central) The first
challenge is finding it (enter from Gladstone

St) and the second is scoring a table. After that, it's easy – seat yourself at the communal table under the bubbly light fixture and ask the waitstaff to suggest delicious drops and snacks to suit your inclinations. Everything's good, so you can't really go wrong.

CRICKETERS ARMS HOTEL   PUB

Map p254 (www.cricketersarmshotel.com.au; 106 Fitzroy St; ⊙2-10pm Sun, 3pm-midnight Mon-Thu, noon-midnight Fri & Sat; ☒; ☐339) A favourite haunt of arts students, dog-owners and locals of all persuasions, you don't even have to know what a silly mid-off is to enjoy this pub. There are open fires for when you need warming up.

SHAKESPEARE HOTEL   PUB

Map p254 (www.shakespearehotel.com.au; 200 Devonshire St; ⊙10am-midnight Mon-Sat, noon-10pm Sun; ☒Central) A classic Sydney pub (1879) with art nouveau–tiled walls, skuzzy carpet, the horses on the TV and cheap bar meals. There are plenty of cosy hidey-holes upstairs.

HOTEL HOLLYWOOD   PUB

Map p254 (☑02-9281 2765; www.facebook.com/hotel.hollywood.sydney; 2 Foster St; ⊙3pm-midnight Mon, noon-midnight Tue & Wed, noon-3am Thu & Fri, 4pm-3am Sat; ☒Museum) A mixed crowd of Surry Hillbillies gets down to serious beer business in this art deco pub that time forgot.

🍷 Darlinghurst

LOCAL TAPHOUSE   PUB

Map p254 (www.thelocal.com.au; 122 Flinders St; ⊙noon-midnight; ☐396-399) Beer lovers can test their palates against the tasting notes as they work their way through dozens of craft beers at this angular old pub. There aren't any views but the little high-sided rooftop is a great spot to catch the breeze.

POCKET   BAR

Map p254 (www.pocketsydney.com.au; 13 Burton St; ⊙4pm-midnight; ☒Museum) Sink into the corner Pocket's comfy leather couches, order a drink from one of the cheery waitstaff, and chat about the day's adventures over a decade-defying indie soundtrack. Pop-art murals and exposed brickwork add to the underground ambience.

HINKY DINKS   COCKTAIL BAR

Map p254 (www.hinkydinks.com.au; 185 Darlinghurst Rd; ⊙1-10pm Sun, 4pm-midnight Mon-Sat; ☒Kings Cross) Everything's just hunky dory in this little cocktail bar styled after a 1950s milkshake parlour. Try the Hinky Fizz, an alcohol-soaked strawberry sorbet served in a waxed paper sundae cup.

SHADY PINES SALOON   BAR

Map p254 (www.shadypinessaloon.com; shop 4, 256 Crown St; ⊙4pm-midnight; ☒Museum) With no sign or street number on the door and entry via a shady back lane (look for the white door before Bikram Yoga on Foley St), this subterranean honky-tonk bar caters to the urban boho. Sip whisky and rye with the good ole hipster boys amid Western memorabilia and taxidermy.

HELLO SAILOR   COCKTAIL BAR

Map p254 (www.hellosailor.com.au; 96 Oxford St; ⊙5pm-3am Tue-Sun; 🛜; ☒Museum) Entered from lanelike Foley St, this 'seafood shack and cocktail bar' gets filled to the gills on the weekends. A diverse but hip crowd drops anchor until the wee hours, partying under maritime flags, navigation maps and sepia pictures of tall ships.

CLIFF DIVE   COCKTAIL BAR

Map p254 (www.thecliffdive.com.au; basement, 16 Oxford Sq; ⊙6pm-3am Thu-Sat; ☒Museum) Head down the stairs and throw yourself into a world of rough-hewn stone walls, glowing tropical-fish lanterns, Polynesian knick-knacks and cocktails served in tiki glasses. There are plenty of nooks to hunker down in after you've worked up a tropical sweat on the dance floor.

VICTORIA ROOM   COCKTAIL BAR

Map p254 (☑02-9357 4488; www.thevictoriaroom.com; Level 1, 235 Victoria St; ⊙6pm-midnight Wed-Fri, noon-2am Sat, 2.30pm-midnight Sun; ☒Kings Cross) Chesterfields, art nouveau wallpaper, dark-wood panelling and bamboo screens – the Victoria Room is the spoilt love child of a 1920s Bombay gin palace and a Hong Kong opium den. Don your white linen suit and panama and order a Raspberry Debonair at the bar. Book ahead for high tea on weekend afternoons (from $45).

EAU-DE-VIE   COCKTAIL BAR

Map p254 (www.eaudevie.com.au; 229 Darlinghurst Rd; ⊙6pm-1am; ☒Kings Cross) Take the door marked 'restrooms' at the back of the

Kirketon Hotel's main bar and enter this sophisticated black-walled speakeasy, where a team of dedicated shirt-and-tie-wearing mixologists concoct the sort of beverages that win best-cocktail gongs.

GREEN PARK HOTEL PUB
Map p254 (www.greenparkhotel.com.au; 360 Victoria St; ☉11am-midnight Sun-Wed, to 2am Thu-Sat; ☒Kings Cross) The ever-rockin' Green Park has pool tables, rolled-arm leather couches, a beer garden with funky Dr Seuss–inspired lighting, and a huge tiled central bar teeming with travellers, gay guys and pierced locals.

DARLO BAR PUB
Map p254 (☑02-9331 3672; www.darlobar.com.au; 306 Liverpool St; ☉10am-midnight Mon-Sat, noon-midnight Sun; ☒Kings Cross) The Darlo's triangular retro room is a magnet for thirsty urban bohemians, fluoro-clad ditch diggers and architects with a hankering for pinball or pool. It's quiet during the day, but DJs fire things up on Saturday nights.

BEAUCHAMP HOTEL PUB
Map p254 (☑02-9331 2575; www.thebeauchamp.com.au; 265 Oxford St; ☉noon-midnight Sun-Thu, to 3am Fri & Sat; ☒Kings Cross) The design lords have transformed this old corner pub into something very hip indeed. On weekends it gets packed – and incredibly noisy – with stylish Eastern Suburbs 20-somethings. There's a cool terrace upstairs. It's pronounced *Beech*-um.

EXCHANGE HOTEL BAR, CLUB
Map p254 (☑02-9331 2956; www.exchangesydney.com.au; 34-44 Oxford St; admission free-$25; ☉24hr; ☒Museum) There's a whole mess of venues here, mashed together under one roof. Q Bar is a loft space, hosting a diverse range of oddball events; Spectrum is an alt-indie club with live bands; and sweaty, sexy Phoenix is home to wild-eyed clubbers, gay and straight. Sandwiched in between, the Vegas and Nevada lounges offer the chance of a cooling beverage and a nice sit-down.

KINSELAS BAR
Map p254 (☑02-9331 3100; www.kinselas.com.au; 383 Bourke St; ☉10am-4am; ☒Museum) A Taylor Sq institution, this converted funeral parlour has come back from the dead more times than we care to recall. The downstairs is all art deco stylings (spot the chapel), while Lo-Fi upstairs is a

chic cocktail bar with the best balcony for posing and people-watching. Continue up to The Standard Bowl for 'Bands! Booze! Bowling!'.

PALMS ON OXFORD GAY, CLUB
Map p254 (☑02-9357 4166; 124 Oxford St; ☉8pm-1am Thu & Sun, to 3am Fri & Sat; ☒Museum) No one admits to coming here, but the lengthy queues prove they are lying. In this underground dance bar, the heyday of Stock Aitken Waterman never ended. It may be uncool, but if you don't scream when Kylie hits the turntables, you'll be the only one.

ARQ GAY, CLUB
Map p254 (www.arqsydney.com.au; 16 Flinders St; ☉9pm-5am Thu & Sun, 9pm-noon Fri & Sat; ☒Museum) If Noah had to fill his Arq with groovy gay clubbers, he'd head here with a big net and some tranquillisers. This flash megaclub has a cocktail bar, a recovery room and two dance floors with high-energy house, drag shows and a hyperactive smoke machine.

MIDNIGHT SHIFT GAY, CLUB
Map p254 (☑02-9358 3848; www.themidnightshift.com.au; 85 Oxford St; admission free-$10; ☉4pm-late Thu-Sun; ☒Museum) The grand dame of the Oxford St gay scene, known for its lavish drag productions, was in the midst of a thorough renovation when we last visited. When the dust has settled expect a much improved downstairs bar to complement the serious tits-to-the-wind club upstairs.

STONEWALL HOTEL GAY, BAR
Map p254 (☑02-9360 1963; www.stonewallhotel.com; 175 Oxford St; ☉noon-3am; ☒Museum) Nicknamed 'Stonehenge' by those who think it's archaic, Stonewall has three levels of bars and dance floors, and attracts a younger crowd. Cabaret, karaoke and quiz nights spice things up; Wednesday's Malebox is an inventive way to bag yourself a boy.

OXFORD HOTEL GAY, PUB
Map p254 (www.theoxfordhotel.com.au; 134 Oxford St; ☉10am-3am; ☒Museum) Over the course of 30 years and numerous facelifts, the main bar at the Oxford has remained the locus of beer-swilling gay blokedom, although the crowd is a little more mixed these days. Upstairs, Ginger's plays host to live music, cabaret, DJs and private functions.

SURRY HILLS & DARLINGHURST DRINKING & NIGHTLIFE

☆ ENTERTAINMENT

★ BELVOIR   THEATRE
Map p254 (☏02-9699 3444; www.belvoir.com.
au; 25 Belvoir St; ⛉Central) In a quiet corner
of Surry Hills, this intimate venue is the
home of an often-experimental and consistently excellent theatre company. Shows
sometimes feature big stars.

SBW STABLES THEATRE   THEATRE
Map p254 (☏02-9361 3817; www.griffintheatre.
com.au; 10 Nimrod St; ⛉King Cross) In the
19th century this place was knee-high in
horse dung; now it's home to the Griffin
Theatre Company, dedicated to nurtur-
ing new Australian writers. It's also where
many actors started out – Cate Blanchett
and David Wenham both trod the boards
here. Monday Rush tickets (two for $20)
are available for certain performances.

ETERNITY PLAYHOUSE   THEATRE
Map p254 (☏02-8356 9987; www.darlinghurst
theatre.com; 39 Burton St; ⛉Museum) Based
in a beautifully restored Baptist tabernacle
(1887), the Darlinghurst Theatre Company
focuses on bringing pithy, intelligent Australian scripts to the stage.

OXFORD ART FACTORY   LIVE MUSIC
Map p254 (www.oxfordartfactory.com; 38-46 Oxford St; ⛉Museum) Indie kids party against an
arty backdrop at this two-room venue mod-
elled on Andy Warhol's NYC creative base.
There's a gallery, a bar and a performance
space that often hosts international acts
and DJs. Check the website for what's on.

VENUE 505   LIVE MUSIC
Map p254 (www.venue505.com; 280 Cleveland St;
⛉doors open 6pm Mon-Sat; ⛉Central) Focusing on jazz, roots, reggae, funk, gypsy and
Latin music, this small, relaxed venue is
artist-run and thoughtfully programmed.
The space features comfortable couches
and murals by a local artist.

SLIDE   CABARET
Map p254 (☏02-8915 1899; www.slide.com.au;
41 Oxford St; ⛉7pm-late Wed-Sat; ⛉Museum)
Slide inside a gorgeously converted banking chamber for dinner and a sexy show:
cabaret, circus, burlesque etc.

GOVINDA'S   CINEMA
Map p254 (☏02-9380 5155; www.govindas.
com.au; 112 Darlinghurst Rd; dinner & movie
$30, movie only $16; ⛉Wed-Sat; ⛉Kings Cross)
The Hare Krishna Govinda's is an all-
you-can-gobble vegetarian smorgasbord,
including admission to the movie room
upstairs. Expect blockbusters, art-house
classics, incense in the air and cushions
on the floor.

🛍 SHOPPING

🛍 Surry Hills

WORKSHOPPED   GIFTS
Map p254 (www.workshopped.com.au; 2/8 Hill
St; ⛉10am-5pm Mon-Sat; ⛉374-6) The work
of Australian designers is showcased in
this funky little store, which focuses on
practical but beautiful things for the home:
ceramics, wood, soft furnishings etc.

HOLY KITSCH!   GIFTS
Map p254 (www.holykitsch.com.au; 321 Crown
St; ⛉10.30am-6pm Wed-Mon; ⛉Central) When
you've a hole that only Day of the Dead

WORTH A DETOUR

WATERLOO

If you're an art buff, a visit to the somewhat gritty suburb of Waterloo can be reward-
ing. From Bourke St continue past the major intersection with Cleveland St for 750m
and you'll hit Danks St, where you'll find the first of our featured galleries. The other is
further south, on the continuation of Elizabeth St.

Aboriginal & Pacific Art (www.aboriginalpacificart.com.au; 2 Danks St, Waterloo;
⛉11am-5pm Tue-Sat; ⛉M20) One of a number of commercial galleries under the same
roof; this one represents community-based Aboriginal and Pacific Islander art.

Darren Knight Gallery (☏02-9699 5353; www.darrenknightgallery.com; 840 Elizabeth
St; ⛉10am-5pm Tue-Sat; ⛉Green Square) This little, off-the-beaten-track, two-storey
gallery showcases established and up-and-coming artists from Australia and New
Zealand, including Ricky Swallow and Louise Weaver.

---

and Mexican wrestling paraphenalia can fill, come here. There's another branch in Newtown (p121).

WHEELS & DOLLBABY CLOTHING
Map p254 (02-9361 3286; www.wheelsanddollbaby.com; 259 Crown St; 10am-6pm Fri-Wed, to 8pm Thu; Museum) 'Clothes to Snare a Millionaire' is the name of the game here, and what a wicked, wicked game it is: lace, leather and leopard print; studs, suspenders and satin. Tight wrapped and trussed up; it won't just be the millionaires who'll be looking your way. Male rockers will have to settle for T-shirts.

HUGHES GALLERY ARTS
Map p254 (02-9698 3200; www.rayhughesgallery.com; 270 Devonshire St; 9am-6pm Tue-Sat; Central) Beyond the corrugated-iron cows and enormous wooden fish, this bohemian warehouse gallery is worth a look, whether you're in the art market or not.

SURRY HILLS MARKETS MARKET
Map p254 (www.shnc.org/events/surry-hills-markets; Shannon Reserve, Crown St; 7am-4pm 1st Sat of month; Central) There's a chipper community vibe at this monthly market, with mainly locals renting stalls to sell/recycle their old stuff: clothes, CDs, books and sundry junk. Bargains aplenty.

Darlinghurst

BLUE SPINACH FASHION
Map p254 (02-9331 3904; www.bluespinach.com.au; 348 Liverpool St; Kings Cross) High-end consignment clothing for penny-pinching label lovers of all genders. If you can make it beyond the shocking blue facade (shocking doesn't really do it justice), you'll find Paul Smith and Gucci at (relatively) bargain prices.

ARTERY ARTS
Map p254 (02-9380 8234; www.artery.com.au; 221 Darlinghurst Rd; 10am-6pm Mon-Fri, to 4pm Sat & Sun; Kings Cross) Step into a world of mesmerising dots and swirls at this small gallery devoted to Aboriginal art. Artery's motto is 'ethical, contemporary, affordable', and while large canvases by more established artists cost in the thousands, small, unstretched canvases start at around $35.

BOOKSHOP DARLINGHURST BOOKS
Map p254 (02-9331 1103; www.thebookshop.com.au; 207 Oxford St; 10am-7pm Sun-Wed, to 9pm Thu-Sat; Kings Cross) This outstanding bookshop specialises in gay and lesbian tomes, with everything from queer crime and lesbian fiction to glossy pictorials and porn. A diverting browse, to say the least (hmm...which would look better on my coffee table: the *Big Book of Breasts* or the *Big Penis Book*?).

HOUSE OF PRISCILLA CLOTHING, ACCESSORIES
Map p254 (02-9286 3023; www.houseofpriscilla.com.au; Level 1, 47 Oxford St; 10am-6pm Mon-Wed, Fri & Sat, to 8pm Thu; Museum) Not only is Priscilla the queen of the desert, she also has her own boutique – not bad for a cinematic bus. Run by some of the city's leading drag artistes, Priscilla is the place for feathered angel wings, naughty nurse outfits, Beyoncé wigs, kinky thigh-high boots and sequinned frocks to fit front-row forwards. Very camp women also welcome.

SAX FETISH CLOTHING, ADULT
Map p254 (02-9331 6105; www.saxfetish.com; 110a Oxford St; 11am-7pm; Museum) No, it's not a bar for jazz obsessives, but rather a sexy, dark-hearted shop selling high-quality leather and rubber gear. All genders are catered for, and the 'accessories' range goes a little further than your standard belts and handbags (cufflinks and ties take on a whole new meaning here).

C'S FLASHBACK VINTAGE
Map p254 (02-9331 7833; www.csflashback.com.au; 316 Crown St; 10am-6pm Fri-Wed, to 8pm Thu; Museum) Looking for a second-hand Hawaiian shirt, some beat-up cowboy boots or a little sequinned 1940s hat like the Queen wears? We're not sure exactly what C was on, but her flashback men's and women's threads are pretty trippy.

Kings Cross & Potts Point

POTTS POINT | ELIZABETH BAY | WOOLLOOMOOLOO | KINGS CROSS

Neighbourhood Top Five

1 Soaking up the sights, sounds and smells of **Darlinghurst Road**, Sydney's seediest strip.

2 Ducking into **Llankelly Place** for a coffee, a cocktail and a view of the passing parade.

3 Admiring the Georgian grace of **Elizabeth Bay House** (p138), a reminder of grander days gone by.

4 Harbour-gazing, fine-dining and celebrity-spotting at **Woolloomooloo Finger Wharf** (p138).

5 Kick-starting a night out you'll never forget (or won't remember) at the **Kings Cross Hotel** (p141).

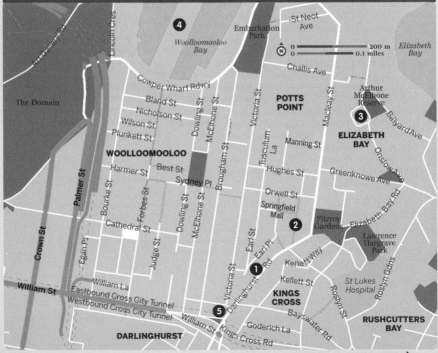

For more detail of this area, see Map p257 ➡

Explore: Kings Cross & Potts Point

The beginning of Sydney's Eastern Suburbs, the city-fringe suburbs of Woolloomooloo, Kings Cross, Potts Point and Elizabeth Bay are a world unto themselves.

Kings Cross is a bizarre, densely populated dichotomy: strip joints, tacky tourist shops and backpacker hostels bang heads with classy restaurants, boozy bars and gorgeous guesthouses. A weird cross-section of society is drawn to the bright lights: buskers, beggars, tourists, prostitutes, pimps, groomed metrosexuals, horny businessmen and underfed artists roam the streets on equal footing. Sometimes the razzle-dazzle has a sideshow appeal; sometimes walking up Darlinghurst Rd is a little depressing. Either way, it's never boring.

Down McElhone Stairs from the Cross, Woolloomooloo has also cleaned up its act. Harry's Cafe de Wheels and the navy base are still here, but drunken sailors are in shorter supply.

Gracious, tree-lined Potts Point and Elizabeth Bay seem worlds away. Well-preserved Victorian, Edwardian and art-deco houses and apartments flank picturesque avenues.

Local Life

➜ **Cafes and pubs** Mainstays include Piccolo Bar (p140) and the Old Fitzroy (p143) but once you get off the Darlinghurst Rd strip, most places are well patronised by locals.

➜ **Parks** Residents of the apartment blocks of Potts Point and Elizabeth Bay can be seen spreading out towels in tiny Arthur McElhone Reserve (p139) or walking their pampered pooches in Embarkation Park (p139).

➜ **Potts Point boys** The subculture of well-heeled, well-groomed, gym-buffed gay men who frequent the local cafes and all of the big dance parties.

Getting There & Away

➜ **Train** Everywhere is within walking distance of Kings Cross station, although the western fringe of Woolloomooloo is closer to St James.

➜ **Bus** Route 311 hooks through Kings Cross, Potts Point, Elizabeth Bay and Woolloomooloo on its way from Railway Sq to the bottom of town. Routes 324 and 325 pass through Kings Cross (Bayswater Rd) en route between Circular Quay and Watsons Bay.

➜ **Car** The city council operates a 24-hour car park at 9a Elizabeth Bay Rd in Kings Cross (entry via Ward Ave; per hour/day $8/40, more on weekends). Street parking is possible, but often metered and limited in duration. Clearways are ruthlessly enforced. Don't leave valuables visible.

Lonely Planet's Top Tip

Where exactly is Kings Cross? Although technically it's just the intersection of William and Victoria Sts, in reality it's more of a mindset than an exact geographical place. What most people call Kings Cross falls within the suburb of Potts Point; businesses tend to use a Potts Point address if they want to sound classy and Kings Cross if they want to emphasise their party cred. Either way, you'll know Kings Cross when you see it.

✖ Best Places to Eat

➜ Ms G's (p140)
➜ Cho Cho San (p140)
➜ Apollo (p140)
➜ Otto Ristorante (p141)
➜ Room 10 (p138)

For reviews, see p138 ➡

🍷 Best Places to Drink

➜ Old Fitzroy Hotel (p143)
➜ Bootleg (p143)
➜ Waterbar (p143)
➜ Jimmy Lik's (p143)
➜ Sugarmill (p142)

For reviews, see p141 ➡

🍷 Best Places to Party

➜ Kings Cross Hotel (p141)
➜ Sugarmill (p142)
➜ World Bar (p142)
➜ Kit & Kaboodle (p142)
➜ Soho (p142)

For reviews, see p141 ➡

KINGS CROSS & POTTS POINT

◉ SIGHTS

◉ Potts Point

FITZROY GARDENS   PARK
Map p257 (cnr Macleay St & Darlinghurst Rd; ℞Kings Cross) It's testimony to the 'cleaning up' of the Cross that this once-dodgy park is now a reasonably safe place to hang out (probably helped by the austere police station in the corner). It still feels seedy, though: malnourished seagulls compete for scraps with pigeons who look like Keith Richards, while bearded homeless guys compile cigarettes from discarded butts.

Known by some local wags as the 'elephant douche', the dandelion-esque El Alamein Fountain (1961) sends waves of chlorinated spray across the open space. An organic food market sets up here on Saturday mornings, while on Sundays a little flea market takes its place.

MCELHONE STAIRS   LANDMARK
Map p257 (Victoria St; ℞Kings Cross) These stone stairs were built in 1870 to connect spiffy Potts Point with the Woolloomooloo slums below. The steep steps run past an apartment block: residents sip tea on their balconies and stare bemusedly at the fitness freaks punishing themselves on the 113-stair uphill climb.

◉ Elizabeth Bay

★ELIZABETH BAY HOUSE   HISTORIC BUILDING
Map p257 (✆02-9356 3022; www.sydneyliving museums.com.au; 7 Onslow Ave; adult/child $8/4; ◷11am-4pm Fri-Sun; ℞Kings Cross) Now dwarfed by 20th-century apartments, Colonial Secretary Alexander Macleay's elegant Greek Revival mansion was one of the finest houses in the colony when it was completed in 1839. The architectural highlight is an exquisite oval entrance saloon with a curved and cantilevered staircase.

The grounds – a sort of botanical garden for Macleay, who collected plants from around the world – extended from the harbour all the way up the hill to Kings Cross. Remnants remain, including a little hidden grotto reached by taking a path leading between 16 and 18 Onslow Ave.

◉ Woolloomooloo

WOOLLOOMOOLOO FINGER WHARF   HISTORIC BUILDING
Map p257 (Cowper Wharf Roadway; ℞Kings Cross) A former wool and cargo dock, this beautiful Edwardian wharf faced oblivion for decades before a 2½-year demolition-workers' green ban on the site in the late 1980s saved it. It received a huge sprucing up in the late 1990s and has emerged as one of Sydney's most exclusive eating, drinking, sleeping and marina addresses.

It's still a public wharf, so feel free to explore the innards, past industrial conveyor-belt relics, a five-star hotel and its designer Water Bar. Along the way the wharf's history is etched into glass walls. You might even squeeze in some star-spotting – songbird Delta Goodrem and everyman-megastar Russell Crowe have both had plush pads here.

ARTSPACE   GALLERY
Map p257 (✆02-9356 0555; www.artspace.org. au; 43-51 Cowper Wharf Rd; ◷11am-5pm Tue-Sun; ℞Kings Cross) FREE Artspace is spacey: its eternal quest is to fill the void with vigorous, engaging Australian and international contemporary art. Things here are decidedly avant-garde – expect lots of conceptual art, audiovisual installations and new-media pieces. It's an admirable attempt to liven things up in Sydney's art scene, experimenting with sometimes-disturbing concepts. Disabled access is excellent.

✕ EATING

With the exception of the phalanx of upmarket restaurants on Woolloomooloo's Finger Wharf, these 'burbs don't have any harbourside razzle-dazzle. Instead you'll find a buzzy set of small bistros and cafes with heaps of charisma. Tiny Llankelly Place has a clutch of hip microcafes.

✕ Kings Cross

ROOM 10   CAFE $
Map p257 (10 Llankelly Pl; mains $9-14; ◷7am-4pm; ℞Kings Cross) If you're wearing a flat cap, sprouting a beard and obsessed by

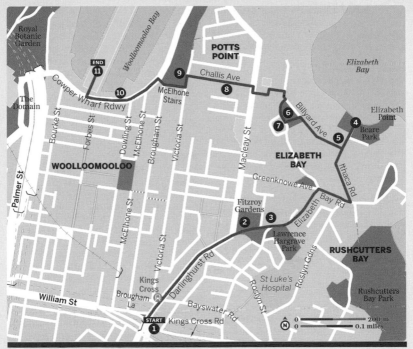

🏃 Neighbourhood Walk
A Risqué Ramble

START WILLIAM ST
END WOOLLOOMOOLOO FINGER WHARF
LENGTH 2.5KM; ONE HOUR

Start under the giant Coca-Cola sign at the William St overpass: the 'Top of the Cross'. It's this intersection, where the streets named after two kings cross, that gives this part of Potts Point its name (OK, so one's a queen but Monarchs Cross doesn't have the same ring). Behind you is Ken Unsworth's much-derided ❶ **Stones Against the Sky** sculpture. Locals call it 'Shits on Sticks', which is maybe why it's changed colour from brown to grey. Take a deep breath and follow Darlinghurst Rd into the dark heart of the Cross. If you don't want to make eye contact with any strip-club touts, dealers or hookers, scan the ground for a series of inscriptions offering titbits of local history. Continue to the spindly ❷ **El Alamein Fountain**.

Cut past the distinctive round ❸ **Gazebo tower**, turn left into Elizabeth Bay Rd and follow it downhill then sharply right at a roundabout. Turn left at Ithaca Rd and head

down to ❹ **Elizabeth Bay** itself, where there's a tiny park by the water.

Backtrack slightly and turn right into Billyard Ave, where you'll pass by the high walls of ❺ **Boomerang**, one of Australia's most expensive private houses. You'll know it by its distinctive multicoloured tiled roof and Spanish Mission stylings. Take the stairs on the left leading up to genteel ❻ **Arthur McElhone Reserve**. Beyond this little park is stately ❼ **Elizabeth Bay House**.

Turn right (downhill) and take the stairs just before 17 Billyard Ave. At the top turn right into Macleay St and then left into caffeinated Challis Ave, where you'll pass an impressive row of ❽ **colonnaded mansions**. At the bottom is ❾ **Embarkation Park**, with photogenic views over Woolloomooloo and the city.

Head down McElhone Stairs to Woolloomooloo, where ❿ **Harry's Cafe de Wheels** (p141) has been a Sydney institution since 1938. Refuel with a pie or continue onto ⓫ **Woolloomooloo Finger Wharf** for a classier finale.

coffee, chances are you'll recognise this tiny room as your spiritual home in the Cross. The food's limited to sandwiches, salads and such – tasty and uncomplicated.

PICCOLO BAR   CAFE $

Map p257 (www.piccolobar.com.au; 6 Roslyn St; mains $6-16; ⊙8am-4pm; 🛜; 🚇Kings Cross) A surviving slice of the old bohemian Cross, this tiny cafe hasn't changed much in over 60 years. The walls are covered in movie-star memorabilia, and Vittorio Bianchi still serves up strong coffee, omelettes and abrasive charm, as he's done for over 40 years.

GUZMAN Y GOMEZ   MEXICAN $

Map p257 (www.guzmanygomez.com; cnr Bayswater Rd & Pennys Ln; mains $7.50-15; ⊙11am-10pm Sun-Thu, to 4am Fri & Sat; 🚇Kings Cross) A branch of the Newtown *taqueria* (p117), offering quality takeaways for sloshy stomachs.

WILBUR'S PLACE   CAFE, BISTRO $$

Map p257 (www.wilbursplace.com; 36 Llankelly Pl; brunch $9-19, dinner $28; ⊙8am-3pm Sat, 5-9.30pm Tue-Sat; 🚇Kings Cross) With limited bench seating inside and a few tables on the lane, tiny Wilbur's is an informal spot for a quick bite on what's become the Cross' coolest cafe strip. Expect simple, straightforward food that is expertly assembled.

✖ Potts Point

ZINC   CAFE $

Map p257 (☑02-9358 6777; 77 Macleay St; breakfast $9-14, lunch $9-19; ⊙7am-4pm; 🖉; 🚇Kings Cross) Zinc was built on breakfasts, which remain excellent. But so are the tasty sandwiches and salads offered at lunchtime. The good-looking staff are full of smiles.

BOURKE STREET BAKERY   BAKERY $

Map p257 (www.bourkestreetbakery.com.au; 46a Macleay St; items $5-14; ⊙7am-4pm; 🚇Kings Cross) Its flagship Surry Hills bakery is a Sydney institution, so Potts Point locals were ecstatic when this new branch opened in one of their leafy side streets. Sit inside the bunkerlike space or claim one of the streetside tables, and enjoy a pie, quiche, sandwich, pastry or cake, accompanied by a good cup of coffee. Enter off Crick Ave.

★MS G'S   ASIAN $$

Map p257 (☑02-9240 3000; www.merivale.com/msgs; 155 Victoria St; mains $25-38; ⊙1-9pm Sun, noon-3pm Fri, 6-11pm Mon-Sat; 🚇Kings Cross) Offering a cheeky, irreverent take on Asian cooking (hence the name – geddit?), Ms G's is nothing if not an experience. It can be loud, frantic and painfully hip, but the adventurous combinations of pan-Asian and European flavours have certainly got Sydney talking.

★CHO CHO SAN   JAPANESE $$

Map p257 (☑02-9331 6601; www.chochosan.com.au; 73 Macleay St; mains $14-36; ⊙noon-3pm Fri-Sun, 6-11pm daily; 🚇Kings Cross) Glide through the shiny brass sliding door and take a seat at the polished-concrete communal table which runs the length of this stylish Japanese restaurant. The food is just as artful as the surrounds, with tasty *izakaya*-style bites emanating from both the raw bar and the hibachi grill.

APOLLO   GREEK $$

Map p257 (☑02-8354 0888; www.theapollo.com.au; 44 Macleay St; mains $26-34; ⊙6-11pm Mon-Thu, noon-11pm Fri & Sat, noon-9.30pm Sun; 🚇Kings Cross) An exemplar of modern Greek cooking, this taverna has fashionably minimalist decor, a well-priced menu of share plates and a bustling vibe. Starters are particularly impressive, especially the pitta bread hot from the oven, the fried *saganaki* cheese with honey and oregano, and the wild weed and cheese pie.

FRATELLI PARADISO   ITALIAN $$

Map p257 (www.fratelliparadiso.com; 12-16 Challis Ave; breakfast $12-14, mains $22-31; ⊙7am-11pm; 🚇Kings Cross) This underlit trattoria has them queuing at the door (especially on weekends). The intimate room showcases seasonal Italian dishes cooked with Mediterranean zing. Lots of busy black-clad waiters, lots of Italian chatter, lots of oversized sunglasses. No bookings.

YELLOW   MODERN AUSTRALIAN $$

Map p257 (☑02-9332 2344; www.yellowsydney.com.au; 57 Macleay St; brunch $14-20, mains $30-34; ⊙8am-3pm Sat & Sun, 6-11pm daily; 🚇Kings Cross) Once a sunflower-yellow symbol of all things Bohemian, this former artists' residence is now a top-notch contemporary restaurant serving sophisticated bistro dishes and, on the weekend, a mean brunch.

CAFE SOPRA ITALIAN $$
Map p257 (www.fratellifresh.com.au; 81 Macleay St; mains $20-30; ⊘noon-10pm; ⊛Kings Cross) Attached to the mightily impressive Fratelli Fresh providore, Sopra serves no-fuss, perfectly prepared Italian food in a bustling atmosphere. The blackboard menu changes seasonally, but some favourites (such as the fabulous *rigatoni alla bolognese*) are constants.

CHESTER WHITE ITALIAN $$
Map p257 (⊘02-9332 3692; 3 Orwell St; mains $12-20; ⊘5-11pm Wed & Thu, noon-11pm Fri & Sat; ⊛Kings Cross) Calling itself a 'cured diner', this diminutive corner eatery serves nine different kinds of cured meats, a large variety of pickled vegetables and a few simple mains (pasta and the like). Grab a chrome stool by the kitchen/bar, sip on an Italian wine and watch the hipster lads slicing and dicing away.

✗ Woolloomooloo

TOBY'S ESTATE CAFE $
Map p257 (⊘02-9358 1196; www.tobysestate. com.au; 129 Cathedral St; meals $10-15; ⊘7am-4pm; ⊛; ⊛St James) Coffee is undoubtedly the main event at this cool little charcoal-coloured roastery, but Toby's is also a great place for a quick sandwich, a veggie wrap or a fat muffin. And the caffeine? Strong, perfectly brewed and usually fair trade.

HARRY'S CAFE DE WHEELS FAST FOOD $
Map p257 (www.harryscafedewheels.com.au; Cowper Wharf Roadway; pies $5-7; ⊘8.30am-3am Mon-Sat, 9am-1am Sun; ⊛Kings Cross) Open since 1938 (except for a few years when founder Harry 'Tiger' Edwards was on active service), Harry's has been serving meat pies to everyone from Frank Sinatra to Colonel Sanders. You can't leave without trying a Tiger: a hot meat pie with sloppy peas, mashed potato, gravy and tomato sauce.

AKI'S INDIAN $$
Map p257 (⊘02-9332 4600; www.akisindian. com.au; 1/6 Cowper Wharf Roadway; mains $22-36; ⊘noon-10pm Sun-Fri, 6-10.30pm Sat; ⊘; ⊛Kings Cross) The first cab off the rank as you walk onto Woolloomooloo's wharf is Aki's. And you need walk no further: this is beautifully presented, intuitively constructed high-Indian cuisine, supple-

mented by a six-page wine list showcasing local and international drops.

OTTO RISTORANTE ITALIAN $$$
Map p257 (⊘02-9368 7488; www.ottoristorante. com.au; 8/6 Cowper Wharf Roadway; mains $41-59; ⊘noon-3pm & 6-11pm; ⊛Kings Cross) Forget the glamorous waterfront location and the A-list crowd – Otto will be remembered for single-handedly dragging Sydney's Italian cooking into the new century with dishes such as *strozzapreti con gamberi* (artisan pasta with fresh Yamba prawns, tomato, chilli and black olives). Bookings essential.

CHINA DOLL ASIAN $$$
Map p257 (⊘02-9380 6744; www.chinadoll.com. au; 4/6 Cowper Wharf Roadway; mains $34-46; ⊘noon-2.30pm & 6pm-late; ⊛Kings Cross) Gaze over the Woolloomooloo marina and city skyline as you tuck into deliciously inventive dishes drawing inspiration from all over Asia. Plates are designed to be shared, although waiters can arrange half serves for solo diners.

🍺 DRINKING & NIGHTLIFE

Traditionally Sydney's premier party precinct, this neighbourhood has stacks of bars ranging from snug locals to superslick posing palaces to raucous booze barns. However, it's been hard-hit by the central Sydney licensing laws introduced in 2014 resulting in 1.30am lockouts and a ban on alcohol service after 3am. Many of the late-night clubs are soldiering on regardless, but some of the heat has moved elsewhere. On the upside, the streets look less like a war zone in the wee hours and certainly feel safer.

🍺 Kings Cross

★**KINGS CROSS HOTEL** PUB, CLUB
Map p257 (www.kingscrosshotel.com.au; 244-248 William St; ⊘noon-1am Sun-Thu, to 3am Fri & Sat; ⊛Kings Cross) With five floors above ground and one below, this grand old pub is a hive of boozy entertainment which positively swarms on weekends. Head up to the roof bar for awesome city views, or drop by the 2nd-floor band room for a blast of live music.

LOCAL KNOWLEDGE

KINGS CROSS CONFIDENTIAL

Mandy Sayer, author of several books set in Kings Cross, on the neighbourhood's raffish charm.

The Soho of Sydney

Every great city has a racy, raffish, artistic village: Paris has Montmartre, New York has The Village, London has Soho, and Sydney has Kings Cross. As an aspiring writer growing up in the area, I discovered my first and most enduring muse: the pulsing vivid neon signs; the buskers and prostitutes; the strip clubs; the many artists, actors and musicians who shared crumbling terrace houses. It also had a history of crime and corruption, dating back to the razor gangs that roamed the back lanes in the early 20th century.

Every Outsider is an Insider

Today the terraces are no longer crumbling but Kings Cross is still known predominantly for its nightlife. The village embraces all sorts of residents, from the loose posse of homeless people on Darlinghurst Rd, to authors and film-makers, to dealers and pimps, to lawyers and doctors, to ex–prime ministers. It's a superlative place for people-watching, which is why I still live here.

Insider Tips

A stroll along Macleay St will reveal some of the most stunning art-deco architecture in Australia, while a walk down Victoria St, below a leafy cathedral of trees, showcases some of the colony's first Victorian houses; and at the end of the street is one of the most breathtaking panoramas of Sydney Harbour. Some venues I'd recommend: Piccolo Bar (p140), a tiny bohemian cafe dating back to the early 1950s; the outdoor restaurants and bars along Kellett St, strung with magical fairy lights; the Old Fitzroy, for an old-fashioned English pub experience; **LL Wine & Dine** (Map p257; ☑02-9356 8393; www.llwineanddine.com.au; 42 Llankelly Pl; mains $27-32; ⊙5-11pm Tue-Fri, 11am-10pm Sat & Sun; ℞Kings Cross), for fine Asian dining and great service; and Hinky Dinks (p132), for luscious cocktails and 1950s ambience.

WORLD BAR   BAR, CLUB

Map p257 (☑02-9357 7700; www.theworldbar.com; 24 Bayswater Rd; ⊙3pm-3am; ℞Kings Cross) World Bar (a reformed bordello) is an unpretentious grungy club with three floors to lure in the backpackers and cheap drinks to loosen things up. DJs play indie, hip hop, power pop and house nightly. There are live bands on Fridays, but Wednesday (The Wall) and Saturday (Cakes) are the big nights.

SUGARMILL   BAR

Map p257 (www.sugarmill.com.au; 33 Darlinghurst Rd; ⊙10am-5am; ℞Kings Cross) For a bloated, late-night, Kings Cross bar, Sugarmill is actually pretty cool. Columns and high pressed-tin ceilings hint at its banking past, while the band posters plastered everywhere do their best to dispel any lingering capitalist vibes. Ten-dollar meals and drag queen–hosted bingo nights pull in the locals. For barbecue with a view, head to **Sweethearts** (www.sweetheartsbbq.com.au) on the rooftop.

KIT & KABOODLE   CLUB

Map p257 (www.kitkaboodle.com.au; 33 Darlinghurst Rd; ⊙8pm-late Thu-Sun; ℞Kings Cross) The club above Sugarmill comes into its own on a Sunday night, when hospitality workers take advantage of the cheap drinks to kick-start their belated weekend.

🍷 Potts Point

SOHO   BAR, CLUB

Map p257 (www.sohobar.com.au; 171 Victoria St; ⊙10am-midnight Mon-Wed, to 4am Thu & Sun, to 6am Fri & Sat; ℞Kings Cross) Housed in the art deco Piccadilly Hotel, Soho is a dark, sexy establishment with smooth leather lounges that have felt the weight of Keanu Reeves', Nicole Kidman's and Ewan McGregor's celebrity booties; it's rumoured to be where Kylie met Michael Hutchence. The downstairs club hosts regular events.

BOOTLEG BAR

Map p257 (www.bootlegbar.com.au; 175 Victoria St; ⏱5-11pm Sun, Tue & Wed, to 1am Thu-Sat; ⓡKings Cross) If you're looking for a quieter, more sophisticated alternative to the Darlinghurst Rd melee (or just a chance to catch your breath), slink into a booth at this bar-cum-Italian eatery and order a wine from the list. The decor's a strange mix of industrial chic and Chicago lounge bar, but it works.

JIMMY LIK'S COCKTAIL BAR

Map p257 (☎02-8354 1400; www.jimmyliks. com; 188 Victoria St; ⏱5-11pm Mon-Thu, noon-midnight Fri-Sun; ⓡKings Cross) Understated, slim and subtle, Jimmy's is very cool, with benches almost as long as the Southeast Asian–influenced cocktail list (try a Mekong Mary with vodka, tomato juice and chilli *nahm jim*).

ⓨ Woolloomooloo

★OLD FITZROY HOTEL PUB

Map p257 (www.oldfitzroy.com.au; 129 Dowling St; ⏱11am-midnight Mon-Sat, 3-10pm Sun; 🛜; ⓡKings Cross) Islington meets Melbourne in the backstreets of Woolloomooloo: this totally unpretentious theatre pub is also a decent old-fashioned boozer in its own right. Prop up the bar, grab a seat at a streetside table or head upstairs to the bistro, pool table and couches.

WATERBAR BAR

Map p257 (www.waterbaratblue.com; 6 Cowper Wharf Roadway; ⏱5-10pm Sun & Mon, to midnight Tue-Sat; ⓡKings Cross) After a few martinis in the heart of Woolloomooloo's

Finger Wharf, time becomes meaningless and escape pointless. This lofty romantic space sucks you in to its pink-love world of candles, corners, deep lounges and ottomans as big as beds. Great for business (if you really must), but better for lurve.

TILBURY PUB

Map p257 (☎02-9368 1955; www.tilbury hotel.com.au; 12-18 Nicholson St; ⏱11am-11pm; ⓡKings Cross) Once the dank domain of burly sailors and salty ne'er-do-wells, the Tilbury now sparkles. Yuppies, yachties, suits, gays and straights alike populate the light, bright interiors. The restaurant, bar and gin garden are particularly popular on lazy Sunday afternoons. And sailors can still get a beer!

☆ ENTERTAINMENT

EL ROCCO JAZZ, COMEDY

Map p257 (www.elrocco.com.au; 154 Brougham St; ⏱5pm-midnight Mon-Sat, to 10pm Sun; ⓡKings Cross) Between 1955 and 1969 this was the city's premier finger-snappin', beret-wearing boho cellar bar, hosting performances by Frank Sinatra and Sarah Vaughan. Those heady days are long gone but live jazz is back on the agenda, along with the **Happy Endings Comedy Club** (www.happyendingscomedyclub.com.au) on Saturday nights.

OLD FITZ THEATRE THEATRE

Map p257 (www.oldfitztheatre.com; 129 Dowling St; ⓡKings Cross) Is it a pub? A theatre? A bistro? Actually, it's all three. Grassroots company Red Line Productions stages loads of new Australian plays here.

Paddington & Centennial Park

PADDINGTON | WOOLLAHRA | CENTENNIAL PARK | MOORE PARK

Neighbourhood Top Five

1 Engaging in a seriously fashionable shopping spree, window or otherwise, in Paddington's boutiques. **Paddington Markets** (p153) is a good place to start.

2 Exploring the vast open space within the gated grounds of **Centennial Park** (p146).

3 Screaming yourself hoarse at a Roosters game at **Sydney Football Stadium** (p155).

4 Hopping between galleries, both commercial and altruistic, including the **Australian Centre for Photography** (p146).

5 Spreading out a picnic under the stars at **Moonlight Cinema** (p152).

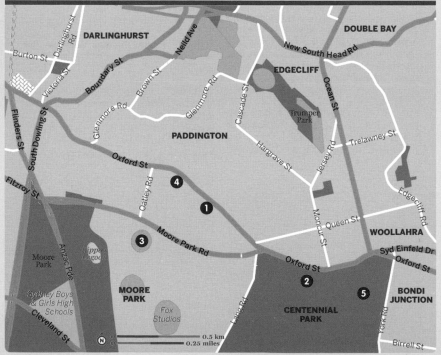

For more detail of this area, see Map p258 ➡

Explore: Paddington & Centennial Park

Paddington, also known as 'Paddo', is an elegant, expensive area of beautifully restored terrace houses and steep leafy streets where fashionable folks drift between designer shops, chic restaurants, art galleries and bookshops. Built over an ancient walking track used by the Gadigal people, the suburb's pulsing artery is Oxford St. The best time to visit is on Saturday, when the markets are at their most effervescent. Rugged bushland until the 1860s, Paddington was built for aspiring Victorian artisans, but following the lemming-like rush to quarter-acre blocks in the outer suburbs after WWII, it became one of Australia's worst slums. A renewed passion for Victorian architecture (and the realisation that the outer suburbs were unspeakably boring) led to Paddington's resurgence in the 1960s. By the 1990s real estate here was beyond all but the lucky and loaded.

In contrast to Paddington, Woollahra was never a slum. This is upper-crust Sydney at its finest: leafy streets, mansions, wall-to-wall BMWs and antique shops. Maybe this is your bag; maybe it isn't – either way, an afternoon here is socially enlightening.

South of Oxford St, the Centennial Parklands spread a giant green blanket over 360 hectares, from Surry Hills to Waverley, enclosing a cluster of famous sports venues.

Local Life

→ **Sports** The cheering, swearing hordes come out in force to support the local lads at the Sydney Football Stadium and Sydney Cricket Ground.

→ **Five Ways** This five-way intersection north of Oxford St is the real heart of the neighbourhood.

→ **Fitness** Sit in Centennial Park for long enough and it will seem like half the neighbourhood has passed by in one big jogging/cycling/in-line-skating blur.

Getting There & Away

→ **Bus** Buses are the main public-transport mode in these parts. Major routes include 355 (Bondi Junction to Newtown via Lang Rd), 373 (Circular Quay to Coogee via Moore Park), 378 (Railway Sq to Bronte via Oxford St), 380 (Circular Quay to Watsons Bay via Oxford St and Bondi) and 389 (Circular Quay to North Bondi via Glenmore Rd, Moncur and Queen Sts).

→ **Train** Walk downhill from Kings Cross or Edgecliff station to Rushcutters Bay and the Paddington and Woollahra lowlands; or from Bondi Junction station to the eastern reaches of Centennial Park.

→ **Car** Street parking is generally possible, although it's usually metered and limited in duration.

Lonely Planet's Top Tip

The street numbers on Oxford St reset themselves with each new suburb. Oxford St Darlinghurst becomes Oxford St Paddington east of Barcom St, which becomes Oxford St Woollahra at Jersey Rd. This can be extremely confusing; if you're looking for the Arts Hotel at 21 Oxford St, for instance, make sure you're in Paddington or you may end up ringing the bell of a private house in Bondi Junction or a gay newspaper in Darlinghurst.

PADDINGTON & CENTENNIAL PARK

✗ Best Places to Eat

→ Four In Hand (p151)
→ Chiswick Restaurant (p151)
→ Vincent (p151)
→ Sonoma (p150)
→ Buon Ricordo (p151)

For reviews, see p150 ➡

☐ Best Places to Drink

→ Wine Library (p152)
→ 10 William Street (p151)
→ Royal Hotel (p151)
→ Lord Dudley Hotel (p152)
→ Four In Hand (p151)

For reviews, see p151 ➡

🔒 Best Places to Shop

→ Paddington Markets (p153)
→ Ariel (p153)
→ Capital L (p153)
→ Corner Shop (p153)
→ Dinosaur Designs (p154)

For reviews, see p153 ➡

◉ SIGHTS

◉ Paddington

VICTORIA BARRACKS
HISTORIC SITE

Map p258 (☏02-8335 5170; www.armymuseum nsw.com.au; Oxford St; ⊙tours 10am Thu; ☐380) FREE A manicured vision from the peak of the British Empire (built 1841 to 1848), these Georgian army barracks have been called the finest of their kind in the colonies. The site is still an active army base, so entry is only possible on a free guided tour. You'll usually get to see a marching band perform (weather permitting) and afterwards you can visit the on-site Army Museum of NSW ($2). Good disabled access.

PADDINGTON RESERVOIR GARDENS
PARK

Map p258 (cnr Oxford St & Oatley Rd; ☐380) 🌿 Opened to much architectural acclaim in 2008, this impressive park makes use of Paddington's long-abandoned 1866 water reservoir, incorporating the brick arches and surviving chamber into an interesting green space featuring a sunken garden, a pond, a boardwalk and lawns. They've even preserved some of the graffiti dating from the many years when it was boarded up and abandoned to feral cats and stealthy spray-can artists.

JUNIPER HALL
HISTORIC BUILDING

Map p258 (www.juniperhall.com.au; 250 Oxford St; ⊙shop 9am-5pm Mon-Fri, gallery 10am-5pm Wed-Sun; ☐380) Australia's oldest villa (1824), this restored Georgian mansion was built by Robert Cooper with profits from his gin business (he named it after the essential gin-making ingredient). The Historic Houses Association of Australia has a small shop downstairs, selling Australian-made gifts and dispensing information about the house. The other main tenant is the Moran Arts Foundation, the gallery of which exhibits the annual Moran Art Prizes (for portraiture and photography).

AUSTRALIAN CENTRE FOR PHOTOGRAPHY
GALLERY

Map p258 (ACP; ☏02-9332 0555; www.acp.org.au; 257 Oxford St; ⊙10am-5pm Tue-Sat, noon-5pm Sun; ☐380) FREE The nonprofit ACP exhibits photographic gems from renowned Sydney and international photographers. It's particularly passionate about photo-media, video and digital-imaging works.

SHERMAN CONTEMPORARY ART FOUNDATION
GALLERY

Map p258 (☏02-9331 1112; www.sherman-scaf.org.au; 16 Goodhope St; ⊙11am-5pm Wed-Sat, closed Jan & Feb; ☐389) FREE After 21 years as a cutting-edge commercial gallery, Sherman celebrated its coming-of-age by reopening as a not-for-profit gallery. The focus is on temporary exhibitions of work by influential and innovative artists from Australia, the Asia-Pacific region and the Middle East.

NEILD AVENUE MAZE
PARK

Map p258 (Neild Ave; ⚆Kings Cross) FREE This tiny maze of thigh-high hedges hides behind a gargantuan plane tree on a Paddington backstreet, squished into a cranny between a textile showroom and someone's back fence. It mightn't take you forever to find your way through, but it will add a smile to your day.

RUSHCUTTERS BAY PARK
PARK

Map p258 (New South Head Rd; ⚆Edgecliff) Surrounded by enormous Moreton Bay fig trees, luxury yachts and pampered pooches, this unpretentious waterfront park is a beaut spot for a quiet stroll, jog or tennis grudge-match. In December the world's greatest yachties prepare for the gruelling Sydney to Hobart race here.

◉ Woollahra

QUEEN STREET
AREA

Map p258 (Queen St; ☐389) Despite its status as the premier antique-shopping strip in Australia (the first shop opened in 1957), Queen St retains a village vibe, with pricey boutiques, delis, summer chestnuts hanging heavy on the bough and kids who say, 'Hey, nice Ferrari!'. There was once a famous annual street fair here, until noise-phobic residents shut it down in the early 1980s.

◉ Centennial Park & Moore Park

CENTENNIAL PARK
PARK

Map p258 (☏02-9339 6699; www.centennial parklands.com.au; Oxford St; ⚆Bondi Junction) Scratched out of the sand in 1888 in grand Victorian style, Sydney's biggest park is a rambling 189-hectare expanse full of horse riders, joggers, cyclists and in-line skaters. During summer Moonlight Cinema (p152) attracts the crowds. Among the wide

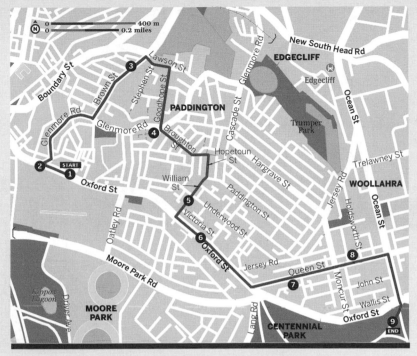

Neighbourhood Walk
Fashionable Footsteps

START VICTORIA BARRACKS
END CENTENNIAL PARK
LENGTH 3.6KM; ONE HOUR

This walk should take around an hour, not including Centennial Park, extended shopping frenzies or getting lost in the Neild Avenue maze. The old **①Victoria Barracks** are still an active army base, so unless you join the tour you'll have to ogle the impressive Georgian sandstone structures from the guarded gates. Cross Oxford St, turn left and head down to **②Glenmore Rd** where temptation comes in the form of sassy boutiques. The boutiques eventually give way to the beautiful Victorian terraced houses which are a defining feature of the neighbourhood.

Follow the curves of Glenmore Rd for several blocks then jag downhill on Brown St to the cute **③Neild Avenue maze**. Turn right into Lawson St, then take the second right into Goodhope St and continue to **④Five Ways** – a roundabout at the confluence of five roads. Oxford St may be the main drag, but the quirky cafes, galleries,

shops and pub here make it the hip heart of Paddington.

From Five Ways, head uphill along Broughton St, turn right into Hopetoun St and follow it around to the bottom of **⑤William St**. This photogenic side street has sprouted a strip of classy boutiques.

Turn left onto **⑥Oxford St**, Sydney's fashionista freeway. Local and international designers fill the shopfronts, selling swanky threads for ladies and lads. Cafes, pubs and homewares stores join the competition to prise the credit card from your wallet.

At the eastern end of the strip hang left into Queen St, the beginning of upmarket Woollahra. Boutiques give way to antique stores and providores as you head downhill. **⑦Simon Johnson** at number 55 sometimes has tastings – drop in for a nibble. At number 132, **⑧Victor Churchill** may look like another boutique but its actually a butcher's – the flashest butcher's you'll ever see. Turn right into Ocean St and head back up to Oxford St. Cross the road and enter the leafy folds of **⑨Centennial Park**.

OLIVER STREWE / GETTY IMAGES ©

1. Dinosaur Designs (p154)
Pick up a statement piece at this vibrant jewellery and homewares shop.

2. Paddington Markets (p153)
Support local designers and craftspeople at this ever-popular market.

3. Paddington Reservoir Gardens (p146)
An abandoned 19th-century reservoir has been transformed into an award-winning green space.

4. William St (p153)
This Paddington street is a premier shopping spot for fashion and home furnishings.

LOCAL KNOWLEDGE

FLYING FOXINESS

If you cast an eye to the twilight sky, don't be surprised if a great black cloud of bats drifts into view. The silent, spectral swoop of fruitbats on the wing might make you want to cower behind a crucifix, but there's really nothing to fear – they'd rather suck on one of Centennial Park's Moreton Bay figs than your jugular. The only damage they're likely to inflict is on the paintwork of your car (their droppings are incredibly corrosive).

These bats are grey-headed flying foxes (*Pteropus ploiocephalus*), and they're an important part of Sydney's ecology, spreading seeds and pollinating flowers as they feed. Unlike other bats, flying foxes don't live in caves, don't use echolocation and can't see particularly well in the dark. Neither do they fly in a jerky manner like their smaller cousins, but rather use their metre-wide wingspan to glide around gracefully, much like birds do. For more information on these critters, check out www.sydneybats.org.au.

formal avenues, ponds and statues is the domed **Federation Pavilion** (Grand Dr) – the spot where Australia was officially proclaimed a nation (on 1 January 1901) – surrounded by the various state flags. **Centennial Parklands Dining** (www.cpdining.com.au; Grand Dr; breakfast $16-21, lunch $19-32, kiosk snacks $5-14; ⊘7am-5pm; ⍰378-380), near the centre of the park, encompasses a cafe, wine bar and kiosk. At the southern edge of the park is Royal Randwick Racecourse (p155), while on its eastern edge the park joins Queens Park.

ENTERTAINMENT QUARTER　　　AREA
Map p258 (☑02-8117 6700; www.eqmoorepark.com.au; 122 Lang Rd; ⍰355) If we were feeling cynical, we might say that the purpose-built Entertainment Quarter is a vacuous, self-perpetuating specimen of lightweight global commercialism, but we'll try to restrain ourselves. Instead, we'll just say that its palm-lined avenues, cinemas, bowling alley, laser strike and markets are a good distraction for the kids. Fox Studios is next door.

MOORE PARK　　　PARK
Map p258 (☑02-9339 6699; www.centennial parklands.com.au; Anzac Pde; ⍰Central) Part of the broader Centennial Parklands, Moore Park covers 115 hectares south of Paddington. With sports fields, tennis courts, an 18-hole public golf course and a site for visiting circuses, there's plenty here to keep you off the streets. The broader precinct also includes the homes of the Sydney Swans Aussie Rules team (the historic Sydney Cricket Ground; p155), the Sydney City Roosters rugby-league team (the Sydney Football Stadium; p155) and the Sydney Mardi Gras Party (Hordern Pavilion; p153) – try not to get them confused! The Entertainment Quarter (p150) spices up the mix.

✕ EATING

This conservative enclave has traditionally offered good eating that shies away from the aggressively modern tendencies of its neighbours – reliable places where the just-so steak paired with the perfect wine is done to perfection and the service is well mannered to match.

✕ Paddington

SONOMA　　　CAFE $
Map p258 (www.sonoma.com.au; 241 Glenmore Rd; mains $6-18; ⊘7am-3pm; ⍰389) 'Artisan sourdough' is the speciality of this mini-chain of bakery-cafes, and the toast with ricotta and the sourdough sandwiches are suitably impressive. There are also branches in Woollahra, Glebe and Bondi.

AMPERSAND CAFE & BOOKSTORE　　CAFE $
Map p258 (☑02-9380 6617; www.facebook.com/AmpersandCafeBookstore; 78 Oxford St; mains $9-17; ⊘7.30am-5pm Mon-Sat, 9am-5pm Sun; ⍰380) Which are better, the books or the cooks? Either way, you're guaranteed to find a good read (30,000 books over three floors) and a good coffee here. Cooked breakfasts, burgers, salads and mezze plates round out the experience.

POPOLO　　　ITALIAN $$
Map p258 (☑02-9361 6641; www.popolo.com.au; 50 McLachlan Ave; breakfast $14-18, mains $21-29; ⊘6-10.30pm Tue-Thu, noon-10.30pm Fri, 8am-10.30pm Sat & Sun; ⍰Kings Cross) Handsome, thickly accented, occasionally arrogant Italian waiters glide about distributing delicious pizza, pasta and, on the weekends, inventive breakfasts to an

adoring clientele. It's set back from a luxury car dealership (naturally) on its own sunny square – or should that be piazza.

FOUR IN HAND   MODERN AUSTRALIAN $$$
Map p258 (☑02-9362 1999; www.fourinhand. com.au; 105 Sutherland St; mains $34-42; ☺noon-2.30pm & 6pm-late Tue-Sun; ☒Edgecliff) You can't go far in Paddington without tripping over a beautiful old pub with amazing food. This is the best of them, famous for its slow-cooked and nose-to-tail meat dishes, although it also offers fabulously fresh seafood dishes and a delectable array of desserts. The bar menu (mains $19 to $29) is a more affordable option.

BUON RICORDO   ITALIAN $$$
Map p258 (☑02-9360 6729; www.buonri cordo.com.au; 108 Boundary St; mains $34-58; ☺noon-2.30pm Fri & Sat, 6.30-10.30pm Tue-Sat, supper to midnight; ☒Kings Cross) You'd need a very *buon ricordo* (good memory) to recall exactly when this Italian stalwart first opened its doors (sometime in the shoulder-pad era), but the critics never forget chef Armando Percuoco when it comes to awarding fine-dining accolades. The menu reflects his Neapolitan origins.

✗ Woollahra

VINCENT   FRENCH $$
Map p258 (☑02-8039 1500; www.vincentfrench. com.au; 14 Queen St; mains $26-36; ☺noon-3pm Fri-Sun, 6-11pm Tue-Sun; ☒380) The glassed-in terrace of the Hughenden Hotel is the charmingly informal setting for this zippy bistro. The menu is excellent, revelling in classics such as cheesy souffles, rich terrines, steak *frites* topped with butter, and fall-apart slow-roasted lamb shoulder.

CHISWICK RESTAURANT   MODERN AUSTRALIAN $$$
Map p258 (☑02-8388 8633; www.chiswick restaurant.com.au; 65 Ocean St; mains $31-38; ☺noon-2.30pm & 6-10pm; ☒389) There may be a celebrity at centre stage (TV regular Matt Moran) but the real star of this show is the pretty kitchen garden, which wraps around the dining room and dictates what's on the menu. Meat from the Moran family farm and local seafood feature prominently too.

BISTRO MONCUR   FRENCH $$$
Map p258 (☑02-9327 9713; www.woollahrahotel. com.au; 116 Queen St; mains $30-45; ☺noon-3pm & 6-10pm; ☒389) Minimoguls and luncheon ladies while away afternoons beneath Bistro Moncur's vaulted ceilings and monochromatic mural. The menu changes seasonally, but signature dishes such as French onion soufflé gratin and Cafe-de-Paris sirloin delight diners year-round. The wine list will make you want to become a mogul.

♥ DRINKING & NIGHTLIFE

Some cool Darlinghurst-style bars spill over into Paddington, but generally this area is a little more refined – and a lot less interesting. Any pretension dissolves when the sports fans pour out of the nearby Sydney Cricket Ground and Sydney Football Stadium and pack into Paddo's pubs.

♥ Paddington

10 WILLIAM STREET   WINE BAR
Map p258 (www.10williamst.com.au; 10 William St; ☺5pm-midnight Mon-Thu, noon-midnight Fri & Sat; ☒380) The Italian boys behind Potts Point's Fratelli Paradiso (p140) are behind this *minuscolo* slice of *la dolce vita* on the fashion strip. Expect excellent imported wines and equally impressive food.

ROYAL HOTEL   PUB
Map p258 (www.royalhotel.com.au; 237 Glenmore Rd; ☺noon-midnight Mon-Sat, to 10pm Sun; ☒389) One of the points on a five-pointed, road-junction star, this beautifully renovated pub is spread over four floors. At the top, both the Elephant Bar and the rooftop enjoy views over the city skyline.

PADDINGTON INN   PUB
Map p258 (www.paddingtoninn.com.au; 338 Oxford St; ☺noon-midnight Mon-Sat, to 10pm Sun; ☒380) The Paddo seems to get a new look every few years, perhaps in keeping with its prime fashion-strip position. Eager locals elbow around the pool table and get stuck into $12 weekday lunches and two-for-one Tuesday meals.

IMPERIAL HOTEL   PUB
Map p258 (www.imperialhotelpaddington.com. au; 252 Oxford St; ☺10am-midnight Mon-Sat, to 10pm Sun; ☒380) This neighbourhood watering hole offers a stylish interior, solicitous service, an extensive wine list and good pub grub.

LONDON   PUB

Map p258 (☎02-9331 3200; www.hotellondon.com.au; 85 Underwood St; ☺noon-midnight Mon-Sat, to 10pm Sun; 🚇380) Among the designer boutique shops of William St, the London draws a fashionable crowd that heads upstairs for a burger or lobster roll. Downstairs punters vie for a stool to watch – or try to ignore – sport on the big screen.

🍷 Woollahra

WINE LIBRARY   WINE BAR

Map p258 (www.wine-library.com.au; 18 Oxford St; ☺noon-11.30pm Mon-Sat, to 10pm Sun; 🚇380) An impressive range of wines by the glass, a smart-casual ambience and a Mediterranean-inclined menu make this the most desirable library in town.

LORD DUDLEY HOTEL   PUB

Map p258 (☎02-9327 5399; www.lorddudley.com.au; 236 Jersey Rd; ☺11am-11pm; 🚉Edgecliff) Popular with rich older geezers and block-shouldered rugby-union types, the Lord Dudley is as close to an English country pub as Sydney gets. Dark woody walls and 18 quality beers on tap, served by the pint.

LIGHT BRIGADE   PUB

Map p258 (☎02-9357 0888; www.lightbrigade.com.au; 2a Oxford St; ☺11am-midnight Mon-Sat, to 10pm Sun; 🚇380) Charge into this curvy art deco pub for its relaxed ground-floor sports bar with a good-value menu ($12 weekday lunch), a pool table, and lots of black tiles and angular stainless steel. Upstairs beyond a huge clock face is chic Italian restaurant and cocktail bar **La Scala On Jersey** (Map p258; ☎02-9357 0815; www.lascalaonjersey.com.au; cnr Jersey Rd & Melrose Lane; mains $28-38; ☺6-11pm Mon-Sat; 🚇380).

WORTH A DETOUR

NIDA

The former stomping ground of Mel Gibson, Cate Blanchett and Geoffrey Rush, the **National Institute of Dramatic Art** (☎02-9697 7600; www.nida.edu.au; 215 Anzac Pde, Randwick; 🚇M50) stage is the place to see stars on the way up. Student and graduate plays happen throughout the year in four intimate performance spaces.

WOOLLAHRA HOTEL   PUB

Map p258 (☎02-9327 9777; www.woollahrahotel.com.au; 116 Queen St; ☺noon-midnight Mon-Sat, to 10pm Sun; 🚇389) It's a bit suity most of the time, but this sports pub is worth checking out for the open-air terrace and the live music on Sunday and Thursday evenings.

☆ ENTERTAINMENT

MOONLIGHT CINEMA   CINEMA

Map p258 (www.moonlight.com.au; Belvedere Amphitheatre, cnr Loch & Broome Aves; adult/child $19/15; ☺sunset Dec-Mar; 🚉Bondi Junction) Take a picnic and join the bats under the stars in magnificent Centennial Park; enter via the Woollahra Gate on Oxford St. A mix of new-release blockbuster, art-house and classic films is screened.

CHAUVEL CINEMA   CINEMA

Map p258 (☎02-9361 5398; www.chauvelcinema.net.au; 249 Oxford St; adult/child $19/14; ☺sessions 10am-9.45pm; 🚇380) Located inside the historic Paddington Town Hall, the Chauvel strives to offer distinctive and alternative cinema experiences, and to foster Sydney's film culture. It plays host to various quirky film festivals.

PALACE VERONA   CINEMA

Map p258 (☎02-9360 6099; www.palacecinemas.com.au; 17 Oxford St; adult/child $19/14; ☺sessions 10am-9pm; ☎; 🚇380) This urbane four-screen cinema has a cool cafe and bar, useful for discussing the merits of the arty flick you've just seen.

HOYTS ENTERTAINMENT QUARTER   CINEMA

Map p258 (☎02-9003 3870; www.hoyts.com.au; Bent St; adult/child $20/15; ☺sessions 9.30am-9.30pm; 🚇355) This hefty movie complex has more than a dozen cinemas, including an IMAX screen and Hoyts Lux, the cinematic equivalent of a 1st-class cabin, with waiter service, lounge chairs, bar access, soft drinks and popcorn included ($35). Art-house films and ethnic film festivals screen in **Cinema Paris** (Map p258; ☎02-9003 3870; www.hoyts.com.au; Bent St; adult/child $20/15; ☺sessions 9.30am-9.30pm; 🚇355), just down Bent St.

COMEDY STORE   COMEDY

Map p258 (☎02-9357 1419; www.comedystore.com.au; Suttor Ave; tickets $10-32; ☺from 8.30pm Thu-Sat; 🚇355) This purpose-built comedy venue lures big-time Australian and overseas stand-ups, and nurtures new talent with open-mic and new-comic nights. US, Irish and Edinburgh Festival performers have 'em rolling in the aisles on a regular basis. Bookings advisable.

HORDERN PAVILION CONCERT VENUE
Map p258 (www.playbillvenues.com; 1 Driver Ave; 373-377) Holding over 5000 heaving music fans, the historic white and grey Hordern (1924) hosts plenty of big-name rock gigs (Smashing Pumpkins, Sam Smith, The Kooks) and, along with neighbouring halls, the massive Mardi Gras Party.

🛍 SHOPPING

As well as three of Sydney's premier shopping strips – Oxford St and William St in Paddington (fashion and homewares) and Queen St in Woollahra (antiques and fashion) – this area also secretes dozens of commercial art galleries in its back streets.

🛍 Paddington

PADDINGTON MARKETS MARKET
Map p258 (www.paddingtonmarkets.com.au; 395 Oxford St; 10am-4pm Sat; 380) Originating in the 1970s, when they were drenched in the scent of patchouli oil, these markets are considerably more mainstream these days. They're still worth exploring for their new and vintage clothing, crafts and jewellery. Expect a crush.

ARIEL BOOKS
Map p258 (02-9332 4581; www.arielbooks. com.au; 42 Oxford St; 9am-10.30pm; 380) Furtive artists, architects and students roam Ariel's aisles late into the evening. 'Underculture' is the thrust here – glossy art, film, fashion and design books, along with kids' books, travel guides and a queer-lit section.

BERKELOUW BOOKS BOOKS
Map p258 (02-9360 3200; www.berkelouw. com.au; 19 Oxford St; 9am-9.45pm; 380) Expecting the dank aroma of secondhand books? Forget it! Follow your nose up to the cafe, then browse through three floors of preloved tomes, new releases, antique maps and Australia's largest collection of rare books. The Berkelouws have specialised in secondhand books and printed rarities over six generations since setting up shop in Holland in 1812.

CAPITAL L FASHION
Map p258 (02-9361 0111; www.capital-l.com; 100 Oxford St; 10.30am-6pm; Kings Cross) This attractive boutique stocks women's clothing by up-and-coming Australian designers. Hip sales staff break from tradition and actually help you find and try on clothes.

CORNER SHOP FASHION
Map p258 (02-9380 9828; www.thecorner-shop.com.au; 43 William St; 10am-6pm Mon-Sat, noon-5pm Sun; 380) This treasure trove of a boutique is stocked with a healthy mix of casual and high-end women's clothing from Australian and international designers, with some jewellery for good measure.

POEPKE FASHION
Map p258 (www.poepke.com; 47 William St; 10am-6pm Mon-Sat, noon-5pm Sun; 380) One of Paddington's more interesting women's boutiques, stocking a curated range from Australian and international designers.

LEONA EDMISTON FASHION
Map p258 (www.leonaedmiston.com; 88 William St; noon-6pm Sun-Tue, 10am-6pm Wed-Sat; 380) Leona Edmiston knows frocks – from little and black to whimsically floral or all-out sexy. Her exuberantly feminine, flirtatious and fun designs are cut from the best cotton, silk and jersey fabrics in colours that range from luscious, sophisticated reds to pinstripes and polka dots. Also at Westfield Bondi Junction, Westfield Sydney, Chifley Plaza and the Strand Arcade.

SASS & BIDE FASHION
Map p258 (www.sassandbide.com; 132 Oxford St; 10am-6pm Fri-Wed, to 8pm Thu; 380) A local success story with boutiques in New York and Auckland, Sass & Bide is known for its sassy low-cut women's jeans, body-hugging jackets and well-constructed dresses. There are further branches in Westfield Sydney and Bondi Junction, and the Strand Arcade.

SCANLAN THEODORE FASHION
Map p258 (02-9380 9388; www.scanlantheo-dore.com.au; 122 Oxford St; 380) Scanlan Theodore excels at beautifully made and finely silhouetted women's outfits for evening or the office. Sophisticated patterns and colours complement fabrics you just can't help but fondle.

154

SHOPPING PADDINGTON & CENTENNIAL PARK

ZIMMERMANN CLOTHING
Map p258 (www.zimmermannwear.com; 2-16 Glenmore Rd; ⊙10am-6pm; 🚇380) Chic and cheeky women's street clothes and swimwear from sisters Nicky and Simone Zimmermann. There are other stores in the Sydney and Bondi Junction Westfields.

CALIBRE FASHION
Map p258 (📞02-9380 5993; www.calibre.com. au; 398 Oxford St; ⊙9.30am-6pm Mon-Wed, Fri & Sat, 9.30am-8pm Thu, 11am-5pm Sun; 🚇380) Hip, high-calibre Calibre fills the wardrobes of Sydney's power players with schmick men's suits and shirts in seasonal fabrics and colours. You'll also find stores in Westfield Bondi Junction and Sydney.

EASTON PEARSON FASHION
Map p258 (www.eastonpearson.com; 30 Glenmore Rd; ⊙10am-6pm Mon-Fri, 11am-5pm Sat & Sun; 🚇380) Brisbane designers who popularised ethno-chic in Australia, and are particularly beloved by women of a slightly fuller figure.

WILLOW FASHION
Map p258 (www.willowltd.com; 3a Glenmore Rd; ⊙noon-5pm Sun, 10am-6pm Mon-Wed, Fri & Sat, 10am-8pm Thu; 🚇380) Local designer Kit Willow has made it big around the globe with the sleek silhouettes of her womenswear. There's another branch in Westfield Sydney.

GINGER & SMART FASHION
Map p258 (📞02-9380 9966; www.ginger andsmart.com; 16a Glenmore Rd; ⊙10am-6pm; 🚇380) Sexy, chic, modern clothes for women, designed by Sydney sisters Alexandra and Genevieve Smart.

DINOSAUR DESIGNS JEWELLERY, HOMEWARES
Map p258 (www.dinosaurdesigns.com.au; 339 Oxford St; 🚇380) If the Flintstones opened a jewellery store, this is what it would look like. Oversized, richly coloured, translucent resin bangles and baubles sit among technicoloured vases and bowls, and chunky sterling-silver rings and necklaces.

VERNE JEWELS JEWELLERY
Map p258 (www.vernejewels.com; 36b Oxford St; ⊙10am-5pm; 🚇380) Nicholas Bullough (there's no actual Verne, more's the pity) assembles the artefacts, stones, pearls and gems he purchases from around the world with an exquisite eye and a wry sense of history.

STILLS GALLERY ARTS
Map p258 (📞02-9331 7775; www.stillsgal lery.com.au; 36 Gosbell St; ⊙11am-5pm Wed-Sat; 🚊Kings Cross) Have a gander at some cutting-edge photography at this spacious backstreet gallery. It represents a swag of internationally recognised photographers, including William Yang and Anne Noble.

ROSLYN OXLEY9 GALLERY ARTS
Map p258 (📞02-9331 1919; www.roslynoxley9. com.au; 8 Soudan Lane; ⊙10am-6pm Tue-Sat; 🚊Edgecliff) For over 30 years this high-powered commercial gallery has showcased innovative contemporary work, representing artists such as Tracey Moffatt, David Noonan and Bill Henson. It's great for a nosy even if you're not looking to buy.

🏠 Woollahra

HERRINGBONE FASHION
Map p258 (📞02-9327 6470; www.herringbone. com; 102 Queen St; ⊙10am-6pm Mon-Sat, 11am-5pm Sun; 🚇389) Combining Australian design with Italian fabric, Herringbone produces something surprisingly English-looking – beautiful men's and women's shirts with crisp collars and bright colours.

AKIRA ISOGAWA FASHION
Map p258 (www.akira.com.au; 12a Queen St; ⊙11am-5pm Wed-Sat; 🚇380) Japanese-born Australian designer Isogawa produces meticulously tailored women's ensembles, featuring gorgeous fabrics. There's another store in the Strand Arcade (p99).

KIDSTUFF TOYS
Map p258 (📞02-9363 2838; www.kidstuff.com. au; 126a Queen St; ⊙9am-5.30pm; 🚇389) This small shop is filled with educational, traditional, low-tech toys and games. Aiming to engage and expand kids' minds, well-known brands mix with costumes, musical instruments, soft toys, doll's houses and magnetic fridge letters.

🏠 Centennial Park & Moore Park

EQ VILLAGE MARKETS MARKET
Map p258 (www.eqmoorepark.com.au; Showring, Bent St; ⊙10am-3pm Wed & Sat; 🚇355) The Entertainment Quarter's markets have loads of regional produce, including delicious cheese and yogurt.

🏃 SPORTS & ACTIVITIES

★**SYDNEY**
FOOTBALL STADIUM   SPECTATOR SPORT
Map p258 (Allianz Stadium; www.allianzsta
dium.com.au; Moore Park Rd; 🚌373-377)
It's now officially named after an insurance company, but these naming rights
change periodically, so we'll stick with
the untainted-by-sponsorship moniker for
this elegant 45,500-capacity stadium. It's
home to local heroes the Sydney Roosters
rugby-league team (www.roosters.com.
au), the NSW Waratahs rugby-union team
(www.waratahs.com.au) and the Sydney
FC A-league football (soccer) team (www.
sydneyfc.com).

All of these teams have passionate fans
(possibly the most vocal are the crazies in
the Roosters' 'chook pen'), so a home game
can be a lot of fun. Book through **Ticketek**
(☎132 849; www.ticketek.com.au).

★**CENTENNIAL PARKLANDS**
EQUESTRIAN CENTRE   HORSE RIDING
Map p258 (www.cpequestrian.com.au; 114-120
Lang Rd; escorted park rides $85-95; 🚌355)
Conveniently located on the edge of Centennial Park, this centre is home to five
different riding stables: **Budapest Riding
School** (☎0419 231 391; www.budapestriding
school.com.au), **Centennial Stables** (☎02-
9360 5650; www.centennialstables.com.au),
Eastside Riding Academy (☎02-9360 7521;
www.eastsideriding.com.au), **Moore Park Stables** (☎02-9360 8747; www.moreparkstables.
com.au) and **Papillon Riding Stables** (☎02-
8356 9866; www.papillonriding.com.au). Each
offers a circuit around the park's tree-lined
3.6km central track. Equine familiarity not
required; bookings essential.

ROYAL RANDWICK
RACECOURSE   HORSE RACING
(www.australianturfclub.com.au; Alison Rd; 🚌339)
The action at Sydney's most famous racecourse peaks in April with the $4-million
Queen Elizabeth Stakes; check the online
calendar for race days.

SYDNEY CRICKET
GROUND   SPECTATOR SPORT
Map p258 (SCG; ☎02-9360 6601; www.sydney
cricketground.com.au; Driver Ave; 🚌373-377)
During the cricket season (October to
March), the stately SCG is the venue for
sparsely attended interstate cricket matches

(featuring the NSW Blues), and sell-out international five-day test, one-day and 20/20
limited-over matches. As the cricket season
ends the Australian Rules (AFL) season
starts and the stadium becomes a blur of
red-and-white-clad **Sydney Swans** (www.
sydneyswans.com.au) fans.

SCG TOUR EXPERIENCE   TOUR
Map p258 (☎1300 724 737; www.sydneycricket
ground.com.au; Venue Services Office, Allianz Stadium, Driver Ave; adult/child/family $30/20/78;
⊙11am & 2pm Mon-Fri, 11am Sat; 🚌373-377)
Run up the players' race from the dressing
rooms in your own sporting fantasy during
this behind-the-scenes guided tour of the
facilities at the Sydney Cricket Ground.

CENTENNIAL PARK CYCLES   BICYCLE RENTAL
Map p258 (☎0401 357 419; www.cyclehire.
com.au; Grand Dr; per day/week from $50/110;
⊙9am-5pm; 🚌380) Hires mountain bikes
and hybrids (per hour/day $15/50), road
bikes ($20/70), kids' bikes ($10/45), tandems
($25/75) and pedal cars (per hour $30–40).

SKATER HQ   SKATING
Map p258 (☎02-8667 7892; www.skaterhq.com.
au; Bent St; ⊙9am-6pm; 🚌355) Handy to Centennial Park, these guys can fix you up with
top-of-the-range in-line skate, roller-skate
and skateboard hire ($20 per hour with safety
gear), or give you a lesson in how to ride 'em
(private/group lesson $70/40 per hour).

MOORE PARK GOLF CLUB   GOLF
Map p258 (☎02-9663 1064; www.mooreparkgolf.
com.au; cnr Anzac Pde & Cleveland St; 18 holes
$40-63, club hire $45-65; 🚌391-399) The 18-
hole, par-70 Moore Park course is the most
central of Sydney's public golf courses.

PARKLANDS TENNIS CENTRE   TENNIS
Map p258 (☎02-9662 7033; www.parklands
sports.com.au; cnr Anzac Pde & Lang Rds; per
hour $20-28; ⊙9am-10pm Mon-Thu, to 6pm Fri-
Sun; 🚌391-399) Moore Park is the perfect
place to release your inner McEnroe, with
plenty of faux grass and hard courts.

RUSHCUTTERS BAY
PARK TENNIS COURTS   TENNIS
(☎02-9357 7332; www.rushcuttersbaytennis.
com.au; Waratah St; per hour $24-29; ⊙7am-10pm;
🚊Kings Cross) The four courts here are open
to the public, with the cheapest rates before
5pm weekdays. It's a relaxed place for a
game, and racket hire is available.

Bondi to Coogee

BONDI | TAMARAMA | BRONTE | CLOVELLY | COOGEE

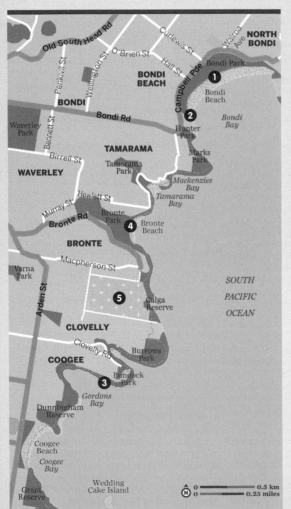

Neighbourhood Top Five

1 Whiling away the day on the golden sands of **Bondi Beach** (p158), periodically cooling off in the surf and cruising the promenade.

2 Revelling in the spectacular coastal scenery of the **Bondi to Coogee walk** (p160).

3 Coming face to face with the slippery and scaly locals on the **Gordons Bay Underwater Nature Trail** (p167).

4 Grilling up a storm (only figuratively, hopefully) at a **Bronte** (p159) beachside barbecue.

5 Waving at the winter parade of whales from the cliffs of **Waverley Cemetery** (p159).

For more detail of this area, see Map p261 and p262 ➡

Explore: Bondi to Coogee

Improbably good-looking arcs of sand framed by jagged cliffs, the Eastern Beaches are a big part of the Sydney experience. Most famous of all is the broad sweep of Bondi Beach, where the distracting scenery and constant procession of beautiful bods never fail to take your mind off whatever it was you were just thinking about... This is where Sydney comes to see and be seen, preferably wearing as little as possible (it's not an affirming place for those with body-image issues).

The unique flavour of Bondi has been greatly influenced by the Jewish, British and Kiwi immigrants who populated it before it became hip. Housing prices on Bondi's strangely treeless slopes have skyrocketed, but the beach remains a priceless constant.

South of Bondi, Bronte is a steep-sided beach 'burb, its bowl-shaped park strewn with picnic tables and barbecues. Further south is the concrete-fringed, safe swimming inlet of Clovelly, a great place to dust off your snorkel. Next stop heading south is Coogee, an Aboriginal word for rotting seaweed... But don't let that deter you: the beach is wide and handsome, and beery backpackers fill the takeaways and pubs.

Local Life

➡ **Beaches** People move to these suburbs to be near the beaches, so don't think they're just for tourists.

➡ **Brunch** On weekends brunchsters descend on the cafes from near and far. Once you step back from Bondi's Campbell Pde, Sydneysiders are in the majority.

➡ **Clovelly Hotel** A proper neighbourhood pub; most of the punters stroll here from the surrounding streets.

Getting There & Away

➡ **Train** The Eastern Suburbs line heads to Bondi Junction, which is 2.5km from Bondi Beach, 3km from Bronte Beach and 4km from Coogee Beach.

➡ **Bus** For Bondi take bus 333 (express) or 380 via Oxford St, or 389 via Woollahra; all depart from Circular Quay. For Bronte take bus 378 from Railway Sq via Oxford St. For Clovelly take bus 339 from the Rocks via Central and Surry Hills. For Coogee take bus 373 from Circular Quay via Oxford St or bus 372 from Railway Sq via Surry Hills. Various routes start at the Bondi Junction interchange, including 381 and 382 to Bondi Beach, 361 to Tamarama, 360 to Clovelly, and 313, 314 and 353 to Coogee.

➡ **Car** Parking is difficult, especially on weekends – be prepared to park, pay and walk.

Lonely Planet's Top Tip

Bondi Junction, situated 2.5km from Bondi Beach and 6km from Circular Quay, is the transport hub for the Eastern Beaches. The Eastern Suburbs train line terminates beneath the main bus station, right next to the Westfield shopping complex. Although you can catch a bus all the way from the city to the beach, it's much quicker to catch the train to Bondi Junction and then head upstairs to finish the journey by bus.

✖ Best Places to Eat

➡ Three Blue Ducks (p164)
➡ Icebergs Dining Room (p164)
➡ Lox, Stock & Barrel (p161)
➡ A Tavola (p164)
➡ The Shop (p161)

For reviews, see p161 ➡

🍷 Best Places to Drink

➡ Neighbourhood (p165)
➡ Anchor (p165)
➡ North Bondi RSL (p165)
➡ Bucket List (p165)
➡ Coogee Pavilion (p166)

For reviews, see p165 ➡

⊙ Best Places To Swim

➡ Bondi Beach (p158)
➡ Bronte Beach (p159)
➡ Mahon Pool (p164)
➡ Clovelly Beach (p159)
➡ Coogee Beach (p161)

For reviews, see p158 ➡

BONDI TO COOGEE

TOP SIGHT
BONDI BEACH

Definitively Sydney, Bondi is one of the world's great beaches: ocean and land collide, the Pacific arrives in great foaming swells and all people are equal, as democratic as sand. It's the closest ocean beach to the city centre (8km away), has consistently good (though crowded) waves, and is great for a rough-and-tumble swim.

Surf's Up

Surfers carve up sandbar breaks at either end of the beach. Two surf clubs – Bondi and North Bondi – patrol the beach between sets of red-and-yellow flags, positioned to avoid the worst rips and holes. Thousands of unfortunates have to be rescued from the surf each year (enough to make a TV show about it), so don't become a statistic – swim between the flags. If the sea's angry or you have small children in tow, try the saltwater sea baths at either end of the beach.

DON'T MISS...

➡ Bodysurfing between the flags
➡ Bondi Pavilion
➡ A beachside barbecue
➡ Learning to surf

PRACTICALITIES

➡ Map p261
➡ Campbell Pde
➡ ☐380

Bondi Pavilion

Built in the Mediterranean Georgian Revival style in 1929, **Bondi Pavilion** (www.waverley.nsw.gov.au; Queen Elizabeth Dr; ⊙9am-5pm) FREE is more a cultural centre than changing shed, although it does have changing rooms, showers and lockers. There's a free art gallery upstairs, a theatre out the back, and various cafes and a bar lining the ocean frontage, including the extremely popular Bucket List (p165).

In the summer **Flickerfest** (☑02-9365 6888; www.flickerfest.com.au; Bondi Pavilion, Queen Elizabeth Dr; ⊙Jan) takes place here, and **Bondi Openair Cinema** (www.openaircinemas.com.au; Dolphin Lawn, next to Bondi Pavilion; tickets $15-45; ⊙Jan & Feb) sets up on the lawn, with live bands providing prescreening entertainment.

Outdoor Facilities

Prefer wheels to fins? There's a **skate ramp** (Queen Elizabeth Dr) at the beach's southern end. If posing in your budgie smugglers (Speedos) isn't having enough impact, there's an outdoor **workout area** (Queen Elizabeth Dr) near the North Bondi Surf Club. Coincidentally (or perhaps not), this is the part of the beach where the gay guys hang out. At the beach's northern end there's a grassy spot with coin-operated barbecues. Booze is banned on the beach.

Surf Lessons

North Bondi is a great place to learn to surf. **Let's Go Surfing** (☑02-9365 1800; www.letsgosurfing.com.au; 128 Ramsgate Ave; board & wetsuit hire 1hr/2hr/day/week $25/30/50/150; ⊙9am-5pm) caters to practically everyone, with classes for grommets aged seven to 16 (1½ hours $49) and adults (two hours $99, women-only classes available), or you can hire a private tutor (1½ hours $175). And if you just want to hire gear to hit the waves, you can do that too.

Bondi Icebergs

With supreme views of Bondi Beach, **Bondi Icebergs Swimming Club** (☑02-9130 4804; www.icebergs.com.au; 1 Notts Ave; adult/child $6/4; ⊙6.30am-6.30pm Fri-Wed) is a Sydney institution. Only hardened winter-swimming fanatics can become fully fledged members, but anyone can pay for a casual entry. Otherwise, soak up the views from the **Crabbe Hole cafe** (Lower Level, 1 Notts Ave; mains $10-12; ⊙7am-5pm) or the very swanky Icebergs (p164) restaurant and bar.

◉ SIGHTS

◉ Bondi

BONDI BEACH BEACH
See p158.

BEN BUCKLER POINT VIEWPOINT
Map p261 (Ramsgate Ave; ☐380) Forming the northern tip of the Bondi horseshoe, this point offers wonderful views of the entire beach. The 235-tonne, car-sized rock near the beach's northern tip was spat out of the sea during a storm in 1912. The lookout is at the end of Ramsgate Ave, or you can follow the trail which runs along the rocks from the beach.

**ABORIGINAL ROCK
ENGRAVINGS** ARCHAEOLOGICAL SITE
Map p261 (5 Military Rd; ☐380) On the clifftop fairways of Bondi Golf & Diggers Club, a short walk north from Bondi Beach, lies a flat patch of rock carved by the Eora Aboriginal people (look for it about 20m southeast of the enormous chimney, and watch out for flying golf balls). Some of the images are hard to distinguish, though you should be able to make out marine life and the figure of a man. The carvings were regrooved in the 1960s to help preserve them.

◉ Tamarama

TAMARAMA BEACH BEACH
Map p261 (Pacific Ave; ☐361) Surrounded by high cliffs, Tamarama has a deep tongue of sand with just 80m of shoreline. Diminutive, yes, but ever-present rips make Tamarama the most dangerous patrolled beach in New South Wales; it's often closed to swimmers. It's hard to picture now, but between 1887 and 1911 a roller coaster looped out over the water as part of an amusement park.

When it earned its nickname 'Glamarama' in the 1980s, Tamarama was probably Sydney's gayest beach. Reflecting increasing acceptance, the gay guys have migrated en masse to North Bondi, leaving the huge waves here to the surfers.

◉ Bronte

BRONTE BEACH BEACH
(Bronte Rd; ☐378) A winning family-oriented beach hemmed in by sandstone cliffs and a grassy park, Bronte lays claims to the title of the oldest surf life-saving club in the world (1903). Contrary to popular belief, the beach is named after Lord Nelson, who doubled as the Duke of Bronte (a place in Sicily), and not the famous literary sorority. There's a kiosk and a changing room attached to the surf club, and covered picnic tables near the public barbecues.

WAVERLEY CEMETERY CEMETERY
Map p262 (www1.waverley.nsw.gov.au/cemetery; St Thomas St; ⊙7am-6pm; ☐378) Many Sydneysiders would die for these views...and that's the only way they're going to get them. Blanketing the cliff tops between Bronte and Coogee, the white marble gravestones here are dazzling in the sunlight. Eighty-thousand people have been interred here since 1877, including writer Henry Lawson and cricketer Victor Trumper. It's an engrossing (and surprisingly uncreepy) place to explore, and maybe to spot a whale offshore during winter.

◉ Clovelly

CLOVELLY BEACH BEACH
Map p262 (Clovelly Rd; ☐339) It might seem odd, but this concrete-edged ocean channel is a great place to swim, sunbathe and snorkel. It's safe for the kids, and despite the swell surging into the inlet, underwater

---

WORTH A DETOUR

CRONULLA

Cronulla is a beachy surf suburb south of Botany Bay, its long surf beach stretching beyond the dunes to the Botany Bay refineries. It can be an edgy place (captured brilliantly in the '70s teen cult novel *Puberty Blues*), with dingy fish-and-chip shops, insomniac teens and a ragged sense of impending 'something', which in 2005 erupted into racial violence. That said the beach is beautiful, with a pleasant promenade, and it's easy to reach by train from Central. In 2008 it became the second Sydney beach to be declared a National Surfing Reserve (after Maroubra, p164).

Neighbourhood Walk
Bondi to Coogee

START BONDI BEACH
END COOGEE BEACH
LENGTH 6KM; TWO TO THREE HOURS

Arguably Sydney's most famous, most popular and best walk, this coastal path really shouldn't be missed. Both ends are well connected to bus routes, as are most points in between should you feel too hot and bothered to continue – although a cooling dip at any of the beaches en route should cure that (pack your swimmers). There's little shade on this track, so make sure you dive into a tub of sunscreen before setting out. A hat's also a good idea.

Starting at ❶**Bondi Beach** (p158), take the stairs up the south end to Notts Ave, passing above the glistening ❷**Icebergs** (p158) pool complex. Step onto the cliff-top trail at the end of Notts Ave.

Walking south, the blustery sandstone cliffs and grinding Pacific Ocean couldn't be more spectacular (watch for dolphins, whales and surfers). Small but perfectly formed ❸**Tamarama** (p159) has a deep reach of sand that is totally disproportion-ate to its width.

Descend from the cliff tops onto ❹**Bronte Beach** (p159). Take a dip, lay out a picnic under the Norfolk Island pines or head to a cafe for a caffeine hit. After your break, pick up the path on the south-ern side of the beach.

Some famous Australians are among the subterranean denizens of the amazing cliff-edge ❺**Waverley Cemetery** (p159). On a clear winter's day this is a prime vantage point for whale watchers.

Pass the locals enjoying a beer or a game of lawn bowls at the Clovelly Bowling Club, then breeze past the cockatoos and canoodling lovers in ❻**Burrows Park** to sheltered ❼**Clovelly Beach** (p159).

Follow the footpath up through the car park, along Cliffbrook Pde, then down the steps to the upturned dinghies lining ❽**Gordons Bay** (p167), one of Sydney's best shore-dive spots.

The trail continues past ❾**Dolphin Point** (p161) then lands you smack-bang on glorious ❿ **Coogee Beach**. Swagger into the Coogee Bay Hotel and toast your efforts with a cold beverage.

visibility is great. A beloved friendly grouper fish lived here for many years until he was speared by a tourist. Bring your goggles, but don't go killing anything...

On the other side of the car park is the entrance to the Gordons Bay Underwater Nature Trail (p167).

⊙ Coogee

COOGEE BEACH
BEACH

Map p262 (Arden St; ☐372-373) Bondi without the glitz and the posers, Coogee (locals pronounce the double *o* as in the word 'took') has a deep sweep of sand, historic ocean baths and plenty of green space for barbecues and frisbee hurling. Between the World Wars, Coogee had an English-style pier, with a 1400-seat theatre and a 600-seat ballroom...until the surf took it.

Offshore, compromising the surf here a little, is craggy Wedding Cake Island, immortalised in a surf-guitar instrumental by Midnight Oil. At Coogee Beach's northern end, below Dolphin Point, **Giles Baths** FREE is what's known as a 'bogey hole' – a semiformal rock pool open to the surging surf. At the beach's southern end, **Ross Jones Memorial Pool** (Carr St) FREE has sandcastle-like concrete turrets.

DOLPHIN POINT
PARK

Map p262 (Baden St; ☐372-373) This grassy tract at Coogee Beach's northern end has superb ocean views and the Giles Baths ocean pool. A sobering shrine commemorates the 2002 Bali bombings. Coogee was hit hard by the tragedy, with 20 of the 89 Australians killed coming from hereabouts. The park's name was changed to honour the six members of the Coogee Dolphins rugby-league team who died in the blast.

 **EATING**

The Eastern Beaches restaurants are as eclectic and unpredictable as the surf. Bondi offers everything from gaudy glamour to funky surfie cafes, while Bronte is a top spot for brunch (spot migrating whales over your flat white). For the Ritz of food halls, check out Westfield Bondi Junction – and while you're there, stock up on snags (sausages) for chucking on the coast's well-maintained coin-operated beachside barbecues. If that all sounds like too much hassle, enjoy some fish and chips on the sand.

✖ Bondi

THE SHOP
CAFE $

Map p261 (www.theshopbondi.com; 78 Curlewis St; mains $10-18; ☺6am-10pm; ☐389) Operating as both a cafe and a wine bar (with a name that reflects neither), this tiny space serves cooked breakfasts, pastries, sandwiches, salads and, in the evening, tapas and burgers. It's a bit self-consciously cool, but the food and coffee are excellent.

SABBABA
MIDDLE EASTERN $

Map p261 (☎02-9365 7500; www.sabbaba.com. au; 82 Hall St; mains $9-17; ☺11am-10pm; ☑; ☐389) There are more board shorts than black coats on view at this Middle Eastern joint in Bondi's main Hassidic strip. Falafels served in pitta are a quick-fire bargain, and there's a sticky-sweet array of baklava to finish off with. There are branches in Westfield Sydney and Newtown.

JED'S FOODSTORE
CAFE $

Map p261 (☎02-9365 0022; 60 Warners Ave; mains $9-19; ☺6.30am-3.30pm Mon-Fri, to 4.40pm Sat & Sun; ☐389) Jed's is so relaxed, you'll feel like you're back in a uni share house. Reggae mellows the tattooed staff, who sing and groove around; dudes sip coffee outside as kids and dogs run amok. Grab a seat for the Caribbean-style jerked potato scramble and a strong coffee.

ORGANIC REPUBLIC
BAKERY $

Map p261 (100 Glenayr Ave; pastries $3-4, sandwiches $7-10; ☺5am-5.30pm; ☐389, 380, 333) ✐ Its motto – 'let the bread speak' – says it all. Fabulous sandwiches on slabs of home-baked organic bread (including spelt) are the signature dish at this bakery cafe in a peaceful pocket of Bondi. You can also enjoy delicious cakes, pastries, pies and biscuits accompanied by free-trade coffee made with organic milk.

LOX, STOCK & BARREL
DINER, DELI $$

Map p261 (☎02-9300 0368; www.loxstock andbarrel.com.au; 140 Glenayr Ave; breakfast & lunch $11-18, dinner $29; ☺7am-3.30pm daily, 6pm-late Wed-Sun) Stare down the barrel of a smoking-hot bagel and ask yourself

1. Bondi to Coogee walk (p160)
Sublime coastal panoramas unfold along this 6km path.

2. Bondi Beach (p158)
Catch some waves at Australia's most famous beach.

3. Coogee Beach (p161)
Coogee's wide stretch of golden sand, historic ocean baths and green parkland will delight sun lovers.

4. Bondi Icebergs Swimming Club (p158)
Swim laps or simply admire the views at this Sydney institution.

WORTH A DETOUR

MAROUBRA

The last major beach before you hit Botany Bay, 'the Bra' is Bondi's match in the waves department, but its location in a working-class suburb provides immunity from Bondi's more pretentious trappings. In 2006 it became the first Australian beach to be declared a National Surfing Reserve.

The notorious Bra Boys surfing gang (documented in the 2007 movie *Bra Boys* by Sunny Abberton) remains entrenched, but don't let it keep you out of the surf.

Hidden within the cliffs, 500m north of Maroubra Beach, **Mahon Pool** (Marine Pde; 📷376-377) is an idyllic rock pool, where the surf crashes over the edges at high tide. It's quite possibly Sydney's most beautiful bogey hole (sea bath).

one question: Wagyu corned-beef Reuben, or homemade pastrami and Russian coleslaw? In the evening the menu sets its sights on steak, lamb shoulder and slow-roasted eggplant.

A TAVOLA   ITALIAN $$

Map p261 (📞02-9130 1246; www.atavola.com.au; 75 Hall St; mains $22-38; ⊙noon-3pm Wed-Sun, 5.30-11pm daily) Carrying on the tradition of its Darlinghurst sister, Bondi's A Tavola centres on a communal marble table where, before the doors open, the pasta-making action happens. Expect robust flavours, sexy waiters and delicious homemade pasta.

BONDI TRATTORIA   ITALIAN $$

Map p261 (📞02-9365 4303; www.bonditrattoria. com.au; 34 Campbell Pde; breakfast $9-19, lunch $17-29, dinner $19-36; ⊙8am-late; 📷380) For a Bondi brunch, you can't go past the trusty 'Trat', as it's known in these parts. Tables spill out onto Campbell Pde for those hungry for beach views, while inside there's a trad trat feel: wooden tables, and the obligatory Tuscan mural and black-and-white photography. As the day progresses, pizza, pasta and risotto dominate the menu.

POMPEI'S   ITALIAN $$

Map p261 (📞02-9365 1233; www.pompeis.com. au; 126-130 Roscoe St; mains $21-34; ⊙noon-11pm Tue-Fri, 8.30am-11pm Sat & Sun; 📷389,

380, 333) The pizza here is among the best in Sydney, but it's the northern Italian dishes whipped up by expat Giorgio Pompei that are really special. Try the handmade ravioli stuffed with spinach, ricotta and nutmeg, and leave some space for a scoop of the legendary gelato.

LA PIADINA   ITALIAN $$

Map p261 (📞02-9300 0160; www.lapiadina.com. au; 106 Glenayr Ave; mains $14-16; ⊙8am-10pm Tue-Sun) A *piadina* is a filled flat bread common in northern Italy, and the Zizioli brothers are the only ones serving them in Sydney. Fillings include prosciutto, rocket, mozzarella and *ndjua,* a kind of spicy sausage. Have them for breakfast, lunch or dinner, but whatever you do, have them – they're delicious!

ICEBERGS DINING ROOM   ITALIAN $$$

Map p261 (📞02-9365 9000; www.idrb.com; 1 Notts Ave; mains $40-48; ⊙noon-3pm & 6.30-11pm Tue-Sun; 📷380) 🍴 Poised above the famous Icebergs swimming pool, Icebergs' views sweep across the Bondi Beach arc to the sea. Inside, bow-tied waiters deliver fresh, sustainably sourced seafood and steaks cooked with élan. To limit the hip-pocket impact, call in at lunchtime for a pasta and salad.

SEAN'S PANAROMA   AUSTRALIAN $$$

Map p261 (📞02-9365 4924; www.seanspan aroma.com.au; 270 Campbell Pde; mains $39-45; ⊙6-11pm Wed-Fri, noon-11pm Sat & Sun; 📷380) Sean Moran's ever-changing menu is chalked on a blackboard in this modest little dining room. Come for the ocean views, hearty seasonal dishes and friendly service, but beware the $5 per person surcharge on weekends.

🍴 Bronte

THREE BLUE DUCKS   CAFE $$

Map p262 (📞02-9389 0010; www.threeblue ducks.com; 141-143 Macpherson St; breakfast $16-25, lunch $24-31, dinner $28-32; ⊙7am-2.30pm Sun-Tue, 7am-2.30pm & 6-11pm Wed-Sat; 📷378) 🍴 These ducks are a fair waddle from the water, but that doesn't stop queues forming outside the graffiti-covered walls for weekend breakfasts. The adventurous chefs have a strong commitment to using local, organic and fair-trade food whenever possible.

✖ Coogee

A FISH CALLED COOGEE   FISH & CHIPS $$

Map p262 (☑02-9664 7700; 229 Coogee Bay Rd; pay per weight of fish; ☺11.30am-9pm; ☐374) This upmarket fish and chipper offers much more than your standard deep-fried cod. There's everything from barbecued shrimp and peppered marlin to swordfish and garlic prawns. Eat in or grab a bag and find a patch of sand.

☻ DRINKING & NIGHTLIFE

If you're a backpacker from anywhere cold and northern hemispheric, it makes sense that you'd want to cram as much beery beach time into your Sydney holiday as possible. You'll find plenty of company in the backpacker haunts along the coast. More cashed-up travellers will find plenty of slick cocktail joints as well.

☻ Bondi

NEIGHBOURHOOD   BAR

Map p261 (www.neighbourhoodbondi.com.au; 143 Curlewis St; ☺5.30-11pm Mon-Thu, noon-11pm Fri, 9am-11pm Sat & Sun; ☐380-382) The natural habitat for the curious species known as the Bondi Hipster, this smart food and wine bar has a brick-lined interior giving way to a wood-lined courtyard. Bondi Radio broadcasts live from a booth near the kitchen.

ANCHOR   BAR

Map p261 (www.anchorbarbondi.com; 8 Campbell Pde; ☺4.30pm-midnight Tue-Fri, 12.30pm-midnight Sat & Sun; ☐380-382) Surfers, backpackers and the local cool kids slurp down icy margaritas at this bustling bar at the south end of the strip. It's also a great spot for a late snack.

NORTH BONDI RSL   BAR

Map p261 (www.northbondirsl.com.au; 120 Ramsgate Ave; ☺noon-10pm Mon-Fri, 10am-midnight Sat, 10am-10pm Sun; ☐; ☐380-382) This Returned & Services League bar ain't fancy, but with views no one can afford and drinks that everyone can, who cares? The

kitchen serves good cheap nosh, including a dedicated kids' menu. Bring ID, as non-members need to prove that they live at least 5km away.

BUCKET LIST   BAR

Map p261 (www.thebucketlistbondi.com; Bondi Pavilion; ☺11am-midnight; ☐380) On a sunny day, fight for a seat on the Bucket List's in-demand terrace. Sip on a ice-cold beverage while watching the passing parade or gazing aimlessly out to sea. If the weather turns, there are plenty of brightly decorated nooks inside where you can shelter from the elements.

CORNER HOUSE   BAR

Map p261 (www.thecornerhouse.com.au; 281 Bondi Rd; ☺5pm-midnight Tue-Sat, 3-10pm Sun; ☐380-382) Three spaces – the Kitchen (wine and pizza bar), Dining Room (restaurant) and Living Room (cocktail bar) – make this a particularly happy house. It's up the hill in Bondi proper so the vibe's more local, attracting an eclectic range of Bondi natives.

ICEBERGS BAR   BAR

Map p261 (www.idrb.com; 1 Notts Ave; ☺noon-midnight Tue-Sat, 10am-10pm Sun; ☐380-382) The neighbouring eatery is more famous, but the ooh-la-la Icebergs Bar is a brilliant place for a drink. Colourful sofas and ritzy cocktails do little to distract from the killer views looking north across Bondi Beach. Dress sexy and make sure your bank account is up to the strain.

BEACH ROAD HOTEL   PUB

Map p261 (www.beachroadbondi.com.au; 71 Beach Rd; ☺11am-midnight Mon-Sat, 10am-10pm Sun; ☐389) Weekends at this big boxy pub are a boisterous, multilevel alcoholiday, with Bondi types (bronzed, buff and brooding) and woozy out-of-towners playing pool, drinking beer and digging live bands and DJs.

☻ Clovelly

CLOVELLY HOTEL   PUB

Map p262 (☑02-9665 1214; www.clovelly hotel.com.au; 381 Clovelly Rd; ☺10am-midnight Mon-Sat, to 10pm Sun; ☐339) A recently renovated megalith on the hill above Clovelly Beach, this pub has a shady terrace and water views – perfect for postbeach

Sunday-afternoon bevvies. Entertainment includes live music, poker comps, quiz nights, happy hours and even a mothers' group.

⚲ Coogee

COOGEE PAVILION   BAR

Map p262 (www.merivale.com.au/coogeepavilion; 169 Dolphin St; ⊙7.30am-late; ⏴; 🚌372-374) With its numerous indoor and outdoor bars, Mediterranean-influenced eatery, kids' play area, giant scrabble set and glorious adults-only rooftop, this vast complex has brought a touch of inner-city glam to Coogee. Built in 1887, the building originally housed an aquarium and swimming pools.

COOGEE BAY HOTEL   PUB, CLUB

Map p262 (www.coogeebayhotel.com.au; 253 Coogee Bay Rd; ⊙7am-late; 🚌374) This rambling, rowdy complex packs in the backpackers for live music, open-mic nights, comedy and big-screen sports in the beaut beer garden, sports bar and Selina's nightclub. Sit on a stool at the window overlooking the beach and sip on a cold one.

🛍 SHOPPING

Surf shops are the mainstay of the beach shopping scene.

★WESTFIELD
BONDI JUNCTION   MALL

(☎02-9947 8000; www.westfield.com.au; 500 Oxford St; ⊙9.30am-6pm Fri-Wed, to 9pm Thu; 🚆Bondi Junction) Vast. That's the only word to describe this upmarket shopping mall. Expect to get lost; the space-time continuum does funny things as you explore the 400-plus stores set over six levels. It's even worse in the underground car park.

Local clothing outlets include branches of Calibre (p154), Oxford (p120), Sass & Bide (p153), Zimmermann (p154), Leona Edmiston (p153) and RM Williams (p100), alongside the big internationals such as Hugo Boss, Gucci and G-Star Raw. Australia's two big department stores – Myer (p100) and David Jones (p100) – do battle here. Plus there are cinemas, bars, cafes, supermarkets, food courts...

SURFECTION   CLOTHING, ACCESSORIES

Map p261 (www.facebook.com/Surfection; 31 Hall St; ⊙10am-5.30pm; 🚌380-382) Selling boardies, bikinis, sunnies, shoes, watches, T-shirts... even luggage – Bondi's coolest surf shop has just about everything the stylish surfer's heart might desire (except for spray-in hair bleach; you'll still need to take your paper bag to a discreet chemist for that). Old boards hang from the ceiling, while new boards fill the racks.

RIP CURL   CLOTHING, ACCESSORIES

Map p261 (☎02-9130 2660; www.ripcurl.com.au; 82 Campbell Pde; ⊙9am-6pm; 🚌380-382) The quintessential Aussie surf shop, Rip Curl began down south in Victoria, but drops in perfectly overlooking the Bondi shore breaks. Beyond huge posters of burly surfer dudes and beach babes, you'll find bikinis, watches, board shorts, wetsuits, sunglasses, hats, T-shirts and (surprise!) surfboards.

BONDI MARKETS   MARKET

Map p261 (www.bondimarkets.com.au; Bondi Beach Public School, Campbell Pde; ⊙9am-1pm Sat, 10am-4pm Sun; 🚌380-382) On Sundays, when the kids are at the beach, their school fills up with Bondi characters rummaging through tie-dyed secondhand clothes, original fashion, books, beads, earrings, aromatherapy oils, candles, old records and more. There's a farmers market here on Saturdays.

GERTRUDE & ALICE   BOOKS

Map p261 (☎02-9130 5155; www.gertrudeandalice.com.au; 46 Hall St; ⊙7.30am-8.30pm; 🚌380-382) This shambolic secondhand bookshop and cafe is so un-Bondi: there's not a model or a surfer in sight. Locals, students and academics hang out reading, drinking coffee and acting like Americans in Paris. Join them for some lentil stew and theological discourse around communal tables.

AQUABUMPS   ARTS

Map p261 (☎02-9130 7788; www.aquabumps.com; 151 Curlewis St) Photographer/surfer Eugene Tan has been snapping photos of Sydney's sunrises, surf and sand for 15 years. His colourful prints hang in this cool space, just a splash from Bondi Beach.

KEMENYS   WINE

(☎138 881; www.kemenys.com.au; 137-147 Bondi Rd; ⊙8am-9pm; 🚌380-382) A short walk up (and then a wobble down) the hill from Bondi Beach, Kemenys occupies a large soft spot in the hearts, minds and livers of Bondi locals. Proffering the best local and imported wines, ales and spirits to the surf set since 1960, it's staunchly resisted being taken over by the big chains. Respect.

SPORTS & ACTIVITIES

★GORDONS BAY
UNDERWATER NATURE TRAIL   DIVING
Map p262 (www.gordonsbayscubadivingclub. com; Clovelly Rd; 339) A 500m underwater chain guiding divers past reefs, sand flats and kelp forests.

WYLIE'S BATHS   SWIMMING
Map p262 (02-9665 2838; www.wylies.com. au; 4b Neptune St; adult/child $4.80/1; 7am-7pm Oct-Mar, to 5pm Apr-Sep; 372-374) On the rocky coast south of Coogee Beach, this superb seawater pool (1907) is targeted at swimmers more than splashabouts. After your swim, take a yoga class ($18), enjoy a massage, or have a coffee at the kiosk, which has magnificent ocean views.

MCIVERS BATHS   SWIMMING
Map p262 (Beach St; admission 20c; 372-374) Perched against the cliffs south of Coogee Beach and well-screened from passers-by, McIvers Baths has been popular for women's bathing since before 1876. Its strict women-only policy has made it popular with an unlikely coalition of nuns, Muslim women and lesbians. Small children of either gender are permitted.

WORTH A DETOUR

KITEBOARDING
....

Sydney Harbour's too busy and the ocean's too rough, but Botany Bay is perfect for strapping yourself onto a parachute and going surfing. Brush up your aqua-aeronautic skills with a lesson from **Kitepower** (1300 732 432; www.kitepower.com.au; 302 The Grand Pde, Sans Souci; 2hr lessons $220; 9am-5.30pm Mon-Sat, 10am-2pm Sun; 303).

DIVE CENTRE BONDI   DIVING
(02-9369 3855; www.divebondi.com.au; 198 Bondi Rd; 9am-6pm Mon-Fri, 7.30am-6pm Sat & Sun; 380) This Professional Association of Diving Instructors (PADI) centre offers learn-to-dive courses (three days $395), plus various boat and shore dives around Sydney.

CLOVELLY BOWLING CLUB   BOWLING
Map p262 (02-9665 1507; www.clovellybowl ingclub.com.au; 1 Ocean St; 10am-7pm; 360) A sunbaked square of cliff-top grass, this lawn-bowls club offers sensational ocean views and something of a hipster scene on weekends. Drop in for a thirst-quenching lager as you traverse the Bondi to Coogee walk. If you want to bowl, it'll cost you $12 (book ahead). Free coaching for beginners.

BONDI GOLF & DIGGERS CLUB   GOLF
Map p261 (02-9130 3170; www.bondigolf.com. au; 5 Military Rd; 9/18 holes $23/28, club hire $15-20; 7.30am-5pm Mon-Fri, 10.30am-5pm Sat & Sun; 380) It's not much of a course (nine holes, par 28) but the views are awesome and hazards include Aboriginal rock engravings (p159) and the Pacific Ocean. Try not to hit any passing whales.

BONDI TO COOGEE SPORTS & ACTIVITIES

Manly

MANLY | BALGOWLAH HEIGHTS | CLONTARF | WARRINGAH

Neighbourhood Top Five

1 Splashing about on long, lovely **Manly Beach** (p170), Sydney's second-most-famous stretch of golden sand. Fully embrace the local lifestyle by learning to surf.

2 Hopping between headlands and beaches along the beautiful **Manly Scenic Walkway** (p174).

3 Exploring the wild, rugged surrounds of the **North Head** (p170) section of Sydney Harbour National Park.

4 Hiring a kayak and paddling to isolated, bushlined **Store Beach** (p171).

5 Delving into the sad and spooky history of the **Quarantine Station** (p171) on a guided tour.

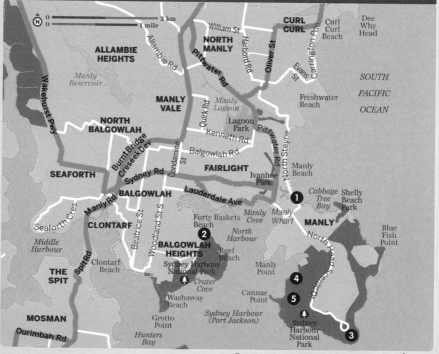

For more detail of this area, see Map p263 ➡

Explore: Manly

Laid-back Manly clings to a narrow isthmus between ocean and harbour beaches abutting North Head, Sydney Harbour's northern gatepost. With its shaggy surfers, dusty labourers and relaxed locals, it makes for a refreshing change from the stuffier harbour suburbs nearby.

Manly's unusual name comes from Governor Phillip's description of the physique of the native people he met here; his Excellency was clearly indulging in an early example of the very Sydney habit of body-scrutinising.

The Corso connects Manly's ocean and harbour beaches; here surf shops, burger joints, juice bars and pubs are plentiful. The refurbished Manly Wharf has classier pubs and restaurants, and there are some good cafes scattered around the backstreets.

In summer, allocate a day to walking and splashing about. In winter, it's worth heading over for a quick look around, if only for Sydney's best ferry journey. Don't bother staying after dark – there are much better eateries and bars elsewhere.

Local Life

→ **Surfing** A fair proportion of Manly residents live to surf, squeezing in a few hours riding the swell before or after work. The beach's three surf life-saving clubs are hubs of community life.

→ **Manly-Warringah Sea Eagles** The local rugby-league team are neighbourhood heroes, having won the premiership twice in the last decade. Home games are played further north at Brookvale, but Manly's pubs are lively places to watch matches.

→ **Cafes** They may not be as self-consciously hip as they are in Surry Hills and Newtown, but Manly has its own dedicated band of baristas bringing quality coffee to those in the know.

Getting There & Away

→ **Ferry** Frequent ferry services head directly from Circular Quay to Manly, making this by far the best (and most scenic) way to get to Manly. Regular Sydney Ferries take 30 minutes for the journey while fast ferries take just 18 minutes.

→ **Bus** PrePay express bus E70 takes 37 minutes to get to Manly Wharf from near Wynyard station, while regular bus 171 takes about an hour. From Manly Wharf, useful routes include 132 and 171 (Balgowlah Heights and Clontarf), 135 (North Head), 139 (Freshwater and Curl Curl) and 140, 143 and 144 (Spit Bridge).

→ **Car** Street parking is restricted and metered in central Manly and near the beach.

Lonely Planet's Top Tip

If you don't have a spare four hours to traverse North Head on foot, hire a bike. Otherwise, rent a kayak and paddle between the secluded bays facing the harbour. Beautiful little Store Beach can only be reached from the water.

✖ Best Places to Eat

→ Pilu at Freshwater (p175)
→ Hugos Manly (p175)
→ Chat Thai (p171)
→ Belgrave Cartel (p175)
→ Barefoot Coffee Traders (p171)

For reviews, see p171 ➡

🍷 Best Places to Drink

→ Manly Wharf Hotel (p175)
→ Hotel Steyne (p175)
→ Bavarian Bier Café (p175)
→ Hugos Manly (p175)

For reviews, see p175 ➡

⊙ Best Beaches

→ Manly Beach (p170)
→ Shelly Beach (p170)
→ Store Beach (p171)
→ Freshwater (p171)
→ Manly Cove (p170)

For reviews, see p170 ➡

MANLY

◉ SIGHTS

◉ Manly

MANLY COVE   BEACH

Map p263 (🚢Manly) Split in two by Manly
Wharf, this sheltered enclave has shark
nets and calm water, making it a popular
choice for families with toddlers. Despite
the busy location, the clear waters have
plenty of appeal.

MANLY ART GALLERY & MUSEUM   MUSEUM

Map p263 (www.manly.nsw.gov.au; West Esplanade; ⊘10am-5pm Tue-Sun; 🚢Manly) FREE A
short stroll from Manly Wharf, this pas-
sionately managed community gallery
maintains a local focus, with exhibits of
surfcraft, camp swimwear and beachy bits
and pieces. There's also a ceramics gallery,
and lots of old Manly photos to peer at.

MANLY SEA LIFE SANCTUARY   AQUARIUM

Map p263 (☑1800 199 742; www.manlysealife
sanctuary.com.au; West Esplanade; adult/child
$25/15; ⊘9.30am-5pm; 🚢Manly) This ain't
the place to come if you're on your way to
Manly Beach for a surf. Underwater glass
tubes enable you to become alarmingly intimate with 3m grey nurse sharks. Reckon
they're not hungry? **Shark Dive Xtreme**
(introductory/certified dives $280/205) enables
you to enter their world. Upstairs, the resi-

WORTH A DETOUR

NORTH HEAD CIRCUIT TRACK

Besides the harbour walk (p174), the
other major segment of the Manly
Scenic Walkway loops around North
Head and takes between three and
four hours (9.5km). From Manly Wharf,
follow Eastern Esplanade and Stuart
St to Spring Cove, head into the North
Head section of Sydney Harbour
National Park, and make your way
through the bush to the spectacular
Fairfax Lookout at the southern tip of
North Head (approximately 45 minutes in total). From the lookout, walk
the Fairfax Loop (1km, 30 minutes)
and then head back via the Cabbage
Tree Bay Walk, which follows the sea-
sprayed shoreline back to Manly Beach
via picturesque Shelly Beach and tiny
Fairy Bower Beach.

---

dents of the penguin enclosure have un-
bridled amounts of fun.

THE CORSO   AREA

Map p263 (🚢Manly) The quickest route from
the Manly ferry terminal to Manly's ocean
beach is along the Corso, a part-pedestrian
mall lined with surf shops, pubs and sushi
bars. Kids splash around in the fountains
and spaced-out surfies shuffle back to the
ferry after a hard day carving up the swell.

★MANLY BEACH   BEACH

Map p263 (🚢Manly) Sydney's second-most-
famous beach stretches for nearly two golden
kilometres, lined by Norfolk Island pines
and scrappy midrise apartment blocks. The
southern end of the beach, nearest the Corso,
is known as South Steyne, with North Steyne
in the centre and Queenscliff at the northern
end; each has its own surf life-saving club.

FAIRY BOWER BEACH   BEACH

Map p263 (Bower Lane; 🚌135) Indulge your
mermaid fantasies (the more seemly ones at
least) in this pretty triangular ocean pool
set into the rocky shoreline. The life-size
sea nymphs of Helen Leete's bronze sculpture *Oceanides* (1997) stand on the edge,
washed by the surf. Fairy Bower is best
reached by the promenade heading around
Manly Beach's southern headland.

ST PATRICK'S COLLEGE   HISTORIC BUILDING

(151 Darley Rd; 🚢Manly) Southeast of Manly's
centre, this Gothic Revival college (1889)
lords it over the rooftops from its hillside
position. It was a seminary for years and
Australia's first Catholic training college. It's
now a management college, but its chapel
was the venue for Nicole Kidman and Keith
Urban's nuptials in 2006. More recently it
doubled as Jay Gatsby's house for Baz Luhrmann's 2013 film version of *The Great Gatsby*.

SHELLY BEACH   BEACH

(🚢Manly) This sheltered north-facing ocean
cove is just a short 1km walk from the busy
Manly beach strip. The tranquil waters are
a protected haven for marine life, so it offers wonderful snorkelling.

NORTH HEAD   NATIONAL PARK

(North Head Scenic Dr; 🚌135) About 3km south
of Manly, spectacular, chunky North Head
offers dramatic cliffs, lookouts and sweeping
views of the ocean, the harbour and the city;
hire a bike and go exploring. The Manly Scenic Walkway (p172) loops around the park;
pick up a brochure from the visitor centre.

QUARANTINE STATION HISTORIC BUILDING
(☑02-9466 1551; www.quarantinestation.com.au; 1 North Head Scenic Dr; ⊙museum 10am-4pm Sun-Thu, to 8pm Fri & Sat; ☐135) FREE From 1835 to 1983 this eerie-but-elegant complex was used to isolate new arrivals suspected of carrying disease, in an attempt to limit the spread of cholera, smallpox and bubonic plague. These days the 'Q Station' has been reborn as a tourist destination with a museum, accommodation, restaurants and a whole swath of tour options.

★STORE BEACH BEACH
(⊙dawn-dusk) A hidden jewel on North Head, magical Store Beach can only be reached by kayak or boat. It's a fairy-penguin breeding ground, so access is prohibited from dusk, when the birds waddle in.

◉ Balgowlah Heights

FORTY BASKETS BEACH BEACH
(Beatty St; ☐171) On the Manly Scenic Walkway, just before heading into the Balgowlah Heights section of Sydney Harbour National Park. The picnic area is cut off at high tide.

REEF BEACH BEACH
(Beatty St; ☐171) Despite what you might have heard, this little cove on the Manly Scenic Walkway is neither nude nor full of dudes; the Manly Council put paid to that in 1993. Now it's often deserted.

◉ Clontarf

WASHAWAY BEACH BEACH
(Cutler Rd; ☐171) Rugged and beautiful, Washaway is a secluded little spot within Sydney Harbour National Park, near Grotto Point on the Manly Scenic Walkway.

CLONTARF BEACH BEACH
(Sandy Bay Rd; ☐132) A low-lapping elbow of sand facing the Spit Bridge. Clontarf is popular with families, and has grassy picnic areas.

◉ Warringah

FRESHWATER BEACH
(Moore Rd; ☐139) This sandy bay just north of Manly has a cool ocean pool and plenty of teenagers. Good for learner surfers.

WORTH A DETOUR

MODERNISM TO THE MAX
Sydney's most famous architect, Harry Seidler, designed the modest 50-sq-metre **Rose Seidler House** (☑02-9989 8020; www.sydneylivingmuseums.com.au; 71 Clissold Rd; adult/child/family $8/4/17; ⊙11am-4pm Sun; ☐575) for his mother and father, Rose and Max. It's a modernist gem from 1950, with free-flowing open spaces, retro colour schemes and hip furnishings. The house is around 30km north of the city and a fair hike from Wahroonga train station – the bus gets closer but you're better off with your own wheels.

CURL CURL BEACH
(Carrington Pde; ☐139) Attracting a mix of family groups and experienced surfers, this is a large beach with rocky saltwater pools at each end, a swampy lagoon and curly waves.

✕ EATING

Salty Manly has dozens of fairly average eateries with a couple of starlets in their midst. Local surf-hippies guarantee a sprinkling of organic and vegetarian options, too.

✕ Manly

BAREFOOT COFFEE TRADERS CAFE $
Map p263 (18 Whistler St; items $3-6; ⊙6.30am-5.30pm; ⛴Manly) Run by surfer lads serving fair-trade organic coffee from a bathroom-sized shop, Barefoot heralds a new wave of Manly cool. Food is limited but the Belgian waffles go magically well with a macchiato.

CHAT THAI THAI $
Map p263 (☑02-9976 2939; www.chatthai.com.au; Manly Wharf; mains $10-18; ⊙11am-9.30pm; ⛴Manly) Set inside Manly Wharf, this branch of the Thaitown favourite (p97) misses out on the harbour views but delivers on flavour.

PURE WHOLEFOODS VEGETARIAN $
Map p263 (☑02-8966 9377; www.facebook.com/PureWholefoods; 10 Darley Rd; mains $10-15; ⊙7am-5pm; ✍; ⛴Manly) ✿ This wholefood minimart has a great street cafe serving organic vegetarian goodies, including

172

ANDREW WATSON / GETTY IMAGES ©

DAVID MESSENT / GETTY IMAGES ©

1. South Steyne (p170)
Grab a surfboard and embrace the local lifestyle.

2. Manly Beach (p170)
This renowned stretch of coast is lined with stately Norfolk Island pines.

3. Manly (p168)
Dine outdoors and enjoy the suburb's laid-back vibe.

4. Quarantine Station (p171)
Examine carvings in the sandstone at this historic site.

SENG CHYE TEO / GETTY IMAGES ©

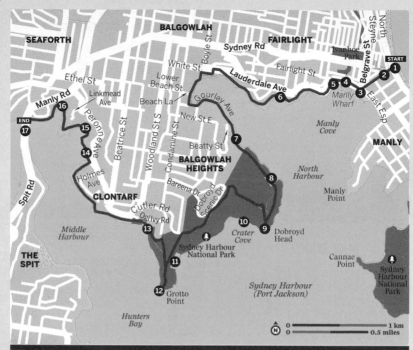

Neighbourhood Walk
Manly Scenic Walkway

START MANLY BEACH
END THE SPIT BRIDGE
LENGTH 10KM; FOUR TO 4½ HOURS

This epic walk traces the coast west from Manly past million-dollar harbour-view properties and then through a rugged 2.5km section of Sydney Harbour National Park that remains much as it was when the First Fleet sailed in. There aren't any eateries en route, so fortify yourself in Manly beforehand or stock up for a picnic. Make sure you carry plenty of water, slop on some sunscreen, slap on a hat and wear sturdy shoes.

Check the surf at ❶ **Manly Beach** (p170) then cruise down the ❷ **Corso** (p170) to the ❸ **Hello Manly information centre** (p225) where you can pick up a walk brochure with a detailed map.

Head down to ❹ **Manly Cove** (p170) and pick up the path near ❺ **Manly Sea Life Sanctuary** (p170). After 700m you'll reach ❻ **Fairlight Beach**, where you can scan the view through the heads. Yachts

tug at their moorings as you trace the North Harbour inlet and after 2km you'll come to ❼ **Forty Baskets Beach** (p171). Kookaburras cackle as you enter the national park and approach ❽ **Reef Beach** (p171).

The track becomes steep, sandy and rocky further into the park – keep an eye out for wildflowers, spiders in bottlebrush trees and fat goannas sunning themselves. The views from ❾ **Dobroyd Head** are unforgettable. Check out the deserted 1930s sea shacks at the base of the ❿ **Crater Cove** cliff, and ⓫ **Aboriginal rock carvings** on an unsigned ledge left of the track before the turn-off to ⓬ **Grotto Point Lighthouse**.

Becalmed ⓭ **Castle Rock Beach** is at the western end of the national park. From here the path winds around the rear of houses to ⓮ **Clontarf Beach** (p171). ⓯ **Sandy Bay** follows and then ⓰ **Fisher Bay** before you reach the ⓱ **Spit Bridge**. From the southern end of the bridge you can either bus it back to Manly (buses 140, 143 or 144) or into the city (176 to 180).

flavoursome flans, salads, nori rolls, cakes, cookies, wraps, burgers and smoothies. Vegan, raw-food, sugar-free, gluten-free and dairy-free purists are also catered for.

BENBRY BURGERS
BURGERS $

Map p263 (www.benbryburgersmanly.com; 5 Sydney Rd; burgers $6.50-14; ⊙11am-9pm; ☑; ⚲Manly) A popular takeaway assembling juicy gourmet burgers.

HUGOS MANLY
ITALIAN $$

Map p263 (☑02-8116 8555; www.hugos.com. au; Manly Wharf; pizzas $20-28, mains $32-38; ⊙noon-midnight; ⚲Manly) Occupying an altogether more glamorous location than its Kings Cross parent, Hugos Manly serves the same acclaimed pizzas but tops them with harbour views and an expanded Italian menu. A dedicated crew mixes cocktails, or you can just slide in for a cold beer.

BELGRAVE CARTEL
CAFE $$

Map p263 (☑02-9976 6548; www.cartelgroup. co; 6 Belgrave St; small plates $6-18, mains $16-26; ⊙7am-10pm Sun, 6am-2pm Mon & Tue, to midnight Wed-Sat; ⚲Manly) Little Cartel may be grungy but it's nowhere as sinister as it sounds; the only drugs being peddled here are pure, unadulterated caffeine and utterly addictive Italian-influenced fare.

BOWER RESTAURANT
MODERN AUSTRALIAN $$

Map p263 (☑02-9977 5451; www.thebowerrestaurant.com.au; 7 Marine Pde; breakfast $14-19, lunch $22-30; ⊙8am-5pm; ⚲Manly) Follow the foreshore east from Manly's ocean beach to this little cafe/restaurant, within spray's breath of the sea. There's lots of seafood on the menu and the surfer-gal staff aren't afraid to let Olivia Newton-John wail on the stereo.

✖ Warringah

PILU KIOSK
CAFE $

(www.piluatfreshwater.com.au; Moore Rd; breakfast $6-9, lunch $11-13; ⊙7am-3pm; ☐139) It may be attached to the pricy Pilu restaurant, but this beach cafe is an altogether more relaxed affair. Board shorts and thongs (flip-flops) are the norm – if you're wearing a shirt, that's a bonus. The coffee is great and the suckling-pig panini are legendary.

PILU AT FRESHWATER
ITALIAN $$$

(☑02-9938 3331; www.piluatfreshwater.com. au; Moore Rd; mains $45; ⊙noon-2.30pm Tue-Sun, 6-11pm Tue-Sat; ☐139) Housed within a heritage-listed beach house overlooking the

WORTH A DETOUR

GO WILD IN THE SUBURBS

Lane Cove National Park (www.nationalparks.nsw.gov.au; Lady Game Dr; per car $7; ⊙9am-6pm; ⚲North Ryde) is a great place to stretch out on some middle-sized bushwalks. It's home to dozens of critters, including some endangered owls and toads. If you visit in spring, the water dragons will be getting horny and the native orchids and lilies will be flowering. There's a boat shed on Lane Cove River that rents out row boats and kayaks, but swimming isn't a good idea. You can also cycle and camp, and some sections are wheelchair accessible.

ocean, this multi-award-winning Sardinian restaurant serves specialities such as oven-roasted suckling pig and traditional flatbread. Your best bet is to plump for the tasting menu (from $105).

🍷 DRINKING & NIGHTLIFE

Manly has a sandy party scene revolving around the Corso and Manly Wharf.

MANLY WHARF HOTEL
PUB

Map p263 (www.manlywharfhotel.com.au; Manly Wharf; ⊙11.30am-midnight; ⚲Manly) Harking back to 1950s design, this waterfront pub is perfect for sunny afternoon beers. Tuck away a few schooners after a hard day in the surf, then pour yourself onto the ferry. Sports games draw a crowd and DJs liven up Sunday afternoons.

HOTEL STEYNE
PUB

Map p263 (☑02-9977 4977; www.steynehotel. com.au; 75 The Corso; ⊙9am-3am Mon-Sat, to midnight Sun; ⚲Manly) Boasting numerous bars over two levels, this pub accommodates everyone from sporty bogans to clubby kids to families. The internal courtyard isn't flash, but the rooftop bar more than makes up for it with wicked views over the beach.

BAVARIAN BIER CAFÉ
BEER HALL

Map p263 (www.bavarianbiercafe.com; Manly Wharf; ⊙11am-midnight Mon-Fri, 9am-midnight Sat & Sun; ⚲Manly) Transplanted from York St (p98) to the beach, the Bavarian offers 10 brews on tap and 10 more imported beers by the bottle.

WORTH A DETOUR

OUTER SUBURB ATTRACTIONS

Wet'n'Wild Sydney (📞13 33 86; www.wetnwildsydney.com.au; 427 Reservoir Rd, Prospect; over/under 110cm tall $80/60; ⏰Sep-Apr, hours & days vary; 🅿️🚻; 🚌shuttle from Parramatta Station) The famous Gold Coast theme park has opened in Sydney with more than 40 slides, including a 360-degree loop slide that hits speeds of up to 60km/h.

Featherdale Wildlife Park (📞02-9622 1644; www.featherdale.com.au; 217-229 Kildare Rd, Doonside; adult/child/family $29/16/82; ⏰9am-5pm; 🚌725, 🚉Doonside) This wildlife park offers opportunities to get better acquainted with koalas, kookaburras, kangaroos and other Aussie critters. It's 45km west of the central city.

🛍 SHOPPING

ALOHA SURF
SPORTS, CLOTHING

Map p263 (📞02-9977 3777; www.alohasurfmanly.com.au; 42 Pittwater Rd; ⏰9am-6pm; 🚢Manly) Longboards, shortboards, bodyboards, skateboards and surfing fashion.

🏃 SPORTS & ACTIVITIES

ECOTREASURES
CULTURAL TOUR

(📞0415 121 648; www.ecotreasures.com.au) 🎫 Small group tours include *Manly Snorkel Walk & Talk* (90 minutes, adult/child $65/40) and longer excursions to the Northern Beaches and Ku-ring-gai Chase National Park, including Aboriginal Heritage Tours lead by Indigenous guides.

MANLY OCEAN ADVENTURES
BOAT TOUR

Map p263 (📞1300 062 659; www.manlyoceanadventures.com.au; 1/40 East Esplanade; from $85; 🚢Manly) Blast out to sea in a speedboat, following the coastline from Manly all the way to Bondi. From May to December it also offers whale-watching excursions.

MANLY BIKE TOURS
CYCLING

Map p263 (📞02-8005 7368; www.manlybiketours.com.au; 54 West Promenade; hire per hour/day from $15/31; ⏰9am-6pm; 🚢Manly) 🎫 Hires bikes and runs daily two-hour bike tours around Manly (10.30am, $89, bookings essential).

MANLY SURF SCHOOL
SURFING

Map p263 (📞02-9932 7000; www.manlysurfschool.com; North Steyne Surf Club; 🚢Manly) Offers two-hour surf lessons year-round (adult/child $70/55), as well as private tuition. Also runs surf safaris up to the Northern Beaches.

MANLY KAYAK CENTRE
KAYAKING

Map p263 (📞1300 529 257; www.manlykayakcentre.com.au; West Esplanade; 1/2/8hr from $25/40/70; ⏰9am-5pm; 🚢Manly) As long as you can swim, you can hire a kayak or paddle board from this stand near Manly Sea Life Sanctuary; there are additional stands near Manly Wharf Hotel (p175) and the Quarantine Station (p171). You'll be provided with a life jacket, paddling instruction and tips on secluded beaches to visit. Three-hour kayak tours cost $89.

DIVE CENTRE MANLY
DIVING

Map p263 (📞02-9977 4355; www.divesydney.com.au; 10 Belgrave St; ⏰8.30am-6pm; 🚢Manly) Offers snorkel safaris ($50), two-day learn-to-dive PADI courses (from $445), guided shore dives (one/two dives $95/125) and boat dives (two dives $175).

PRO DIVE
DIVING

Map p263 (📞02-9977 5966; www.prodivesydneymanly.com; 169 Pittwater Rd; ⏰9am-6pm; 🚌155-9) This outfit offers everything from introductory Discover Scuba dives (from $197) to three-day open-water courses ($399).

MANLY WATERWORKS
WATER PARK

Map p263 (📞02-9949 1088; www.manlywaterworks.com.au; cnr West Esplanade & Commonwealth Pde; per hour/day $18/30; ⏰10am-5pm Sat & Sun; 🚢Manly) The twisting, turning water slides at Manly Waterworks are surefire kid-pleasers.

SKATER HQ
SKATEBOARDING

Map p263 (📞02-8667 7892; www.skaterhq.com.au; 49 North Steyne; ⏰9am-6pm; 🚢Manly) The Manly branch of Skater HQ (p155) offers the same deals as its Entertainment Quarter sibling.

DRIPPING WET
SURFING

Map p263 (📞02-9977 3549; www.facebook.com/drippingwet.surfco; 95 North Steyne; ⏰9am-6pm; 🚢Manly) This beachside surf shop hires out surfboards (per hour/day/week $15/50/150), bodyboards (per hour/day/week $5/20/60) and wetsuits (same as bodyboards).

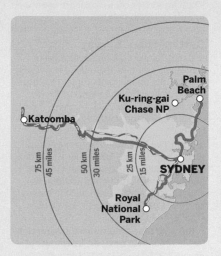

Day Trips from Sydney

The Blue Mountains p178

For more than a century, the Blue Mountains has lured Sydneysiders up from the sweltering plains with promises of cool-climate relief, naughty fireside weekends, astounding scenery and brilliant bushwalks.

Royal National Park p180

A prime stretch of wilderness at the city's doorstep, encompassing secluded beaches, vertiginous cliffs, scrub, heath, rainforest, swamp wallabies, lyrebirds and raucous flocks of yellow-tailed black cockatoos.

Northern Beaches p181

It requires a little effort to reach them (no trains run here and buses seem to take forever), but the Northern Beaches are some of Sydney's very best suburbs. Especially if you're a *Home & Away* fan.

The Blue Mountains

Explore

Climbing west from Sydney, the Blue Mountains (named after the purple haze of eucalyptus oils) is actually a vast sandstone plateau riddled with steep gullies and dark forests cloaked in mist.

Plenty of people make a day trip just to gawp at this classic Australian vista, but with the wondrous bushwalks (lasting from a few minutes to a few days), fine food and cosy lodgings it's a magical escape worth extra time.

Katoomba, with the dramatic Three Sisters rock formation, is the main port of call for day-trippers. But if you're staying overnight, romantic Leura and earthy Black-

heath are better choices. All are connected to Sydney's train network.

Getting There & Away

➜ **Car** Head west on Parramatta Rd to Strathfield and take the tolled M4. West of Penrith, the motorway becomes the Great Western Hwy. Depending on traffic it's just under two hours to Katoomba. A less direct route is the pretty 90km Bells Line of Road.

➜ **Train** The Blue Mountains line departs hourly from Central station for Glenbrook, Faulconbridge, Wentworth Falls, Leura and Katoomba (adult/child $8.60/4.30, two hours). Roughly every second train continues on to Blackheath, Mt Victoria, Zig Zag and Lithgow.

➜ **Bus** The **Blue Mountains ExplorerLink** (☑13 15 00; www.cityrail.info/tickets/which/explorerlink; 1-day pass adult/child from $55.20/24.90, 3-day pass adult/child from

Blue Mountains

$78.20/39.10) combines a train ticket to Katoomba and day access to the hop-on, hop-off bus that drives between 30 attractions around the Blue Mountains.

 SIGHTS

WENTWORTH
FALLS RESERVE
WATERFALL, PARK

(Falls Rd; 🚆Wentworth Falls) The falls that lend the town its name launch a plume of droplets over a 300m drop. This is the starting point of a network of walking tracks, which delve into the sublime Valley of the Waters, with waterfalls, gorges, woodlands and rainforests. Be sure to stretch your legs along the 1km return to Princes Rock, which offers excellent views of Wentworth Falls and the Jamison Valley.

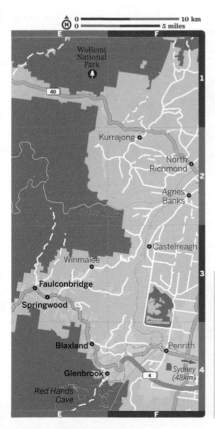

LEURA
TOWN

Leura, 3km east of Katoomba, is a gracious, affluent town, fashioned around undulating streets, unparalleled gardens and sweeping Victorian verandahs. The Mall, the tree-lined main street, offers rows of country craft stores and cafes for the daily tourist influx.

ECHO POINT
LOOKOUT

(Echo Point Rd, Katoomba) Echo Point's cliff-top viewing platform is the busiest spot in the Blue Mountains thanks to the views it offers of the area's most essential sight: a rocky trio called the **Three Sisters**. The story goes that the sisters were turned to stone by a sorcerer to protect them from the unwanted advances of three young men, but the sorcerer died before he could turn them back into humans.

SCENIC WORLD
CABLE CAR

(📞02-4780 0200; www.scenicworld.com.au; cnr Violet St & Cliff Dr, Katoomba; adult/child $35/18; ⊗9am-5pm) Take the glass-floored Skyway gondola out across the gorge and then ride what's billed as the steepest railway in the world down the 52-degree incline to the Jamison Valley floor. From here you can wander a 2.5km forest boardwalk (or hike the 12km, six-hour return track to the Ruined Castle rock formation) before catching a cable car back up the slope.

KATOOMBA
TOWN

From Leura, it's only 2km to Katoomba, the region's main town, whose often-misty steep streets are lined with art deco buildings. The population here is an odd mix of working-class battlers and hippyish refugees from the big smoke, all of whom seem to cope with the huge numbers of tour buses and tourists who come here to ooh-and-aah at the spectacular view of the Jamison Valley and Three Sisters rock formation

Blue Mountains

towers from the Echo Point viewing platforms. There are a number of short walks from Echo Point that allow you to escape the bulk of the crowds. Parking is expensive ($3.80 for first hour, $4.40 for subsequent hours); if you're walking here from the town centre, Lurline St is the most attractive route.

BLACKHEATH   TOWN

The next town to the west is Blackheath, where you can enjoy amazing views from Perrys Lookdown, Pulpit Rock, Govetts Leap and Evans Lookout. Crowds here aren't as oppressive as at Echo Point. Blackheath is also the gastronomic centre of the region, with some excellent restaurants operating between Thursday and Sunday.

Sleeping in the Blue Mountains

The Blue Mountains is the home of the B&B, with most places requiring a minimum two-night stay at the weekend. Visit www.bluemtns.com.au for an exhaustive list. Alternatively, try the much-lauded **Blue Mountains YHA** (☑02-4782 1416; www.yha.com.au; 207 Katoomba St; dm $30, d with/without bathroom $112/99; @☎), with spotlessly bright dorms and family rooms.

Royal National Park

Explore

Forming Sydney's southern border is the 165-sq-km Royal National Park. The world's second-oldest national park is home to Aboriginal rock art (it was the traditional lands of the Dharawal people),

Royal National Park

KU-RING-GAI CHASE NATIONAL PARK

Across the peninsula from Palm Beach is **Ku-ring-gai Chase National Park** (📞02-9472 8949; www.nationalparks.nsw.gov.au; Bobbin Head Rd, Mount Colah; per car per day $11, landing fee by boat adult/child $3/2), where over 100km of shoreline meets rainforest and eucalypts, rocky cliffs and mangroves. Camp at **The Basin** (📞02-9974 1011; www.nationalparks.nsw.gov.au/ku-ring-gai-chase-national-park/the-basin-campground/camping; adult/child per night $14/7; 🚢Palm Beach) or explore walking tracks, bike trails, dramatic lookouts (the view from West Head to Barrenjoey Lighthouse is a winner) and significant Aboriginal sites.

About 2.5km from the Mt Colah entrance, **Kalkari Discovery Centre** (📞02-9472 9300; Ku-ring-gai Chase Rd, Mt Colah; ⏲9am-5pm) offers guided walking and kayaking tours. On the **Aboriginal Heritage Walk** you'll come across the best-known site in the park: **Red Hands Cave** with its rock engravings and art of the Guringai Nation.

vibrant wildflowers, isolated beaches and the charming community of Bundeena.

There are a variety of bracing coastal hikes and cycling tracks in the park, leading to waterfalls, freshwater swimming holes and picnic spots; the visitors centre has maps and camping permits. **Audley Boat Shed** (📞02-9545 4967; www.audleyboatshed.com; 6 Farnell Ave) hires canoes and kayaks (per hour/day $20/45) for a paddle up Kangaroo Creek or the Hacking River.

Getting There & Away

→ **Car** You'll need a car to explore the park easily. From Sydney, take the Princes Hwy 30km south.

→ **Ferry** Catch the train to Cronulla, then a **Cronulla National Park Ferry** (📞02-9523 2990; www.cronullaferries.com.au; Cronulla Wharf; adult/child one way $6.40/$3.20; ⏲hourly between 5.30am-6.30pm Mon-Fri, 8.30am-6.30pm Sat, 8.30am-5.30pm Sun) from Cronulla to Bundeena (30 minutes).

→ **Train** If you're prepared for a lengthy hike from the station, take the Eastern Suburbs & Illawarra line to Loftus, Engadine, Heathcote or Waterfall, or continue on the South Coast line to Helensburgh or Otford (adult/child $6.80/3.40).

SIGHTS & ACTIVITIES

BUNDEENA   TOWN

(Bundeena Dr) The sizeable town of Bundeena, on the southern shore of Port Hacking opposite Sydney's southern suburb of Cronulla, is surrounded by the park. From here you can walk 30 minutes towards the ocean to **Jibbon Head**, which has a good beach and interesting Aboriginal rock art. Bundeena is the starting point of the coastal walk.

WATTAMOLLA BEACH   BEACH

(www.nationalparks.nsw.gov.au/royal-national-park/wattamolla-picnic-area/picnic-bbq; Wattamolla Rd) About halfway along the coast, Wattamolla Beach is one of the park's favourite picnic spots. It has the great advantage of having both a surf beach and a lagoon, allowing for safe swimming.

GARIE BEACH   BEACH

(Garie Beach Rd) An excellent surf beach with road access. Like all of these surf beaches, swimming can be treacherous.

Sleeping in Royal National Park

Aside from some B&Bs in Bundeena, camping is the main sleeping option within the park and there are both drive-in and walk-in sites available. Bookings are essential; call 📞02-9542 0683.

Northern Beaches

Explore

Sydney's northern coastline is truly special, with idyllic beaches, bush and an endless-summer vibe. An hour's drive from the city

Northern Beaches

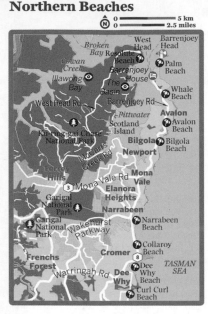

(best avoided during peak hour), the region makes for a cruisey day trip.

Driving north, **Dee Why** is a no-fuss family beach while **Collaroy** has great swimming conditions and is excellent for beginner surfers. The beachside **YHA** (✆02-9981 1177; www.sydneybeachouse.com. au; 4 Collaroy St, Collaroy; dm/d from $27/72; @ ⊠; ☐E88) offers free boards. Once you've got some experience you can head to **Narrabeen**, which is hard-core surf turf. **Avalon** is getting a reputation for great little

cafes, bars and boutiques, and exclusive **Whale Beach**, a paradisiacal slice of sand flanked by steep cliffs, is popular with celebrities and families.

Palm Beach, the farthest flung, is the least built up and the best. It's also the setting of Summer Bay, the fictional town in soap opera *Home & Away*. Hike up to the 1881 **Barrenjoey Lighthouse** at the northern tip of the headland for stunning views across Pittwater.

For a leisurely lunch try **Barrenjoey House** (✆02-9974 4001; www.barrenjoeyhouse. com; 1108 Barrenjoey Rd, Palm Beach; mains $30-39; ◷11.30am-late; ☐L90, 190) opposite the ferry wharf or the equally alluring **Boathouse** (www.theboathousepb.com.au; Governor Phillip Park, Palm Beach; mains $25; ◷7.30am-4pm; ☐L90, 190).

Getting There & Away

Ku-ring-gai Chase National Park has several through roads from the northern suburbs of Turramurra, Mt Colah and Terrey Hills.

➡ **Car** From the city, take the bridge or tunnel north and exit at Military Rd. Continue on to Spit Rd across the Spit Bridge and keep heading straight. This eventually becomes Pittwater Rd, which reaches the coast at Dee Why.

➡ **Bus** Various routes terminate along the way but L90 (from Railway Sq and Wynyard) goes all the way to Palm Beach ($4.50, 1¾ hours).

➡ **Ferry** Catch the Palm Beach Ferry from Palm Beach Wharf to The Basin.

Sleeping

Sydney offers a vast quantity and variety of accommodation in every price range. Even so, the supply shrivels up under the summer sun, particularly around weekends and big events, so be sure to book ahead.

Rates & Seasons

These days, all but the smallest hotels vary their prices depending on the season, special events, day of the week (weekends tend to be more expensive) and, most importantly, occupancy. Where prices vary widely, we've listed a 'from' amount, basing this on the cheapest room available given a reasonable amount of notice in the high (but not necessarily peak) season. If you leave booking until the last minute, you may find yourself paying considerably more.

The summer high season lasts from around December to March, with the absolute peak being between Christmas and New Year (especially New Year's Eve). Prices also shoot up again in late February/early March in the lead up to Mardi Gras.

Hotels

There are hotels scattered throughout Sydney, but you'll find the international chains with all their bells and whistles in Circular Quay and the city centre. The suburbs and beaches host a diverse bunch of boutique escapes, from heritage-listed terrace houses to sleek apartments and beach bungalows.

Hostels

Sydney's hostels range from the sublime to the sublimely grotty. A clump of flashpacker-style blocks encircling Central station have raised the bar, offering en suites, air-conditioning, rooftop decks and, in one case, a pool. Private rooms in such places are often on par with midrange hotels – and in many cases the prices aren't all that different either. You'll find smaller, cheaper hostels in Kings Cross, Glebe and at the beaches.

B&Bs & Guesthouses

We've used the term guesthouses to refer to places that are bigger and less personal than the average B&B, but are smaller and offer less services than your average hotel. Guesthouses may or may not offer free breakfast.

NEED TO KNOW

Price Ranges
In reviews the following codes represent the price of accommodation for two people in high season (except for hostels, which are based on the per-person dorm rate):

$ doubles under $100

$$ doubles $100 to $200

$$$ doubles over $200

Checking In & Out
Check in is normally 2pm, although most places are flexible if the room is ready, or at least let you stow your luggage. Check out is often as early as 10am; it doesn't hurt to request a later time.

Breakfast
Many hotels offer a continental buffet breakfast, but it's worth asking about room-only rates, as they can be much cheaper – and exploring Sydney's cafes is part of the fun. Some hostels offer free toast and cereal. Not all B&Bs offer full cooked breakfasts; check in advance.

Websites
➡ **Wotif** (www.wotif.com) Bookings, including 'mystery deals'.

➡ **sydney.com** (www.sydney.com) Official tourism website, including accommodation listings.

➡ **Lonely Planet** (www.lonelyplanet.com/australia/sydney/hotels) Accommodation listings.

➡ **HomeCamp** (www.home-camp.com.au) Budget option; camp in suburban house gardens.

Lonely Planet's Top Choices

Sydney Harbour YHA (p186) Million-dollar harbour views on a youth-hostel budget.

QT Sydney (p188) Fun, sexy and completely over the top.

Cockatoo Island (p186) Island camping in the heart of the city.

ADGE Boutique Apartment Hotel (p190) A kaleidoscopic twist on the ubiquitous serviced apartment.

Park Hyatt (p186) There's no better location for Sydney razzle-dazzle.

Best by Budget

$
Bounce (p189)
Railway Square YHA (p187)

$$
1888 Hotel (p188)
Dive Hotel (p192)

$$$
QT Sydney (p188)
Park Hyatt (p186)

Best for Views

Shangri-La (p186)
Quay West (p186)
Park Hyatt (p186)
Meriton Serviced Apartments Kent Street (p187)

Best for Heritage

Lord Nelson Brewery Hotel (p186)
Russell (p186)
Sydney Harbour Bed & Breakfast (p186)

1888 Hotel (p188)
Harbour Rocks (p186)

Best Serviced Apartments

Pullman Quay Grand (p186)
ADGE Boutique Apartment Hotel (p190)
Fraser Suites (p188)
Adina Bondi Beach (p191)

Best Boutique Hotels

QT Sydney (p188)
Establishment Hotel (p188)
1888 Hotel (p188)
Dive Hotel (p192)

Best B&Bs

Tara Guest House (p189)
Forsyth B&B (p189)
Simpsons of Potts Point (p191)
Bondi Beach House (p191)

Best for Swimming Pools

The Langham (p186)
Quay West (p186)
Fraser Suites Sydney (p188)
InterContinental Double Bay (p187)

Best Hostels

Wake Up! (p187)
Railway Square YHA (p187)
Blue Parrot (p190)
Bounce (p189)
Bondi Beachouse YHA (p191)

Where to Stay

Neighbourhood	For	Against
Circular Quay & The Rocks	Big-ticket sights; vibrant nightlife; top hotels and restaurants	Tourist central; expensive
Sydney Harbour	Everywhere is a pleasant ferry journey from town	Can be isolated
City Centre & Haymarket	Good transport links; lots of sights, bars, fantastic Asian restaurants	Can be noisy and, in parts, ugly
Darling Harbour & Pyrmont	Plenty to see and do; lively nightlife	Soulless; few affordable restaurants
Inner West	Bohemian; great coffee; interesting shops; priced for locals	Few sights; getting to beaches requires effort
Surry Hills & Darlinghurst	Sydney's hippest eating and drinking precinct; heart of gay scene	Few actual sights
Kings Cross & Potts Point	Interesting and idiosyncratic; numerous hostels, bars and clubs; good transport links	Sleazy stripclubs; regular alcohol-fuelled stoushes
Paddington & Centennial Park	Leafy and genteel; bus access to city and beaches	Few sights; limited accommodation options
Bondi to Coogee	Sand, surf and sexy bods	Slow bus ride to the city
Manly	Beautiful beaches; community feel	Not much to do if the weather's bad

🛏 Circular Quay & The Rocks

★SYDNEY HARBOUR YHA
HOSTEL $

Map p240 (☑02-8272 0900; www.yha.com.au; 110 Cumberland St; dm/r from $52/192; ⓡCircular Quay) 🍃 Any qualms about the unhostel-like prices will be shelved the moment you head up to the rooftop of this YHA and see the million-dollar views of Circular Quay. All of the spacious rooms, including the dorms, have private bathrooms and there are a host of sustainability initiatives in place.

RUSSELL
HOTEL $$

Map p240 (☑02-9241 3543; www.therussell.com. au; 143a George St; s without bathroom $159, d without bathroom $169-209, d $259-299; ⓡCircular Quay) Old-world charm meets gentle contemporary styling at this long-standing favourite. The rooftop garden, downstairs wine bar and Circular Quay location are major drawcards. Next door to the historic Fortune of War pub, front rooms can be noisy on weekends.

SYDNEY HARBOUR BED & BREAKFAST
B&B $$

Map p240 (☑02-9247 1130; www.bbsydneyhar bour.com.au; 142 Cumberland St; r with/without bathroom $240/165; ⓡCircular Quay) This quaint 100-year-old guesthouse offers lovely rooms which have an Australian flavour without straying into twee territory. Rooms come in a variety of configurations, have tea- and coffee-making facilities and feature handcrafted furnishings and polished floors. Rates include a cooked breakfast.

LORD NELSON BREWERY HOTEL
PUB $$

Map p240 (☑02-9251 4044; www.lordnelson brewery.com; 19 Kent St; r from $180; ⓡCircular Quay) Built in 1836, this sandstone pub has a tidy set of upstairs rooms, with exposed stone walls and dormer windows with harbour glimpses. Most of the nine rooms have en suites; there are also cheaper rooms with shared facilities. Rates include breakfast.

★PARK HYATT
HOTEL $$$

Map p240 (☑02-9256 1234; www.sydney.park. hyatt.com; 7 Hickson Rd; r from $860; ⓡCircular Quay; ⓢ) At Sydney's most expensive hotel the impeccable service levels and facilities are second to none. With full-frontal views across Circular Quay, you can catch all the action from your bed, balcony or bathtub. From the rooftop pool you feel you can almost touch the Harbour Bridge.

LANGHAM
HOTEL $$$

Map p240 (☑02-8248 5200; www.sydney.lang hamhotels.com; 89-113 Kent St; r from $635; ⓡWynyard; ⓢ) Recently reopened after a $30-million revamp, this opulent hotel eschews excessive glitz in favour of an elegant antique ambience. This is where you head for a true five-star stay featuring afternoon turn-down service, in-house pastry kitchen, page-long pillow menu and an extravagant pool and day-spa experience.

HARBOUR ROCKS
BOUTIQUE HOTEL $$$

Map p240 (☑02-8220 9999; www.harbourrocks. com.au; 34 Harrington Street; r from $350; ⓡCircular Quay) This deluxe boutique hotel on the site of Sydney's first hospital has undergone a chic and sympathetic transformation from colonial warehouse to a series of New York loft–style rooms, with high ceilings, charcoal brick walls and elegant furnishings.

SHANGRI-LA
HOTEL $$$

Map p240 (☑02-9250 6000; www.shangri-la.com; 176 Cumberland St; r from $350; ⓡCircular Quay) The Hong Kong–based chain's Sydney offering is a sleek tower with palatial rooms and seriously spectacular views. As expected, service is efficient and discreet, whatever the request. The acclaimed Altitude Restaurant on the 36th floor offers a well-edited menu focusing on seasonal produce.

QUAY WEST SUITES
APARTMENT $$$

Map p240 (☑02-9240 6000; www.quaywestsuites sydney.com.au; 98 Gloucester St; apt from $387; ⓡCircular Quay) One of the older high-rise hotels, Quay West's early-1990s decor could just about qualify as retro. The roomy apartments are a home away from home, each with a full kitchen, lounge and laundry room. The views are extraordinary.

PULLMAN QUAY GRAND SYDNEY HARBOUR
APARTMENT $$$

Map p240 (☑02-9256 4000; www.pullmanhotels. com; 61 Macquarie St; apt from $472; ⓡCircular Quay) With the Opera House as its neighbour, the building known locally as 'the toaster' has a scorching-hot location. These well-designed contemporary apartments set you in the glitzy heart of Sydney.

🛏 Sydney Harbour

★COCKATOO ISLAND
CAMPGROUND $

Map p242 (☑02-8898 9774; www.cockatooisland. gov.au; camp sites from $45, 2-bed tents from $150, apt from $225, houses from $595; ⓢCockatoo

Island) Waking up on an island in the middle of the harbour is an extraordinary Sydney experience. Bring your own tent or 'glamp' in a two-person tent complete with a double bed on the water's edge. Non-campers will enjoy the elegant garden apartments. For self-caterers, there's a well-equipped camp kitchen; for everyone else, there are three cafes and bars.

SAVOY HOTEL
HOTEL $$

Map p242 (☑02-9326 1411; www.savoyhotel. com.au; 41 Knox St; d $125-195, ste from $230; ☑Double Bay) Double Bay may be undergoing a renaissance but thankfully the Savoy remains unpretentious, friendly and great value. Rooms are dated but comfortable for the price. Strive for a loft or a suite looking towards the bay. A large breakfast is served at the iconic D'Bees cafe.

WATSONS BAY
BOUTIQUE HOTEL
BOUTIQUE HOTEL $$

Map p242 (☑02-9337 5444; www.watsonsbayho tel.com.au; 10 Marine Parade; r $190-390, ste $400-620; ☑Watsons Bay) The ferry pulls up to the doorstep of this chic, Hampton's-inspired hotel in a charming beachside hamlet. Expect luxuries such as crisp linen, trendy bathroom accessories and slick glassed-in en suites. The hotel's multilevel Beach Club hums on weekends, and despite double glazing noise can be an issue. Rates include breakfast.

INTERCONTINENTAL
SYDNEY DOUBLE BAY
HOTEL $$$

Map p242 (☑02-8388 8388; www.ihg.com; 30 Cross St, Double Bay; d/ste from $570/850; ☑Double Bay; ☒) Following a lavish renovation, this resort has been restored to the grandeur that first made it a celebrity hotspot back in the day. Swathed in Italian marble and twinkling chandeliers, it's all class from the Stillery gin bar to the slick rooftop pool. Many of the guest rooms have superb harbour views.

🛏 City Centre & Haymarket

WAKE UP!
HOSTEL $

Map p245 (☑02-9288 7888; www.wakeup.com. au; 509 Pitt St; dm $38-44, s $98, d with/without bathroom $148/118; ☑Central) Flashpackers sleep soundly in this converted 1900 department store on top of Sydney's busiest intersection. It's a convivial, colourful, professionally run hostel with 520 beds, lots of activities, a tour desk, 24-hour check-in, a sunny cafe, a bar and no excuse for neglecting your inner party animal.

RAILWAY SQUARE YHA
HOSTEL $

Map p245 (☑02-9281 9666; www.yha.com.au; 8-10 Lee St; dm from $39, d with/without bathroom from $130/116; ☑Central) This hostel's not just central, it's actually *in* Central station. A nouveau-industrial renovation has turned a former parcel shed into a hip hostel. You can even sleep in dorms in converted train carriages (bring earplugs). Private en suite rooms also available.

SYDNEY CENTRAL YHA
HOSTEL $

Map p245 (☑02-9218 9000; www.yha.com.au; 11 Rawson Pl; dm from $39, d with/without bathroom from $125/115; ☑Central; ☒) 🏊 This 1913 heritage-listed monolith is the mother of all Sydney YHA properties. The renovated hostel includes everything from a travel agency to an in-house cinema. The rooms are brightly painted and the kitchens are great but the highlight is sweating it out in the sauna, then cooling off in the rooftop pool.

PENSIONE HOTEL
BOUTIQUE HOTEL $$

Map p245 (☑02-9265 8888; www.pensione.com. au; 631-635 George St; s/d from $115/149; ☑Central) This reworked post office features smart, if bland rooms with TVs and fridges. Mark Rothko prints and a wooden staircase warm the simple, restrained surrounds. The windows facing George St are double glazed but don't open. The quietest rooms are those facing the central light-well.

HYDE PARK INN
HOTEL $$

Map p246 (☑02-9264 6001; www.hydeparkinn. com.au; 271 Elizabeth St; s/d from $165/176; ☑Museum) Right on the park, this relaxed place offers studio rooms with kitchenettes, deluxe rooms with balconies and full kitchens, and some two-bedroom apartments. All have flat-screen TVs with cable access. Breakfast and parking are included in the rate.

ADINA APARTMENT
HOTEL SYDNEY
APARTMENT $$

Map p246 (☑02-9274 0000; www.adinahotels .com.au; 511 Kent St; studio from $180, 1-/2-bedroom apt from $240/280; ☑Town Hall) Near both Chinatown and Darling Harbour but with double-glazed windows to ensure a good night's sleep, Adina offers spacious, fully equipped apartments and smaller studio rooms with kitchenettes.

MERITON SERVICED
APARTMENTS KENT STREET
APARTMENT $$

Map p246 (☑02-8263 5500; www.staymsa. com/kent; 528 Kent St; apt from $195; ☑Town Hall) There's a lot to be said for staying in a serviced apartment, not least the ability to be able to wash your smalls whenever the need arises. Each of the one- to three-bedroom apartments in this modern tower has laundry facilities and a full kitchen complete with a dishwasher.

★ QT SYDNEY
BOUTIQUE HOTEL $$$

Map p246 (☑02-8262 0000; www.qtsydney.com.au; 49 Market St; r from $380; ☒St James) Fun, sexy and completely OTT, this hotel is in the historic State Theatre. Art deco eccentricity is complemented by retro games and DIY martini kits in all the rooms, which have 12 madcap styles. There's also a spa complete with hammam (Turkish bath) and old-school barber, plus a bar and grill operated by one of the city's most fashionable restaurateurs.

PARK8
BOUTIQUE HOTEL $$$

Map p246 (☑02-9283 2488; www.8hotels.com; 185 Castlereagh St; r $225-275; ☒Town Hall) Hidden in plain sight behind a hole-in-the-wall cafe in the centre of town, this boutique hotel has perky staff. The rooms are comfortable and chic; choose between quieter standard rooms with frosted-glass windows or deluxe rooms with windows opening on to the noisy-by-day street. Families will want to check out the loft apartments.

HILTON
HOTEL $$$

Map p246 (☑02-9266 2000; www.sydney.hilton.com; 488 George St; r from $279; ☒Town Hall) A glitzy high-rise in the centre of town, the Hilton has luxury laden over every feature: spoiling spa, star-chef restaurant, mega health club – and city views to swoon over. Swanky, modernist rooms feature wood floors and flat-screens, frosted-glass bathrooms and ergonomic work desks. Superchef Luke Mangan handles the restaurant; Zeta and Marble Bar lure the beautiful people.

FRASER SUITES SYDNEY
APARTMENT $$$

Map p246 (☑02-8823 8888; sydney.frasershospitality.com; 488 Kent St; apt from $295) The spectacular 6m rainfall chandelier in the foyer sets the tone for this luxe all-suite apartment hotel which offers well-appointed rooms, a lap pool and kitchen facilities complete with fine bone china and hand-crafted French teas. The views are impressive and there are generous inclusions like free wi-fi and Molton Brown bath products.

WESTIN SYDNEY
HOTEL $$$

Map p246 (☑02-8223 1111; www.westinsydney.com; 1 Martin Pl; r from $310; ☒Martin Place) This luxury address is popular with business travellers who choose between elegant heritage rooms in the grand General Post Office building or bedding down in a modern high-rise. Thoughtful extras like lending guests exercise gear are impressive.

ESTABLISHMENT HOTEL
BOUTIQUE HOTEL $$$

Map p246 (☑02-9240 3100; www.merivale.com.au; 5 Bridge Lane; r from $350; ☒Wynyard) A room at this so-hip-it-hurts hotel is your VIP pass to the city's most decadent nights out. What Establishment lacks in facilities it makes up for with its fabulous clutch of acclaimed bars and restaurants, not to mention designer good looks that wander from Japanese-style rooms to muted, tranquil abodes, both with massive bathrooms stocked with Bulgari toiletries.

🛏 Darling Harbour & Pyrmont

★ 1888 HOTEL
BOUTIQUE HOTEL $$

Map p250 (☑02-8586 1888; www.1888hotel.com.au; 139 Murray St; d/ste from $169/249; ☒Town Hall) In a heritage-listed wool store, this stylish gem combines stark industrial minimalism with the warmth of ironbark wood beams and luxury appointments. Rooms range from the aptly named shoebox to the airy lofts and attic suites with harbour views. The cool but casual staff point out the hip hotel must-haves: lobby space set up for Instagram selfies, bikes for hire and an iPad in every room.

THE DARLING
CASINO HOTEL $$$

Map p250 (☑02-9777 9000; www.thedarling.com.au; 80 Pyrmont St, Pyrmont; r from $430; ☒Pyrmont Bay) Beyond the bling of Star City Casino lies the sumptuous Darling. Sink into beds laid with 400-thread-count Egyptian cotton sheets and choose from a menu of 12 pillows. Hard to get up? No problem. Guests can adjust the lighting, air temperature and select a time for the blinds to open in the morning via remote control.

🛏 Inner West

GLEBE VILLAGE
HOSTEL $

Map p252 (☑02-9660 8878; www.glebevillage.com; 256 Glebe Point Rd, Glebe; dm $23-27, s/d $65/90; ☒431) Straddling four Victorian houses, grungy Glebe Village is perfect for those less hung-up on comfort and cleanliness than good times. That said, the 10pm curfew can be a bit of dampener when you're enjoying the lively communal area. It offers a mix of shared bathrooms and en suites. Breakfast is included.

GLEBE POINT YHA HOSTEL **$**
Map p252 (☎02-9692 8418; www.yha.com.au; 262-264 Glebe Point Rd, Glebe; dm $28-45, s without bathroom $70, d without bathroom $84-105; ⊟431) A great choice for working travellers, this chilled-out hostel has decent facilities, plenty of organised activities and simple rooms with sinks. Less uptight than some YHAs, there's a convivial vibe, particularly on the rooftop terrace, which is popular on barbecue nights. A real plus are the surrounding cafes and easy access to public transport into town.

ALISHAN INTERNATIONAL GUEST HOUSE GUESTHOUSE **$**
Map p252 (☎02-9566 4048; www.alishan.com. au; 100 Glebe Point Rd, Glebe; dm/s/d from $35/75/95; ⊟431-434) In a substantial Victorian house in the centre of Glebe, the homely Alishan is clean, quiet and well run, with spacious communal areas including a modern kitchen and a garden with a barbecue. All rooms have TVs and fridges, although some of the cheapies share bathrooms.

★TARA GUEST HOUSE B&B **$$**
Map p252 (☎02-9519 4809; www.taraguest house.com.au; 13 Edgeware Rd, Enmore; d with/ without bathroom $215/185; ☒Newtown) When you stay at a guesthouse run by designers with a passion for cooking and gardening, you know you're in for a good time. Brom and Julian have created a peaceful retreat with four graceful spaces with soaring ceilings and French doors opening onto large verandahs. The communal breakfast is a highlight. Rates include airport transfers.

VULCAN HOTEL BOUTIQUE HOTEL **$$**
Map p252 (☎02-9211 3283; www.vulcanhotel. com.au; 500 Wattle St, Ultimo; r from $140; ☒Central) Vulcan was a watering hole well into the 1990s before the pub rooms were converted into a family-owned boutique budget hotel. The minimalist beige guest rooms are small but nicely appointed with attractive bathrooms. Breakfast (extra cost) is served in the sunny ground-floor cafe.

URBAN HOTEL BOUTIQUE HOTEL **$$**
Map p252 (☎02-8960 7800; www.theurbanhotel. com.au; 52-60 Enmore Rd, Newtown; r from $148; ☒Newtown) A minute's walk from Newtown station and a bunch of great bars and eats, this brand-new hotel in a former RSL Club offers industrial-sleek studio accommodation. The Urban stands out from the crowd with a slew of extras like free wi-fi, free landline calls Australia-wide and relaxed check-in/-out options.

FORSYTH BED & BREAKFAST B&B **$$**
Map p252 (☎02-9552 2110; www.forsythbnb.com; 3 Forsyth St, Glebe; d $195-225; ⊟431) Count yourself lucky if you nab one of the two guest rooms at this bijou escape in Glebe's leafy backstreets. Forsyth B&B has light, art-filled rooms, one with a balcony overlooking the city. The accommodating owners provide personalised itineraries, airport transfers and help with public transport. Breakfast is served in the Japanese-inspired garden. Minimum three-night stay.

🛏 Surry Hills & Darlinghurst

BOUNCE HOSTEL **$**
Map p254 (☎02-9281 2222; www.bouncehotel. com.au; 28 Chalmers St, Surry Hills; dm/r from $40/149; ☒Central) 🐾 This popular hostel has scooped up a pile of awards for its boutique take on budget accommodation. Beyond the standard dorms there are double rooms with sleek en suites, luxury-hotel-quality beds and TVs. Soak up those skyline views on the rooftop terrace.

BIG HOSTEL HOSTEL **$**
Map p254 (☎02-9281 6030; www.bighostel. com; 212 Elizabeth St, Surry Hills; dm $32-36, s/d $89/110; ☒Central; 🛜) A great, no-frills hostel experience with a cool rooftop terrace and a snazzy communal area. A plus is the free breakfast and free wi-fi on the ground floor.

KIRKETON HOTEL BOUTIQUE HOTEL **$$**
Map p254 (☎02-9332 2011; www.kirketon.com. au; 229 Darlinghurst Rd, Darlinghurst; r $124-394; ☒Kings Cross) You might feel like you're in a David Lynch movie as you wander the red-lit mirrored corridors. Inside the rooms you'll find ornate trimmings, superior linen and expensive toiletries, but even the oversized gilt-edged mirror bedheads can't hide the fact the rooms are cramped. Staff, however, are incredibly friendly and both the bar and on-site restaurant are top shelf.

CAMBRIDGE HOTEL HOTEL **$$**
Map p254 (☎02-9212 1111; www.cambridge-hotel.com.au; 212 Riley St, Surry Hills; r from

$170; (🖳380) You couldn't wish for a more conveniently situated hotel than this urban bolt-hole. Most of the spacious, contemporary rooms have private balconies with city-skyline vistas. Downstairs the happening Baccomatto Osteria serves brilliant Italian food, including the hotel breakfast.

★ADGE BOUTIQUE
APARTMENT HOTEL   APARTMENT $$$
Map p254 (📞02-8093 9888; www.adgehotel.com.au; 222 Riley St, Surry Hills; apt from $374; 🖳380; 🛜) As soon as you spot the bold wall murals, it's clear the ADGE is all about putting a clever twist on the ubiquitous serviced-apartment experience. The 12 idiosyncratic but extremely comfortable two-bedroom apartments are bedecked with garishly striped carpets, smart TVs and colourful retro fridges. Free wi-fi, a welcome drink and a nightly turn-down service make this hotel one of Sydney's best boutique options.

MEDUSA   BOUTIQUE HOTEL $$$
Map p254 (📞02-9331 1000; www.medusa.com.au; 267 Darlinghurst Rd, Darlinghurst; r from $310; 🚇Kings Cross) Medusa's shocking pink exterior and witty, luscious decor was once the height of hotel hipsterdom. Today the small colour-saturated suites with large beds and regal furnishings (the best face the courtyard) are looking less decadent. Thankfully the staff are as energetic as ever and small touches like the Aesop toiletries go a long way. So does the tremendous location.

🛏 Kings Cross & Potts Point

ORIGINAL BACKPACKERS LODGE   HOSTEL $
Map p257 (📞02-9356 3232; www.originalbackpackers.com.au; 160-162 Victoria St, Kings Cross; dm $22-34, s $65-85, d $70-95; 🚇Kings Cross) This long-standing hostel meanders through two historic mansions, offering dozens of beds and great outdoor spaces. Rooms have high ceilings, fridges, fans and shared bathrooms (some doubles have en suites).

BLUE PARROT   HOSTEL $
Map p257 (📞02-9356 4888; www.blueparrot.com.au; 87 Macleay St, Potts Point; dm $35-42; 🚇Kings Cross) This well-maintained, secure little place feels more like a share house (albeit a rather clean one!) rather than a backpackers. There are no private rooms, just dorms – and as a 'genuine' youth hostel, Blue Parrot only accepts 18- to 35-year-olds.

JACKAROO   HOSTEL $
Map p257 (📞02-9332 2244; www.jackaroohostel.com; 107-109 Darlinghurst Rd, Kings Cross; dm $34-36, r with/without bathroom $90/80; 🚇Kings Cross) There's no accommodation positioned closer to the heart of the action than this hostel directly above Kings Cross station. Ordinarily that wouldn't be a good thing, but Jackaroo passes muster. While communal spaces are lacklustre and rooms cramped, they are very clean. Pack earplugs. A no-frills breakfast is included.

EVA'S BACKPACKERS   HOSTEL $
Map p257 (📞02-9358 2185; www.evasbackpackers.com.au; 6-8 Orwell St, Kings Cross; dm from $34-36, r from $89; 🚇Kings Cross; 🛜) Far enough from the Kings Cross fray, Eva's is a long-time favourite offering free breakfast and wi-fi, plus an ace rooftop barbecue area and a sociable kitchen-dining room. Clean and secure.

MAISONETTE HOTEL   HOTEL $$
Map p257 (📞02-9357 3878; www.sydneylodges.com/lodges/the-maisonette-hotel/; 31 Challis Ave, Potts Point; s/d from $59/98; 🚇Kings Cross) If you're travelling on the cheap and have had your fill of dorms, check out the small, bright en suite rooms at the Maisonette. They are more than adequate for a short stay; all have TVs and kitchenette.

HOTEL 59   B&B $$
Map p257 (📞02-9360 5900; www.hotel59.com.au; 59 Bayswater Rd, Rushcutters Bay; s $99, d $130-140; 🚇Kings Cross) In the style of a European *pensione*, Hotel 59 offers good bang for your buck on the quiet part of Bayswater Rd. The cafe downstairs does whopping cooked breakfasts (included in the price). Two-night minimum.

MARINERS COURT   HOTEL $$
Map p257 (📞02-9320 3888; www.marinerscourt.com.au; 44-50 McElhone St, Woolloomooloo; r $110-160; 🚇Kings Cross) This won't be the flashest place you'll stay in Sydney (the vibe is kinda 1994), but it offers that rare combination of location, price and a bit of elbow room. Not to mention a complimentary hot breakfast buffet. Good wheelchair access.

BAYSWATER   BOUTIQUE HOTEL $$
Map p257 (📞02-8070 0100; www.sydneylodges.com; 17 Bayswater Rd, Kings Cross; r from $120; 🚇Kings Cross) This smart hotel tries for the boutique experience but unfortunately misses the mark when it comes to the small details. What it does offer is attractive and affordable lodgings with a great address. It can get noisy on weekend nights.

DIAMANT HOTEL $$

Map p257 (☏02-9295 8888; www.diamant.com. au; 14 Kings Cross Rd, Kings Cross; r $159-375, ste $315-425, apt $500-3200; ▣Kings Cross) This swish high-rise bridges the junction between Kings Cross and Darlinghurst. Space-age corridors open onto slick, spacious black-and-white rooms – all have king-size beds, quality linen, huge plasma screens and iPads. Guests have free 24-hour access to a public gym in the building.

MACLEAY HOTEL HOTEL $$

Map p257 (☏02-9357 7755; www.themacleay.com; 28 Macleay St, Elizabeth Bay; r from $165; ▣Kings Cross; ☒) At the posh end of Potts Point, surrounded by fabulous restaurants, is this understated hotel. The studios are a bit faded but all have small kitchenettes and there's a laundry on each floor. An added plus is the rooftop pool and gym. Ask for a room on a higher floor for city and harbour views.

VICTORIA COURT HOTEL B&B $$

Map p257 (☏02-9357 3200; www.victoriacourt. com.au; 122 Victoria St; r from $169; ▣Kings Cross) Chintzy charm reigns supreme at this faded but well-run B&B, which has 25 rooms in a pair of three-storey 1881 terrace houses. Continental breakfast is served in the courtyard.

BLUE SYDNEY HOTEL $$$

Map p257 (☏02-9331 9000; www.bluehotel.com. au; 6 Cowper Wharf Roadway, Woolloomooloo; r from $250; ▣311) Carved out of the historic Woolloomooloo Finger Wharf, now home to some top restaurants, much of the industrial machinery has been left exposed, to be admired over cocktails in the Water Bar. Rooms are mostly split-level, with king-size beds perched above living areas.

SIMPSONS OF POTTS POINT BOUTIQUE HOTEL $$$

Map p257 (☏02-9356 2199; www.simpsonshotel. com; 8 Challis Ave; r from $255; ▣Kings Cross) At the quiet end of a busy cafe strip, this 1892 villa has been affectionately restored. The perennially popular Simpsons is widely loved for its charming service and the cosy luxury of the 12 guest rooms.

🛏 Paddington & Centennial Park

HUGHENDEN HOTEL $$

Map p258 (☏02-9363 4863; www.thehughenden. com.au; 14 Queen St, Woollahra; r/apt from $138/225; ▣380) This quirky Victorian Ital-ianate guesthouse has plenty of eccentric charm without much style. Room range from 'cosy' (a euphemism for small and dark with a window facing the corridor) to spacious terrace apartments on the roof.

ARTS HOTEL $$

Map p258 (☏02-9361 0211; www.artshotel.com. au; 21 Oxford St, Paddington; r from $174; ▣380; ☒) A well-managed 64-room hotel with simple but comfortable rooms in a handy location on the Paddington–Darlinghurst border. There's heavy-duty triple glazing on the Oxford St frontage, while the rear rooms face a quiet lane. The central courtyard has a small solar-heated pool.

KATHRYN'S ON QUEEN B&B $$

Map p258 (☏02-9327 4535; www.kathryns.com. au; 20 Queen St, Woollahra; r $180-260; ▣380) Deftly run by the ever-smiley Kathryn, this grandiose 1888 Victorian terrace opposite Centennial Park has two tastefully decorated rooms dotted with antiques; choose between the en suite attic room or the 1st-floor room with a balcony.

🛏 Bondi to Coogee

BONDI BEACHOUSE YHA HOSTEL $

Map p261 (☏02-9365 2088; www.yha.com.au; 63 Fletcher St, Bondi; dm $26-37, tw/d without bath-room $65-90, tw/d with bathroom $90-110, f with bathroom $162-180; ▣361 from Bondi Junction) Perched on a hillside between Bondi and Tamarama Beaches, this 95-bed art-deco hostel is the best in Bondi. Dorms sleep four to eight, and some of the private rooms have ocean views – all are well maintained.

ADINA APARTMENTS BONDI BEACH APARTMENT $$

Map p261 (☏02-9300 4800; adinahotels.com.au; 69-73 Hall St; ▣389) Bondi's newest hotel is super modern, smartly appointed and just a barefoot dash to the surf. The apartments all have balconies and there's a fabulous retail and restaurant precinct downstairs. The hotel offers small conveniences such as grocery delivery to the rooms, a lap-pool, gym and in-house movies.

BONDI BEACH HOUSE GUESTHOUSE $$

Map p261 (☏0417 336 444; www.bondibeach-house.com.au; 28 Sir Thomas Mitchell Rd, Bondi; s $100-125, d $135-230, ste $270-300; ▣380) This charming place offers a homely atmosphere with rustic-chic furnishings and a well-equipped communal kitchen. Though only a

AIRPORT BEDS

Plane-spotters will love the view from **Rydges Sydney Airport Hotel** (☎02-9313 2500; www.rydges.com; 8 Arrival Ct; r from $160; 🚇International Airport), situated within the international terminal. If you have an early flight to catch, the comfy beds and black-out curtains will ensure the ultimate night's sleep. A free shuttle runs to the domestic airport.

two-minute walk from the beach, you may well be tempted to stay in all day – the courtyard and terrace are great spots for relaxing.

HOTEL BONDI   HOTEL **$$**
Map p261 (☎02-9130 3271; www.hotelbondi. com.au; 178 Campbell Pde, Bondi; s $140, d $185-200, ste $270-300; 🚇380) After an extreme makeover Bondi's grand dame is now fantastic, affordable and a place to sleep well, thanks to the double glazing now installed throughout. Most of the rooms look into an internal courtyard, so pay extra for an ocean view. While it still feels like a pub hotel, the relaxed staff and stellar location make it great value for money.

COOGEE SANDS   APARTMENT **$$**
Map p262 (☎02-9665 8588; www.coogeesands. com.au; 161 Dolphin St, Coogee; apt from $175; 🚇372-374) The golden sands of Coogee Beach are just across the street from this unpretentious apartment hotel. Many of the studios and one-bed apartments have recently been refurbished and you can pay extra for a shady courtyard or an ocean view. Alternatively, save your coin and make use of the superb rooftop deck.

DIVE HOTEL   BOUTIQUE HOTEL **$$**
Map p262 (☎02-9665 5538; www.divehotel. com.au; 234 Arden St, Coogee; r from $190; 🚇372-374) Plenty of hotels don't live up to their name and thankfully neither does this one. Right across the road from the beach, the 17 contemporary rooms at this relaxed, family-run affair are well designed. Breakfast included.

RAVESI'S   BOUTIQUE HOTEL **$$$**
Map p261 (☎02-9365 4422; www.ravesis.com.au; 118 Campbell Pde, Bondi; d $209-389, ste $289-549; 🚇389, 380 or 333) The perfectly placed Ravesi's is right across from the beach. Pick of the guest rooms are the deluxe split-level suites and those up top with amazing views of the sea. That said, it's a great spot and the

more moderately priced side-view rooms are good value.

🛌 Manly

MANLY BUNKHOUSE   HOSTEL **$**
Map p263 (☎02-9976 0472; www.bunkhouse.com. au; 35 Pine St; dm $38, tw & d $90; 🚇Manly) Backpackers (mainly Dutch) mix it up with international students and holiday workers at this laid-back hostel minutes from Manly Beach. The bright and clean four-person dorms with en suite are the way to go, as the overpriced private rooms are in need of sprucing up.

CECIL STREET B&B   B&B **$$**
(☎02-9977 8036; www.cecilstreetbb.com.au; 18 Cecil St, Manly; s/d $110/$130; 🚇Manly) This low-key bed and breakfast is in a handsome federation-style home on a hill above Manly. The two simple but tastefully decorated rooms make the most of high ceilings, leadlight windows and polished-timber floors.

101 ADDISON ROAD   B&B **$$**
Map p263 (☎02-9977 6216; www.bb-manly.com; 101 Addison Rd; s/d $165/185; 🚇Manly) This sumptuously decorated 1880s cottage is perched on a quiet street close to the beach and ferry wharf. Two rooms are available but the delightful host only takes single bookings (from one to four people) – meaning you'll have free reign of the antique-strewn accommodation.

NOVOTEL SYDNEY MANLY PACIFIC   HOTEL **$$$**
Map p263 (☎9977 7666; www.novotelmanly-pacific.com.au; 55 North Steyne; r from $279; 🚇Manly; 🅿) Right on Manly's ocean beach, this midriser has a dated corporate vibe but is a million miles from the city's business hustle. Check the surf from ocean-front balconies, or hit the rooftop pool.

🛌 Other Suburbs

LANE COVE RIVER TOURIST PARK   CAMPGROUND **$**
(☎02-9888 9133; www.lcrtp.com.au; Plassey Rd, Macquarie Park; unpowered/powered camp sites per 2 people $37/39, cabins from $135, luxury tents $200; 🚇North Ryde) 🍃 Have a back-to-nature experience in the heart of suburbia, staying in this national-park campsite 14km northwest of the CBD. There are caravan and camping sites, cabins and a pool. For a romantic bush getaway, the Tandara luxury glamping option is worth the price.

Understand Sydney

Sydney Today

With around 4.8 million residents, Sydney is Oceania's biggest and brightest city, and it dominates its home state of New South Wales politically and economically. Australia may have escaped recession during the global economic turmoil of the last decade but much of that was due to a resources boom on the other side of the country. With that boom now a receding echo, Sydneysiders who are already feeling the pinch are bracing themselves for tougher economic times.

Best on Film

Finding Nemo (2003) Animated feature following an adventurous clownfish who finds himself captive in a Sydney aquarium.
The Adventures of Priscilla, Queen of the Desert (1994) Sydney drag queens road-tripping to Alice Springs.
Muriel's Wedding (1994) Both a good laugh and genuinely affecting; Toni Collette's Muriel reinvents her frumpy Abba-tragic self.
Strictly Ballroom (1992) Breakthrough Aussie comedy set in the surreal world of competitive ballroom dancing.

Best in Print

The Lieutenant (Kate Grenville, 2008) The names are changed but Grenville's fascinating chronicle of first contacts with the Eora people rings true.
Leviathan (John Birmingham, 1999) A gritty history exploring Sydney's seamier side, written in the tone of an unauthorised biography.
The Playmaker (Thomas Keneally, 1987) A fictionalised account of First Fleet life.
Voss (Patrick White, 1957) Nobel Prize–winner White contrasts the unforgiving outback with Sydney colonial life.

The Sydney Seige

On 15 December 2014, what Sydney had long feared appeared to be coming true when a lone gunman took 18 people hostage in the Lindt cafe in Martin Place. Shortly after, a black flag with an Islamic message was held against the window. After a 16-hour stand-off, shots were heard from inside and police stormed the cafe and killed the gunman. Two of the hostages were also killed – one by the gunman and one from the ricochet of a police bullet.

While the siege bore some of the hallmarks of a terrorist attack, it was soon revealed that the gunman was a lone mentally disturbed person with a criminal record, unaligned with any terrorist group.

Sydney's Muslim community roundly condemned the attack and fears of a backlash were dissipated by messages of solidarity from leaders of other faiths and everyday Australians. The hashtag 'illridewithyou' quickly became a Twitter phenomenon, with tens of thousands of non-Muslim Australians offering their support to Muslims who felt nervous of retaliation.

Housing Woes

If Sydneysiders seem utterly obsessed by real estate, it's for good reason. A 2015 Demographia survey rated Sydney as the third-least-affordable city (behind Vancouver and Hong Kong) in which to buy a house within the English-speaking world. Median house prices ($812,000) are 9.8 times higher than median household incomes ($82,800) – a ratio of 3:1 is considered affordable, above 5:1 severely unaffordable.

For those Sydneysiders for whom home ownership seems like an unattainable dream, there's a double whammy to face: renting is increasingly unaffordable too. The median asking price for a house is now $500 per week (in Melbourne it's $380) and stories abound of hordes of people turning up to showings of even the crummiest flats. For those on the fringes, it's hardest: Anglicare estimated that out of 12,164 properties advertised for rent in April 2014, only 33 were affordable and appropriate for households on income-support payments.

Part of the challenge is geographical. The city is hemmed in between ocean, mountains and national parks, restraining the ability for new housing to expand on its fringes. Then there's Australia's perennial problem – how to provide enough water for an expanding city?

The silver lining? In most surveys of the world's most liveable cities, Sydney rates in the top 10.

Transport

Transport is one of the city's biggest political hot potatoes. Most travellers will find it surprisingly easy and reasonably pleasant to get around using public transport, but for those residents not living in suburbs served by train lines, the daily commute involves traffic snarls or expensive tolls...or both.

Recent improvements have included the introduction of a new smart ticketing system operating on all trains, ferries, buses and trams (the Opal card), and an extension of the light-rail line to Dulwich Hill in the Inner West. Plans are afoot to create a new line from Circular Quay to Central and on to Surry Hills, Moore Park and Randwick.

Sydney Style

Despite recent events, Sydneysiders are an optimistic lot. Most Sydney living happens under the sun and the stars: street cafes, alfresco restaurants, moonlight cinemas, beer gardens, parades... It follows that locals have an almost pathological disdain for overdressing. As the innumerable supermodel-spangled billboards around town attest, less is more in the Sydney fashion stakes, and showing some skin is de rigueur. And if you've got a hot bod, why not decorate it? Full-sleeve tattoos have become mainstream, while hospitality workers sans piercings are rare. Smoking is as popular as ever – will future Sydney echo with an emphysematic death rattle?

Ultimately, Sydney's relentlessly chipper attitude tends to bowl over (or at least distract from) any obstacle. A swim in the surf, a bucket of prawns by the harbour, a kickin' DJ set or a multicultural meal goes a long way towards convincing the majority of residents that life here is pretty darn good.

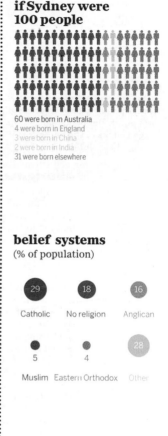

if Sydney were 100 people

60 were born in Australia
4 were born in England
3 were born in China
2 were born in India
31 were born elsewhere

belief systems
(% of population)

29 Catholic
18 No religion
16 Anglican
5 Muslim
4 Eastern Orthodox
28 Other

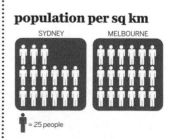

population per sq km

SYDNEY   MELBOURNE

≈ 25 people

History

Although go-getting modern Sydney may not seem particularly interested in the past, it's surprisingly easy to catch glimpses of what's gone before. Ancient rock carvings still adorn the headlands, people continue to travel along convict-hewn roads, and large chunks of the harbour look much as they did when the First Fleet breezed in and changed absolutely everything.

Australia's Aborigines were the first people in the world to make polished, edge-ground stone tools; to cremate their dead; and to engrave and paint representations of themselves and the animals they hunted.

Aboriginal Australia

Australian Aboriginal society has the longest continuous cultural history in the world, its origins dating back to at least the last ice age. Mystery shrouds many aspects of Australian prehistory, but it's thought that the first humans probably came here from Southeast Asia more than 50,000 years ago. Archaeological evidence suggests that descendants of these first arrivals colonised the continent within a few thousand years.

Aborigines were traditionally tribal people, living in extended family groups. Knowledge and skills obtained over millennia enabled them to use their environment extensively and sustainably. Their intimate knowledge of animal behaviour and plant harvesting ensured that food shortages were rare.

The simplicity of Aboriginal technology contrasted with a sophisticated cultural life. Religion, history, law and art were integrated in complex ceremonies, which depicted ancestral beings who created the land and its people, as well as prescribing codes of behaviour. Aboriginal people continue to perform traditional ceremonies in many parts of Australia.

When the British arrived at Sydney Cove in 1788, it's estimated that there were between 500,000 and one million Aboriginal people across Australia, with between 200 and 250 distinct regional languages. Governor Arthur Phillip estimated that around 1500 Aborigines lived around Sydney at first contact, but his figures can't be relied upon.

The coastal people around Sydney were known as the Eora (which literally means 'from this place'), broken into clans such as the Gadigal

TIMELINE	40,000 BC	AD 1770	1788
	The Eora people live in Sydney, split into several separate tribes including the Dharug-speaking Gadigal around Sydney Cove. Ku-ring-gai people occupy the North Shore.	Lieutenant James Cook lands at Botany Bay and claims Australia for the British. He writes of the Indigenous population: 'all they seem'd to want was us to be gone'.	The First Fleet drops anchor in Botany Bay, followed by Frenchman La Pérouse five days later; the British decide Botany Bay is unsuitable and head north to Port Jackson.

and the Wangal. Three main languages were used by Aboriginal people in the area, encompassing several dialects and subgroups. Although there was considerable overlap, Ku-ring-gai was generally spoken on the northern shore, Dharawal along the coast south of Botany Bay, and Dharug and its dialects from the harbour to the Blue Mountains.

As Aboriginal society was based on tribal family groups, a coordinated response to the European colonisers wasn't possible. Without any 'legal right' to the lands they lived on – the British declared Australia to be *terra nullius*, meaning 'land belonging to no one' – Australia's Aboriginal people were dispossessed. Some were driven away by force, some were killed, many were shifted onto government reserves and missions, and thousands, including most of the Gadigal, succumbed to foreign diseases introduced by the Europeans.

Communities that had survived for millennia before the arrival of the settlers were changed – often shattered – forever.

The Bloom of British Sails

When the American War of Independence disrupted the transportation of convicts to North America, Britain lost its main dumping ground for undesirables and needed somewhere else to put them. Joseph Banks, who had been Lieutenant James Cook's scientific leader during the expedition in 1770, piped up with the suggestion that Botany Bay would be a fine new site for criminals.

The 11 ships of the First Fleet landed at Botany Bay in January 1788 – a motley crew of 730 male and female convicts, 400 sailors, four companies of marines, and enough livestock and booze to last two years. Captain Arthur Phillip, eager to be the colony's first governor, didn't take to Botany Bay's meagre natural supplies. He weighed anchor after only a few days and sailed 25km north to the harbour Cook had named Port Jackson, where he discovered a crucial source of fresh water in what he called Sydney Cove (Circular Quay). The day was 26 January 1788, now celebrated as Australia Day (many Aboriginal people refer to it as 'Invasion Day' or 'Survival Day').

Convicts were put to work on farms, roads and government building projects, but Governor Phillip was convinced that the colony wouldn't progress if it relied solely on convict blood and sweat. He believed prosperity depended on attracting free settlers (to whom convicts would be assigned as labourers) and on the granting of land to officers, soldiers and worthy emancipists (convicts who had served their time). In 1791 James Ruse was the first former convict to be granted land by Governor Phillip; he was given 12 hectares as reward for his successful work in agriculture.

The early days of the colony weren't for softies – the threat of starvation hung over the settlement for at least 16 years. The Second Fleet arrived in 1790 with more convicts and supplies. A year later, following the landing of the Third Fleet, Sydney's population had swelled to around 4000.

1790	1791	1842	1861
A Bidjigal man, Pemulwuy, spears to death a convict game hunter. A British revenge mission fails and Pemulwuy goes on to lead Indigenous resistance until he's shot in 1802.	It's estimated that only three Gadigal people survive, their numbers decimated by the smallpox that arrived with the First Fleet. The Gadigal have no natural immunity to the disease.	The transportation of convicts to New South Wales effectively ceases; over the course of the previous half-century 150,000 people had been dumped in the colony.	The Government enacts the White Australia Policy, aimed at restricting the number of Chinese immigrants. The policy isn't completely dismantled until 1973.

Wild Colonial Boys

When Governor Phillip went back to England in 1792 due to failing health, Francis Grose took over. Grose granted land to officers of the New South Wales Corps, nicknamed the Rum Corps. With so much money, land and cheap labour in their hands, this military leadership made huge profits at the expense of small farmers. They began paying for labour and local products in rum. Meeting little resistance (everyone was drunk), they managed to upset, defy, outmanoeuvre and outlast three governors, the last of which was William Bligh, the famed captain of the mutinous ship HMAV *Bounty*. In 1808 the Rum Corps, in cahoots with powerful agriculturalist John Macarthur, ousted Bligh from power in what became known as the Rum Rebellion.

The Rum Rebellion was the final straw for the British government – in 1809 it decided to punish its unruly child. Lieutenant Colonel Lachlan Macquarie was dispatched with his own regiment and ordered the New South Wales Corps to return to London to get their knuckles rapped. Having broken the stranglehold of the Rum Corps, Governor Macquarie began laying the groundwork for social reforms.

Until 1803, when a second penal outpost was established in Van Diemen's Land (today's Tasmania), Sydney was still the only European settlement in Australia. Inroads into the vast interior of the continent were only made in the ensuing 40 years.

In 1851 the discovery of large gold deposits near Bathurst, 200km west of Sydney, sparked Australia's first gold rush. Another massive find in the southern colony of Victoria shortly afterwards reduced Sydney to secondary size and importance to Melbourne. Melbourne's ascendency lasted from the 1850s until the economic depression of the 1890s, when Sydney swung back into national favour...and so the Sydney–Melbourne rivalry began.

Early History Online

Barani (www.cityofsydney.nsw.gov.au/barani)

Dictionary of Sydney (www.dictionaryofsydney.org)

First Fleet Online (http://firstfleet.uow.edu.au)

First Australians (www.sbs.com.au/firstaustralians) TV documentary, only viewable from within Australia.

The Australian Century

The Commonwealth of Australia came into being on 1 January 1901 and New South Wales (NSW) became a state of the new Australian nation. Yet Australia's legal ties with, loyalty to, and dependency on Britain remained strong. When WWI broke out in Europe, Australian troops were sent to fight in the trenches of France, at Gallipoli in Turkey and in the Middle East. This was a first test of physical stamina and strength for the nation, and it held its own, although almost 60,000 of the 330,000 troops perished in the war. A renewed patriotism cemented the country's confidence in itself. But, in the wake of so much slaughter, many Australians also questioned their relationship with their old colonial overlords. The bond between Britain and Australia was never quite the same.

1900	1902	1932	1942
Bubonic plague kills 103 people in Sydney's overcrowded and unhygienic slums; as a result, large areas of substandard housing, particularly around the Rocks, are cleared and rebuilt.	Women are granted the right to vote; the same right isn't extended to Indigenous Australians until after a referendum held almost 70 years later.	Sydney's second-most-famous icon, the Sydney Harbour Bridge, opens to traffic; the vast structure is immediately loved by Sydney residents for both aesthetic and practical reasons.	Japanese submarines enter Sydney Harbour and fire torpedos. Two subs are destroyed in the harbour boom net; the wreckage of a third is discovered off Sydney's Northern Beaches in 2006.

If Australia was now notionally independent, the same could not be said for its Indigenous peoples. From 1910 to the end of the 1960s, a policy of 'cultural assimilation' allowed Aboriginal children (usually of mixed race) to be forcibly removed from their families and schooled in the ways of white society and Christianity. Around 100,000 children (dubbed the 'stolen generations') were separated from their parents in this way, causing untold stress and damage to the nation's Indigenous community.

Meanwhile, Australia's economy grew through the 1920s until the Great Depression hit the country hard. By 1932, however, Australia was starting to recover due to rises in wool prices and a revival of manufacturing. With the opening of the Harbour Bridge in the same year, Sydney's building industry gained momentum and its northern suburbs began to develop.

In the years before WWII, Australia became increasingly fearful of the threat to national security posed by expansionist Japan. When war broke out, Australian troops again fought beside the British in Europe. Only after the Japanese bombed Pearl Harbor did Australia's own national security begin to take priority. A boom with a net barrage to prevent submarine access was stretched across the entrance channels of Sydney Harbour, and gun fortifications were set up on rocky harbour headlands.

Unlike the Northern Territory's capital city, Darwin, which was pretty much razed by Japanese bombings, Sydney escaped WWII virtually unscathed – although on 31 May 1942, three Japanese M24 midget submarines entered Sydney Harbour, sank a small supply vessel and lobbed a few shells into the suburbs of Bondi and Rose Bay.

Ultimately, the US victory in the Battle of the Coral Sea protected Australia from Japanese invasion and accelerated Australia's shift of allegiance from mother Britain to the USA.

The aftermath of WWII, along with postwar immigration programs, made Australia more appealing to migrants from Europe. Australia experienced new growth and prosperity, Sydney's population exploded and the city's borders spread west.

Eventually Australia came to accept the US view that communism threatened the increasingly Americanised Australian way of life. The trade-union movement remained strong, however, particularly in the big cities such as Sydney. In 1965 the Liberal Party government sent troops to serve in the Vietnam War, even though Britain did not.

In 1967 a national referendum was held on whether to allow Aboriginal people the right to vote, which was passed by 90% of eligible voters. Meanwhile, civil unrest over conscription to Vietnam eventually helped to bring about the election of the left-wing Australian Labor Party (ALP) in 1972, the first time in 23 years that it had held power.

During the Vietnam War years, the face of Sydney changed again, as American GIs flooded the city. Kings Cross provided the kind of belt-level R&R the troops desired.

HISTORY THE AUSTRALIAN CENTURY

1959	1984	1990s	1999
Construction of the much-admired Sydney Opera House gets underway, but it doesn't open for performances until 1973, after a long and turbulent period of construction.	Homosexuality is decriminalised in NSW; an age of consent equal with that for heterosexuals isn't achieved until 2003.	Sydney booms as a film-making centre, churning out classics such as *The Matrix*, *Strictly Ballroom*, *Shine*, *Muriel's Wedding* and *The Adventures* of *Priscilla, Queen of the Desert*.	A referendum seeking to abandon the monarchy and turn Australia into a republic is defeated, with 55% of voters against. However, in Sydney, 68% vote in favour of a republic.

During Labor leader Gough Whitlam's short stint as prime minister, the government withdrew Australian troops from Vietnam, abolished national military service and put the final nail in the coffin of the White Australia Policy. His ousting by the governor-general in 1975 fuelled unease with the constitutional system and generated calls for a republic (a referendum on the issue was voted down in 1999).

Into the New Millennium

A booming 1980s economy saw Sydney skyscrapers spring up, while the bicentennial celebrations in 1988 also boosted the city's ego. The subsequent economic bust in 1989 left abandoned construction holes in the city centre, but with the announcement of the 2000 Olympic Games, Sydney reinvigorated itself once again and put on a spectacular show for the world. In the meantime, Aboriginal issues slowly started to make their way into the national debate. In 1992 a landmark High Court case overturned the principle of *terra nullius*, and in a later court case, the Wik decision declared that pastoral leases do not necessarily extinguish native title, and that Aborigines could still claim ancestral land under white ownership. The implications of this ruling are still being resolved.

In 1997 the damning *Bringing Them Home* report was tabled in federal parliament, which graphically detailed the harm done to the stolen generations of Indigenous Australians. A quarter of a million Sydneysiders marched across Sydney Harbour Bridge in 2000, calling on the government to apologise for the historical systematic ill treatment of Australia's first people. It took until 2008 and a change of federal government for the apology to take place.

Sydney welcomed the new millennium with a boom of fireworks and a combination of excitement and scepticism about the upcoming Olympics. Once they rolled around, all doubts were dispelled and Sydneysiders embraced the Games with much passion and good cheer. The rosy glow lingered long after the flame was extinguished, and the effect on tourism to the city has been pronounced.

The 2004 election of colourful Clover Moore as lord mayor was perhaps a reaction to a growing frustration with state politics. An independent politician, she came with none of the baggage of her rivals on either side of Australia's left–right divide. She also embraces many of the issues for which Sydney is famed, such as environmental sustainability and gay rights.

In the 2011 state elections, the Liberal–National Coalition celebrated a landslide win over Labor, who had been in power for the previous 16 years (but had been through four leaders since 2008). When it comes to politics, Sydneysiders are a cynical bunch, and many view both major political parties with similar mistrust.

Riveting Historical Reads

....

The Lieutenant (Kate Grenville)

....

The Playmaker (Thomas Keneally)

....

Oscar & Lucinda (Peter Carey)

....

The Harp in the South (Ruth Park)

2000	2003	2005	2008
Sydney stages a dazzling Olympic Games, at which Australia wins 16 gold medals – in fourth place overall after traditional powerhouse nations USA, Russia and China.	Linda Burney, a member of the stolen generations who didn't meet her father until she was 28, becomes the first Indigenous member of the NSW state parliament.	Race riots break out in Cronulla following an assault on local surf life-savers, with drunken mob attacks on people of Middle Eastern appearance.	Architect Jørn Utzon dies, having never seen his famous Sydney Opera House. The lights on the Opera House sails are dimmed to mourn his passing.

Food Culture

Food is so hot right now – even the cold stuff. It's almost as if Sydneysiders couldn't live without it. Switch on Australian TV and every other show is a cooking competition or a celebrity-chef-led expedition to discover the taste sensations of outer Mongolia. This chapter aims to help you make sense of the city's dynamic dining scene.

Advance Australian Fare

Australia is blessed with brilliant produce from farms and fisheries across the nation. The tropical north provides pineapples, mangoes and even winter strawberries, while cooler southern climes lend themselves to fine wines and cheeses. These come together in a fresh, flavoursome, multicultural collision on dining tables across Sydney.

It's through food that the last lingering limitations of colonial Australia are being dissolved. These days Sharon and Darren from Rooty Hill are just as likely to head out for Thai, Vietnamese or Lebanese as they are for fish and chips or a roast.

History & Cultural Influences

While the First Fleeters came close to starvation in the early years of Sydney Town, the local Aboriginal tribes had millennia of experience in living from the land. You can check out examples of edible plants harvested by the Cadigal, Dharug and Dharawal peoples in the Cadi Jam Ora (First Encounters) beds of the Royal Botanic Gardens. The existence of huge middens under the city centre shows that shellfish were a staple, with fish, birds, snakes and kangaroo providing further protein.

The colonists, though, hankered for their bland English food – roast meat, pies and boiled vegetables. In lean times, the city's poor would fall back on rabbit. Eventually, 'meat and three veg' followed by tinned fruit with cream became the standard Australian home-cooked meal, with 'throwing some prawns on the barbie' the domain of the adventurous.

Waves of immigrants brought their cuisine with them, starting with the Chinese in the 1850s. Mediterranean migrants (particularly Italians, Greeks and southern Slavs) influenced local fare from the early 20th century, especially around Kings Cross. They also started Sydney's love affair with coffee, which has spread to every corner of the city.

In the latter half of last century, wars in Vietnam and Lebanon brought new refugees and new ways of cooking – although it's only recently that these cuisines have crossed into the mainstream. In the 1980s and '90s the number of young Thai students burgeoned, firmly establishing Thai as one of Sydney's most popular ethnic cuisines.

In Sydney today you can experience a different culture's cuisine every night for a month without doubling up – everything from Cambodian to Colombian can be found within a few kilometres of the city centre.

The nearest wine-growing region to Sydney is the Hunter Valley, 150km north of the city. It's the oldest wine region in Australia, with the first vines planted here in 1831. Semillon, shiraz and, more recently, chardonnay are the specialities, with more than 100 vineyards blanketing the valley slopes.

Mod Oz

Those making the case for a distinctly Australian cuisine might point to 'bush tucker' or a degustation menu of pavlova, lamingtons, Vegemite sandwiches and Anzac biscuits. Patriots might suggest eating the coat of arms – kangaroo and emu – with a crocodile starter. A more reasoned approach has been taken by Australia's more innovative chefs, reverting to convict stereotypes: eyeing the surroundings, determining what to steal and weaving it all into something better than the sum of its parts – something perfect for the location and the climate.

This mix of European traditions with exotic flavours is casually termed Modern Australian cuisine – an amalgamation of Mediterranean, Asian, Middle Eastern and Californian cooking practices that emphasise lightness, experimentation and healthy eating. It's a hybrid style, shaped by migrant influences, climatic conditions and local ingredients – a culinary adventure built around local, seasonal produce that plays freely with imported ingredients and their accompanying cooking techniques and traditions. In Sydney this light-fingered culinary style has filtered down from sophisticated restaurants to modest main-street bistros and pubs.

The once-ubiquitous phrase 'Mod Oz' may have fallen out of vogue, but the style of cooking is very much alive and well.

Food Festivals

Sydney Cellar Door (www.nswfoodandwine.com.au/sydneycellardoor; late February)

Taste of Sydney (www.tasteofsydney.com.au; early March)

Crave (www.cravesydney.com; October)

Current Trends

A craze for Latin American street food has seen tangy soft-shell tacos replace salt and pepper squid as the bar snack of choice in hipper establishments. A similar fad for 'dude food' has seen posh places adding fancy burgers (called 'sliders' by those chefs who watch far too much American TV), pulled-pork sandwiches and big slabs of meat to their menus, often with a liberal side-serve of irony.

In an extension of the tapas trend that's been rolling for several years, 'shared plates' are all the rage. Bigger than tapas and not necessarily Spanish, this style of eating favours groups with adventurous palates. Fussy eaters and those from cultures that prefer their own portions on their own plates might find it more challenging.

The move towards favouring quality local, seasonal, organic, sustainable, free-range and fair-trade produce is now so ingrained in the culture of the very best restaurants that it can barely be called a trend any more. While ethical eating seems to be here to stay, you'll still see unsustainable fish species and controversial fish products like foie gras popping up on Sydney menus. Cheaper restaurants with lower margins are usually less inclined to pay the premium for ethical products, but there are worthy exceptions. Fair-trade coffee and free-range eggs are quickly becoming the norm at the better cafes.

ETHNIC EAT STREETS

→ **Thai** Campbell St, Haymarket; King St, Newtown
→ **Chinese** Chinatown; Chatswood
→ **Korean** Pitt St near Liverpool St in the city
→ **Indian** Cleveland St, Surry Hills
→ **Italian** Norton St, Leichhardt; Stanley St, East Sydney
→ **Vietnamese** Chinatown; King St, Newtown; Cabramatta

VEGETARIANS & VEGANS

Sydney is great for herbivores. Unless you wander into a steakhouse by mistake, vegetarians should have no trouble finding satisfying choices on most menus. Some leading restaurants offer separate vegetarian menus; at Tetsuya's (p96) and the Bathers' Pavilion (p82) these stretch to multiple-course degustation.

At Asian eateries it pays to ask whether the vegetable dishes are cooked with oyster or fish sauce – they'll usually be happy to make soy-based substitutions. Many of the more established restaurants such as Thai Pothong (p117) in Newtown specifically mark strictly vegetarian options on the menu. Southeast Asian vegetarian dishes are usually a good option for vegans also, but again, it pays to check.

The more socially progressive suburbs such as Newtown and Glebe have the widest range of vegie options. Also worth checking out is the cluster of mainly vegetarian South Indian restaurants on Cleveland St, Surry Hills, between Crown and Bourke Sts.

Catering specifically to vegans is the chain **Iku Wholefood** (www.ikuwholefood.com), which has 13 cafes throughout Sydney, and Pure Wholefoods (p171).

Celebrity Chefs

Not content with proving themselves world-beaters in the swimming pool, on the cricket pitch and on the big screen, Australians have taken the competition into the kitchen, where old-fashioned Aussie hero worship has turned a crop of local chefs into minor celebrities. You might find this glossy cult of the celebrity chef a bit nauseating – the food isn't always unbeatable, and unless you book weeks in advance you mightn't even be able to get a table. Still, such competitive kitchen vigour makes for interesting conversation.

Major players include the following:

➡ **Adriano Zumbo** Australia's highest-profile pastry chef introduced the nation to macarons during a stint on TV's *MasterChef*, and has gone on to sell his 'zumbarons' through four eponymous patisseries.

➡ **Luke Nguyen** Mainstream fame came with SBS TV series *Luke Nguyen's Vietnam*; try his food at Red Lantern in Darlinghurst.

➡ **Peter Gilmore** Gilmore's Quay restaurant is currently the only one in Australia to make *Restaurant* magazine's prestigious list of the top 50 restaurants in the world.

➡ **Matt Moran** Handsome, bald-headed, former *MasterChef* judge, and chef at Aria, Chiswick Restaurant and Chiswick at the Gallery.

➡ **Kylie Kwong** Flying the flag for both sustainable food and modern Chinese cuisine, Kylie runs Billy Kwong restaurant (named after her father) and can often be spotted cooking up a storm at Eveleigh Farmers' Market in the Inner West.

➡ **Bill Granger** Credited with kicking Sydney's brunch scene into high gear; taste Mr Scrambled Eggs' handiwork at his three 'bills' cafes, the original of which is in Darlinghurst.

➡ **Tetsuya Wakuda** His landmark Tetsuya's, in the city centre, was once ranked among the top five restaurants in the world. His innovative blend of Japanese and French cuisine raised standards in Sydney, so much so that he's now forced to share the limelight with several protégés.

➡ **Neil Perry** Pony-tailed veteran with a passion for seafood and Chinese flavours, and with numerous books and TV shows under his apron. Sample his stuff at Rockpool, Rockpool Bar & Grill and Spice Temple in the city centre.

How Sydneysiders Eat

It might be something to do with long nights of partying, but breakfast is something Sydney cafes do particularly well. Many locals prefer to conduct business over a morning latte instead of a power lunch or an upmarket dinner, and friends often launch the day with scrambled eggs, carrot juice and a few laughs. The prime breakfasting 'hoods are Potts Point, Surry Hills and the beaches, but it'd be weird not to find a decent brekky cafe in any inner-city 'burb.

Breakfast can happen anytime from 6am to late morning, although many cafes serve all-day breakfasts, especially on weekends. The all-day option is perfect for hardened party animals, and is therefore more common in the inner east and west. If you're an early riser, pull up a window seat in Darlinghurst or Kings Cross and watch the nocturnal detritus spilling out of the clubs – think of yourself as a seat warmer for when they wake up in the afternoon. Yum cha in Chinatown is also a hugely popular weekend brunch option (expect to queue).

It's in the caffeine stakes that Sydney wipes the floor with London and Los Angeles (as do most Australasian cities). You won't have to settle for wussy drip-filtered pap here – it's espresso all the way. The big international chains have sprouted up, but they're generally considered the last refuge of the unimaginative. Choose a local cafe instead and order a flat white (espresso with milk that's been perfectly warmed but not bubbled – it's an art all of its own), caffe latte (similar but milkier, often served in a glass), a cappuccino (espresso topped with frothed milk and chocolate or cinnamon), a long or short black (espresso without milk and with varying amounts of water), a macchiato (a short black with a tiny splash of milk) or a ristretto (very concentrated espresso). Most cafes also offer soy or 'skinny' (skim) milk.

For Sydney's workaday warriors, lunch means a quick sandwich or salad inhaled at their desk or in a nearby park. Others hit the shopping-centre food courts, which offer ethnically diverse bain-marie fodder – though many restaurants provide more atmospheric versions of the same. Chinatown, in particular, sees corporate-casual lunchtime crowds jamming its good-value eateries.

Dinner weighs more heavily on the social scales, but unless it's a special event, casual is usually the go: jeans, T-shirts and trainers are usually OK in all but the most ritzy joints.

At many restaurants, but particularly Asian, Middle Eastern and Indian restaurants, sharing dishes is the norm (unless you're the only vegetarian). At European-style restaurants many Sydneysiders stop at two courses, only ordering an entrée (Americans take note: this is the starter served before the main course, not the main course, which is called a 'main') or dessert on special occasions (or when the boss is paying).

When it comes to the pointy end of the night, there's usually a discussion as to whether to split the bill or pay for your own. Splitting is common, but if you've knocked back the crayfish and a bottle of Dom Perignon you'd better shell out some extra. Unlike in some cultures, there's no expectation that the person doing the inviting will pay the whole bill. Even if you're out on a date, women shouldn't expect that their meal will be bought for them. Gender inequality is *soooo* last millennium.

The Arts

While it can't match New York or London in terms of the volume of theatres, galleries or performance venues, Sydney nevertheless lays claim to a robust arts scene. And as opposed to taking the sniffy, superior attitude so prevalent in many artsy societies, Sydney has a laid-back, open-minded approach to its artistic pursuits. Influencing the local arts scene is the constant redefinition of the city's identity, with the beach and Sydney's many multicultural facets also chiming in.

Cinema

Since Fox Studios opened in Moore Park in 1998, Sydney has starred in various big-budget blockbusters such as *The Matrix* trilogy (featuring numerous Sydney skyscrapers), *Mission Impossible 2* (Elizabeth Bay and Sydney Harbour) and *X-Men Origins: Wolverine* (Cockatoo Island). Sydneysider Baz Luhrmann's *Moulin Rouge*, *Australia* and *The Great Gatsby* were made here, as were numerous other films set everywhere from Antarctica *(Happy Feet II)* to a galaxy far, far away (the *Star Wars* prequels).

Yet more emblematic of the soul of Sydney cinema is the decidedly low-budget Tropfest (www.tropfest.com), where thousands of locals shake out their blankets in Centennial Park to watch entries in the largest short-film festival (p23) in the world.

One of the most successful early Australian films was *The Sentimental Bloke* (1919), which included scenes filmed in Manly, the Royal Botanic Gardens and Woolloomooloo. The cavalry epic *Forty Thousand Horsemen* (1940), in which Cronulla's sand dunes stood in for the Sinai, was a highlight of the locally produced films of the 1930s to the 1950s, many of which were based on Australian history or literature.

Government intervention reshaped the future of the country's film industry through the 1970s. This took the form of both state and federal subsidies, tax breaks and the creation of the Australian Film Commission (AFC) in 1975. Sydneysiders who benefited from the subsequent renaissance in the Australian industry included Oscar-nominated director Peter Weir (who made such films as *Gallipoli*, *Dead Poets Society*, *The Truman Show* and *Master and Commander*) and Oscar-winners Mel Gibson and Nicole Kidman.

The 1990s saw films that cemented Australia's reputation as a producer of quirky comedies about local misfits: *Strictly Ballroom* (with locations in Pyrmont and Marrickville), *Muriel's Wedding* (Parramatta, Darlinghurst, Darling Point and Ryde) and *The Adventures of Priscilla, Queen of the Desert* (Erskineville). Sydney actors who got their cinematic start around this time include Hugo Weaving, David Wenham, NZ-born Russell Crowe, Cate Blanchett, Heath Ledger and Toni Collette.

The new millennium got off to a good start with the likes of *Lantana* and *Finding Nemo*, but since then it's fair to say that Sydney has failed to set big screens alight.

Australia saw some of the world's earliest attempts at cinematography. In 1896, just one year after the Lumière brothers opened the world's first cinema in Paris, one of their photographers, Maurice Sestier, came to Sydney where he made the country's first films and opened its first cinema.

SYDNEY CINEMA

Sydney sure is good-lookin' – a fact not overlooked in its filmography.

➡ *Puberty Blues* (1981) Southern Sydney's 1970s surf culture at its most 'perf'. Directed by Bruce Beresford.

➡ *The Sum of Us* (1994) A touching father-son tale where a young Russell Crowe jogs round Sydney in his footie shorts as the gay lead. Directed by Geoff Burton and Kevin Dowling Lucas.

➡ *Two Hands* (1999) A black-humoured look at the Kings Cross criminal underworld, starring a young Heath Ledger. Directed by Gregor Jordan.

➡ *The Matrix* trilogy (1999–2003) A trio of futuristic, mind-bending flicks with plenty of martial-arts action, slick costumes and noir themes. Filmed in Sydney's streets and soundstages. Directed by Andy and Larry Wachowski.

➡ *Looking for Alibrandi* (2000) An endearing story about growing up Italian in modern Sydney. Directed by Kate Woods.

➡ *Lantana* (2001) 'Mystery for grown-ups', this extraordinary ensemble piece is a deeply moving meditation on life, love, truth and grief. Directed by Ray Lawrence.

➡ *Candy* (2006) Abbie Cornish and Heath Ledger play drug-addicted lovers in the film adaptation of Luke Davies' 1998 grunge novel. Directed by Neil Armfield.

➡ *Bra Boys* (2007) Maroubra's bad-boy surf gang in stark profile. Narrated by the dulcet Russell Crowe; directed by real-life Bra Boy Sunny Abberton.

Theatre

Sydney provides something for all thespian tastes, from mainstream blockbuster musicals at major venues to small theatre companies staging experimental, exciting works in the inner-city suburbs. That said, Sydney's theatrical tastes do tend towards the unadventurous end of the spectrum.

Australian Aboriginal art is one of the oldest forms of creativity in the world, dating back more than 50,000 years. Art has always been integral to Aboriginal life – a connection between the past and the present, the supernatural and the earthly, the people and the land.

While the bulk of Australian actors live and work in Sydney, Australia's geographic isolation and a lingering sense of 'cultural cringe' mean that truly local theatre gigs are thin on the ground and not particularly well paid. Thus, many actors prefer to get as much film and TV work as they can or, better yet, go overseas. The National Institute of Dramatic Art (NIDA) in Kensington is a breeding ground for new talent, and stages performances of students' work.

The city's biggest name in theatre is the Sydney Theatre Company (STC). Established in 1978, it provides a balanced program of modern, classical, local and foreign drama, and attracts solid talent across the board. Until 2013, Cate Blanchett and playwright hubbie Andrew Upton were the company's artistic codirectors, their star-power bringing plenty of media attention to the company; now Upton continues solo in the role. Smaller theatre companies presenting genuinely innovative work include the much-loved Company B at the Belvoir St Theatre; the Griffin Theatre Co at the Stables; and Red Line Productions at the Old Fitz Theatre.

Stage performers to watch for in local productions include Deborah Mailman, Oscar-nominee Jackie Weaver, Marcus Graham, John Howard (not that one), Robyn Nevin and Barry Otto. And, of course, Sydney's resident colony of movie stars pop up from time to time in stage roles.

Visual Art

Sydney's first artists were the people of the Indigenous Eora nation. Figures of animals, fish and humans can still be seen engraved into sandstone outcrops in Bondi and around the harbour. In the Blue Mountains, ancient hand stencils decorate cave walls.

In the colony's early days, the first foreign-born painters applied traditional European aesthetic standards to Australia's bleached light, raggedy forests and earthy colours: as such, they failed to capture the landscape with any certainty. In the early 19th century, John Glover (a convict) adopted a different Australian landscape-painting style, using warm earth tones and more precise depictions of gum trees and mountains in his work. Conrad Martens, a friend of Charles Darwin, painted accurate landscapes of a surprisingly busy Sydney Harbour in the 1850s (where did all the trees go?).

The first significant art movement in Australia, the Heidelberg School, emerged around the 1890s. Using impressionistic techniques and favouring outdoor painting, the school represented a major break with prevailing European tastes. Painters such as Tom Roberts and Arthur Streeton were the first to render Australian light and colour in this naturalistic fashion. Originally from Melbourne, they came to Sydney and established an artists camp at Little Sirius Cove in Mosman in 1891, which became a focal point for Sydney artists. Roberts and Streeton depicted what are now considered typically Australian scenes: sheep shearers, pioneers, bushrangers...all powerful stimulants in the development of an enduring national mythology.

At the beginning of the 20th century, Sydney painters such as Grace Cossington Smith and Margaret Preston began to flirt with modernism. French-influenced Nora Simpson kick-started the innovative movement, experimenting with cubism and expressionism.

In the 1960s Australian art drew on multiculturalism and abstract trends, an eclecticism best represented by the work of Sydney artist Brett Whiteley, an internationally celebrated enfant terrible who died in 1992. He painted sexy, colourful canvases, often depicting distorted figures, as well as landscapes of Sydney Harbour. His Surry Hills studio, containing many of his works, has been preserved as a gallery.

Drawing on pop-culture images for much of his work, Martin Sharp rose to prominence in the 1960s as cofounder of the satirical magazine *Oz*. In the 1970s he helped restore the 'face' at Luna Park, but he is most famous for his theatrical posters and record covers (including Cream's *Disraeli Gears* and *Wheels of Fire*).

Performance art happens at galleries around Sydney, including Artspace in Woolloomooloo – some of it is most certainly not for the faint-hearted. In 2003 Mike Parr performed a piece at Artspace titled *Democratic Torture*, in which people could deliver electric shocks to him via the internet; he also nailed himself to a wall here in *Malevich: A Political Arm*.

Other contemporary artists of note include photographers Tracey Moffatt and William Yang, and painters Tim Storrier, Ben Quilty, Keith Looby, Judy Cassab and John Olsen. For some quirky wearable art, check out artist Reg Mombassa's work for surfwear label Mambo, available at most surf shops.

On the design front, Australia's most successful export has been the work of Marc Newson, a graduate of the Sydney College of the Arts. His aerodynamic Lockheed Lounge (1985–86) has been snapped up by savvy furniture collectors and design buffs worldwide.

Literature

Australia's literary history harks back to Sydney's convict days. New experiences and landscapes inspired the colonists to commit their stories to the page. Though many early works have been lost, some – like Marcus Clarke's convict drama *For the Term of His Natural Life* (1870) – have become legendary.

By the late 19th century, a more formal Australian literary movement was developing with the *Bulletin*, an influential magazine promoting egalitarian and unionist thinking. Well-known contributing authors of the time included Henry Lawson (1867–1922), who wrote short stories about the Australian bush, and poet AB 'Banjo' Paterson (1864–1941), who penned *Waltzing Matilda* and *The Man from Snowy River*.

My Brilliant Career (1901), by Miles Franklin (1879–1954), is considered the first authentic Australian novel. The book caused a sensation when it was revealed that Miles was actually a woman.

Multi-award-winning Australian authors of international stature include Patrick White (Nobel Prize in Literature, 1973), Thomas Keneally (Booker Prize winner, 1982), Peter Carey (Booker Prize winner 1988 and 2001) and Kate Grenville (Commonwealth Writers' Prize winner 2006). Other Sydney authors of note include David Malouf, Mandy Sayer, Shirley Hazzard, Eleanor Dark and Ruth Park.

Music

Sydney offers the traveller everything from world-class opera and intimate jazz to Indigenous hip hop, live electronic beats and raucous pub rock. Gigs happen every night in the city's pubs and performance halls, with plenty of big-name touring artists enriching the mix.

In the 1970s and '80s, Australia churned out a swag of iconic pub rockers, with Sydney bands INXS and Midnight Oil at the forefront. During the '90s and noughties, when guitar bands came back into vogue, contrary Sydney popped a pill and headed to the disco. Most of the significant Australian acts of the era formed elsewhere, with the exception of garage rockers the Vines and the Cops, cartoon punks Frenzal Rhomb, singer-songwriter Alex Lloyd and jangly sentimentalists the Whitlams. In the meantime, Sydney's most successful musical export was children's novelty act the Wiggles.

SYDNEY ON THE SHELF

Sydney has been a rich setting and source material for the written word.

➡ *Sydney* (Delia Falconer; 2010) An insightful dissection of the Harbour City by one of its own.

➡ *The Secret River* (Kate Grenville; 2005) Grenville's Commonwealth Prize–winning and Booker-nominated story of 19th-century convict life in Sydney and around the Hawkesbury River.

➡ *Sydney Architecture* (Paul McGillick and Patrick Bingham-Hall; 2005) One for the coffee table, with beautiful photographs and text showcasing 100-plus stunning Sydney buildings.

➡ *30 Days in Sydney* (Peter Carey; 2001) A richly nostalgic account of Carey's return to Sydney after 10 years in New York. His emotions and experiences read like a diary, thematically spanning the four elements of earth, air, fire and water.

➡ *Quill* (Neal Drinnan; 2001) A sassy and moving tale of gay love, life and death in Sydney, with party scenes that many Sydneysiders will relate to.

➡ *In the Gutter...Looking at the Stars* (ed Mandy Sayer and Louis Nowra; 2000) A spellbinding compilation of Kings Cross musings, painting a vivid, decade-by-decade portrait of the area.

➡ *The Cross* (Mandy Sayer; 1995) Set in Kings Cross, and based on the life and unsolved 1975 disappearance of Sydney publisher Juanita Nielson.

➡ *Oscar & Lucinda* (Peter Carey; 1988) This unusual tale of 19th-century misfits won Carey his first Booker prize.

➡ *The Bodysurfers* (Robert Drewe; 1983) Seductive stories from Sydney's Northern Beaches, calmly tearing shreds off the Australian suburban idyll.

➡ *The Harp in the South* and *Poor Man's Orange* (Ruth Park; 1948 and 1949) Gripping and touching accounts of impoverished family life in Surry Hills when the suburb was a crowded slum.

SYDNEY PLAYLIST

➡ 'Khe Sanh' (Cold Chisel, 1978) Classic Oz rock song about a Vietnam vet's return. Other Sydney songs by Cold Chisel include 'Tomorrow', 'Numbers Fall' and 'Letter to Alan'.

➡ 'Bliss' (Th' Dudes, 1979) Kiwi rockers score speed in Coogee and falafels in Kings Cross.

➡ 'Power and the Passion' (Midnight Oil, 1982) Peter Garrett, a former federal MP, vents about Sydney 'wasting away in paradise'. Listen also to Midnight Oil songs 'Wedding Cake Island' and 'Section 5 (Bus to Bondi)'.

➡ 'Reckless' (Australian Crawl, 1983) Glacial '80s pop: 'as the Manly ferry cuts its way to Circular Quay'.

➡ 'Incident on South Dowling' (Paul Kelly, 1986) The Melbourne bard turns his pen to Sydney. Listen also to Kelly's 'From St Kilda to Kings Cross', 'Randwick Bells' and 'Darlin' It Hurts'.

➡ 'My Drug Buddy' (the Lemonheads, 1992) Evan Dando gets wasted in Newtown.

➡ 'Purple Sneakers' (You Am I, 1995) 'Had a scratch only you could itch, underneath the Glebe Point Bridge'.

➡ 'God Drinks at the Sando' (the Whitlams, 1999) The band named after Australia's grooviest Prime Minister digs into Sydney's best and worst on *Love this City*.

➡ 'Never Had So Much Fun' (Frenzal Rhomb, 1999) Local punks advise against drinking the water.

➡ 'Sydney Song' (Eskimo Joe, 2001) Ode to Sydney wannabes.

➡ 'Darlinghurst Nights' (the Go-Betweens, 2005) Sad Darlinghurst memories get an airing.

However, things have been looking up in recent years, with the city turning out the likes of electro popsters the Presets, hard rockers Front End Loader, folky siblings Angus & Julia Stone, alternative rock lads Boy & Bear and indie disco kids the Jezabels.

Australia loves its pop stars and dance divas, and is currently churning them out at a rate of knots in reality TV shows. Others have taken the more traditional route to pop stardom: starring in a cheesy soap opera. Melbourne can lay claim to Kylie Minogue, but Sydney makes do with Delta Goodrem and Natalie Imbruglia. Then there's home-grown boy-band 5 Seconds of Summer, who hit number one in 11 countries in 2014 with their self-titled debut album.

Sydney loves to cut a rug, and you'll find a bit of everything being played around the dance clubs, from drum and bass to electro. Homegrown dance music is made by the likes of RÜFÜS, Flume, Flight Facilities, Bag Raiders and Art vs Science, and spun by popular DJs such as Timmy Trumpet, Tigerlily, Alison Wonderland and J-Trick.

With an opera house as its very symbol, no discussion of Sydney's musical legacy is complete without mentioning Dame Joan Sutherland (1926–2010), the Eastern Beaches lass who became one of the greatest opera singers of the 20th century. Her legacy can be seen in the success of Opera Australia and singers such as Cheryl Barker.

Architecture

Modern Sydney began life in Sydney Cove and the area immediately around it has been the hub of the city ever since. It's no surprise, then, that central Sydney gives the best insight into how the city's architecture has matured from shaky, poorly crafted imitation to confident autonomy, peaking with its glorious opera house.

The Lay of the Land

Ever since Captain Arthur Phillip slurped from the Tank Stream, water has shaped Sydney's development. The Tank Stream now runs in brick culverts beneath the city, but in the early days of the First Fleet it defined Sydney. Phillip used the stream to separate convicts on the rocky west from the officers on the gentler eastern slopes, hemming in the convicts between the sea on one side and the soldiers on the other. Following this pattern, government institutions were concentrated to the east of the

Above Interior of Sydney Opera House (p54)

stream, while industry set up shop on the western side of town. Social differences were thus articulated, establishing a pattern that can still be seen in Sydney more than 200 years later.

According to scientist and author Dr Tim Flannery, many Aboriginal camp sites used to lie near fresh water on Sydney Harbour's north-facing shore – and the colonists took their cue from the original inhabitants. Topographically, it makes sense. The area catches the winter sun, and is relatively sheltered from chilly southerly and bullying westerly winds. The northeasterly breeze, meanwhile, comes straight through the mouth of the harbour, delivering warm winter and cool summer breezes.

In one of history's great coincidences, Frenchman Jean Compte de la Pérouse arrived at Botany Bay days after the First Fleet. That event and fierce competition from other colonial powers meant there was a perceived threat of invasion from the outset. As a consequence, the navy appropriated much of the harbour foreshore. This was fortunate indeed – much of the land was not built upon, conserving these regions as wilderness while the rest of Sydney clambered up around them.

Little Britain

The men and women who arrived in the First Fleet were staggeringly ill-prepared for the realities of building in their new, raw environment. The British powers that be had failed to include an architect on board, so design and construction duties largely fell to the convict bricklayer James Bloodsworth. Inevitably the early builders looked to the 'mother' country for inspiration, but shoddy workmanship, poor tools and the colony's temporary vibe conspired against long-term success.

A significant change to this ad-hoc approach was heralded by the appointment of Governor Lachlan Macquarie in 1810, who viewed good architecture as an essential component of a thriving, healthy society. The arrival of several architects, including the transfigurative Francis Greenway, a convict transported for forgery, helped change Sydney's built environment. The prevailing Georgian architecture of Britain was echoed in many buildings that sprang up at this time. As the 19th century kicked on, colonial architects still looked to Britain for inspiration, but broader European influences were also seen, from the neoclassical Town Hall to the early-Gothic-style spires of St Mary's Cathedral.

When Australia became a fully fledged country in its own right in 1901, increasing architectural autonomy ensued. Architects questioned traditional approaches and sought new ways to adapt buildings to Sydney's extraordinary setting – particularly in the residential areas. In the city centre, meanwhile, the scrapping of height restrictions in the 1950s sparked Sydney's love affair with skyscrapers. Modernism was influential, with such architects as Harry Seidler focusing on Sydney Harbour and embracing diverse international attitudes. Of course, a walk around central Sydney still shows the legacy of British influence. Today's buildings, however, are much more locally sensitive.

If the city centre is ideal for tracing the development of institutional and financial building styles, the Rocks is the place to gain an understanding of the social structures behind Sydney architecture. Millers Point highlights some impressive social housing policies and the area's strong industrial maritime heritage.

The Utilitarian Harbour

Sydney has always relied on its harbour. All sorts of cargo (including human) has been unloaded here, and some of the more interesting Sydney buildings are the utilitarian wharves and warehouses still lining parts of the harbour's inner shores. After the bubonic plague arrived in Sydney in 1900 (killing 103 Sydneysiders), the government took control of the old, privately owned wharves. Many ageing neoclassical warehouses were razed and replaced with new utilitarian buildings, but the 'containerisation' of shipping in the 1960s and '70s made many of these facilities redundant almost overnight.

Now, Sydneysiders' obsession with harbourside living is also putting many of these historic sites at risk. Fortunately, some have been transformed through inspired redevelopment – once-dilapidated sheds morphing into top-notch cafes, restaurants and apartments. Woolloomooloo's Finger Wharf, and the Walsh Bay and Pyrmont wharves are classic examples. One of Sydney's big architectural challenges is to retain the richness of a working harbour and to ensure these sites have a successful, working role in the modern city.

Modernism Arrives

Between the two world wars Sydney boomed, and Australia looked to the USA for architectural inspiration. Martin Place, with its granite-faced, art-deco temples to commerce, is a well-preserved example. Similarly lavish buildings began to dot the eastern suburban skyline, giving a stylish look to many suburbs, although there have since been some hideous modern incursions.

The opening of the Sydney Harbour Bridge in 1932 was a seminal moment for Sydney architecture, opening up the densely forested North Shore to development. Much of this shoreline retains a bushy character, reflecting local architects' determination to engage with Sydney's natural charms.

Some good news in the 1950s and '60s came via the Sydney School, which pioneered a distinctively Australian architecture, characterised by the appreciation of native landscapes and natural materials, and the avoidance of conventional and historic features. Further steps were taken as 'new Australians' such as Seidler and Hugh Buhrich brought to the local architectural scene a sensitivity to place, infused with Bauhaus and modernist concepts.

Since the 1960s, central Sydney has become a mini-Manhattan of tall buildings vying for harbour views, thanks to the lifting in the late 1950s of the 150ft (46m) height limit. The best early modernist examples are Seidler's Australia Square and MLC buildings. Plans for an almost total redevelopment of the city's historic districts were afoot in the 1960s as the irascible Askin Liberal Government (which kicked Sydney Opera House designer Jørn Utzon out of Sydney) deemed many Victorian and early-20th-century buildings undesirable in its race to construct an 'all new' metropolis. Thankfully, union green bans and plenty of vociferous

For some glimpses of typical Sydney inner-city residential styles, make your way to Paddington, Potts Point or Elizabeth Bay. The backstreets of these dense suburbs include superbly restored Victorian terrace houses, art-deco apartments and modern housing.

SYDNEY OPERA HOUSE

Frank Lloyd Wright called it a 'circus tent' and Mies van der Rohe thought it the work of the devil, yet Danish architect Jørn Utzon (1918–2008) bequeathed Sydney one of the 20th century's defining architectural monuments.

Utzon was 38 when he entered the NSW government's competition to design the Opera House in 1956 and, remarkably, had only realised a few small houses by this age. Working from navigational maps of the site and memories of his travels to the great pre-Columbian platforms in Mexico, Utzon achieved the unimaginable. His great architectural gesture – billowing white sails hovering above a heavy stone platform – tapped into the essence of Sydney, almost as if both building and site had grown from the same founding principles.

Eight years on, having realised his designs for the platform, concrete shells and ceramic skin, Utzon had a change of client following the election of new NSW Premier Robert Askin. By April 1966, owed hundreds of thousands of dollars in unpaid fees, Utzon was unceremoniously forced to leave his building half-finished. He afterwards commented that the six years he spent developing the house's interiors and glass walls, for which there is nothing to show, were the most productive of his working life.

Attempts at reconciliation with Utzon began in the 1990s, and in 1999 he agreed to be taken on as a consultant for a new acoustic interior for the building. Sadly, Utzon died in 2008 having never returned to Australia to see his masterpiece.

GREEN BUILDINGS

Environmental concerns have rocketed up the agenda in Sydney over the past decade, and local architecture hasn't been immune. The Olympic Games quickened architects' thinking on sustainability issues, and there are several developments around Olympic Park that highlight the 'sustainable' agenda of the Games. The first thing you'll probably see when you arrive is the Olympic Park Rail Station, admired for its natural light, ventilation and striking shell-like design. The modernist blocks of Newington Apartments, originally the Olympic Village, also emphasise natural light, energy conservation and water recycling. While you're in the 'hood, sneak a peek at the grace of Peter Stutchbury's Archery Pavilion.

Since the Olympics, buildings like 30 The Bond on Hickson Rd in Millers Point and One Central Park on Broadway in Chippendale have raised the bar for ecofriendly design and energy efficiency. Of course, sustainable building isn't limited to big financial and infra-structure developments – new and recycled 'green' residential projects are also coming on apace. One stellar example is the converted 19th-century Chippendale terrace house at 58 Myrtle St, which the owner/designer bills as 'Sydney's first sustainable house' (see www.sustainablehouse.com.au).

It seems like a regulation Sydney terrace from the front, one of thousands in the inner city, but some ingenious and surprisingly simple design means that all the house's requi-site energy and water needs are supplied on-site. The house consumes just 220L of water per day (the Sydney average is 274L), and only six kilowatts of electricity, down from an average of 24. In fact, the house exports more energy to the national grid than it uses. Simple but effective fittings include rooftop solar panels, a rainwater filter on the drain-pipe, a doorbell on a string, a super-energy-efficient fridge, and stainless-steel benches that magnify sunlight and prevent the need for daytime electric light during the day. Check it out in the book *Sustainable House* by owner Michael Mobbs.

local protests managed to save large chunks of the Rocks and areas such as Kings Cross, Paddington and Woolloomooloo.

Many buildings from the 1970s and '80s are forgettable, but striking exceptions include the Capita Centre on Castlereagh St and Governors Phillip and Macquarie Towers on Phillip St.

Contemporary Design

The spate of skyscraper construction that hit central Sydney following the lifting of height restrictions has defined the skyline. For a while, the city's older buildings were in danger of being neglected. That changed for the bicentennial celebrations of 1988, when cultural heritage soared up the agenda. As well as the refurbishment of Macquarie St and Circular Quay, developers turned their eye towards Darling Harbour. Critics con-demn today's Darling Harbour as a tacky Las Vegan aberration, but few fail to be amazed at how completely this once-disused industrial space has been transformed. At the time of writing, Darling Harbour is being redeveloped once again.

Historic buildings that have been redeveloped for new uses with effect include the Mint and the Sydney Conservatorium of Music on Macquarie St, the Customs House at Circular Quay and the wharves at Walsh Bay – all great examples of how thoughtful and sympathetic con-temporary design can inject new life and energy into an area.

The other defining event that cemented Sydney architecture's place on the world map was the 2000 Olympic Games. Many of the buildings and infrastructure developed around Homebush Bay, where the Games were based, were world class. The most significant recent constructions sit on either side of Broadway on the city's southern flank: One Central Park by internationally acclaimed architect Jean Nouvel, and Frank Gehry's Dr Chau Chak Wing Building at the University of Technology, Sydney.

Some of the more innovative contemporary work in Sydney happens far from the public gaze in the realm of the family house, where progressive clients bankroll the creative ambitions of architects.

Sporty Sydney

Sydneysiders – like most Aussies – are nuts about sport: watching it, playing it and betting on it. Australia's national self-esteem is so intertwined with sporting success that locals worship their teams as they would a religion. This national obsession makes for heady times in front of the big screen at the local pub, and certainly contributed to Sydney's overwhelmingly successful 2000 Olympic Games. Sport dominates weekend TV schedules, but nothing beats catching a game live. Sydney's all-consuming passion is rugby league – a superfast, supermacho game with a frenzied atmosphere for spectators.

Not many people have a ferry and a swimming pool named after them, but Dawn Fraser is quite extraordinary. One of Sydney's most loved sportspeople, she is one of only two swimmers to have won the same event at three successive Olympics (the 100m freestyle in 1956, 1960 and 1964).

Rugby League

There's plenty to yell about if you arrive during the winter footy season. 'Footy' can mean a number of things: in Sydney it's usually rugby league, but the term is also used for Australian Rules football (Aussie Rules), rugby union and soccer.

In this big, dirty city, rugby league is the big, dirty game: mud, swearing, broken bones, cheerleaders...and that's just in the stands! Rugby league is king in New South Wales (NSW), and Sydney is considered one of the world capitals for the code. The pinnacle of the game is widely held to be the annual State of Origin where NSW battles Queensland (and Queensland usually wins). This best-of-three series even overshadows test matches, such as the annual Anzac Test between Australia's Kangaroos and New Zealand's Kiwis.

The **National Rugby League** (www.nrl.com.au) comp runs from March to October, climaxing in the sell-out Grand Final at ANZ Stadium. You can catch games every weekend during the season, played at the home grounds of Sydney's various tribes. The easiest ground to access is the 45,500-seat Sydney Football Stadium, home of the Sydney Roosters, but nothing beats a Wests Tigers home match at Leichhardt Oval.

The main Sydney teams are the Sydney Roosters, the South Sydney Rabbitohs, the Wests Tigers, the Canterbury Bulldogs, the Cronulla Sharks, the Parramatta Eels, the Manly-Warringah Sea Eagles and the Penrith Panthers. The St George Illawarra Dragons are based in Wollongong, but also in Kogarah in Sydney's southern 'burbs.

Netball

Despite Australia being world champs since 2007, and it being one of the most-played sports in the country, netball gets neither the coverage nor the money that the football boys rake in. During the winter season, catch test internationals or Sydney's team the **NSW Swifts** (www.nswswifts.com.au) in the trans-Tasman **ANZ Championship** (www.anz-championship.com). The team won the inaugural championship when it was held in 2008; catch them at Sydney Olympic Park Sports Centre.

GO RABBITOHS! GO RUSS!

For a rugby-league team in need of friends in high places, South Sydney (aka Souths, aka the Rabbitohs) has certainly managed to pull some bunnies out of the hat. Big-name fans waving their green and red scarves around include TV host Ray Martin, comedian Andrew Denton, Australia's favourite ex-son-in-law Tom Cruise and actor Russell Crowe, who loved the team so much he bought the franchise in 2006.

Despite being the only surviving team from the seminal 1908 season and having won more premierships than any other team (20), South Sydney was on the scrap heap in the late 1990s. The ill-fated '1997 Super League' saw the competition slashed from 17 teams to 14, omitting the Rabbitohs. Souths' passionate supporters didn't appreciate this 'redundancy' and weren't going to go quietly. In June 2001, 80,000 green-and-red-clad supporters paraded from Redfern Oval to the Town Hall in a 'Save the Game' rally. On 6 July 2001 the Federal Court of Australia gave the Bunnies back their footy-playing rights and the number of teams in the comp was raised to 15.

Since Russ bought the club, its run of bad luck and heavy on-field losses seems to have ended. After waiting 43 years to qualify for the final, the Rabbitohs took the 2014 NRL Premiership. For current Bunny stats, see www.rabbitohs.com.au.

Cricket

Cricket is the major summer sport, and one in which Australia does very well – at the time of writing, the national team ranked fourth in the world for test matches and first for One Day Internationals (ODIs). From October to March, Sydney hosts interstate Sheffield Shield and one-day matches, and international Test, ODI and 20/20 cricket matches; see **Cricinfo** (www.cricinfo.com.au) for details. Cricket matches are held at the elegant old Sydney Cricket Ground.

Rugby Union

Despite its punishing physical component, **rugby union** (www.rugby.com.au) has a more upper-class rep than rugby league and a less fanatical following in Sydney. Since winning the Rugby World Cup in 1991 and 1999, Australia's national team, the Wallabies, has been a bit off the boil. The annual southern hemisphere Rugby Championship (formerly the Tri-Nations) between Australia's Wallabies, New Zealand's All Blacks, South Africa's Springboks and Argentina's Pumas provokes plenty of passion – particularly the matches against New Zealand which determine the holders of the ultimate symbol of Trans-Tasman rivalry, the Bledisloe Cup (mostly because the Aussies haven't won it since 2002).

In the SuperRugby competition, the NSW Waratahs bang heads with 14 other teams from Australia, New Zealand and South Africa.

Australian Rules

In Aussie Rules football, the **Australian Football League** (AFL; www.afl.com.au) is growing in popularity since Sydney's beloved Swans won the 2005 premiership – the first time the Swans had won it since 1933, when they were still the South Melbourne Swans (they relocated to Sydney in 1982). Traditionally much more popular in the southern states and Western Australia, the future of Aussie Rules is looking rosy in NSW, with the addition of the new Greater Western Sydney Giants team to the AFL in 2012.

Soccer (Football)

Soccer comes a lowly fourth in the popularity race between Sydney's football codes, but received a boost when Australia qualified for the FIFA World Cup in 2006, 2010 and 2014 – before that was 1974.

European immigrants kick-started many of the city's local teams, which became strongly associated with particular ethnicities. Fan tensions were particularly pronounced in matches between the Croatian-dominated Sydney United and Serbian-dominated Bonnyrigg White Eagles, culminating in a riot in 2005.

Things have settled down since the creation of the **A-League** (www.aleague.com.au), consisting of nine Australian and one New Zealand team, and the multi-ethnic **Sydney FC** (www.sydneyfc.com), which won the championship in 2006 and 2010. The league bucks convention, playing games from late August to February rather than through the depths of winter.

Basketball

Formerly the domain of dapper septuagenarians, lawn bowls has become inexplicably hip for a certain demographic in recent years. Young folks have learned to appreciate the sport's affordability, retro-kitsch vibe and the time-honoured traditions of drinking and smoking while the balls are rolling. Jack high!

Sydney is represented in the **National Basketball League** (www.nbl.com.au) by the Sydney Kings, who had a run of three wins in the first decade of this century. In the **Women's National Basketball League** (www.wnbl.com.au), the Sydney Flames haven't won a championship since 1997.

Surf Life-Saving

Surf life-saving originated in Sydney, although red-and-yellow-capped volunteer life-savers have since assumed iconic status across Australia. Despite the macho image, many life-savers are women, and a contingent of gay and lesbian life-savers march in the Sydney Mardi Gras Parade.

At summer surf carnivals all along the coast you can see these dedicated athletes wedge their Speedos up their butt cracks and launch their surf boats (butt cheeks grip the seats better than speedos, apparently). Ask a local surf life-saving club for dates, or contact **Surf Life Saving Australia** (☑02-9471 8000; www.surflifesaving.com.au) for info.

Sailing

The racing season for 18ft skiff yachts runs from September to April, with a whole messy wake of races across the harbour. South Head offers a good vantage point or head out on a **Sydney Flying Squadron** (Map p242; ☑02-9955 8350; www.sydneyflyingsquadron.com.au; 76 McDougall St, Milsons Point; ⏢North Sydney) viewing boat. On Boxing Day (26 December), Sydney Harbour hosts the start of the harrowing **Sydney to Hobart Yacht Race** (www.rolexsydneyhobart.com).

Tennis

Tennis is much played in Sydney, with plenty of good courts scattered about, but Melbourne is home to the Australian Open. A prelude to that event, January's **Apia International Sydney tennis tournament** (www.apiainternational.com.au) takes place at Sydney Olympic Park.

Survival Guide

Transport

ARRIVING IN SYDNEY

The vast majority of visitors to Sydney (and to Australia, for that matter) arrive at Sydney Airport, 10km south of the city centre. Around 40 airlines fly here from numerous international and domestic cities.

Trains chug into Sydney's Central station from as far north as Brisbane (13½ hours), as far south as Melbourne (11½ hours) and as far west as Perth (four days!); see **NSW TrainLink** (☑13 22 32; www.nswtrainlink.info) and the **Indian Pacific** (☑1800 703 357; www.greatsouthernrail. com.au) for details.

Long-distance buses pull up to the Sydney Coach Terminal beneath Central station. Operators include **Australia Wide** (☑02-9516 1300; www.austwidecoaches. com.au), **Firefly** (☑1300 730 740; www.fireflyexpress.com. au), **Greyhound** (☑1300 473 946; www.greyhound.com. au), **Murrays** (☑13 22 51; www.murrays.com.au), **Port Stephens Coaches** (☑02-4982 2940; www.pscoaches. com.au) and **Premier Motor Service** (☑133 410; www. premierms.com.au). Direct buses head here from as far afield as Adelaide and Cairns, although you can connect via Greyhound to services reaching all major cities.

Flights, cars and tours can be booked online at lonely planet.com.

Sydney Airport

Also known as Kingsford Smith Airport, **Sydney Airport** (☑02-9667 9111; www.sydneyairport.com. au; Airport Dr, Mascot) has separate international (T1) and domestic (T2 and T3) sections, 4km apart on either side of the runway. Each has left-luggage services, ATMs, currency-exchange bureaux and rental-car counters, and buses and shuttles depart from both.

Bus

Services from the airport are limited but there is a direct bus to Bondi Junction (routes 400 and 410, $4.50, 1¼ hours) which departs roughly every 20 minutes.

Shuttle

Airport shuttles head to hotels and hostels in the city centre, and some reach surrounding suburbs and beach destinations. Operators include **Sydney Airporter** (☑02-9666 9988; www.kst. com.au; adult/child $15/10),

---

INTEGRATED TICKETS & PASSES

Although you can still buy individual tickets for most public-transport services, a smartcard system called **Opal** (www.opal.com.au) also operates.

The card can be obtained (for free) and loaded with credit at numerous newsagencies and convenience stores across Sydney. When commencing a journey you'll need to touch the card to an electronic reader, which are located at the train-station gates, near the doors of buses and light-rail carriages, and at the ferry wharves. You then need to touch a reader when you complete your journey so that the system can deduct the correct fare. Advantages include cheaper single journeys, daily charges capped at $15 ($2.50 on Sundays) and free travel after taking any eight journeys in a week (it resets itself every Monday). You can use the Opal card at the airport train stations, but none of the aforementioned bonuses apply.

Paper-based MyMulti passes can be purchased at ferry and train ticket offices and many newsagencies and convenience stores, but you're much better off getting an Opal card instead. For instance, the MyMulti Day Pass costs $24 as opposed to the $15 Opal cap.

CLIMATE CHANGE & TRAVEL

Every form of transport that relies on carbon-based fuel generates CO_2, the main cause of human-induced climate change. Modern travel is dependent on aeroplanes, which might use less fuel per kilometre per person than most cars but travel much greater distances. The altitude at which aircraft emit gases (including CO_2) and particles also contributes to their climate change impact. Many websites offer 'carbon calculators' that allow people to estimate the carbon emissions generated by their journey and, for those who wish to do so, to offset the impact of the greenhouse gases emitted with contributions to portfolios of climate-friendly initiatives throughout the world. Lonely Planet offsets the carbon footprint of all staff and author travel.

Super Shuttle Sydney (SSS; ☑1300 018 460; www.signaturelimousinessydney.com.au), **Airport Shuttle North** (☑1300 505 100; www.airportshuttlenorth.com; to Manly 1/2/3 people $41/51/61) and **Manly Express** (☑02-8068 8473; www.manlyexpress.com.au; to Manly 1/2/3 people $43/58/68).

Taxi

Fares from the airport are approximately $45 to $55 to the city centre, $55 to $65 to North Sydney and $90 to $100 to Manly.

Train

Trains from both the domestic and international terminals, connecting into the main train network, are run by **Airport Link** (www.airportlink.com.au; adult/child $18/14; ☺4.30am-12.30am). They're frequent (every 10 minutes), quick (13 minutes to Central) and easy to use, but airport tickets are charged at a hefty premium. If there are a few of you it's cheaper to catch a cab. Another alternative is to catch the bus to Rockdale station (routes 400 and 410, $3.50, 12 minutes) and then catch the regular train to Central ($3, 15 minutes).

Central Station

Intercity trains pull into the old section of Sydney's historic **Central station** (Map p245; Eddy Ave; ℝCentral), in

the Haymarket area of the inner city. From here you can connect to the suburban train network or follow the signs to Railway Sq for suburban buses.

Sydney Coach Terminal

Long-distance coaches arrive at **Sydney Coach Terminal** (Map p245; ☑02-9281 9366; www.sydneycoachterminal.com.au; Eddy Ave; ☺6am-6pm; ℝCentral), underneath Central station. From here you can walk along Eddy Ave for the suburban trains or turn left onto Pitt St for the major bus stop on Railway Sq.

GETTING AROUND SYDNEY

Sydneysiders love to complain about their public-transport system, but visitors should find it surprisingly easy to navigate. The train system is the linchpin, with lines radiating out from Central station. Ferries head all around the harbour and up the river to Parramatta; light rail is useful for Pyrmont and Glebe; and buses are particularly useful for getting to the beaches.

Transport NSW (☑131 500; www.transportnsw.info) is the body that coordinates all the state-run bus, ferry, train and light-rail services. You'll find a useful journey planner on its website.

Train

Sydney Trains (☑131 500; www.sydneytrains.info) has a large suburban railway web with relatively frequent services, although there are no lines to the northern or eastern beaches.

➡ Trains run from around 5am to 1am; check timetables for your line.

➡ A short inner-city one-way trip costs $4.

➡ If you don't have an Opal card, purchase your ticket in advance from an automated machine or a counter at the bigger stations.

Bus

Sydney Buses (☑131 500; www.sydneybuses.info) has an extensive network, operating from around 5am to midnight, when less frequent NightRide services commence.

➡ Bus routes starting with an X indicate limited-stop express routes; those with an L have limited stops.

➡ You can buy a ticket from the driver on most services ($2.40 to $4.70, depending on the length of the journey) but you'll need an Opal card or prepaid paper ticket (available at newsagents, convenience stores and supermarkets) for prepay-only services.

➡ Prepaid tickets need to be dunked into the green ticket machines as you enter the bus. If you'll be catching buses a lot (but not trains or ferries), consider a prepaid 10-ride TravelTen ticket (sections 1–2 $20, 3–5 $31, 6+ $38).

➡ Route 555 is a free service which heads up and down George St, from Circular Quay to Central station.

Ferry

Most **Sydney Ferries** (Map p240; ☑131 500; www. transportnsw.info) operate between 6am and midnight. The standard single fare for most harbour destinations is $6.20; boats to Manly, Sydney Olympic Park and Parramatta cost $7.60. If you're heading to Taronga Zoo by ferry, consider the all-inclusive ZooPass (adult/child $53/27).

Private companies **Manly Fast Ferry** (☑02-9583 1199; www.manlyfastferry.com.au; adult/child $9/6) and **Sydney Fast Ferries** (☑02-9818 6000; www.sydneyfastferries. com.au; adult/child $9.75/7.50; ☎) both offer boats that blast from Circular Quay to Manly in 18 minutes.

Light Rail

➡ Trams run between Central station and Dulwich Hill, stopping in Chinatown, Darling Harbour, The Star casino, Sydney Fish Market and Glebe en route.

➡ Tickets cost $3.80 for a short journey and $4.80 for a longer one, and can be purchased from the conductor.

Taxi

➡ Metered taxis are easy to flag down in the central city and inner suburbs, except for at changeover times (3pm and 3am).

➡ Fares are regulated, so all companies charge the same. Flagfall is $3.50, with a $2.50 'night owl surcharge' after 10pm on a Friday and Saturday until 6am the following morning.

The fare thereafter is $2.14 per kilometre, with an additional surcharge of 20% between 10pm and 6am nightly. There's also a $2.40 fee for bookings.

➡ The UberX ride-sharing app operates in Sydney but the state government maintains that it is illegal for drivers to offer the service.

➡ For more on Sydney's taxis, see www.nswtaxi.org.au.

Major taxi companies include the following:

Legion Cabs (☑13 14 51; www.legioncabs.com.au)

Premier Cabs (☑13 10 17; www.premiercabs.com.au)

RSL Cabs (☑02-9581 1111; www.rslcabs.com.au)

Taxis Combined (☑133 300; www.taxiscombined.com.au)

Car & Motorcycle

Avoid driving in central Sydney if you can: there's a confusing one-way street system, parking's elusive and expensive (even at hotels), and parking inspectors, tolls and tow-away zones proliferate. Conversely, a car is handy for accessing Sydney's outer reaches and for day trips.

Driving & Parking

Australians drive on the left-hand side of the road; the minimum driving age (unassisted) is 18. Overseas visitors can drive with their domestic driving licences for up to three months but must obtain a NSW driving licence after that. Speed limits in Sydney are generally 60km/h (50km/h in some areas), rising to 100km/h or 110km/h on motorways. Seat belts are compulsory; using hand-held mobile phones is prohibited. A blood-alcohol limit of 0.05% is enforced with random breath tests and hefty punishments. If you're in an accident (even if you didn't

cause it) and you're over the alcohol limit, your insurance will be invalidated. For further information, see www. rms.nsw.gov.au.

Sydney's private car parks are expensive (around $15 per hour); public car parks are more affordable (sometimes under $10 per hour). The city centre and Darling Harbour have the greatest number of private car parks, but these are also the priciest. Street parking devours coins (from $2.50 to $5 per hour), although some take credit cards.

Toll Roads

There are hefty tolls on most of Sydney's motorways and major links (including the Harbour Bridge, Harbour Tunnel, Cross City Tunnel and Eastern Distributor). The tolling system is electronic, meaning that it's up to you to organise an electronic tag or visitor's pass through any of the following websites: www. roam.com.au, www.roam express.com.au or www. myetoll.com.au. Note that some car-hire companies now supply etags.

Hire

Car-rental prices vary depending on season and demand. Read the small print to check age restrictions, exactly what your insurance covers and where you can take the car.

The big players have airport desks and city offices (mostly around William St, Darlinghurst). The *Yellow Pages* lists other local car-hire companies, some specialising in renting near-wrecks at rock-bottom prices – study the fine print to ensure you're not being lumped with a lemon.

For motorbike hire, try **Bikescape** (☑02-9569 4111; www.bikescape.com.au; cnr Parramatta Rd & Young St, Annandale; ☒Stanmore).

Ace Rentals (☑02-8338 1055; www.acerentalcars.com.au)

Avis (☎136 333; www.avis.
com.au)

Bayswater Car Rental
(☎02-9360 3622; www.bays
watercarrental.com.au)

Budget (☎02-8295 9600;
www.budget.com.au; 93
William St; ☺7.30am-5.45pm
Mon-Fri, to 3.45pm Sat & Sun;
🚇Kings Cross)

Europcar (☎1300 131 390;
www.europcar.com.au)

Hertz (☎02-9360 6621; www.
hertz.com.au; 65 William St;
☺7.30am-5.30pm Mon-Fri,
8am-3pm Sat & Sun; 🚇St
James)

Jucy Rentals (☎1800 150
850; www.jucy.com.au)

Thrifty (☎02-8374 6177; www.
thrifty.com.au; 85 William St;
☺7.30am-5.30pm Mon-Fri, to
4pm Sat & Sun; 🚇Kings Cross)

Automobile Association

The **National Roads & Motorists Association** (NRMA;
Map p246; ☎132 132; www.
nrma.com.au; 74 King St; ☺9am-
5pm Mon-Fri; 🚇Wynyard)
provides 24-hour emergency
roadside assistance, maps,
travel advice, insurance and
accommodation discounts. It
has reciprocal arrangements
with similar organisations
interstate and overseas (bring
proof of membership).

Bicycle

Sydney traffic can be in-
timidating, but there are
an increasing number of
separated bike lanes; see
www.cityofsydney.nsw.gov.
au. Helmets are compulsory.

Bicycles can travel on
suburban trains for free if
you have an Opal card or
if it's a fold-up bike. If not,
you'll need to by a separate
kid's ticket for your bike during peak hours; off-peak is
free. Bikes also ride for free
on Sydney's ferries but are
banned from buses.

Many cycle-hire shops
require a credit-card deposit.
For hire, see the following:
➡ Bike Buffs (p68)
➡ Bike Hire @ Sydney Olympic
Park (p111)
➡ Bonza Bike Tours (p68)
➡ Centennial Park Cycles (p155)
➡ Inner City Cycles (p121)
➡ Manly Bike Tours (p176)
➡ Skater HQ Centennial
Park (p155)
➡ Skater HQ Manly (p176)

Water Taxis

Water taxis are a fast way to
shunt around the harbour
(Circular Quay to Watsons
Bay in as little as 15 minutes). Companies will quote
on any pick-up point within
the harbour and the river,
including private jetties,
islands and other boats.

Aussie Water Taxis (Map
p250;☎02-9211 7730; www.aus-
siewatertaxis.com; Cockle Bay
Wharf) The smallest seats 16
passengers and can be rented
per hour or point to point.

H2O Maxi Taxis (☎1300
420 829; www.h2owatertaxis.
com.au) Smallest seats 21
people. Harbour Islands a
speciality: Fort Denison/
Cockatoo Island/Shark Island
costs $110/125/150 for up to 10
people from Circular Quay. Has
a quote calculator on its website.

Water Taxis Combined
(☎02-9555 8888; www.water
taxis.com.au) Fares based on
up to four passengers: Circular
Quay to Watsons Bay $110;
to Rose Bay $110; to Wool-
loomooloo $70. It also offers
harbour cruise packages.

Yellow Water Taxis (☎02-
9299 0199; www.yellowwater
taxis.com.au) Set price for
up to four passengers, then
$10 per person for additional
people. Sample fares from King
St Wharf: Circular Quay and
Fort Denison $83; Taronga Zoo
$95; Cockatoo Island and Shark
Island $121; Watsons Bay $127.

TOURS

Organised tours can be a
useful way to get around if
you're short on time or prefer to have things organised
for you. For localised tours,
refer to the neighbourhood
chapters.

Real Sydney Tours
(☎0402 049 426; www.real
sydneytours.com.au; 1-3 passengers from $465, additional
passengers from $135) Private
minibus tours around Sydney
or to further-flung locations
such as the Blue Mountains
and the Hunter Valley.

Bailey's Sydney (☎0409
008 767; www.baileys-sydney.
com; full day from $395) Offers
highly personalised private
tours of Sydney 'for people who
don't like tours'.

Runaway Tours (☎0410
545 117; www.runawaytours.
com.au; price on application)
Small-group half- or full-day
City Sights and Sydney By
Night tours, plus day trips to
the Blue Mountains, Hunter
Valley and other destinations.

City Sightseeing (☎02-
9567 8400; www.city-sight
seeing.com; 24/48hr ticket
$40/60) Open-topped double-
decker buses running along
two interlinked, 90-minute,
hop-on/hop-off loops every 15
to 45 minutes from 8.30am to
7.30pm.

Bikescape (☎02-9569 4111;
www.bikescape.com.au; cnr
Parramatta Rd & Young St,
Annandale; tours from $195;
🚇Stanmore) Harley-Davidson
city tours, road trips and
motorbike hire (from $80 for
a 150cc scooter to $280 for a
BMW R1200RT).

Blue Sky Helicopters
(☎02-9700 7888; www.
blueskyhelicopters.com)
Departing from the airport, this
experienced crew offers scenic
flights, ranging from a 15-minute
Bridge & Back trip ($330) to
a five-hour *Blue Mountains
Helitour* (from $2500).

Directory A–Z

Customs Regulations

➡ Entering Australia you can bring in most articles free of duty, provided the **Australian Customs Service** (☎1300 363 263; www.customs.gov.au) is satisfied they're for personal use and that you'll be taking them with you when you leave.

➡ There's a duty-free quota per person of 2.25L of alcohol (if you're over 18), 50 cigarettes (ditto) and dutiable goods up to the value of $900 ($450 if you're under 18).

➡ Amounts of more than A$10,000 cash (or its equivalent) must be declared.

➡ Authorities take biosecurity very seriously, and are vigilant in their efforts to prevent introduced pests getting into the country. Be sure to declare all goods of animal or vegetable origin. Dispose of any fresh food and flowers. If you've recently visited farmland or rural areas, it's best to scrub your shoes before you get to the airport; you'll also need to declare them to Customs.

➡ Weapons and firearms are either prohibited or require a permit and safety testing. Other restricted goods include products made from protected wildlife species, nonapproved telecommunications devices and live animals.

➡ When you leave, don't take any protected flora or fauna with you. Customs comes down hard on smugglers.

Discount Cards

➡ **Sydney Museums Pass** (www.sydneylivingmuseums.com.au/sydney-museums-pass; adult/child $18/9) Allows a single visit to four boutique museums: Museum of Sydney, Hyde Park Barracks, Justice & Police Museum and Susannah Place Museum. It's valid for three months and available at each of the participating museums.

➡ **Ultimate Sydney Pass** (adult/child $99/70) Provides access to the high-profile, costly attractions operated by British-based Merlin Entertainment: Sydney Tower Eye (including the Skywalk), Sydney Sea Life Aquarium, Wild Life Sydney Zoo, Madame Tussauds and Manly Sea Life Sanctuary. It's available from each of the venues, but is often considerably cheaper online through the venue websites. If you plan on visiting only some of these attractions, discounted Sydney Attractions Passes are available in any combination you desire.

Electricity

240V/50Hz

Emergency

In the event of an emergency, call ☎000 for the police, the ambulance or the fire brigade. Other useful contacts:

Lifeline (☎13 11 14; www.lifelinesydney.org; ⊘24hr) Round-the-clock phone counselling services, including suicide prevention.

National Roads & Motorists Association (NRMA; Map p246;☎13 21 32; www.nrma.com.au; 74 King St; ⊘9am-5pm Mon-Fri;

(⊠Wynyard) Provides 24-hour emergency roadside assistance, maps, travel advice, insurance and accommodation discounts. It has reciprocal arrangements with similar organisations interstate and overseas (bring proof of membership).

NSW Rape Crisis (☎1800 424 017; www.nswrapecrisis.com.au; ⊗24hr) Offers counselling, 24 hours a day.

Internet Access

➡ Most hotels and hostels now provide wi-fi connections, although many, especially top-end places, charge for the service. Many larger hotels have an in-room cable connection.

➡ The majority of hostels and some hotels provide computers for guest use. Access may or may not be charged.

➡ Many cafes and bars offer free wi-fi, particularly the big international chains (including Starbucks and McDonald's). Most public libraries offer it, and the Broadway Shopping Centre has it in its foodcourt.

➡ Pay-as-you-go internet hot spots are common in busy areas.

➡ Because of the greater access to free connections, internet cafes are not as ubiquitous as they once were, although you'll still find them around touristy areas such as Central station, Kings Cross and Bondi. One reliable chain is **Global Gossip** (☎1300 738 353; www.globalgossip.com), which has terminals in many hostels.

Legal Matters

➡ Australia is very strict when it comes to driving under the influence of alcohol or other drugs. There is a significant

police presence on the roads, and they have the power to stop your car and see your licence (you're required to carry it), check your vehicle for roadworthiness and insist that you take a breath test for alcohol. The legal limit is 0.05 blood-alcohol content. If you're over, you may face a hefty fine.

➡ First offenders caught with small amounts of illegal drugs are likely to receive a fine rather than go to jail, but a conviction may affect your visa status.

➡ If you remain in Australia after your visa expires, you will officially be an 'overstayer' and could face detention and expulsion, and then be prevented from returning to Australia for up to three years.

Medical Services

Visitors from Belgium, Finland, Ireland, Italy, Malta, the Netherlands, New Zealand, Norway, Slovenia, Sweden and the UK have reciprocal health rights, entitling them to 'limited subsidised health services for medically necessary treatment', including free public-hospital access" and subsidised medicines. In some cases you'll need to

pay upfront, then be reimbursed once you've registered with **Medicare** (☎13 20 11; www.medicareaustralia.gov.au). Travel insurance is advisable to cover other expenses (such as ambulance and repatriation).

Clinics

If you need a dentist pronto, visit www.dentist.com.au.

Kings Cross Clinic (☎02-9358 3066; www.kingscross-clinic.com.au; 13 Springfield Ave; ⊗9am-6pm Mon-Fri, 10am-1pm Sat; ⊠Kings Cross) General and travel-related medical services.

Travellers Medical Vaccination Centre (☎02-9221 7133; www.traveldoctor.com.au; L7, 428 George St; ⊗9am-5.30pm Mon-Wed & Fri, to 8pm Thu, to 1pm Sat; ⊠St James) Travel-related shots and medical advice.

Emergency Rooms

Hospitals with 24-hour accident and emergency departments include the following:

Royal Prince Alfred Hospital (RPA; ☎02-9515 6111; www.sswahs.nsw.gov.au/rpa; Missenden Rd, Camperdown; ⊠Macdonaldtown)

St Vincent's Hospital
(☑02-8382 1111; www.st
vincents.com.au; 390 Victoria
St; ⊠Kings Cross)

Sydney Children's Hospital (☑02-9382 1111; www.
sch.edu.au; High St, Randwick;
☐400)

Sydney Hospital (☑02-
9382 7111; www.seslhd.health.
nsw.gov.au/SHSEH; 8 Macquarie St; ⊠Martin Place)

Pharmacies

Every shopping strip and
mall has a pharmacy. The
following have conveniently
long hours:

Blakes Pharmacy
(☑02-9358 6712; www.
blakespharmacy.com.au; 20
Darlinghurst Rd, Kings Cross;
☺9am-11pm Mon-Fri, to 9pm
Sat & Sun; ⊠Kings Cross)

Wu's Pharmacy (☑02-9281
9431; 629 George St, Haymarket; ☺9am-9pm Mon-Sat, to
7pm Sun; ⊠Town Hall)

Money

➡ The unit of currency is the
Australian dollar, which is divided into 100 cents.

➡ Notes are colourful, plastic
and washing-machine-proof, in
denominations of $100, $50,
$20, $10 and $5.

➡ Coins come in $2, $1, 50c,
20c, 10c and 5c. The old 2c
and 1c coins have been out of
circulation for years, so shops
round prices up (or down) to the
nearest 5c. Curiously, $2 coins
are smaller than $1.

➡ Travellers cheques are something of a dinosaur these days,
and they won't be accepted
everywhere. It's easier not to
bother with them.

ATMs

Central Sydney is chock-
full of banks with 24-hour
ATMs that will accept debit
and credit cards linked to

international network systems (Cirrus, Maestro, Visa,
MasterCard etc). Most banks
place a $1000 limit on the
amount you can withdraw
daily. You'll also find ATMs
in pubs and clubs, although
these usually charge slightly
higher fees. Shops and retail
outlets usually have Eftpos
facilities, which allow you to
pay for purchases with your
debit or credit card.

Changing Money

➡ Exchange bureaux are dotted
around the city centre, Kings
Cross and Bondi.

➡ Shop around, as rates vary
and most charge some sort of
commission.

➡ The counters at the airport
are open until the last flight
comes in; rates here aren't quite
as good as they are in the city.

Credit Cards

Visa and MasterCard are
widely accepted at larger
shops, restaurants and hotels, but not necessarily at
smaller shops or cafes. Diners
Club and American Express
are less widely accepted.

Tipping

In Sydney most service
providers don't expect a tip,
so you shouldn't feel pressured into giving one, even
at fancy restaurants. If the
service is good, however, it is
customary to tip wait staff in
restaurants (up to 10%, but
only for good service) and
taxi drivers (round up to the
nearest dollar).

Opening Hours

Banks 9.30am–4pm Monday–
Thursday, 9.30am–5pm Friday
Cafes 8am–4pm
Offices 9am–5.30pm
Pubs 11am–midnight Monday–
Saturday, 11am–10pm Sunday
Restaurants noon–3pm and
6pm–10pm, sometimes shut
Sunday or Monday

Shops 9.30am–6pm Monday–
Wednesday, Friday and Saturday, 9.30am–9pm Thursday,
11am–5pm Sunday

Post

Australia Post (☑13 76
78; www.auspost.com.au) is
efficient and has branches
throughout the city. It costs
70c to send a postcard or
a standard letter within
Australia. Airmail letters or
postcards cost $1.85 to New
Zealand, $1.95 to the Asia
Pacific region and $2.75 to
the rest of the world.

Public Holidays

On public holidays, government departments, banks,
offices and post offices shut
up shop. On Good Friday,
Easter Sunday, Anzac Day
and Christmas Day, most
shops are closed.

New Year's Day 1 January

Australia Day 26 January

Easter (Good Friday, Easter
Saturday, Easter Monday)
March/April

Anzac Day 25 April

Queen's Birthday Second
Monday in June

Bank Holiday First Monday in
August (only banks are closed)

Labour Day First Monday in
October

Christmas Day 25 December

Boxing Day 26 December

Most public holidays cleverly
morph into long weekends
(three days), so if a holiday
such as New Year's Day falls
on a weekend, the following
Monday is usually a holiday.

Something else to consider when planning a Sydney
visit is school holidays, when
accommodation rates soar
and everything gets hectic.
Sydney students have a long
summer break that includes
Christmas and most of January. Other school holidays
fall around March to April

(Easter), late June to mid-July, and late September to early October.

Taxes & Refunds

There's a 10% goods and services tax (GST) automatically added to almost everything you buy, Australia-wide. If you purchase goods with a total minimum value of $300 from any one store within 60 days of departure from Australia, the Tourist Refund Scheme entitles you to a refund of any GST paid.

Keep your receipts and carry the items on board your flight as hand luggage; you can get a cheque refund or a credit-card refund at the designated booth located past Customs at Sydney airport (see www.customs.gov.au for more information).

Telephone

➝ Public telephones, which can be found all over the city, take phonecards, credit cards and occasionally (if the coin slots aren't jammed up) coins.

➝ Australia's country code is 🔊61

➝ Sydney's area code is 🔊02 (drop the zero when dialling into Australia)

➝ International access code is 🔊0011 (used when dialling other countries from Australia)

➝ Toll-free numbers start with the prefix 🔊1800, while numbers that start with 🔊1300 are only the cost of a local call.

Mobile Phones

➝ Australian mobile-phone numbers have four-digit prefixes starting with 🔊04.

➝ Australia's digital network is compatible with most international phones, with the exception being some phones from the USA and Japan. Quadband US/Japanese phones

will work, but to avoid global-roaming charges, you'll need an unlocked handset that takes prepaid SIM cards from Australian providers.

➝ It's illegal to talk on a hand-held mobile phone while driving.

Phonecards

Local and international phonecards range in value from $5 to $50 – look for the phonecard logo at retail outlets, such as newsagents. There is a bewildering variety of cards available, with all sorts of deals aimed at visitors wanting to get in touch with loved ones in Europe, Asia and the Americas. Shop around.

Time

Sydney is on Eastern Standard Time (EST), which is 10 hours ahead of GMT/UTC. That means that when it's noon in Sydney it's 6pm the day before in Los Angeles, 9pm the day before in New York, 2am in London, 4am in Johannesburg, 11am in Tokyo and 2pm in Auckland. Running from the first Sunday in October to the first Sunday in April, Daylight Savings Time is one hour ahead of standard time.

Tourist Information

City Host Information Kiosks (www.cityofsydney.nsw.gov.au) Circular Quay (Map p240; cnr Pitt & Alfred Sts; ⊘9am-5pm; ⊛Circular Quay) Haymarket (Map p245; Dixon St; ⊘11am-7pm; ⊛Town Hall) Kings Cross (Map p257; cnr Darlinghurst Rd & Springfield Ave; ⊘9am-5pm; ⊛Kings Cross) Town Hall (Map p246; George St; ⊘9am-5pm; ⊛Town Hall)

Hello Manly (Map p263; 🔊02-9976 1430; www.hellomanly.com.au; Manly Wharf;

⊘9am-5pm; ⊛Manly) This helpful visitors centre, just outside the ferry wharf and alongside the bus interchange, has free pamphlets covering the Manly Scenic Walkway (www.manly.nsw.gov.au) and other Manly attractions, plus loads of local bus information.

Parramatta Heritage & Visitor Information Centre (🔊1300 889 714; www.discoverparramatta.com; 346a Church St; ⊘9am-5pm; ⊛Parramatta) Knowledgeable staff will point you in the right direction with loads of brochures and leaflets, info on access for visitors with impaired mobility, and details on local Aboriginal cultural sites.

Sydney Visitor Centres (www.bestof.com.au; 🔊02-8273 0000) Darling Harbour (Palm Grove, behind IMAX; ⊘9.30am-5.30pm; ⊛Town Hall) The Rocks (cnr Argyle & Playfair Sts; ⊛Circular Quay) Has a range of brochures, and staff can book accommodation, tours and attractions.

Travellers with Disabilities

Compared with many other major cities, Sydney has great access for citizens and visitors with disabilities.

Wheelchair access Most of Sydney's main attractions are accessible by wheelchair, and all new or renovated buildings must, by law, include wheelchair access. Older buildings can pose some problems, however, and some restaurants and entertainment venues aren't quite up to scratch. Most of the National Trust's historic houses are at least partially accessible, and abashed attendants can usually show you photos of inaccessible areas. Some taxis accommodate wheelchairs – request them when you make your booking.

Hearing-impaired travellers
Most of Sydney's major attractions offer hearing loops and sign-language interpreters. To expedite proceedings, make contact with venue staff in advance.

Vision-impaired travellers
Many new buildings incorporate architectural features that are helpful, such as textured floor details at the top and bottom of stairs. Sydney's pedestrian crossings feature catchy beep-and-buzz sound cues.

Parking Sydney also has lots of parking spaces reserved for drivers with disabilities; see the **City of Sydney** (⌨02-9265 9333; www.cityofsydney.nsw. gov.au) website for information.

Organisations

Deaf Society of NSW
(⌨TTY 02-8833 3691; www. deafsocietynsw.org.au)

Roads & Maritime (⌨13 22 13; www.rms.nsw.gov.au) Supplies temporary parking permits for international drivers with disabilities.

Spinal Cord Injuries Australia (SCIA; ⌨1800 819 775; www.spinalcordinjuries. com.au)

Vision Australia (⌨1300 847 466; www.vision australia.org)

Visas

➧ All visitors to Australia need a visa – only New Zealand nationals are exempt, and even they receive a 'special category' visa on arrival. Visa application forms are available from Australian diplomatic missions overseas, travel agents or the website of the **Department of Immigration and Citizenship** (DIAC; ⌨13 18 81; www.immi.gov.au).

➧ Citizens of European Union member countries, Andorra, Iceland, Liechtenstein, Mo-

naco, Norway, San Marino and Switzerland are eligible for an eVisitor, which is free and allows visitors to stay in Australia for up to three months. These must be applied for online, and they are electronically stored and linked to individual passport numbers, so no stamp in your passport is required. It's advisable to apply at least 14 days prior to the proposed date of travel to Australia. Applications are made on the Department of Immigration and Citizenship website.

➧ An Electronic Travel Authority (ETA) allows visitors to enter Australia any time within a 12-month period and stay for up to three months at a time (unlike eVisitor, multiple entries are permitted). Travellers from qualifying countries can get an ETA through any travel agent or overseas airline registered with the International Air Transport Association (IATA). They make the application for you when you buy a ticket and they issue the ETA, which replaces the usual visa stamped in your passport. It's common practice for travel agents to charge a fee for issuing an ETA (in the vicinity of US$25). This system is available to passport holders of some 33 countries, including all of the countries that are eligible for eVisitor.

➧ The eight countries that are eligible for ETA but not eVisitor can make their application online at www.eta.immi.gov.au, where a $20 fee applies. Those countries are Brunei, Canada, Hong Kong, Japan, Malaysia, Singapore, South Korea and the USA.

➧ If you are from a country not covered by eVisitor or ETA, or you want to stay longer than three months, you'll need to apply for a visa. Tourist visas cost from $130 and allow single or multiple entry for stays of three, six or 12 months and are

valid for use within 12 months of issue.

➧ Visitors are allowed a maximum stay of 12 months, including extensions. Visa extensions are made through the Department of Immigration and Citizenship, and it's best to apply at least two or three weeks before your visa expires.

➧ Young (aged 18 to 30) visitors from Belgium, Canada, Cyprus, Denmark, Estonia, Finland, France, Germany, Hong Kong, Ireland, Italy, Japan, South Korea, Malta, the Netherlands, Norway, Sweden, Taiwan and the UK are eligible for a Working Holiday Maker (WHM) Visa (417), which allows you to visit for up to one year and gain casual employment. The emphasis of this visa is on casual and not full-time employment, so you're only supposed to work for any one employer for a maximum of six months. A first WHM visa must be obtained prior to entry to Australia and can be applied for at Australian diplomatic missions abroad or online. You can't change from a tourist visa to a WHM visa once you're in Australia. You can apply for this visa up to a year in advance, which is worthwhile doing, as there's a limit on the number issued each year. Conditions include having a return air ticket or sufficient funds for a return or onward fare, and a fee of $420 is charged.

➧ Nationals from Argentina, Bangladesh, Chile, Indonesia, Malaysia, Poland, Portugal, Spain, Thailand, Turkey, the USA and Uruguay between the ages of 18 and 30 can apply for a Work and Holiday Visa (462) prior to entry to Australia. Once granted, this visa allows the holder to stay for up to 12 months and undertake temporary employment to supplement a trip. Conditions vary depending on nationality. The application fee is also $420.

Behind the Scenes

SEND US YOUR FEEDBACK

We love to hear from travellers – your comments keep us on our toes and help make our books better. Our well-travelled team reads every word on what you loved or loathed about this book. Although we cannot reply individually to your submissions, we always guarantee that your feedback goes straight to the appropriate authors, in time for the next edition. Each person who sends us information is thanked in the next edition – and the most useful submissions are rewarded with a selection of digital PDF chapters.

Visit **lonelyplanet.com/contact** to submit your updates and suggestions or to ask for help. Our award-winning website also features inspirational travel stories, news and discussions.

Note: We may edit, reproduce and incorporate your comments in Lonely Planet products such as guidebooks, websites and digital products, so let us know If you don't want your comments reproduced or your name acknowledged. For a copy of our privacy policy visit lonelyplanet.com/privacy.

OUR READERS

Many thanks to the travellers who used the last edition and wrote to us with helpful hints, useful advice and interesting anecdotes:

Franziska Feldmann, Hana Murr, Brian Scanlan, Vicki Stanton

AUTHOR THANKS

Peter Dragicevich

I owe a great debt of thanks to all my Sydney support crew, particularly David Mills, Barry Sawtell, Tony Dragicevich, Debbie Debono, Tim Moyes and Michael Woodhouse. Thanks for sacrificing your stomachs and livers so enthusiastically for this book.

Miriam Raphael

Thank you Tasmin Waby for getting in touch, Di Schallmeiner and Lauren Wellicome for your insanely quick responses to my Christo crises (real and imagined), and the editing team for their flexibility around the birth of baby Raph. Cheers to all the north-coast locals who so happily shared their secrets. A huge thanks to Ken's red pen (let that ink never run out) and my wing-peeps Marcel and Pearl.

ACKNOWLEDGMENTS

Illustrations p72–3 by Javier Zarracina. Cover photograph: Sydney Opera House, Kimberly Coole/Getty.

THIS BOOK

This 11th edition of Lonely Planet's *Sydney* guidebook was researched and written by Peter Dragicevich and Miriam Raphael. The previous edition was also written by Peter. This guidebook was produced by the following:

Destination Editor
Tasmin Waby
Product Editors
Carolyn Boicos, Katie O'Connell
Senior Cartographers
Mark Griffiths, Julie Sheridan
Book Designer
Virginia Moreno
Assisting Editors Judith Bamber, Imogen Bannister, Melanie Dankel, Anne Mason,

Charlotte Orr, Monique Perrin, Victoria Smith
Cover Researcher
Naomi Parker
Thanks to Daniel Corbett, Anna Harris, Wayne Murphy, Claire Naylor, Karyn Noble, Sarah Reid, Ellie Simpson, Gabrielle Stefanos, Angela Tinson, Lauren Wellicome, Tony Wheeler

See also separate subindexes for:

EATING P233

DRINKING & NIGHTLIFE P234

ENTERTAINMENT P235

SHOPPING P235

SPORTS & ACTIVITIES P236

SLEEPING P236

Index

🏃 **SPORTS & ACTIVITIES**

🛏 **SLEEPING**

Sydney Maps

Sights
- Beach
- Bird Sanctuary
- Buddhist
- Castle/Palace
- Christian
- Confucian
- Hindu
- Islamic
- Jain
- Jewish
- Monument
- Museum/Gallery/Historic Building
- Ruin
- Shinto
- Sikh
- Taoist
- Winery/Vineyard
- Zoo/Wildlife Sanctuary
- Other Sight

Activities, Courses & Tours
- Bodysurfing
- Diving
- Canoeing/Kayaking
- Course/Tour
- Sento Hot Baths/Onsen
- Skiing
- Snorkelling
- Surfing
- Swimming/Pool
- Walking
- Windsurfing
- Other Activity

Sleeping
- Sleeping
- Camping

Eating
- Eating

Drinking & Nightlife
- Drinking & Nightlife
- Cafe

Entertainment
- Entertainment

Shopping
- Shopping

Information
- Bank
- Embassy/Consulate
- Hospital/Medical
- Internet
- Police
- Post Office
- Telephone
- Toilet
- Tourist Information
- Other Information

Geographic
- Beach
- Hut/Shelter
- Lighthouse
- Lookout
- Mountain/Volcano
- Oasis
- Park
- Pass
- Picnic Area
- Waterfall

Population
- Capital (National)
- Capital (State/Province)
- City/Large Town
- Town/Village

Transport
- Airport
- Border crossing
- Bus
- Cable car/Funicular
- Cycling
- Ferry
- Metro station
- Monorail
- Parking
- Petrol station
- Subway station
- Taxi
- Train station/Railway
- Tram
- Underground station
- Other Transport

Note: Not all symbols displayed above appear on the maps in this book

Routes
- Tollway
- Freeway
- Primary
- Secondary
- Tertiary
- Lane
- Unsealed road
- Road under construction
- Plaza/Mall
- Steps
- Tunnel
- Pedestrian overpass
- Walking Tour
- Walking Tour detour
- Path/Walking Trail

Boundaries
- International
- State/Province
- Disputed
- Regional/Suburb
- Marine Park
- Cliff
- Wall

Hydrography
- River, Creek
- Intermittent River
- Canal
- Water
- Dry/Salt/Intermittent Lake
- Reef

Areas

- Airport/Runway
- Beach/Desert
- Cemetery (Christian)
- Cemetery (Other)
- Glacier
- Mudflat
- Park/Forest
- Sight (Building)
- Sportsground
- Swamp/Mangrove

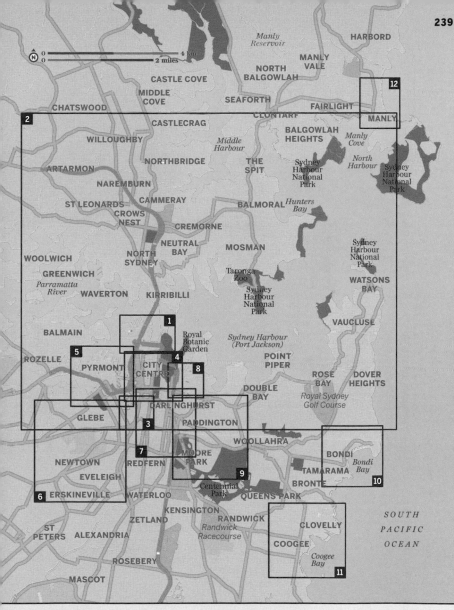

MAP INDEX

CIRCULAR QUAY & THE ROCKS

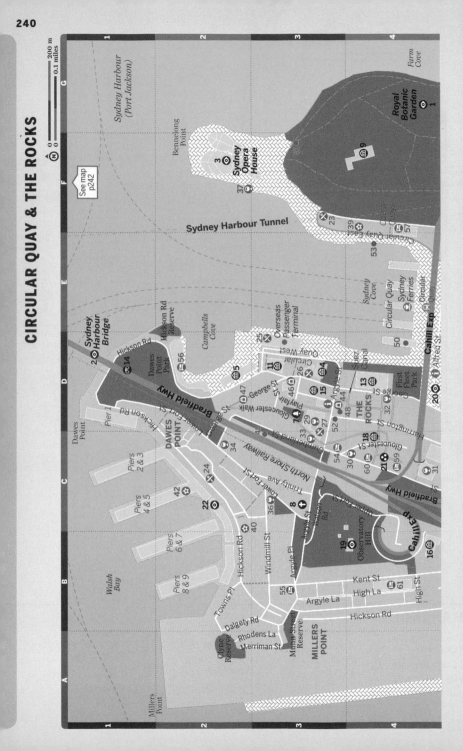

200 m
0.1 miles

See map p242

Sydney Harbour (Port Jackson)

Farm Cove

Royal Botanic Garden

Bennelong Point

Sydney Opera House

Sydney Harbour Tunnel

Circular Quay East

Opera Quays

Sydney Cove

Circular Quay

Sydney Ferries

Circular Quay

Alfred St

Cahill Exp

Sydney Harbour Bridge

Hickson Rd Reserve

Campbells Cove

Overseas Passenger Terminal

Dawes Point Park

Hickson Rd

Suez Canal

First Fleet Park

Dawes Point

Bradfield Hwy

DAWES POINT

Pier 1

Lower Fort St

George St

Playfair St

Gloucester Walk

Circular Quay West

THE ROCKS

George St

Harrington St

Piers 2 & 3

North Shore Railway

Cumberland St

Dumbarton St

Gloucester St

Bradfield Hwy

Piers 4 & 5

Trinity Ave

Lower Fort St

Piers 6 & 7

Windmill St

Argyle Pl

Watson Rd

Upper Fort St

Observatory Hill

Cahill Exp

Piers 8 & 9

Walsh Bay

Towns Pl

Hickson Rd

Argyle La

Kent St

High La

High St

Dalgety Rd

Rhodens La

Merriman St

Munn Street Reserve

MILLERS POINT

Hickson Rd

Clyne Reserve

Millers Point

1
9
3
37
23
39
57
53
2
14
56
5
25
26
11
46
47
7
29
33
34
36
24
42
22
40
8
55
19
16
61
4
15
13
32
50
20
48
52
27
44
18
30
54
60
21
59
31

CIRCULAR QUAY & THE ROCKS

See map
p246

Open Air Cinema (300m);
Mrs Macquaries Point (600m)

Key on p244

SYDNEY HARBOUR

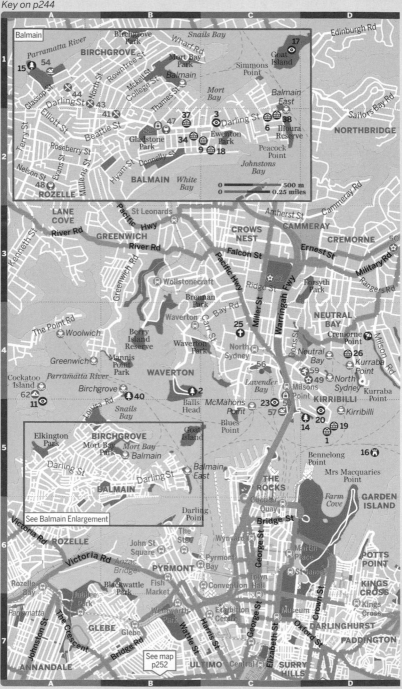

Balmain

Parramatta River
BIRCHGROVE
Birchgrove Park
Snails Bay
Wharf Rd
Edinburgh Rd

15 54
Glassop St
North St
Rowntree St
McKell St College St
Mort Bay Park
17
Goat Island

Darling St
44
43
Thames St
Balmain
Mort Bay
Simmons Point
Balmain East
Sailors Bay Rd

Elliott St
Beattie St
41
47
37
3 Darling St
38
NORTHBRIDGE

Terry St
Roseberry St
Millers St
Hyam St
Gladstone Park
34
9
18
Ewenton Park
6 Illoura Reserve

Nelson St
Donnelly St
Peacock Point

48
ROZELLE
BALMAIN
White Bay
Johnstons Bay

0   500 m
0   0.25 miles

Kenneth St
LANE COVE
Pacific Hwy
St Leonards
Amherst St
Cammeray Rd

River Rd
GREENWICH
River Rd
CROWS NEST
CAMMERAY
CREMORNE 50

Greenwich Rd
Falcon St
Ernest St
Military Rd

Pacific Hwy
Ridge St
51
Forsyth Park
Rangers Rd

Wollstonecraft
Bronman Park
Miller St
Warringah Fwy

The Point Rd
Woolwich
Waverton
Bay Rd
Carr St
NEUTRAL BAY
Cremorne Point

Greenwich
Berry Island Reserve
Waverton Park
25
North Sydney
Doris St
Neutral Bay
26
Milson Rd
Kurraba Point

Mannis Point Park
WAVERTON
56
59
North Sydney
Kurraba Point

Cockatoo Island
Parramatta River
Birchgrove
40
2
Lavender Bay
49
KIRRIBILLI

62
11
Louisa Rd
Snails Bay
Balls Head
Goat Island
McMahons Point
23 58
57
Kirribilli

Elkington Park
BIRCHGROVE
Mort Bay Park
Mort Bay
Balmain
Blues Point
14
20 19
1

Darling St
Darling St
Balmain East
THE ROCKS
Bennelong Point
16

See Balmain Enlargement
BALMAIN
Darling Point
Mrs Macquaries Point
GARDEN ISLAND

Victoria Rd
ROZELLE
John St Square
The Star
Circular Quay
Bridge St
Farm Cove

Rozelle Bay
Anzac Bridge
PYRMONT
Pyrmont Bay
Wynyard
George St
Martin Place
St James
POTTS POINT

Parramatta
The Crescent
Jubilee Park
Blackwattle Park
Fish Market
Convention Hall
Town Hall
Exhibition Centre
Museum
Crown St
Oxford St
KINGS CROSS
Kings Cross
DARLINGHURST

Johnston St
GLEBE
Glebe
Bridge Rd
Wentworth Park
Harris St
Wattle St
George St
Elizabeth St
SURRY HILLS
PADDINGTON

ANNANDALE
ULTIMO
See map p252
Central

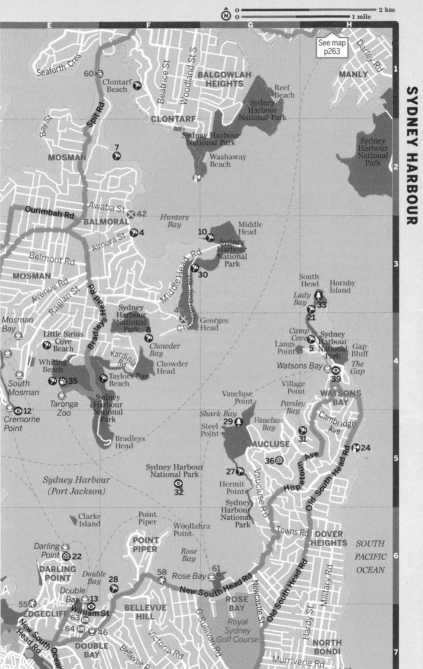

SYDNEY HARBOUR *Map on p242*

HAYMARKET

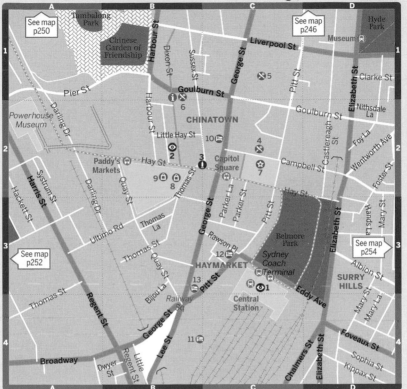

CITY CENTRE

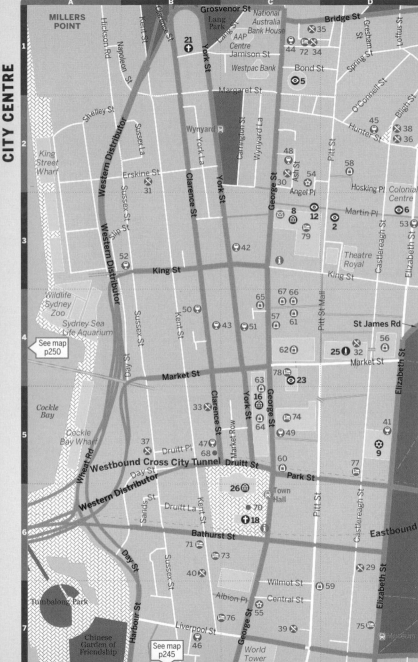

MILLERS POINT

Grosvenor St
Lang Park
National Australia Bank House
Bridge St
21
AAP Centre
Jamison St
Westpac Bank
35
44 72 34
York St
Gresham St
Loftus St
Spring St
O'Connell St
Bligh St
Bond St
5
Margaret St
Hickson Rd
Napoleon St
Kent St
Clarence St
Shelley St
Wynyard
Hunter St
45
38
36
Erskine St
31
York La
York St
Sussex La
Carrington St
Wynyard La
George St
48
Ash St
30
54
Angel Pl
58
Pitt St
Hosking Pl
Colonial Centre
King Street Wharf
Western Distributor
Martin Pl
6
8
12
2
79
53
Clarence St
Slip St
Sussex St
42
King St
Theatre Royal
King St
52
Wildlife Sydney Zoo
Sydney Sea Life Aquarium
50
43
51
65
67 66
57
61
Pitt St Mall
St James Rd
See map p250
Kent St
Day St
Sussex St
62
78
63
23
25
32
56
Market St
Elizabeth St
Castlereagh St
Market St
Cockle Bay
Cockle Bay Wharf
33
Clarence St
Market Row
York St
George St
16
64
74
49
41
9
37
Druitt Pl
47
68
Westbound Cross City Tunnel
Druitt St
60
Park St
Town Hall
77
Western Distributor
Day St
Spring St
26
Druitt La
Kent St
70
18
Pitt St
Castlereagh St
Eastbound
Bathurst St
71
73
Sussex St
40
Wilmot St
29
Elizabeth St
Tumbalong Park
Harbour St
Day St
Albion Pl
Central St
55
59
Chinese Garden of Friendship
See map p245
Liverpool St
46
76
George St
39
World Tower
75
Museum

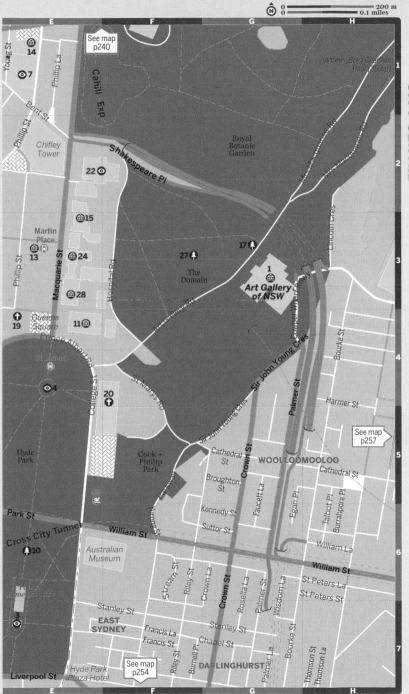

N 0 _____ 200 m
0 _____ 0.1 miles

Young St

14
7

Phillip La

Bent St

Phillip St

Cahill Exp

See map
p240

Chifley
Tower

Shakespeare Pl

22

Royal
Botanic
Garden

Andrew (Boy) Charlton
Pool (250m)

Mrs Macquaries Rd

Mrs Macquaries Rd

Lincoln Cres

15

Martin
Place

13

Macquarie St

24

Phillip St

28

Hospital Rd

27

The
Domain

17

Art Gallery
of NSW

1

Cowper Wharf Rdwy

19
Queens
Square

Prince Albert Rd

11

Art Gallery Rd

Bourke St

St James

College St

Sir Albert Rd

4

St Marys Rd

20

St John Young Cres

Sir John Young Cres

Palmer St

Harmer St

See map
p257

Hyde
Park

Sir John Young Cres

Cathedral
St

WOOLLOOMOOLOO

Cathedral St

Cook +
Phillip
Park

Broughton
St

Faucett La

Egan Pl

Talbot Pl

Burrahpore Pl

Park St

Cross City Tunnel

10

Nimrod St

Kennedy St

Suttor St

William La

William St

William St

William St

Australian
Museum

Stream St

Riley St

Crown La

Crown St

Rosella La

Palmer St

Wisdom La

St Peters La

St Peters St

3

Stanley St

EAST
SYDNEY

Francis La
Francis St

Riley St

Burnett Pl

Stanley St

Chapel St

Crown St

Bourke St

Palmer La

Thomson St
Thomson La

Liverpool St

Hyde Park
Plaza Hotel

See map
p254

DARLINGHURST

CITY CENTRE *Map on p246*

CITY CENTRE

DARLING HARBOUR & PYRMONT

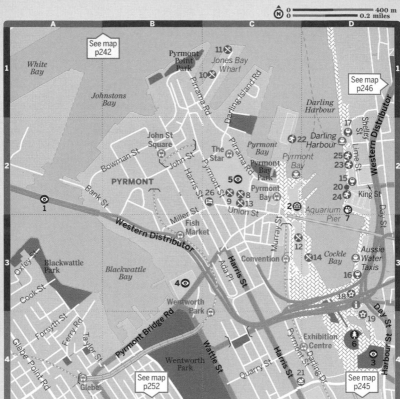

INNER WEST *Map on p252*

INNER WEST

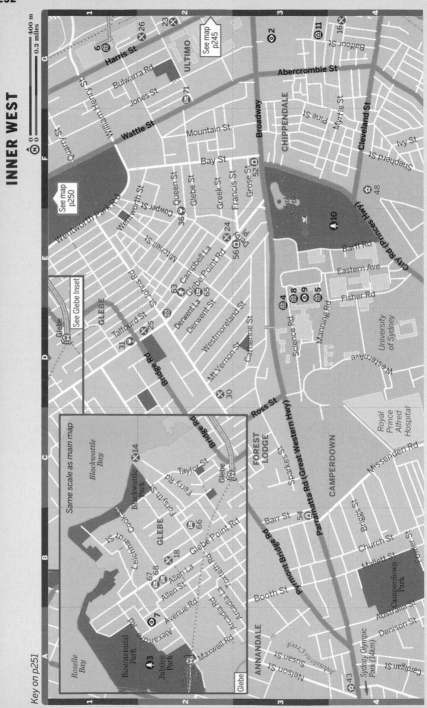

Key on p251

400 m
0.2 miles

ULTIMO

Harris St

26
23
6
Bulwarra Rd
Jones St
71

Quarry St

William Henry St

Wattle St

See map
p245

2

11
16
Balfour St

Abercrombie St

CHIPPENDALE

Mountain St

Bay St

Pine St

Myrtle St

Cleveland St

Ivy St

Shepherd St

Broadway

Glebe St
Queen St
Greek St
Francis St
Grose St
52

36

See map
p250

Wentworth Park Rd

GLEBE

Mitchell St

Wentworth St

Cowper St

St Johns Rd

Campbell La
Glebe Point Rd
55

24
56
53

Derwent La
Derwent St

Westmoreland St

Catherine St

City Rd (Princes Hwy)

10

Barff Rd

Eastern Ave

Fisher Rd

48

4
8
9
5

Science Rd

Manning Rd

University
of Sydney

Western Ave

See Glebe Inset

Glebe

Talfourd St
37
25

Bridge Rd

Mt Vernon St

30

Ross St

FOREST
LODGE

Sparkes St

Parramatta Rd (Great Western Hwy)

Pyrmont Bridge Rd

Barr St
54

CAMPERDOWN

Missenden Rd

Royal
Prince
Alfred
Hospital

Briggs St

Church St

Mallett St

Fowler St

Camperdown
Park

Australia St

Denison St

Cardigan St

Same scale as main map

Blackwattle
Bay

Blackwattle
Park

Taylor St

Ferry Rd

Forsyth's St

14

Cook's St

Leichhardt St

Glebe

GLEBE

67
68
18

Allen La
Allen St

66

Toxteth Rd

Arcadia Rd

Arcadia La

Avenue Rd

Booth St

ANNANDALE

Nelson St
Susan St

Johnston's Creek

43

Sydney Olympic
Park (14km)

Rozelle
Bay

Bicentennial
Park

Alexandra Rd

7

Jubilee
Park

3

Maxwell Rd

Glebe

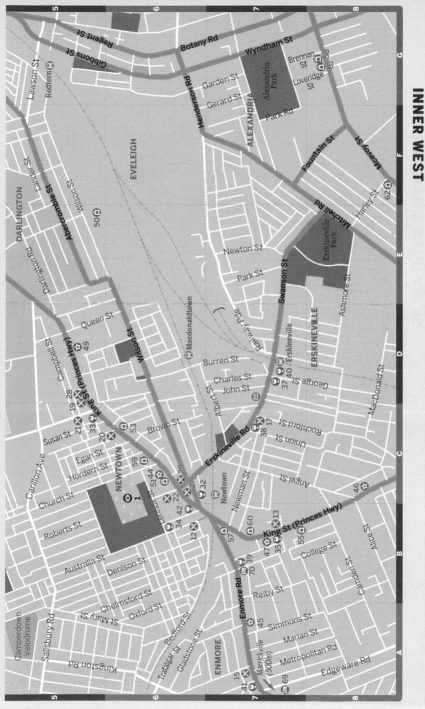

SURRY HILLS & DARLINGHURST

Key on p256

See map p256

Eastbound Cross City Tunnel

See map p246

See map p257

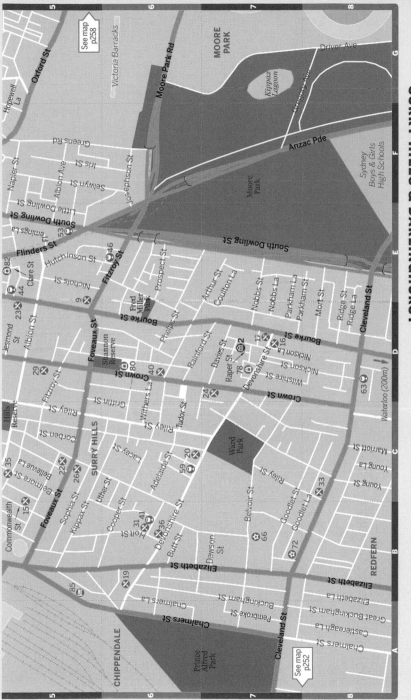

See map p258

See map p252

Oxford St

Hopewell La

Napier St

South Dowling St

Little Dowling St

Flinders St

Clare St

Hutchinson St

Nichols St

Albion Ave

Iris St

Selwyn St

Greens Rd

Josephson St

Moore Park Rd

Victoria Barracks

MOORE
PARK

Driver Ave

Kippax
Lagoon

Anzac Pde

Moore
Park

Sydney
Boys & Girls
High Schools

Fitzroy St

Prospect St

Bourke St

Phelps St

Arthur St

Coulton La

Nobbs St

Nobbs La

Parkham La

Parkham La

Mort St

Ridge St

Ridge La

Cleveland St

South Dowling St

Rainford St

Davies St

Wiltshire St

Nickson St

Nickson La

Devonshire St

Raper St

Crown St

Waterloo (200m)

Fred
Miller
Park

Foveaux St

Shannon
Reserve

Crown St

Withers La

Tudor St

Griffin St

Riley St

Fitzroy St

Riley St

Corben St

Hills
Reserve

Ward
Park

Lacey St

Adelaide St

Belvoir St

Riley St

Goodlet St

Goodlet La

Marriott St

Young La

Young St

Belmore St

Bellevue La

SURRY HILLS

REDFERN

Commonwealth
St

Foveaux St

Sophia St

Kippax St

Uther St

Cooper St

Holt St

Devonshire St

Butt St

Dawson St

Elizabeth St

Elizabeth St

Elizabeth La

Great Buckingham St

Castlereagh La

Chalmers St

Chalmers La

Pembroke St

Buckingham St

Chalmers St

CHIPPENDALE

Prince
Alfred
Park

Cleveland St

82

44

23

9

53

46

6

80

40

24

2

78

17

16

63

29

35

15

22

26

31

41

36

19

85

59

20

33

66

72

SURRY HILLS & DARLINGHURST Map on p254

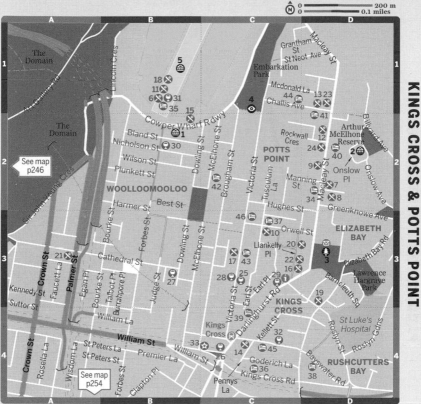

⊚ Sights (p138)

1 Artspace....................B2
2 Elizabeth Bay House D2
3 Fitzroy Gardens.........D3
4 McElhone Stairs............C1
5 Woolloomooloo
   Finger Wharf..............B1

⊗ Eating (p138)

6 Aki's..........................B1
7 Apollo........................D2
8 Bourke Street
   Bakery D2
9 Cafe Sopra.................D2
10 Chester White...............C3
11 China Doll....................B1
12 Cho Cho San.................D2
13 Fratelli Paradiso............D1
14 Guzman y Gomez C4
15 Harry's Cafe de
   Wheels.....................B2

16 LL Wine & Dine.............C3
17 Ms G's........................C3
18 Otto Ristorante B1
19 Piccolo Bar...................D3
20 Room 10 ....D3
21 Toby's Estate...............A3
22 Wilbur's Place...............C3
23 Yellow.........................D1
24 Zinc............................D2

⊙ Drinking & Nightlife (p141)

   Bootleg.................(see 28)
25 Jimmy Lik's..................C3
26 Kings Cross Hotel C4
   Kit & Kaboodle.....(see 29)
27 Old Fitzroy Hotel B3
28 Soho...........................C3
29 Sugarmill.....................C3
30 Tilbury........................B2
31 Waterbar.....................B1
32 World Bar.....................C4

⊙ Entertainment (p143)

33 El Rocco.......................C4
   Old Fitz Theatre...(see 27)

⊟ Sleeping (p190)

34 Blue Parrot...................D2
35 BLUE Sydney................B1
36 Diamant.......................C4
37 Eva's Backpackers.........C3
38 Hotel 59......................D4
39 Jackaroo.....................C4
40 Macleay Hotel D2
41 Maisonette Hotel...........D2
42 Mariners Court..............C2
43 Original
   Backpackers
   Lodge.......................C3
44 Simpsons of Potts
   Point........................C1
45 The Bayswater C4
46 Victoria Court Hotel......C3

PADDINGTON & CENTENNIAL PARK

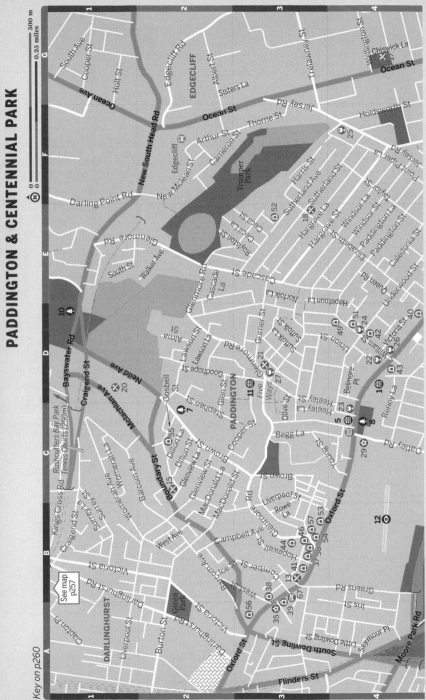

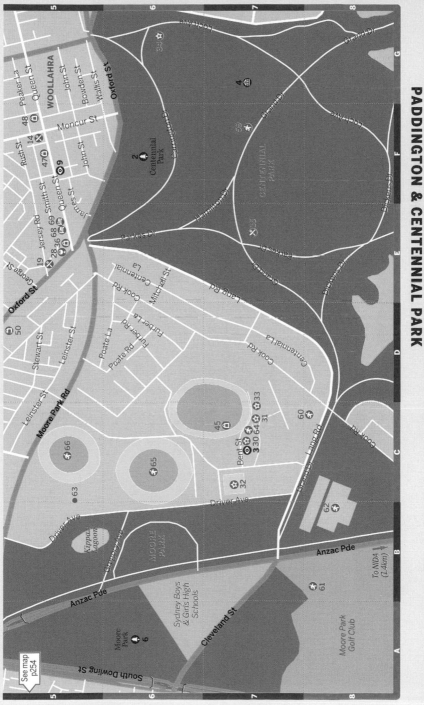

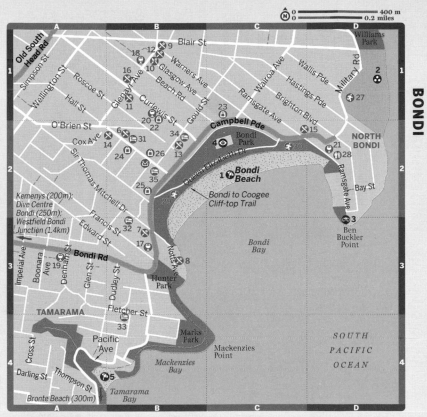

BONDI

COOGEE

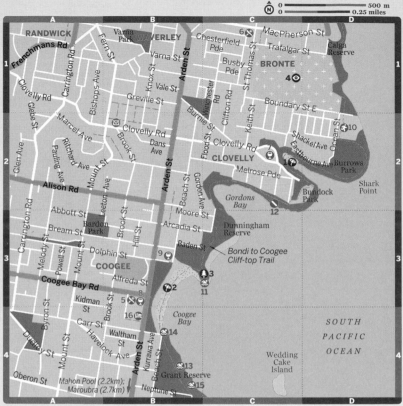

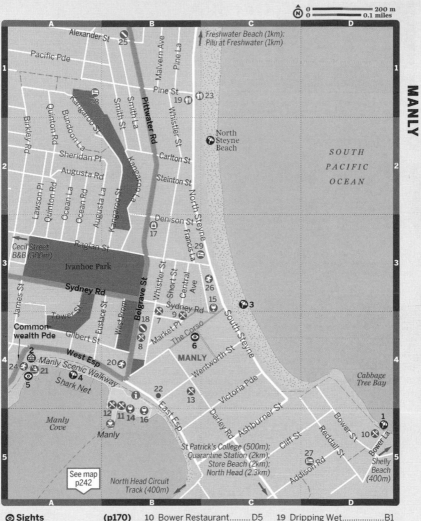

0 ———— 200 m
0 ———— 0.1 miles

Our Story

A beat-up old car, a few dollars in the pocket and a sense of adventure. In 1972 that's all Tony and Maureen Wheeler needed for the trip of a lifetime – across Europe and Asia overland to Australia. It took several months, and at the end – broke but inspired – they sat at their kitchen table writing and stapling together their first travel guide, *Across Asia on the Cheap*. Within a week they'd sold 1500 copies. Lonely Planet was born.

Today, Lonely Planet has offices in Franklin, London, Melbourne, Oakland, Beijing and Delhi, with more than 600 staff and writers. We share Tony's belief that 'a great guidebook should do three things: inform, educate and amuse'.

Our Writers

Peter Dragicevich

After a decade of frequent flights between his native New Zealand and Sydney, the lure of the bright lights and endless beach days drew Peter across the Tasman on a more permanent basis. For the best part of the next decade he would call Sydney's inner suburbs home, while managing the city's most popular gay and lesbian newspaper, followed by a stable of upmarket food, fashion and photography magazines. More recently he's coauthored dozens of titles for Lonely Planet, including two previous editions of this guide and five other Australian titles. Peter wrote the Plan Your Trip and Explore Sydney chapters (excluding Sydney with Kids, Like a Local, For Free, Beaches, Day Trips from Sydney and Sleeping), along with the Understand Sydney and Survival Guide sections.

Read more about Peter at:
lonelyplanet.com/members/peterdragicevich

Miriam Raphael

Miriam has authored over a dozen books for Lonely Planet, racking up thousands of kilometres driving across Australia's wide brown lands in pursuit of the greatest hidden beaches, outback-pub meals and curious characters. She regularly enthuses on all things travel for a range of Australian and international publications, while blogging about intrepid journeys with kids at SevenSuitcases.com. After many years living in Australia's extraordinary Northern Territory she has recently returned to her hometown of Sydney. Miriam wrote the Sydney with Kids, Like a Local, For Free, Beaches, Day Trips from Sydney and Sleeping chapters.

Published by Lonely Planet Publications Pty Ltd
ABN 36 005 607 983
11th edition – Dec 2015
ISBN 978 1 74321 576 0
© Lonely Planet 2015   Photographs © as indicated 2015
10 9 8 7 6 5 4 3 2 1
Printed in China

Although the authors and Lonely Planet have taken all reasonable care in preparing this book, we make no warranty about the accuracy or completeness of its content and, to the maximum extent permitted, disclaim all liability arising from its use.